THE

ENTREPRENEURSHIP

DYNAMIC

THE

ENTREPRENEURSHIP

DYNAMIC

ORIGINS OF ENTREPRENEURSHIP
AND THE EVOLUTION OF INDUSTRIES

EDITORS

CLAUDIA BIRD SCHOONHOVEN

AND ELAINE ROMANELLI

STANFORD UNIVERSITY PRESS · STANFORD, CALIFORNIA

Stanford University Press
Stanford, California

© 2001 by the Board of Trustees of the
Leland Stanford Junior University

Printed in the United States of America
On acid-free, archival-quality paper

Library of Congress Cataloging-in-Publication Data
The entrepreneurship dynamic : origins of entrepreneurship and the
evolution of industries / editors, Claudia Bird Schoonhoven and Elaine
Romanelli.

    p.   cm.

    Papers presented at the Balboa Bay Conference on the Entrepre-
neurship Dynamic held in Newport Beach, Calif. in Nov. 1998.

    Includes bibliographical references and index.

    ISBN 0-8047-3789-4 (alk. paper)—ISBN 0-8047-3790-8
(pbk. : alk. paper)

    1. Entrepreneurship—Congresses.   2. New business
enterprises—Congresses.   I. Schoonhoven, Claudia Bird.
II. Romanelli, Elaine.   III. Balboa Bay Conference on the
Entrepreneurship Dynamic (1998 : Newport Beach, Calif.)
HB615 .E6333   2001
338'.04—dc21   2001041153

Original Printing 2001
Last figure below indicates year of this printing:
10 09 08 07 06 05 04 03 02 01
Typeset by BookMatters in Adobe Garamond 11/15

For Scott G. Schoonhoven, in appreciation for your love and support   **C. B. S.**

For my parents, Jean and Joe Romanelli   **E. R.**

CONTENTS

PREFACE *xi*

CONTRIBUTORS *xv*

1   Introduction:
          Premises of the Entrepreneurship Dynamic *1*
          CLAUDIA BIRD SCHOONHOVEN and ELAINE
          ROMANELLI

PART I The Origins of Entrepreneurial Activity and
          New Organizations

2   The Company They Keep: Founders' Models for
          Organizing New Firms *13*
          M. DIANE BURTON

3   The Local Origins of New Firms *40*
          ELAINE ROMANELLI and CLAUDIA BIRD
          SCHOONHOVEN

4   The Role of Immigrant Entrepreneurs in
          New Venture Creation *68*
          ANNALEE SAXENIAN

5   The Magic Beanstalk Vision: Commercializing University Inventions and Research *109*
ANNE S. MINER, DALE T. EESLEY, MICHAEL DEVAUGHN, and THEKLA RURA-POLLEY

6   Knowledge Industries and Idea Entrepreneurs: New Dimensions of Innovative Products, Services, and Organizations *147*
ERIC ABRAHAMSON and GREGORY FAIRCHILD

7   From the Technology Cycle to the Entrepreneurship Dynamic: The Social Context of Entrepreneurial Innovation *178*
JOHANN PETER MURMANN and MICHAEL L. TUSHMAN

PART II   Entrepreneurship in the Evolution of Industries

8   Learning and Legitimacy: Entrepreneurial Responses to Constraints on the Emergence of New Populations and Organizations *207*
HOWARD E. ALDRICH and TED BAKER

9   Entrepreneurial Action in the Creation of the Specialty Coffee Niche *236*
VIOLINA P. RINDOVA and CHARLES J. FOMBRUN

10   The Power of Public Competition: Promoting
Cognitive Legitimacy Through Certification
Contests   *262*
HAYAGREEVA RAO

11   Social Movement Theory and the Evolution of New
Organizational Forms   *286*
ANAND SWAMINATHAN and JAMES B. WADE

12   Entrepreneurship in Context: Strategic Interaction
and the Emergence of Regional Economies   *314*
ARI GINSBERG, ERIK R. LARSEN, and ALESSANDRO
LOMI

13   The Legal Environment of Entrepreneurship:
Observations on the Legitimation of Venture
Finance in Silicon Valley   *349*
MARK C. SUCHMAN, DANIEL J. STEWARD, and
CLIFFORD A. WESTFALL

14   Emergent Themes and the Next Wave of
Entrepreneurship Research   *383*
CLAUDIA BIRD SCHOONHOVEN and ELAINE
ROMANELLI

REFERENCES   *409*
INDEX   *441*

PREFACE

Entrepreneurship is an old subject in social science. Appearing regularly and early in every discipline from psychology to economics, the entrepreneur and the new organization hold places of special scholarly attention because they signify the creation of something new in the world, the potential for transforming change in the economic and social structures of society. Entrepreneurs, we collectively believe, at least in our myths, are rare individuals whose unique personalities and uncommon motivations drive the innovation of new products and services that directly change the everyday habits and activities of people in a society. New organizations, the means of innovation in the entrepreneurial story, are both directly the engines of new wealth and new knowledge in society and, more indirectly, through their incitement of what Schumpeter (1950, 81–84) termed a "perennial gale of creative destruction," the causes of revolutions in the economic structures of society. To cite some common examples from American history, who can doubt that John D. Rockefeller, Ray Kroc, and Bill Gates, through their creation of Standard Oil, McDonald's, and Microsoft have, for better or worse, altered the face of American business and society?

The source of our long fascination with the subject of entrepreneurship is thus abundantly clear. Entrepreneurship, both the people and processes of organizational creation, is a fundamental dynamic of change in society. We study entrepreneurship because we believe it is essential to the creation and renewal of economic wealth and well-being.

And yet, there is a paradox. Despite centuries of scholarly attention, and the persistent conviction that entrepreneurship is an essential driver of growth and change, there has emerged no general theory.[1] Psychologists (e.g., McClelland

---

1. Hebert and Link (1988) traced the earliest systematic use of the term "entrepreneurship" to an essay, *Essai Sur la Nature du Commerce en General* (1755), by Richard Cantillon, a Paris banker and finan-

1961; Brockhaus 1982) have studied the personalities and social backgrounds of entrepreneurs because they believe that the idiosyncratic prevalence of such presumably rare individuals in a society is prerequisite to and deterministic of rates of entrepreneurial activity. Sociologists (e.g., Weber 1958; Geertz 1963; Waldinger, Aldrich, and Ward 1990) have explored the cultures of "entrepreneurial" societies because they believe that the social norms and celebrations of societies circumscribe the legitimate activities of individuals. Economists (e.g., Schumpeter 1934; 1950) and organizational theorists (e.g., Astley 1985; Barnett and Carroll 1987; Baum and Singh 1994a; Tushman and Anderson 1986) have examined the structures of competition among organizational populations because they believe that entrepreneurial opportunity arises from changes in the concentration of capital and resources produced by ongoing economic activity. Even within these disciplines—and we admit to having grossly simplified their major arguments and differences—it would be difficult to specify any major theories of entrepreneurship. Thus, we cannot even systematically compare the arguments and findings of alternative theories. This situation must change.

As we began to explore the need for change with colleagues both across the U.S. and throughout the world, and in the aftermath of our presenting our ideas at the 1994 Academy of Management meetings, we discovered a broad consensus. Although scholars were working on many different ideas about the origins and outcomes of entrepreneurial activity, including specifying the location of entrepreneurs in organizations and regions and the processes by which new industries emerge in particular times and places, there was also an emerging agreement about entrepreneurship as a pivotal dynamic in industry and regional development. Much of the research was empirical. And, perhaps most important, it appeared that the research was progressing from a necessarily eclectic theoretical foundation that nonetheless had its roots firmly grounded in the disciplinary social sciences. While the motivations for entrepreneurship research are almost inescapably practical—the outcomes of entrepreneurship are just too pragmatically important—these scholars were insistent that a better understanding of entrepreneurial phenomena must proceed

---

cier who made a fortune speculating in trade stocks during the early eighteenth century. Cantillon specified the entrepreneur as a person who assumes the risk of current assets for future profits.

from and contribute to theoretical understanding. Thus, we thought, the time is right for a collection.

We organized a mini-conference and invited more than thirty of our colleagues to present their research and to discuss the future and development of entrepreneurship theory and studies. The Balboa Bay Conference on the Entrepreneurship Dynamic was held at the Balboa Bay Club in Newport Beach, California, in November of 1998. The papers included in this book, which include many of those presented at the conference as well as several others by researchers who were attracted to our project as word began to spread, are the fruit of that conference.

This book could not have been written without the help and encouragement of many colleagues at the Graduate School of Management, University of California, Irvine, and the McDonough School of Business, Georgetown University. We feel lucky to find ourselves in such superb academic institutions. Thanks also go to the Tuck School of Business Administration, Dartmouth University, for funding that supported some of the early work. Linda Johanson, managing editor of the *Administrative Science Quarterly*, read through the entire manuscript and offered many insightful suggestions that substantially improved the quality of each chapter as well as the integration of ideas and arguments presented throughout the volume. Her incomparable copyediting also saved many of us from inadvertent gaps in logic and thoroughly enhanced the readability of this volume. Most especially, though, we are grateful to the authors in this volume who contributed not only their excellent scholarship but also their creative commentary on all the chapters in this volume. The Balboa Bay Conference on the Entrepreneurship Dynamic was one of the most exciting three-day conversations in which we've ever had the pleasure of engaging. We are grateful to all who participated.

CLAUDIA BIRD SCHOONHOVEN

ELAINE ROMANELLI

2001

CONTRIBUTORS

CLAUDIA BIRD SCHOONHOVEN is professor of organization and strategy at the Graduate School of Management, University of California, Irvine. She earned a Ph.D. and an M.A. from Stanford University, a B.A. from the University of Illinois, Champaign-Urbana, and an M.A. from Dartmouth College. Professor Schoonhoven's research focuses on the evolutionary dynamics of technology-based firms, innovation, and entrepreneurship. She is currently investigating the influence of strategic partnerships on new venture outcomes and the effects of entrepreneurship on the creation and evolution of industries. The editor-in-chief of *Organization Science*, Professor Schoonhoven was elected a Fellow of the Academy of Management, to the Academy's Board of Governors, chair of the Organization and Management Theory Division of the Academy, and president of the Western Academy of Management.

ELAINE ROMANELLI is an associate professor at the Georgetown University McDonough School of Business and director of the Global Entrepreneurship Program there. She holds a Ph.D and an M.B.A. from the Columbia University Graduate School of Business and an A.B. degree from the University of California, Berkeley. Professor Romanelli specializes in entrepreneurship and organizational strategy; her work has focused on the minicomputer, biotechnology, and motion picture industries. She received a four-year Presidential Young Investigator Award from the National Science Foundation to support her research. Professor Romanelli has published articles in the *Administrative Science Quarterly*, the *Academy of Management Journal*, the *Annual Review of Sociology*, *Organization Science*, and *Research in Organizational Behavior*. She has served on the editorial boards of a number of journals, including the *Academy of Management Review*, the *Academy of Management Review*, the *Journal of Business Venturing*, *Organization Science*, and the *Administrative Science Quarterly*.

ERIC ABRAHAMSON is a professor of management at Columbia Business School. He holds a Ph.D. and an M.Ph. from New York University. Professor Abrahamson is internationally recognized for his research on innovation diffusion generally, and fashions in management techniques, more particularly. His work has won two of the most prestigious awards in the management area, the Award for the Best Article published in the *Academy of Management Journal* (1995) and two Best Paper Awards of the Academy of Management Organization and Management Theory Division (1990; 1997). He is a past consulting editor for the *Academy of Management Review* and an upcoming program chair of the Organizational and Management Theory division of the Academy of Management.

HOWARD E. ALDRICH is Kenan Professor of Sociology, chair of the Management and Society curriculum, and adjunct professor of business at the University of North Carolina, Chapel Hill. Professor Aldrich is studying how women- and men-owned businesses differ in their human resource practices and orientations toward growth; the role of social networks and gender in entrepreneurship; the emerging Application Service Provider industry; high-tech firms' dependence on key employees; and the contributions of social networks and personal wealth to new firm formation. His latest book, *Organizations Evolving* (Sage, 1999), won the George Terry Award as the best Academy of Management book published in 1998–99 and was co-winner of the American Sociological Association's Max Weber Award as the best book published in 1997–99. He earned a Ph.D. from the University of Michigan.

TED BAKER is an assistant professor at School of Business at the University of Wisconsin (Madison) School of Business. He teaches graduate courses in entrepreneurial management and is director of the Weinert Applied Ventures in Entrepreneurship (*WAVE*) Program. Baker's research focuses on organizational and employment strategies in high-growth start-ups and on electronic commerce. He holds an M.A. and Ph.D. from the University of North Carolina, Chapel Hill, and an M.B.A. from the University of Chicago. Prior to starting his academic career, Baker worked in private industry for 15 years, most recently as general manager of APPEX Corporation, which was named fastest-growing "high tech hot shot" in the U.S. by *Business Week* in 1990.

M. DIANE BURTON is an assistant professor at the MIT Sloan School of Management. She earned her undergraduate degree in Social and Decision Sciences from Carnegie Mellon University, an M.Ed. from Harvard University Graduate School of Education, and an A.M. and Ph.D. from the Department of Sociology at Stanford University. Professor Burton studies employment relations and organizational change in entrepreneurial companies.

MICHAEL DEVAUGHN is a Ph.D. candidate in the School of Business at the University of Wisconsin, Madison. His research interests include organizational learning, managerial decision making, and ethnic entrepreneurship.

DALE T. EESLEY is a doctoral student at the University of Wisconsin (Madison) School of Business. His research interests include the relation of universities to new venture creation, high-technology start-ups, and how the various paths to entrepreneurship affect new ventures. He is a research assistant at the Weinert Center for Entrepreneurship and has taught his own courses in organizational management, strategy, and small business planning. He holds a B.A. in Economics and English from Gordon College and an M.A. in Religion from Westminster Seminary. Previously, he worked on the Producer Price Index as an economist for the Federal Bureau of Labor Statistics.

GREGORY FAIRCHILD is an assistant professor of business administration at the University of Virginia's Darden School. He holds a Ph.D. from the Columbia Business School, a B.S. from Virginia Commonwealth University, and an M.B.A. from the University of Virginia. He studies management fashions, entrepreneurship in developing economies, and organizational justice.

CHARLES J. FOMBRUN is executive director of the Reputation Institute and professor of management at the Stern School of Business, New York University. He earned a B.S. in physics from Queen's University (Canada) and a Ph.D. at Columbia University. Professor Fombrun has published over fifty articles in leading research and professional journals such as the *Administrative Science Quarterly*, the *Academy of Management Journal*, the *Sloan Management Review*, the *Strategic Management Journal*, and *Organizational Dynamics*. His research addresses three questions: how companies build and sustain valuable reputations; how they plan and execute radical change; and how they manage their resources strategically. He is editor-in-chief of the *Corporate Reputation Review*, a quarterly journal, and founded the Reputation Institute, an organization devoted to research, measurement, and valuation of corporate reputations.

ARI GINSBERG is professor of management, Harold Price Professor of Entrepreneurship, and director of the Berkley Center for Entrepreneurial Studies at the Stern School of Business, New York University. He received his M.B.A. and his Ph.D. in strategic planning and policy from the University of Pittsburgh, and a Master's degree in human learning and cognition from Columbia University. Professor Ginsberg's research and consulting activities focus on entrepreneurial initiatives in ongoing businesses, and he has published widely on the challenges of organizational adaptation and renewal and on how managers think about emerging and dynamically complex business environments. He has received the Citibank Excellence in Teaching Award and the Peter Drucker Fellowship, and has served as chairman of the Management Department at the Stern School.

ERIK R. LARSEN is professor of management and systems at City University Business School, London. He received a Ph.D. in economics from Copenhagen Business School and an M.Sc. in engineering from the Technical University of Denmark. His main research interests include computational organizational theory and strategy (micro-macro problems and modeling with management teams), electricity deregulation (the formulation of strategy in newly deregulated companies), and scenario planning as well as nonlinear dynamics. He has consulted with companies, governments, and international organizations in these areas. From 1996 to 1998 he was an EU Marie Curie Fellow at the University of Bologna.

ALESSANDRO LOMI is a professor of organization theory and behavior at the School of Economics of the University of Bologna (Italy). His research interests include ecological models of organizations, computational theories of organizations, and the analysis of social networks. With Erik Larsen he recently edited *Simulating Organizational Societies*, a volume on simulation and computational models of organizations that will be published by the American Association for Artificial Intelligence and the MIT Press. He received his M.S. and Ph.D. from Cornell University.

ANNE S. MINER is The Ford Motor Company Distinguished Professor of Management and Human Resources at the University of Wisconsin (Madison) School of Business. She has a Ph.D. and M.A. from Stanford University and B.A. from Radcliffe/Harvard. Her research on improvisation and organizational and population-level learning has appeared in journals such as the *Academy of Management Review*, the *Administrative Science Quarterly*, and the *Strategic Management Journal.* Miner co-directed the Technology Enterprise Cooperative, a cross-campus group that facilitates technology entrepreneurship. She is an affiliate of the Weinert Center for Entrepreneurship and teaches courses on technology strategy.

JOHANN PETER MURMANN is an assistant professor of management and organizations at the Kellogg Graduate School of Management at Northwestern University. He received his Ph.D. in management and organization from Columbia University. Currently he is finishing his book *Knowledge and Competitive Advantage: The Coevolution of Firms, Technology, and National Institutions in the Synthetic Dye Industry, 1850–1914.*

HAYAGREEVA RAO is professor of organization and management, Goizeuta Business School, and an adjunct professor in the department of sociology, Emory University. He completed his Ph.D. in organizational behavior at Case Western Reserve University. His research analyzes the social foundations of economic outcomes and has been published in the *American Journal of Sociology*, the *Administrative Science Quarterly*, the *Academy of Management Journal, Organization Science*, the *Strategic Management Journal,* and the *Journal of Marketing.* He is a consulting editor of the *American Journal of Sociology* and senior editor at *Organization Science*, and serves on the editorial boards of the *Administrative Science Quarterly* and the *Academy of Management Review.*

VIOLINA P. RINDOVA is an assistant professor at the Smith School of Business, University of Maryland. She received a J.D. from University of Sofia, an M.B.A. from Madrid Business School–University of Houston, and a Ph.D. from the Stern School of Business, New York University. She teaches strategy and does research on reputation management, value creation, and competitive advantage. Her recent work focuses on Internet exemplars, such as Amazon.com, Yahoo!, and other on-line leaders. She has published several book chapters, as well as articles in scholarly journals such as the *Corporate Reputation Review*, the *Journal of Management Inquiry*, the *Journal of Management Studies*, and the *Strategic Management Journal*, and has presented her work at numerous conferences.

THEKLA RURA-POLLEY received her Ph.D. from the University of Wisconsin, Madison. She is currently a senior lecturer in management at the University of Technology, Sydney. Her research interests include population-level learning, innovation, and emergent technologies. She has studied Catholic children's institutions as well as the film, construction, and conference industries.

ANNALEE SAXENIAN is a professor of city and regional planning at the University of California, Berkeley, and an internationally recognized expert on regional economies and the information technology sector. She has a Ph.D. in political science from MIT, a Master's degree in regional planning from the University of California, Berkeley, and a B.A. in economics from Williams College. Saxenian has written extensively about innovation and regional development, urbanization, and the organization of labor markets in Silicon Valley. Her current research examines the contributions of skilled immigrants to Silicon Valley and their growing ties to regions in Asia. She is the current Gordon Cain Senior Fellow at the Stanford Institute for Economic Policy Research.

DANIEL J. STEWARD is a Ph.D. candidate in the department of sociology at the University of Wisconsin, Madison. He holds a J.D. from the Columbia University School of Law and has practiced as a transactional lawyer in the San Francisco/Silicon Valley area of California. He works with Mark Suchman to study the roles of attorneys, entrepreneurs, and financiers in Silicon Valley. This research, together with studies of the history of censorship discourse and the development of intellectual property law, informs an ongoing theoretical interest in the relations between the legal system and civil society.

MARK C. SUCHMAN is an associate professor of sociology and law at the University of Wisconsin, Madison. His primary research interests center on the legal environments of organizational activity in general, and on the role of law firms in the development of Silicon Valley in particular. He has also written on organizational legitimacy, on ecological and institutional models of organizations, on the interrelationship of economic and sociological explanations of legal phenomena, and on the impact of changing professional structures on corporate litigation ethics. He holds an A.B. from Harvard University, a J.D. from the Yale Law School, and a Ph.D. in sociology from Stanford University.

ANAND SWAMINATHAN is an associate professor of management in the Graduate School of Management at the University of California, Davis. He received his Ph.D. in business administration from the University of California, Berkeley. His current research focuses on the resource-partitioning model in organizational ecology, the influence of network structure on organizational survival, the emergence of institutional constraints and their consequences for firm performance, and the social movement aspects of industry evolution. His research has appeared in journals such as the *Academy of Management Journal, Acta Sociologica*, the *American Journal of Sociology*, the *American Sociological Review*, the *Administrative Science Quarterly, Industrial and Corporate Change, Organization Studies*, and the *Strategic Management Journal*. Professor Swaminathan is a member of the editorial board for the *Administrative Science Quarterly* and *Organization Science*.

MICHAEL L. TUSHMAN is the Paul R. Lawrence, Class of 1942 Professor of Business Administration at the Harvard University Graduate School of Business. He earned a B.S.E.E. from Northeastern University, an M.S. from Cornell University, and a Ph.D. from the Sloan School of Management at MIT. Professor Tushman is internationally recognized for his work on the relations between technological change, executive leadership, and organization adaptation, and for his work on managing R&D laboratories. He has served on the boards of many scholarly journals, including the *Administrative Science Quarterly, Management Science,* the *Academy of Management Journal, Human Relations,* the *Journal of Business Venturing,* the *Journal of Product Innovation Management,* and *IEEE Transactions on Engineering Management.* Tushman was elected Fellow of the Academy of Management and has served as past chairperson of the Organization and Management Theory and the R&D and Innovation Divisions of the Academy of Management.

JAMES B. WADE is associate professor of management and human resources in the School of Business at the University of Wisconsin, Madison. He received his Ph.D. in business administration from the University of California, Berkeley. His articles have been published in the *Administrative Science Quarterly,* the *Strategic Management Journal,* the *Academy of Management Journal,* the *Rand Journal of Economics,* the *Journal of Labor Economics,* and other outlets. His research interests include top management team issues, organizational ecology, social movement aspects of industry evolution, the technological evolution of standards, and how knowledge is transferred through alliances and inter- and intra-organizational personnel flows. Currently he is investigating the evolution of standards in the flexible disk drive industry, the role of personnel mobility in knowledge transfer in the U.S. paper industry, the determinants of shareholder resolutions and option repricings, the evolution of the HDTV standard in the United States, and how strategic contingencies affect executive pay and promotion rates.

CLIFFORD A. WESTFALL holds a J.D. from New York University and is a graduate student in sociology at the University of Wisconsin, Madison. His primary research interests include sociological theory, the sociology of legal and bureaucratic institutions, and the sociology of culture.

THE ENTREPRENEURSHIP DYNAMIC

1

Introduction

Premises of the Entrepreneurship Dynamic

CLAUDIA BIRD SCHOONHOVEN

AND ELAINE ROMANELLI

This book developed from the basic idea that it is both necessary and the right time to focus theoretical and empirical attention on the key questions of entrepreneurship research rather than on the differing assumptions and emphases of the disciplines. We think there are two major questions that cut across the disciplines and animate the abiding fascination of entrepreneurship research.

First, what are the conditions, including economic, cultural, and even personal situations and proclivities, that prompt the founding of new organizations? In other words, what are the origins of new organizations? Especially, what are the conditions in industries, economies, and societies that generate large numbers of new organizations being founded in particular times and places? This question, while motivating the majority of entrepreneurship studies, has rarely been asked objectively or systematically. Instead, disparate theories of origins—that is, the personal, the cultural, and the economic—have been posited and tested for their influence in isolation from one another. The unsurprising result is that we find evidence in the literature of a myriad of factors that, sometimes, for some industries, in some nations or regions, and in certain periods of history, appear to promote the rise of new organizations, especially in large numbers. Still, no one today can predict when and where large numbers of new organizations will emerge. We still don't know which factors to emphasize or when different factors will be important. And, of course, the factors themselves may be changing over time. Research needs to be directed to the study of organizational origins in a way that is independent of disciplinary biases. Organization theory, which cuts across the various disciplines, seems a good scholarly venue for approaching this research.

Second, what are the real and important outcomes of entrepreneurial activity? Somewhat surprisingly, since outcomes, including the economic and social transformation of whole societies, are the only reasonable motivation for research into origins, little research has directly explored outcomes. Birley (1986) verified the general and seemingly indisputable observation that new organizations produce new jobs and economic wealth in greater proportion than established organizations. Popular statistics, like those from the U.S. Small Business Administration and Department of Commerce, seem to confirm the idea that new organizations produce innovation, and reap profits from major innovations, to a much greater extent than established organizations. Organizational ecologists (e.g., Hannan and Freeman 1989) have explored organizational foundings as a key dynamic in the development of organizational populations. Aldrich (1979; 1999), echoing Schumpeter's (1934) arguments about the business cycle, has maintained that the effects of organizational foundings, especially in large numbers, on the competitive conditions of industry is one of the most important questions in all of the social sciences. Nonetheless, outcomes themselves have been little examined.

At the nexus of these two fundamental questions, we believe, lies a still more basic understanding, or perhaps only belief, about entrepreneurship as a root dynamic of change in industries, economies, and societies. New organizations do not emerge *de novo* from the idiosyncratic and isolated invention of individual entrepreneurs. Their ideas for new organizations, their ability to acquire capital and other important material and human resources, and their new organization's likelihood of surviving derive from the contexts in which individuals live and work. Context, even assuming a special and broad influence of distinctive and uncommon individual inclinations, must exert a constraining influence on rates and kinds of organization creation at the same time that it motivates organization creation. New organizations are both users of existing resources and creators of new resources—knowledge, skills, and needs—that drive markets for new products and services. The very process of organization creation, although it is the product of context, we argue, fundamentally and immediately transforms the context. New organizations, in other words, are both the products of conditions already evolved and the producers of change. Entrepreneurship is a pivotal dynamic of economic and social change.

The Entrepreneurship Dynamic is organized into two parts, the first addressing the question of organizational origins in context and the second exploring the role of entrepreneurial activity in the transformation of contexts. We admit up front, and it should come as no surprise, that the chapters actually produced for this book do not fit neatly under the two questions posed as independent issues. As we have briefly discussed, origins and outcomes are not independent issues. Rather, the origins, and perhaps we should say the processes, rather than the outcomes of entrepreneurial activity are two sides of one overarching process of industry transformation in regions and economies. Sometimes the origins lie in established systems of industry knowledge and production, systems that may have outlived their capacities for incorporating new ideas or innovations. Sometimes, though, they lie in the very conditions and processes of new industry creation. We thus organized this book to reflect the predominant emphases of the chapters on either the contextual origins of entrepreneurial activity or the role and influence of entrepreneurial activity on processes of industry development. As the reader will discover, there are both many overlapping and newly emerging themes in these chapters. In our closing chapter, we try to highlight some of these themes and outline an agenda for new research that holds promise for transforming the study of entrepreneurship itself.

The six papers in Part One, "The Origins of Entrepreneurial Activity and New Organizations," directly tackle the questions, "Where do new firms come from, and what are the conditions that promote the rise of entrepreneurial activity in general?" Each paper examines entrepreneurial origins empirically and provides insight into the creation of new organizations in context.

The first three chapters—"The Company They Keep: Founders' Models for Organizing New Firms," by M. Diane Burton, "The Local Origins of New Firms," by Elaine Romanelli and Claudia Bird Schoonhoven, and "The Role of Immigrant Entrepreneurs in New Venture Creation," by AnnaLee Saxenian—all directly address the question of where founders come from and, more important, how the originating contexts affect both the kinds of organizations the founders create and the influence of their new organizations on regional and industrial contexts. In Chapter 2, Burton explores how founders' experiences in previous organizations, and the mental models they develop about appropriate employment relationships as a result of those experiences, influence the forms of organizations they create. In focusing on founders' experiences in existing organizations as the incubators of ideas about organizational forms, Burton both fuses the individual and contextual influences on organizational creation and at least partially locates the origins of organizational diversity in the forms of existing organizations. The chapter develops theory and tests hypotheses about the origins of entrepreneurs' employment models, using a sample of 173 young high-technology firms in Silicon Valley. Mental models about appropriate modes of organization creation, held by entrepreneurs as well as institutional players such as venture capitalists, lawyers, and professional organizations, emerged as a central theme in discussions and debates at the Balboa Bay Conference, as we will discuss in Chapter 14.

In Chapter 3, we draw on similar premises about the importance of existing organizations in the entrepreneurial process, but we shift perspective to the organization community circumscribed by major metropolitan regions. In this chapter, we argue that entrepreneurs' ideas for new ventures, while based in their experiences in established organizations, also acquire character from the nature of the surrounding organizational community. In particular, the formation of an idea for a new venture proceeds not merely from experience in the design or marketing of a particular product or service in an existing organization but also from knowledge about local markets and competitive conditions for new products or services. The importance of understanding entrepreneurial activity as a predominantly local process and phenomenon was a second major theme of the conference. This chapter explores the geographically local character of organizational creation and develops a theory of the local origins of entrepreneurial activity.

Saxenian, in Chapter 4, adds another dimension to this developing perspective about the regional origins of entrepreneurial activity. Focusing on Silicon Valley and its now-legendary capacity for generating innovation through homegrown entrepreneurial activity, she explores the role of immigration as a central feature of the region's penchant for entrepreneurial experimentation. Saxenian explores the regular influx and outflow of immigrant entrepreneurs in Silicon Valley as a persistent dynamic of industry and regional transformation. Partly as a result of a perceived glass-ceiling effect for non-White technology workers, immigrant entrepreneurs in Silicon Valley have increasingly established their own organizations and professional associations to promote exchanges of information and personnel. Moreover, as immigrant entrepreneurs in Silicon Valley show a persistent concern for economic development in their home countries, Saxenian explores how the knowledge and experiences they gained in California may diffuse throughout the world.

The last three chapters in Part One—"The Magic Beanstalk Vision: Commercializing University Inventions and Research," by Anne S. Miner, Dale T. Eesley, Michael DeVaughn, and Thekla Rura-Polley, "Knowledge Industries and Idea Entrepreneurs: New Dimensions of Innovative Products, Services, and Organizations," by Eric Abrahamson and Gregory Fairchild, and "From the Technology Cycles to the Entrepreneurship Dynamic: The Social Context of Entrepreneurial Innovation," by Johann Peter Murmann and Michael L. Tushman—shift our perspective on entrepreneurial origins from the somewhat personalized location of the individual entrepreneur to a broader notion of originating contexts: the university, the knowledge industry, and the technology cycle, respectively. In distinct but related ways, these chapters explore communities of knowledge or learning as venues for the generation of entrepreneurial ideas.

In Chapter 5, Miner and her colleagues explore universities as popularly presumed prolific producers of new organizations. Building on interviews with senior university officers and technology transfer administrators at universities and research institutions in seven countries, these authors document the prevalence of a theory in use about the close relationship between university research and organizational formation. They explore both the cultural origins of this pervasive belief about universities as producers of entrepreneurial activity and consequent regional wealth, as well as the broad empirical literature about the actual influences of universities. While the authors are systematically and insightfully critical of the mental model of the university as a "magic beanstalk" of new organizations, they also extend a theory of how population-level learning from shared (even if erroneous) assumptions can generate real change. Like most of the chapters in this section, the authors found it impossible to consider origins in isolation from outcomes. One produces the other.

Abrahamson and Fairchild, in Chapter 6, explore an intriguing new question about how entrepreneurship arises in what they call the knowledge industries—book publishing, consulting, mass media, and education, among many others. Entrepreneurship, they argue, lies not only in the domain of innovative products and services but also in the ideas that govern our understandings about how organizations and industries should function. Asking questions about the sources of ideas for new knowledge ventures as well as the timing and development of new industry segments from the activities of idea entrepreneurs, these authors again emphasize the inseparability of entrepreneurial individuals and the contexts from which they emerge.

Finally, in Chapter 7, Murmann and Tushman examine technological systems as dynamic sources of knowledge or ideas for new organizations. While much research on innovation and technology has focused on the emergence of a dominant design as a singular event from which mainly process innovations follow, these authors argue that such breakthroughs establish merely the *first* interesting event in a nested hierarchy of dominant designs in technological subsystems. Dominant designs, which are typically first identified at the product level, give way over time, through learning by the technologists, to whole new technologies and dominant designs in the technological subsystems of the original dominant design. In this chapter, Murmann and Tushman build on their earlier work to focus here on the social context of entrepreneurial innovation, emphasizing the influence of networks of relationships among academic and industry scientists as well as decisions and policies of players in the institutional environments of nations.

Taken together, these six chapters seek to locate the origins of new organizations in (1) the organizational contexts in which individuals live and work, and (2) the knowledge and resource communities that, through the interactions and learning of the individuals within the communities, produce the conceptual raw material of new ideas. Community, whether bounded by geography, knowledge, or technology, is a rich, emergent theme in organizational theory writ large, and one that conference participants considered might develop generally as a unifying theme for future investigation of the origins of entrepreneurship. Perhaps precisely the problem in decades and centuries of previous research has been a failure to properly or richly enough define the context of entrepreneurial origins.

As we argued at the outset of this chapter, there is but one inescapably important reason to care about the origins of entrepreneurial activity: the outcomes that new organizations produce for economies and societies. While many sorts of outcomes—such as jobs, innovation, and economic wealth— have been examined as important products of entrepreneurial activity, the chapters in this section focus on ways in which new organizations affect the development of industries and the creation of new organizational populations. The six chapters contained in Part Two, "Entrepreneurship in the Evolution of Industries," diversely address this issue.

The first four papers—"Learning and Legitimacy: Entrepreneurial Responses to Constraints on the Emergence of New Populations and Organizations," by Howard E. Aldrich and Ted Baker, "Entrepreneurial Action in the Creation of the Specialty Coffee Niche," by Violina P. Rindova and Charles J. Fombrun, "The Power of Public Competition: Promoting Cognitive Legitimacy Through Certification Contests," by Hayagreeva Rao, and "Social Movement Theory and the Evolution of New Organizational Forms," by Anand Swaminathan and James B. Wade—examine the processes and tools that entrepreneurs use to create and legitimate new organizational populations. These chapters develop the third major insight from the Balboa Bay Conference, that entrepreneurs play an active and purposive role in the creation and development of new industries and new organizations.

Aldrich and Baker, in Chapter 8, examine this question directly in an exploration of strategies that entrepreneurs have used to establish the cognitive and sociopolitical legitimacy of new forms of business and consumer transactions in the emerging community of Internet organizations. Legitimacy, which refers to the establishment of new organizational forms as both taken-for-granted and appropriate ways of conducting business, is not easily or naturally granted in society. Rather, entrepreneurs must systematically and strategically promote the legitimacy of their new organizational forms. Aldrich and Baker emphasize the collective nature of this activity. Entrepreneurs, at the same time as they may compete in particular product or service domains of the Internet, also share information and act collectively to legitimate the organizational form.

In Chapter 9, Rindova and Fombrun, through a detailed history of the U.S. coffee industry and the relatively recent creation of the specialty coffee niche, also explore the proposition that new structures (or niches) within established industries are endogenously produced by the activities of entrepreneurs. Entrepreneurs, they stress, systematically educate consumers about the benefits of new products and services to actively carve out new market spaces. These authors describe the strategies of specialty coffee entrepreneurs—perhaps we could call them idea entrepreneurs of a different sort—to promote and create demand for coffee...as if taste mattered. Where Aldrich and Baker focus on the formation of new communities as the substance of new population creation, Rindova and Fombrun focus on the creation of markets.

In Chapter 10, Rao investigates the role and influence of product certification contests as a key strategy for promoting the cognitive and sociopolitical legitimacy of a new organizational form. Drawing on a rich history of the early automobile industry in the United States, he shows how public contests—races and other comparisons of performance and reliability—among early competitors in the industry not only promoted debate about relative benefits of their individual products, but also educated the public about the benefits in general. As an interesting proof of the importance of certification contests in creating cognitive and sociopolitical legitimacy, Rao notes the disappearance of the formal contests once automobiles were established as a taken-for-granted and appropriate mode of transportation.

Finally, Swaminathan and Wade, in Chapter 11, draw on the rich literature of social movements to explore how entrepreneurs, especially those seeking to establish new organizational forms, mobilize resources to overcome liabilities of newness and establish cognitive and sociopolitical legitimacy. Drawing on data from the development of specialized brewing populations, these authors examine both the structure of opportunities and constraints that promote or retard the mobilization of resources and the generation of collective action frames that overcome such constraints. In contrast to Rao, who emphasizes public competition as a form of collective strategy for generating legitimacy, these authors stress cooperation. At the same time, these authors point out, collective activity for the formation of a new population is more likely to emerge in the presence of a strong, incumbent population that competes for resources with the new population.

The next two chapters in Part Two—"Entrepreneurship in Context: Strategic Interaction and the Emergence of Regional Economies," by Ari Ginsberg, Erik R. Larsen, and Alessandro Lomi, and "The Legal Environment of Entrepreneurship: Observations on the Legitimation of Venture Finance in Silicon Valley," by Mark C. Suchman, Daniel J. Steward, and Clifford A. Westfall—both continue the theme of collective action as an essential process in the development of a new organizational population and return us to the theme of entrepreneurship in local context that was explored in the first several chapters of this volume. Whereas the earlier chapters examine the influence of local context on the formation of individual organizations, these chapters focus on local cooperation and institutionalization as key processes in the development of industry clusters.

Ginsberg, Larsen, and Lomi, in Chapter 12, use a computational model to examine the rise and sustainability of industry clusters as a function of both the initial size of the cluster and the decisions that entrepreneurs make about appropriate strategic interaction. Entrepreneurs make strategic decisions about whether to cooperate with other organizations in a geographic cluster by conforming to an emerging common organizational form or by defecting from that form based on their understandings of local competitive conditions. More cooperative clusters, if they reach a threshold size, will tend to persist and will also become increasingly stable in the established organizational form.

Finally, Suchman and his colleagues, in Chapter 13, explore the role of law—venture capital financing contracts in particular—in the development of persistent entrepreneurial activity in regions. Legal institutions, these authors argue, promulgate perceived-to-be-effective and thus legitimate forms of organizational activity through their active participation in the structuring of financial deals and their development of a broad, if socially constructed, knowledge about kinds of organizational forms that have succeeded (or failed) in the past. Venture capital financing contracts in Silicon Valley, especially as they became more standardized over time, tended to reduce uncertainties about both the processes and likely outcomes of start-up activity, thus encouraging a steady release of entrepreneurial activity and investment.

As the above brief descriptions make clear, and as a close reading of the chapters in this volume will reveal, there is perhaps a surprising consensus among the authors about important new themes for theory and new directions for entrepreneurship research. Though our authors arrived at the Conference with ideas about entrepreneurship research that initially seemed disparate, a collective understanding emerged about a few core ideas that appeared repeatedly in the papers. First, entrepreneurship is a local process, bounded fundamentally by the resources and cultural understandings of local environments. Second, the mental models of effective organization creation and population development, which are held by both entrepreneurs and institutional actors, systematically influence the character of both new organizations and the industries or populations of which they are a part. Finally, both the creation of new organizations and the institutional establishment of new populations are the result of purposive and collective strategies by entrepreneurs and institutional actors. Together, these themes, which we examine in the final chapter of this book, set the stage for new research and conversation about the *Entrepreneurship Dynamic.*

We conceived the Balboa Bay Conference as a convocation for emerging ideas about entrepreneurship as a vital dynamic in the evolution of industries, and in the same way, we offer this book as call for future research. Entrepreneurship studies have gone on for too long and the issues have been too varied and complex for us to suggest the emergence of any unified theory. The themes described above, however, along with several others that emerge from this collection of papers, we believe create a foundation for a new era in entrepreneurship research, one that attends to important and cross-disciplinary questions and one that takes seriously the importance of theory. We invite other interested scholars to carry on the conversation.

The Origins of Entrepreneurial Activity and New Organizations

2

The Company They Keep

Founders' Models for Organizing New Firms

M. DIANE BURTON

In starting a company, entrepreneurs pursue courses of action that, intentionally or unintentionally, embody different assumptions about the nature of work, the nature of people, the appropriate bases for attaching people to organizations, and the best methods for controlling and coordinating work. Such differing premises lead entrepreneurs to build different types of firms, particularly with respect to the employment relationship. Early employment-related choices—which crystallize organizational culture, authority relations, and routines concerning work—are among the most difficult to undo (Hannan and Freeman 1984). Furthermore, there is ample empirical evidence demonstrating that decisions about whom to employ and how to organize their work is related to the earliest viability of a firm (Boeker 1988; Cooper, Gimeno-Gascon, and Woo 1994; Eisenhardt and Schoonhoven 1990; MacMillan, Siegel, and Subba Narasimha 1985). Yet despite consensus that these early employment-related choices are important, there has been little systematic research on the factors that influence founders' decisions. Instead, most research on how founders launch new ventures has emphasized the entrepreneurs' strategies for products, markets, technology, operations, and finance

This research was supported by the Division of Research of Harvard Business School, the Stanford Graduate School of Business (particularly the Center for Entrepreneurial Studies), and the Alfred P. Sloan Foundation. I am deeply indebted to Mike Hannan and Jim Baron for support of many kinds. I also benefited greatly from discussions with and comments from Karen Aschaffenburg, Nitin Nohria, Mike Tushman, Marc Ventresca, and Stephanie Woerner.

(e.g., Romanelli 1989a). Yet a new venture's capacity to recruit the appropriate people and build an effective organization around them arguably has as much if not more to do with ultimate success (Stinchcombe 1965).

In making organizational and employment-related decisions, founders necessarily rely on a mental model of the correct and appropriate ways to organize and to manage (DiMaggio 1997; Fligstein 1990; Karpik 1978). These models are culturally and historically situated prescriptions for organizing and managing (Barley and Kunda 1992; Guillen 1994). Organizational theory provides a strong prediction that, taking into account the environmental conditions facing the firm (Pfeffer and Salancik 1978) and the technical demands of the task (Thompson 1967; Woodward 1965), there will be a dominant model, especially within the boundaries of a particular industry (DiMaggio and Powell 1983). Interestingly, despite this prediction, observers have found different employment models across seemingly similar firms (Applebaum and Batt 1994; Henderson and Cockburn 1994; Kochan, Katz, and McKersie 1992). The question of what accounts for this heterogeneity is largely unanswered (Romanelli 1991). An important first step is to understand different mental models and their sources.

Although extant theory implies that organizations founded at particular times in particular industries tend to exhibit similar employment models, differences in founders' educational and employment experiences may produce diversity in their understanding of what the normative employment models are. Novel models may arise by accident, invented by those who are either inexperienced or disconnected or both (March and Olsen 1976; Hannan and Freeman 1989). Alternatively, founders might intentionally deviate from the normative models because of unhappy experiences. They may also strategically avoid such models out of a belief than an atypical employment model may lead to competitive advantages. Thus, novel models may arise when leaders believe that they can prosper by deliberately choosing a distinctive approach to organizing and managing (DiMaggio 1988; Fligstein 1987; Schein 1983). Without a clear understanding of how variation in employment models arises, we cannot begin to understand how particular choices may relate to the development of the firm or to its performance.

This chapter examines the employment models founders use as they begin to construct new firms. The empirical setting is a sample of emerging high-technology firms in Silicon Valley. This chapter focuses on two questions: (1) Why are new firms founded under different conceptual models? and (2) What are the factors that lead a founding team to espouse a particular employment model?

Nascent organizations, start-ups, are ideal subjects for studying variations in employment models. The founding team members must immediately make a series of staffing and organization-building decisions that necessarily embody the employment relationship. Moreover, in a new firm, the choices are not limited by prior decisions nor do they build on existing policies; instead, the decisions arise directly from the founders' mental models. The initial employment model and the organizational strategy are simultaneously set as a firm is founded; thus, one can examine contemporaneous associations without concern for causality. Finally, because new firms have not yet established either a reputation or a track record, they depend on external ties to provide both resources and legitimacy (Starr and Macmillan 1990). Because of this dependency, new firms may be especially receptive to external influences that impose normative models (Scott 1995).

EMPLOYMENT MODELS IN START-UPS

The data for this chapter come from information collected as part of the Stanford Project on Emerging Companies (SPEC).[1] SPEC is a panel study examining the founding conditions, the evolution of employment practices, organizational designs, and business strategies, and the longer-term consequences of early organization building in a sample of 173 young high-technology firms in Silicon Valley. The firms in the study were founded between 1982 and 1994 and had at least 10 employees at the time of sampling in 1994–95.

The design of the SPEC study deliberately narrows some of the possible sources of variation in founders' models. For example, focusing on firms in a single region and sector of economic activity necessarily controls for labor mar-

---

1. The description draws heavily from published research papers by M. Diane Burton, James Baron, Michael Hannan, and others affiliated with the Stanford Project on Emerging Companies (SPEC).

ket and environmental conditions, as well as for some of the institutional influences asserted to shape organizations. There are other reasons to expect a great deal of homogeneity in organizational models among young Silicon Valley technology companies. Compared with the economy as a whole, the tasks of high-technology companies are relatively similar. For the most part, firms in Silicon Valley are subject to the same state and regional legal and regulatory environment. The accessibility of capital and the tightly interconnected infrastructure of service providers such as lawyers, headhunters, accountants, and consultants that fuel the start-up creation process should, in theory, create relatively standardized organizations (cf. Suchman 1994a). All of the firms are in rapidly changing environments, and all of them are critically dependent on technical talent, a resource that tends to be in short supply. Both employees and founders in Silicon Valley are highly mobile (Rogers and Larsen 1984; Saxenian 1994).

Prior SPEC research has demonstrated that there is heterogeneity in founders' employment models. Researchers have identified archetypal employment models that are associated with distinctive human resources practices (Baron, Burton, and Hannan 1996) and that predict subsequent organizational development, including the timing of an initial public stock offering, the transition to a non-founder CEO (Hannan, Burton, and Baron 1996), the amount of managerial and administrative overhead (Baron, Hannan, and Burton 1999), and the extent of bureaucratization (Baron, Burton, and Hannan 1999). This prior research documents that the employment models are real: they are empirically observable and have measurable and predictable consequences for firms. This chapter assesses whether there is a dominant model within particular industry segments and attempts to identify the factors that account for conformity to or deviance from what may be normatively prescribed.

The primary data for this chapter come from open-ended interviews that I and several research associates conducted with founders. These interviews typically lasted 60 minutes, during which time the founder was first asked to describe the impetus for forming a company, how the founding team was put together, and the planned source of competitive advantage. Each founder was then asked whether he or she had "an organizational model or blueprint in mind" when he or she founded the company. Founders described models retrospectively in the context of a semi-structured interview in which the questions and probes were open-ended and were part of an informal dialogue.

Detailed qualitative analysis of the transcripts revealed three recurring dimensions along which founders' descriptions varied: (1) the nature of the employees' attachment to the firm, (2) the basis for selecting new employees, and (3) the mode of coordinating and controlling work (for additional details, see Burton 1995).

Attachment. Founders articulated three different bases of employees' attachment: love, work, and money. Some founders envisioned creating a strong family-like feeling and an intense emotional bond with the workforce that would inspire superior effort and help retain highly sought employees. In these firms, what binds the employee is a sense of personal belonging and identification with the company that is labeled love. Other founders believed that the primary motivator for their employees was the desire to work at the technological frontier. These founders relied on providing interesting and challenging work as the basis for attracting, motivating, and perhaps retaining employees. Finally, other founders stated that they regarded the employment relationship as a simple exchange of labor for money.

Selection. Founders described three bases for selecting employees: skills, potential, and fit. Some founders seemed to think of the firm as a bundle of tasks and sought employees with the requisite skills and experience needed to accomplish some immediate tasks. Other founders focused less on immediate and well-defined tasks than on a series of projects, often not yet even envisioned, through which employees would move over time. Accordingly, they focused on long-term potential. Finally, another group of founders focused primarily on values or cultural fit and placed heavy emphasis on how a prospective hire would connect with others in the organization.

Mode of coordination and control. The most common blueprint for controlling and coordinating work involved extensive reliance on informal control through peers or the organizational culture. Other founders appeared to take for granted the fact that workers were committed to excellence in their work and could perform at high levels because they had been professionally socialized to do so. Professional control emphasizes autonomy and independence, rather than inculcation, and founders using this approach tended to recruit high-potential individuals from elite institutions. A third group of founders espoused a more traditional view of control as being embedded in formal procedures and systems. Finally, some founders stated that they intended to control and coordinate work personally, by direct oversight, reminiscent of the simple control paradigm that Edwards (1979) identified as characteristic of small capitalist firms in the late-nineteenth and early twentieth century.

Founders' employment models are made up of one of three possible variants of both attachment and selection and one of four possible variants of control, yielding the potential for $3 \times 3 \times 4 = 36$ unique employment models. But iterative inductive analyses of the interview transcripts suggested that founders drew on a small number of salient cultural institutions—universities and research laboratories, project teams, traditional hierarchies, and communities—to describe their models, and many of the observations in the SPEC sample cluster into five of the 36 cells, which neatly correspond to the cultural institutions and account for 57% (88 of 154) of the ventures.[2] Table 2.1 shows these basic archetypal models, which are here labeled engineering, star, commitment, bureaucracy, and autocracy, with their corresponding dimensions and prevalence in the sample.

Each of the archetypal models exemplifies a well-understood mode of organizing. The engineering model, which involves attachment through challenging work, peer-group control, and selection based on specific task abilities, resembles a task-focused project team. The star model resembles the organizing mode of science and academia, wherein attachment derives from challenging work, there is a reliance on autonomy and professional control, and personnel are selected based on their long-term potential. The commitment model is family-like and relies on emotional attachments of employees to the organization, selection based on cultural fit, and peer-group control. The bureaucracy model is a modern, rationalized, organization and involves attachment based on providing challenging work and/or opportunities for development, selecting individuals based on their qualifications for a particular role, and relying on formalized control. Finally, the autocracy model is reminiscent

---

2. We were able to code the component dimensions of the founding employment model for 154 of the 173 firms. In some cases we were unable to interview a founder. In other cases the transcripts lacked sufficient detail to code reliably all three dimensions (attachment, selection, and control).

Table 2.1

Five Archetypal Employment Models Based on Three Dimensions

Dimensions			*Employment Model*	*Percent of Firms*
ATTACHMENT	SELECTION	COORDINATION/ CONTROL		
Work	Potential	Professional	Star	8.4%
Work	Skills	Peer/cultural	Engineering	32.5%
Love	Fit	Peer/cultural	Commitment	7.1%
Work	Skills	Formal	Bureaucracy	5.2%
Money	Skills	Direct	Autocracy	3.9%

of turn-of-the-century factories, in which employment is premised on purely monetary motivations, control and coordination are achieved through close personal oversight, and employees are selected based on their ability to perform prespecified tasks.

The remaining 43% of the sample—those firms that are located in one of the 31 cells other than the five cells representing the basic types—can be characterized according to their distance from the archetypes by counting the number of dimensions that would need to change in order to transform a firm in a given cell into a basic model. For example, a firm with money as the basis of attachment, skill-oriented selection criteria, and formal control systems (money, skill, formal control) would be three dimensions from a commitment firm (love, fit, normative control), two dimensions from an engineering firm (work, skill, normative control), but only one dimension from either a bureaucracy (work, skill, formal control) or an autocracy (money, skill, direct control).

Under this formulation, one can argue that virtually all of the firms in the SPEC sample are conceptually close to at least one of the five basic models. Eighty-eight of the 154 firms (57%) are accounted for by the basic types. Another 64 firms (42%) are within a single dimension of at least one basic type of employment model. Within this group, it is useful to differentiate hybrid models, those that are one dimension from two or more basic types (47 firms, or 31%, use hybrid models), and quasi models, those that are one dimension from a single basic type (15 firms, or 10%, have quasi models). Only two firms out of 154 (1%) are aberrant or incongruent (two dimensions away from a basic employment model). Table 2.2 presents a diagram of all 36 cells indicating the distance of each model from basic employment models as well as counts of the number of firms in each cell.

From the numbers in Table 2.2, one might conclude that the engineering model is dominant in Silicon Valley—nearly one-third of the firms exhibit basic engineering models and an additional third (50 of 154) are within a single dimension of the engineering model. But what of the remaining third of the firms? A closer examination of the firms' environment or strategy may account for such model variations without having to take into account the unique biography of each firm, as Kimberly and Bouchikhi (1995) suggested, because the SPEC sample design controls for history and geography. The most salient environmental feature is the industry, and although all of the SPEC firms are technology related, they operate in different industries that are subject to different regulatory environments and face different domestic and international competition. Different industries may also have different norms and cultures. The firms were coded into broad industry categories that capture the major sources of environmental variation that they faced: computer related, semiconductor, networking and telecommunications, medical related, research, and manufacturing.[3] Within the SPEC sample, there is a strong association between the founding employment model and the firm's industry, as shown in Table 2.3.

Among the 88 firms that were founded with a basic model, there appears to be a clear dominant archetype. For example, at least one-third of the firms in the electronics industries—computers (37.5%), semiconductors (37.5%), and networking (33.3%)—were founded with the engineering model. Over 40% of the firms in the medical and research industries were founded under the star model, which resembles the universities and laboratories from which much of their talent is recruited. Among manufacturing firms the only archetype exhibited in the SPEC sample is the commitment model. In subsequent analyses (except one assessing the effect of strategy), industries that have the same dominant industry model are combined and relabeled, resulting in three

---

3. These industry categories are rather coarse. For example, the medical-related industry category includes both medical device companies and biotechnology companies. For purposes of characterizing the environment, both types of firms are subject to regulation by the Food and Drug Administration. In this way, they are similar to one another yet distinct from other electronics and high-tech companies in the sample.

Table 2.2
Firm Classification According to a Three-Way Crosstabulation of
Employment Model Dimensions (including cell counts)

Control	Selection	Attachment			
		LOVE	WORK	MONEY	TOTAL
Professional	Skills	0 *Unclassified*	6 *Hybrid Star/ Engineering/ Bureaucracy*	2 *Quasi Autocracy*	8
	Potential	0 *Quasi Star*	13 *Archetypal Star*	0 *Quasi Star*	13
	Fit	0 *Quasi Commitment*	1 *Quasi Star*	0 *Unclassified*	1
Normative	Skills	9 *Hybrid Commitment/ Engineering*	50 *Archetypal Engineering*	6 *Hybrid Engineering/ Autocracy*	65
	Potential	2 *Quasi Commitment*	8 *Hybrid Star/ Engineering*	0 *Unclassified*	10
	Fit	11 *Archetypal Commitment*	9 *Hybrid Commitment/ Engineering*	2 *Quasi Commitment*	22
Formal	Skills	0 *Quasi Bureaucracy*	8 *Archetypal Bureaucracy*	4 *Hybrid Bureaucracy/ Autocracy*	12
	Potential	0 *Unclassified*	1 *Hybrid Star/Bureaucracy*	0 *Unclassified*	1
	Fit	1 *Quasi Commitment*	1 *Quasi Bureaucracy*	2 *Unclassified*	4
Direct	Skills	2 *Quasi Autocracy*	4 *Hybrid Engineer/ Bureaucracy/ Autocracy*	6 *Archetypal Autocracy*	12
	Potential	0 *Unclassified*	1 *Quasi Star*	0 *Quasi Autocracy*	1
	Fit	5 *Quasi Commitment*	0 *Unclassified*	0 *Quasi Autocracy*	5
TOTAL AT FOUNDING		29	103	22	154

Table 2.3
Industry and Archetype Model Association
(cell counts and row percentages)

	Engineering	Star	Commitment	Autocracy	Bureaucracy	Other	Total
Computer-related	27	2	5	3	4	31	72
	(37.5%)	(2.8%)	(6.9%)	(4.2%)	(5.6%)	(43.1%)	
Semiconductor	6	0	2	1	1	6	16
	(37.5%)	(0.0%)	(12.5%)	(6.3%)	(6.3%)	(37.5%)	
Networking and Telecommunications	11	0	2	2	2	16	33
	(33.3%)	(0.0%)	(6.1%)	(6.1%)	(6.1%)	(8.5%)	
Medical related	5	9	0	0	1	7	22
	(22.7%)	(40.9%)	(0.0%)	(0.0%)	(4.5%)	(31.8%)	
Research	1	2	0	0	0	1	4
	(25.0%)	(50.0%)	(0.0%)	(0.0%)	(0.0%)	(25.0%)	
Manufacturing	0	0	2	0	0	5	7
	(0.0%)	(0.0%)	(28.6%)	(0.0%)	(0.0%)	(71.4%)	
TOTAL	50	13	11	6	8	66	154
	(30.8%)	(8.4%)	(7.1%)	(3.9%)	(5.2%)	(42.9%)	

NOTE: Pearson chi-square = 59.08, d.f. = 25, p = .000

broad industry categories: (1) the electronics industry (computers, semiconductors, and networking firms), (2) the medical-related and research industries, and (3) the manufacturing industry.

A closer examination of the firms that do not conform to the industry-dominant model offers additional empirical support for dominant industry models. Table 2.4 reveals that excluding the firms that are founded with any of the five basic models, the majority of firms are conceptually close to their industry's dominant model: the star model for the medical-related and research firms, and the engineering model for companies in all other industries in the sample, with the exception of manufacturing.

Nearly two-thirds of the firms (42 of 66) are within a single dimension of their industry's dominant model. The pattern is most pronounced in the electronics industry, in which the majority of firms not founded with one of the basic employment models are within one dimension of the dominant engineering model. Similarly, half of the firms in the medical or research industries

Table 2.4
Distance from Dominant Employment Model by Industry Group

		Variant		Deviant	
INDUSTRY	INDUSTRY-DOMINANT MODEL	OTHER ARCHETYPAL MODEL	1 DIMENSION FROM DOMINANT MODEL	2 DIMENSIONS FROM DOMINANT MODEL	3 DIMENSIONS FROM DOMINANT MODEL
Electronics[a]	Engineering 44	24	36	12	5
Medical-related or Research	Star 11	7	4	2	2
Manufacturing	Commitment 2	0	2	1	2
TOTAL	57	31	42	15	9

[a]Computer related, Semiconductors, Networking, or Telecommunications

are conceptually close to the dominant star model. Just under half of the manufacturing firms are within a single dimension of the commitment model. Thus, there is empirical support for dominant organizational models within broadly defined industry categories.

These industry archetypes, prevalent in the SPEC sample, also have validity from rich descriptions provided by others who have analyzed these industries. For example, medical-related firms rely heavily on scientific achievement and thus have been described as being strongly influenced by science-oriented cultures (Latour and Woolgar 1986; Henderson and Cockburn 1994; Werth 1994). The organizational model of the computer industry, in which work is accomplished primarily in project teams, has been carefully chronicled by Kidder (1981) and Kunda (1992). Furthermore, the electronics industry, particularly the Silicon Valley electronics industry, has a distinctive and dominant cultural model that one commentator has described as the "triumph of the nerds" (Cringely 1996, 17). Some of the commonly described features of this Silicon Valley organizing mode include relatively flat organizational structures, incentive systems that encourage (rather than penalize) risktaking, and team-based projects that encourage communication and coordination (Sager 1997). The strong technology-oriented organizational cultures are purported to have loose organizational boundaries, weak organization-to-employee relationships yet strong project (or task) affiliations, and status hierarchies that reflect technical ability (Saxenian 1994). Finally, high-commitment work systems, particularly for manufacturing organizations, were commonly described (and prescribed) by management gurus throughout much of the '80s and '90s (Applebaum and Batt 1994; Pfeffer 1994; Womack et al. 1990). Three factors may account for deviations from these dominant models: strategy, founding team characteristics, and external partners.

Strategy

Organizational scholars have asserted that human resource strategy (the employment model) and corporate strategy should be aligned (Lawrence and Lorsch 1967; Nadler and Tushman 1997; Schuler 1992; Sonnenfeld and Peiperl 1988; Pfeffer 1994). Both strategy and the employment model are core features of an organization that are established early in the life cycle, are difficult to reorient, and are among the foundational characteristics that shape future organizational evolution (Hannan and Freeman 1984; Romanelli and Tushman 1994). Prior research has documented the association between strategy and the employment model (Hannan, Burton, and Baron 1996); thus, it is both a theoretical and a logical extension to presume that within a given industry, some of the variation in employment models can be explained by differences in strategy.

The firms in the SPEC sample varied in their dominant strategic focus. SPEC researchers categorized initial strategies by content by analyzing interviews with founders, supplemented in some cases by other sources such as newspaper articles, industry analysts' reports, or business plans (see Hannan, Burton, and Baron 1996 for more information). Founders were asked in the interviews to report their firms' distinctive source of competitive advantage. From their responses firms could be grouped into four main categories: (1) innovator, (2) enhancer, (3) marketer or marketing hybrid, and (4) low-cost producer.

Innovator. Innovator firms seek competitive advantage through innovation or technological leadership. Such firms seek first-mover advantages by winning a technology race. The emphasis in these firms is on revolutionary technology, which often involves gaining a crucial patent or patents. Among firms in the SPEC study that could be classified according to the founder's human resource model, roughly 50% were coded as belonging in this category, which is hardly surprising given the high-tech industries involved.

Enhancer. Some firms set out to enhance existing technologies. These firms seek to produce a product or product line similar to those of other companies but make some general modification to the technology to gain competitive advantage. Distinctive competencies can include system integration (e.g., of software and hardware), superior quality (in terms of dependability or availability of features desired by customers), and the like. Just under 20% percent of the firms fell into the enhancer category.

Marketer. Some of the SPEC firms planned to compete on the basis of superior sales, marketing, or customer service. Firms in the marketer category seek competitive advantage by developing or capitalizing on superior relations with customers, achieved through custom design of products, nonstandard methods of sales or distribution, or simply by developing superior capabilities in marketing, sales, branding, and/or customer service. Often, this strategy entailed firms creating products in direct response to customers' idiosyncratic needs, frequently working interactively with customers toward that end. In the SPEC sample, 13.6% were classified as having strategies driven by marketing, sales, and/or service. For the purposes of this chapter, an additional 10.4% of the sample that reported combining a marketing-service focus with an emphasis either on enhancing an existing technology or on technological leadership is included. Thus, in the SPEC sample 24% of the firms can be considered marketers.

Low-cost producer. Firms that are low-cost producers seek cost advantages through superior production techniques, economies of scale, and the like. Only a small number of firms were classified as having a pure low-cost strategy, but several others combined an emphasis on cost minimization with some other focus (generally marketing or service) and were classified by the researchers into this category as well, resulting in a total of 7.1% of the companies.

As is evident in Table 2.5, among the firms in the SPEC sample, there is a strong association between industry and strategy, and much of the statistical association can be accounted for by the overrepresentation of medical-related firms pursuing an innovator strategy and manufacturing firms pursuing a low-cost strategy. Despite a strong association between industry and strategy, however, there is also a fair amount of strategic diversity. The computer-

Table 2.5
Association Between Industry and Strategy Among SPEC Sample Firms
(cell counts and row percentages)

	Innovator	Enhancer	Marketing/ Hybrid	Cost	Total
Computer related	36	16	14	6	72
	50.0%	22.2%	19.4%	8.3%	100.0%
Semiconductor	8	4	4		16
	50.0%	25.0%	25.0%		100.0%
Networking and Telecommunications	11	8	12	2	34
	33.3%	24.2%	36.4%	6.1%	100.0%
Medical related	18	1	3		22
	81.8%	4.5%	13.6%		100.0%
Research	3		1		4
	75.0%		25.0%		100.0%
Manufacturing		1	3	3	7
		14.3%	42.9%	42.9%	100.0%
Total	76	30	37	11	154
	49.4%	19.5%	24.0%	7.1%	100.0%

NOTE: Pearson chi-square = 33.91, d.f. = 15, p = .004

related and networking and telecommunications industries have firms represented in all four strategy categories. The semiconductor, medical-related, and manufacturing industries have firms represented in three of the four strategy categories. It is only the research industry, the most sparsely represented industry, that exhibits limited strategic range.

As described above, most of the high-technology firms in the SPEC sample reported pursuing a technology-driven strategy, either enhancing existing technology or developing innovative new technology. These firms focus on product development rather than organizational development and thus should be most likely to conform to the dominant industry model. In contrast, those firms founded to compete on the basis of superior sales, marketing, or service, or on having lower costs rely on an organizational competence to achieve their strategic goals, which suggests that they will pay greater attention to organizational design and architecture.

Hypothesis 1: *Firms pursuing organizational as opposed to technological strategies will be more likely to deviate from the industry dominant model.*

A preliminary test of this hypothesis can be done by cross-classifying strategy and initial employment model by industry, given that the associations between strategy and industry and between industry and employment model are strong (see Tables 2.3 and 2.5). A more fine-grained analysis revealed that the overall association between strategy and employment model is modest (chi-square = 22.75, d.f. = 15, p = .10). Within industries, however, the association between strategy and employment model is nonexistent, producing no statistically significant associations (electronics: chi-square = 15.34, d.f. = 15, p = 0.43; medical: chi-square = 2.37, d.f. = 6, p = 0.88; manufacturing: chi-square = 3.73, d.f. = 2, p = 0.12). This implies that there is a great deal of model variation to be explained by factors other than technical or strategic considerations, including characteristics of the founding team.

Founding Team Characteristics

There is a long-standing stream of research suggesting that organizational founders exert a powerful and lasting influence on the firms that they create (Boeker 1988; DiMaggio 1991; Eisenhardt and Schoonhoven 1990; Schein 1983). Furthermore, there is ample empirical evidence supporting the contention that top management team characteristics are powerful predictors of organizational features (Finkelstein and Hambrick 1996; Fligstein 1987). Obviously, prior experience is likely to be related to organization-building models (Cooper 1985). With experience comes knowledge of different organizational models as well as an appreciation for how employees fare under different alternatives. Archival sources, including newspaper and magazine articles, internal company documents, and published directories, were used to gather career history information for each founding team member. The career history data were used to identify three types of experience: prior founding experience, senior management experience, and nontechnical (sales, marketing, finance, or administrative) experience, all of which are likely to lead founders away from industry-dominant models. Senior management experience is defined as holding a title of vice president or higher prior to founding the focal firm. Prior founding experience is likely to be undercounted in these sources, however, since successful ventures tend to be mentioned in executive biographies whereas failures do not.

There are two mechanisms by which experience leads to deviance: confidence and exposure to alternatives. Experienced founders who have either founded a firm in the past and/or held senior executive positions have presumably had the benefit of operating under at least one model and may feel confident in their ability to construct or invent a model that suits them. By analogy, first-time parents are more likely to raise their child by the book than are experienced parents. Exposure to alternative models may also liberate founders to deviate from the industry norm. Founders with nontechnical backgrounds are more likely to have had experience in other industries and therefore will be less well socialized to the dominant industry model. Similarly, founders who have held senior management roles are likely to have held positions in multiple firms and thus may have experience with multiple employment models.

Hypothesis 2: *Firms founded by experienced teams will be more likely to deviate from the industry dominant model.*

Experience need not be embodied in a single founder but, rather, can be the aggregate experience of all members of the founding team. In the SPEC sample, the size and composition of the founding team, as well as how the team members came together, varied dramatically across the sample. Founding teams ranged in size from one to twelve. A relatively small fraction (15.9%) were founded by a solo entrepreneur. The most typical SPEC firms were founded by two (32.3%), three (22.6%), or four (14.6%) people. The remaining firms (14.6%) were founded by teams of five or more. One of the most striking features of the founders in this sample is the diversity of experience. The majority of the firms had at least one member of the founding team with technical experience (76.2%). Just over half of the firms (55.4%) had at least one team member who had earlier held a senior management position (vice president or higher) in another company. Roughly one-third of the firms (36.9%) had at least one founder who had prior start-up experience. Fewer than one-third of the firms had a founder with experience in either sales (29.8%) or finance (10.7%).

External Partners

It is often asserted that interorganizational relationships are important determinants of organizational characteristics (e.g., Haunschild 1994). Firms scan the environment and adopt organizational features that others have adopted. This process of organizational imitation is accelerated when there are network ties linking firms (DiMaggio and Powell 1983). While most of the empirical research on this topic has assessed the diffusion of organizational structures and practices, it is reasonable to assume that the same processes operate in the diffusion of employment models. Furthermore, the influence of significant others is likely to be dramatic in very young firms, given their lack of legitimacy and need for resources (Nohria 1992). External partners, such as venture capitalists, who help bring cash to new firms, may be important influences on the structure of new firms (Suchman 1994).

Hypothesis 3: *Firms whose important external partners include venture capitalists will be less likely to deviate from the dominant industry model.*

As described above, founders were asked in a written survey about the external partners and advisors who were involved in the founding. The survey item asked the respondent to list "important actors and the roles they played in the founding process." Beyond listing the members of the founding team, respondents identified 12 types of external partners: four types of investors (venture capitalists, private investors, corporate investors, other), lawyers, accountants, board members, customers, employees, friends or family, previous employers, and other advisors. The frequencies of different types of external partners are reported in Table 2.6.

In Table 2.6, partners have been aggregated for each firm so that each type of partnership variable has a discrete yes-or-no value. In other words, the variables simply indicate whether the founder mentioned *any* individuals who fulfilled a particular role.[4] While lawyer, board member, and venture capitalist are the most frequently mentioned categories of external partnership, each was

---

4. This coding does not account for either multiple roles by a single individual, such as a venture capitalist who is also an advisor and a board member, or for multiple individuals playing a single role, as is the case when a respondent listed several private investors.

Table 2.6
Frequency of Different Types of
External Partners Among SPEC Sample Firms

Partner Role	Number of Firms	Percent of Firms
Investors	89	77.4%
Venture capital	59	51.3%
Private	30	26.1%
Corporate	23	20.0%
Other	3	2.6%
Lawyers	62	53.9%
Board members	59	51.3%
Advisors	57	49.6%
Accountants	15	13.0%
Customers	13	11.3%
Employees	11	9.6%
Friends and family	6	5.2%
Previous employer	5	4.3%

listed by just over half of the firms (53.9%, 51.3%, and 51.3% of the firms, respectively). Similarly, advisors were mentioned by 49.6% of the firms. Other types of partners were mentioned less frequently. It is worth noting that partnership types seem to cluster. A simple similarity ratio computed from a correlation-type matrix reveals that venture capitalist, lawyer, advisor, and board member tend to be co-present.[5]

ANALYSES

Multinomial logistic regression analyses were used to examine conformity to and deviance from the dominant industry model. The empirical strategy distinguishes, at one extreme, those firms that adopt their industry's model and, at the other extreme, those firms that are not adopting any of the five basic employment models (nor anything conceptually close to any of the five basic

---

5. This analysis used a Jaccard measure for binary variables. This is an index based on a 2 × 2 table of variable 1 (present, absent) crossed by variable 2 (present, absent). In the Jaccard measure, joint absences are excluded from consideration and equal weight is given to matches and nonmatches.

types) and are two or more dimensions from the dominant industry model. The intermediate category, described as variants, includes the firms that are founded under a basic employment model or are within one dimension of the dominant industry model. This empirical strategy was driven by an interest in identifying the sources of novel organizational forms, which occurs when firms are founded with extremely deviant employment models. The analytic strategy allows novelty (deviance) to be distinguished empirically from well-understood archetypal employment models or models that are conceptually close to such models. Industry-dummy variables were included to control for the different strengths of the industry-specific dominant models. As shown above, the greatest propensity to conform to an industry template was evident in the electronics industry, while firms in the medical-related industry were most likely to be founded with a basic (or near) star model. A substantial number of firms were organized with an engineering model. In contrast, the only basic model that is apparent in the SPEC manufacturing firms is the commitment model. Furthermore, the firms founded with nonbasic models are more likely to be distant from the commitment model (three firms are two or more dimensions from commitment) than they are to be close to it (two firms are only one dimension from commitment).

To account for two potential sources of heterogeneity—initial scale and idiosyncratic time variations from things like short-term labor market fluctuations—we included a measure of the firm size (the natural logarithm of the number of employees at the end of the first year of operations) and the age of the firm when we first interviewed the founder.

RESULTS

Table 2.7 presents the results of a multinomial logistic regression predicting the initial employment model. The baseline (omitted) category is for firms conforming to their industry's dominant model. The two panels in the table represent the varying degrees of deviance from the normative prescription. The first panel represents the most extreme deviance, in which firms adopt a model that is conceptually distant from both the dominant model and the four alternative archetypes. The second panel represents variants, more modest devia-

Table 2.7

Multinomial Logistic Regression Predicting Deviation from
Industry-Dominant Model (N = 123)

(omitted category = industry-dominant model)

Deviant: Model Is Two or More Dimensions from the Industry-Dominant Model	Model 1 Cofficient (standard error)	Model 2 Coefficient (standard error)
Initial organizational size	−0.19 (0.42)	−0.69 (0.52)
Age	−0.32 + (0.20)	−0.27 (0.20)
Medical or research industry	0.73 (1.35)	0.82 (1.66)
Manufacturing industry	1.15 (1.21)	3.21[b] (1.64)
Nontechnology strategy	3.22[c] (1.22)	3.79[c] (1.56)
Number of founders		−1.09 (0.68)
Number of founders with finance, sales, or marketing experience		1.50[a] (0.81)
Number of founders with senior management experience		1.39[b] (0.68)
Constant	−1.52 (1.92)	−1.27 (2.29)

(continued)

tions, in which the founders have avoided the dominant model but have adopted a model that is (or is close to) one of the four archetypes. Model 1 includes only technical and environmental determinants of the employment model. Model 2 adds characteristics of the founding team. The results indicate that much of the tendency toward nonstandard employment models can be explained by differences in strategy, supporting hypothesis 1. This is particularly true when the firm dramatically deviates from the industry's dominant model.

An interesting and unanticipated finding is that, controlling for functional

Table 2.7 *(continued)*

Variant: One of the Four Other Archetypal Models or Within One Dimension of the Industry-Dominant Model	Model 1 Coefficient (standard error)	Model 2 Coefficient (standard error)
Initial organizational size	−0.19 (0.19)	−0.15 (0.21)
Age	0.05 (0.07)	0.06 (0.08)
Medical or research industry	−0.75 (0.52)	−0.67 (0.55)
Manufacturing industry	−0.94 (1.07)	−0.76 (1.08)
Nontechnology strategy	0.38 (0.49)	0.23 (0.50)
Number of founders		−0.25[b] (0.12)
Number of founders with finance, sales, or marketing experience		0.33 (0.28)
Number of founders with senior management experience		0.05 (0.20)
Constant	0.81 (0.76)	1.18 (0.83)
Model chi-square	24.89[c]	37.07[c]
Degrees of freedom	10	16

NOTE: + p < .15; [a]p < .10; [b]p < .05; [c]p < .01

heterogeneity, larger teams are less likely to deviate from the dominant industry model. This coefficient is a statistically significant predictor of modest deviations and is close to being statistically significant (p = 0.11) for more dramatic deviations. One plausible explanation for these findings is rooted in group dynamics. Developing an initial employment model in a group setting may require that all parties converge. It is highly likely that through a process of consensus building and compromising, the emergent model will closely resemble a dominant industry model.

The most intriguing finding is that there are key experience differences among those founding teams whose initial employment model differs dramatically from the industry archetype. Founding teams with more senior management experience and more nontechnical experience (controlling for the total number of founders) are the most likely to deviate from the dominant industry model, net of strategic considerations, supporting hypothesis 2. In other words, experienced executives who are part of a functionally well-rounded founding team are the most likely to adopt an employment model that is different from either the dominant industry model or any other well-understood cultural archetype. An interpretation of this finding is that those firms that begin with functionally heterogeneous teams do so because they differ in the complexity or diversity of their operations. This diversity may have implications for which model is most appropriate, and it may require deviating from an industry's dominant model. An alternative explanation for the finding is that it is driven by the presence of industry outsiders. Comparing two founding teams of the same size, a team that includes broad business experience (senior management, finance, sales, or marketing) has a higher probability of drawing on industry outsiders than one of primarily technical founders. An interesting topic for future research is determining the consequences of adopting a novel model.

In other analyses of the survey data, I tested hypothesis 3, on the role of external partners, such as lawyers and venture capitalists. As Table 2.8 shows, although there are bivariate associations between having a venture capitalist as an important partner and adopting a particular employment model, in multivariate analyses that included dummy variables to indicate whether either a lawyer or a venture capitalist was listed as a partner, neither coefficient was statistically significant. Furthermore, including the variables did not change the results described above. I omit them from the reported results because they decrease the usable sample (54 cases are dropped due to missing partner data).

One possible explanation of the lack of effect for the influence of external partners is that, as posited above, the salience of particular external actors may vary both by industry and by strategy. It is also possible that external influences are not directly in the form of partner relationships but, rather, are indirect, coming through more subtle mechanisms such as executive migration (Boeker 1997) or broader field-level conflicts and contests (Ventresca and Washington

Table 2.8
Association Between External Influences and Employment Model

Partner	Autocracy N = 7 (6.3%)	Commitment N = 12 (10.7%)	Star N = 13 (11.6%)	Engineering N = 41 (36.6%)	Bureaucracy N = 5 (4.5%)	Other N = 34 (30.4%)	Likelihood Ratio Chi-square (5 d.f.)
Private investor	1	3	6	10	0	9	6.08
(N = 30)	(3.4%)	(10.3%)	(20.7%)	(34.5%)	(0.0%)	(31.0%)	
Venture capitalist	2	4	7	23	5	17	10.16[a]
(N = 59)	(3.4%)	(6.9%)	(12.1%)	(39.7%)	(8.6%)	(29.3%)	
Corporate investor	2	2	3	9	2	4	3.22
(N = 23)	(9.1%)	(9.1%)	(13.6%)	(40.9%)	(9.1%)	(18.2%)	
Other investor	1	1	0	0	0	1	5.99
(N = 3)	(33.3%)	(33.3%)	(0.0%)	(0.0%)	(0.0%)	(33.3%)	
Lawyer	2	3	6	25	4	20	8.96
(N = 62)	(3.3%)	(5.0%)	(10.0%)	(41.7%)	(6.7%)	(33.3%)	
Advisor	1	5	7	25	4	14	9.36[a]
(N = 57)	(1.9%)	(9.4%)	(12.5%)	(44.6%)	(7.1%)	(25.0%)	
Accountant	1	2	1	6	0	4	2.02
(N = 15)	(7.1%)	(14.3%)	(7.1%)	(42.9%)	(0.0%)	(28.6%)	
Board member	5	8	4	24	2	16	5.86
(N = 59)	(8.5%)	(13.6%)	(6.8%)	(40.7%)	(3.4%)	(39.0%)	
Customer	1	1	0	6	1	4	4.02
(N = 13)	(7.7%)	(7.7%)	(0.0%)	(46.2%)	(7.7%)	(30.8%)	
Founder	3	6	3	12	0	9	6.69
(N = 34)	(9.1%)	(18.2%)	(9.1%)	(36.4%)	(0.0%)	(27.3%)	
Employee	0	0	2	5	0	4	5.74
(N = 11)	(0.0%)	(0.0%)	(18.2%)	(45.5%)	(0.0%)	(36.4%)	
Kin	1	3	0	1	0	1	9.13[a]
(N = 6)	(16.7%)	(50.0%)	(0.0%)	(16.7%)	(0.0%)	(16.7%)	
Previous company	0	0	1	2	0	1	2.46
(N = 5)	(0.0%)	(0.0%)	(25.0%)	(50.0%)	(0.0%)	(25.0%)	

NOTE: [a]p<.10

1998). Another interesting possibility is that external partnerships may be most important when founders lack experience or legitimacy, as do founders who are young scientists or engineers. These founders are most likely to adopt an industry dominant model and are least likely to have venture backing. The process of choosing that model may or may not be related to the influence of external partners.

DISCUSSION

This research raises two broad issues related to organizational models and entrepreneurship. First, treatments of entrepreneurial strategy have tended to focus exclusively on the product or financing domains. If we are to take seriously the organization-building side of entrepreneurial strategy, however, we must consider both the options available to entrepreneurs (e.g., the labor markets in which they compete) and the available models for organizing. Second, understanding strategic organization-building choices may require alternative conceptualizations.

This research concentrates on models used by entrepreneurs to guide the ways in which they build their firms. There is evidence that dominant models of the employment relationship vary among industries, even within the relatively homogenous high-technology sector. There is also strong evidence of considerable variation around the dominant models. This chapter begins to explore the sources of variation in the models. The evidence presented here indicates that strategy matters: firms pursuing a nontechnology strategy are more likely to deviate from the dominant industry model than are firms that are pursuing a more purely technical path. Further, the demographic composition of the founding team makes a difference. Smaller founding teams are more likely to deviate from an industry-dominant model as are teams whose members have backgrounds in finance, sales, or marketing or that include founders with senior-level management experience.

At a minimum, the findings reported here suggest that broad interpretations of institutional theory particularly, and organizational theory more generally, may systematically underestimate the patterned variation in organizational models present in a given field. Entrepreneurs do not appear to be overly constrained by overarching cultural pressures, as represented in institutional theory, or by the expectations of those people and other firms on whom they depend, as in resource dependence theory, or by the technical requirements of the task. Rather, entrepreneurs with broader business experience may in fact devise novel organizational forms that resonate with particular business strategies or that are consistent with their own personal values (DiMaggio 1991; Fombrun 1988).

A second issue raised by this research concerns the strategic use of models of the employment relation. Deviant employment models may be mistakes, and they may result from founders being disconnected, but they do not appear to stem from a lack of experience. Instead, it appears that novel employment models are tolerated when the founding team has extensive experience, both across functions and at the highest level of organizations. It is these seasoned professionals who are credibly able to devise their own employment model.

The second alternative is that nonstandard employment models reflect deliberate strategic choices by entrepreneurs trying to differentiate their firm in the labor market. Although this explanation finds some support here, the factors appear to be more complex than is typically imagined (e.g., Sonnenfeld and Peiperl 1988). The interviews with founders revealed clearly that some entrepreneurs truly operated in default mode in building their organizations, reporting that they didn't give any attention to such issues. Other founders reported that they operated quite deliberately in choosing models of the employment relation and in initial organization building. Among the latter were two types. Some founders chose models for ideological reasons; they reported strong beliefs in the intrinsic value of the models they implemented and made no reference to performance implications or consequences. Others reported that their choice of model was based on business rationales about which models can attract key personnel in the current labor market or about the link between model and product strategy, with an eye toward improving the organizations' competitive chances or enhancing performance. Table 2.9 provides some illustrative quotes for each of these approaches.

The co-existence of these three modes of choosing models has potentially important consequences that have not yet been explored. For example, these different modes may influence the amount of diversity in the community of organizations. The default mode will tend to reproduce the dominant industry mode, especially when new ventures are guided by relatively large teams of technical founders. Such a process will produce stability over time within industries and maintain differences between industries, particularly when there is little cross-industry mobility among executives. The ideological mode would likely increase the variance within industries. The interviews revealed a strong oppositional component in the ideological mode: entrepreneurs expressed considerable distaste for the models used in the firms with which they had experience and a desire to create an organization that was the polar

Table 2.9

Sample Statements Illustrating Different Approaches to
Choosing an Employment Model

Unintended/Default	Ideological	Strategic
We did not really spend a lot of time on organization. Not because it's not important, but because you are in survival mode and it's like a platoon, it's not an army. You're thinking like a platoon, you're a command operation, and you know that you are, and you don't worry about it, because you're not an army. So don't try to be like an army, because you'll be a very lousy platoon. (19)	The initial plan or blueprint was to be different than the typical Silicon Valley company. We were not looking to establish a "get rich quick" company. We wanted to follow an Eastern model of treating people well. And we didn't want to grow at the expense of our people. (1)	The two key determinants of early success for biotechnology companies are science and capital. The best scientists attract investors and capital, and capital attracts good scientists. The two complement and enforce each other, and you need both to succeed. That's it. Inadequate funding leads to bad science because you can't attract the best people. You won't attract or retain the best people because they can go somewhere that has the money, and they will. Secondly, when you start without the money, you start cutting corners. You have no choice. That ultimately comes back to bite you in the rear end. (104)
The culture was a de facto culture of hard work and long hours. Not much of a culture. (3)	We wanted a strong participatory culture with an enormous amount of ground up information, not only from the management team, but also the people on the floor. (23)	We know our size, our name, our business won't attract any top-notch people. So you have to use your relationships. People who know you can be successful. They believe in you more than they believe in the business. (39)
Absolutely zero plan [for the employment relationship]. The biggest things on our minds were customers and products. We started paying deeper attention when we crossed the 50-people barrier. (110)	I wanted to build a company that walked its talk. A company that mistreats its suppliers, for instance, but says it treats its customers well is lying. You have to build partners inside and build partners for your suppliers and partners for your customers. You can't do that if the basic culture of the company is "I just want to get rich and screw you." And what I've just described is probably closer to the Silicon Valley norm. (132)	Basically, to work for us you have to be really, really good and you have to be willing to work for pretty much nothing. That eliminates all but the fanatics. People who come in here to work for us get lots of advantages. Mostly we hire engineers, people who make products. The ability to come in and write a product from the ground up that's your baby, and that's going to sell, and you'll have influence all the way through, from the design to artwork to packaging to distribution, is rare. (164)

opposite. Such a mode will tend to increase the variance of organizational models within industries, assuming that entrepreneurs tend to remain within the same industries. The strategic mode is also likely to increase variability within industries. The most interesting case involves the strategic choice of organizational models directed toward attaining a distinctive position in the labor market. If entrepreneurs follow this logic, they will tend to move away from the dominant industry models and thereby increase the variance in models within industries.

Within the academy, there is strong consensus that organizational diversity is important and valuable. The value of heterogeneous organizational forms has been linked to public policy (Van de Ven and Garud 1989), industry dynamics (Delacroix, Swaminathan, and Solt 1989), organizational viability (Hannan and Freeman 1989), and individual career mobility (Carroll, Haveman, and Swaminathan 1992; Hannan 1988). Yet despite this consensus, there is still relatively little research that addresses the sources of organizational diversity. In this small sample of technology start-ups in Silicon Valley there is startling variation in founders' employment models, even among start-up companies in the same industry, competing directly against one another. This chapter is only a first step toward understanding the factors that create this diversity. There is still much work to be done.

3

The Local Origins of New Firms

ELAINE ROMANELLI AND

CLAUDIA BIRD SCHOONHOVEN

Where do new organizations come from? What accounts for the formation of new organizational populations? Why do we observe that new organizations arise in large numbers only occasionally and in a few particular times and places? Interest in these age-old questions has spurred countless investigations, in virtually every social science discipline, into the human and environmental factors that promote the rise of new organizations. New organizations produce new jobs, new wealth, and innovation (Freeman 1982; Birley 1986) that fuel the economic vitality of regions and societies. We care about the origins of new organizations because we care about their outcomes.

Despite a long history of research and the undeniable importance of the questions, however, we are still not very good at predicting when and where, in social or economic space, new organizations will arise in large numbers. And although we have numerous general theories about entrepreneurial personalities (e.g., McClelland 1961) and entrepreneurial environments (Aldrich and Wiedenmayer 1993; Thornton 1999), we still cannot explain the particular rise, especially within regions, of large numbers of new organizations. A phenomenon such as Silicon Valley, which is today the nonpareil of regional

We are grateful to the Global Entrepreneurship Program at the McDonough School of Business, Georgetown University, and grants from the Graduate School of Management at the University of California, Irvine, and the Tuck School of Business Administration, Dartmouth University, for support of this research. Several colleagues, including Jacques Delacroix and the other authors of this volume, provided helpful comments and insights that substantially improved our arguments.

entrepreneurial and innovative vitality, still comes as a surprise. As academics rush to explain the phenomenon and business and civic leaders invest vast resources to try to recreate the phenomenon elsewhere, theory is needed first to explain and then, perhaps, to predict and influence the development of regional entrepreneurial environments.

Two problems, we believe, underlie the difficulty of answering these questions. First, with few and fairly recent exceptions (e.g., Aldrich 1999; Granovetter 1995), academics have largely avoided investigating entrepreneurship as a fundamentally local process, born of individual, potential entrepreneurs taking advantage of local information and resources both to identify opportunities for new business formation and to collect the resources necessary for building new organizations. People found organizations when they have information that a market opportunity exists for a new product or service, when they can obtain resources for building the new organization, and when they believe that the social or financial benefits of the new organization will be sufficient to repay them for the trouble of building it (Stinchcombe 1965). Information about opportunities for new business formation and resources for building a new organization develop primarily in the local environments in which individuals live and work (Aldrich and Wiedenmayer 1993; Freeman 1982; Jacobs 1969; Romanelli 1989b). Thus, to understand when and where new organizations will be founded, especially in large numbers, theory must explain how information and resources for entrepreneurial activity come to be disproportionately massed in some places and at some times. As Venkataraman (1997) stated, our most fundamental questions about organizational origins will never be answered until we tackle, theoretically, the rise of entrepreneurial opportunity.

Specifying the distribution, over time and geographic space, of entrepreneurial information and resources is a daunting and perhaps impossible task. Herein lies the second problem. How can we discern, from the immense quantities of information flowing both locally and globally, which information might be relevant to entrepreneurs? How can we even think about locating the information as being more available in some places than in others? These questions are, of course, rhetorical. No theory of entrepreneurial opportunity or development can be built from the raw ingredients of information and resources.

Perhaps, however, we can conceive of structures of information and resources, especially in the work lives of individuals, that may be more or less likely to promote entrepreneurial activity. Perhaps if we understood better how individuals acquire, construct, and act on information about entrepreneurial activity, we would be better able to characterize the contexts most likely to produce such activity. We can begin with the assumption that individuals gain most of their ideas, construct networks of contacts, and develop reputations that will be needed for actually building an organization primarily through their work in organizations before founding. Since organizations vary, more or less observably, in the kinds of information they routinely process, organizations may serve as useful local contexts for understanding the general origins of entrepreneurial activity. Then, since organizations also operate in systematically and identifiably different regional and ecological populations and communities, we can begin to investigate when and where new organizations will arise, especially in large numbers.

The theory developed in this chapter is based on these two basic ideas—that individuals learn about opportunities for new business formation primarily in their pre-founding work and educational organizations, and that characteristics of existing organizations and the environments surrounding the organizations influence foundings. These ideas have been mentioned often in the organizational literature, but they have been little investigated to date.

THE LOCAL CONTEXTS OF ENTREPRENEURIAL ACTIVITY

The idea that environments are critical, conditioning agents of entrepreneurial activity is, of course, not new. Two broad theories, what Peterson (1980) perhaps first termed the supply and demand theories of entrepreneurship, summarize the literature reasonably well.[1] Entrepreneurial supply theorists, especially psychologists (e.g., McClelland 1961; Brockhaus 1982), have focused on identifying the distinguishing personality traits of entrepreneurs, such as the need for achievement and risk-taking propensity. According to this

---

1. See Aldrich and Wiedenmeyer (1993) and Thornton (1999) for more recent reviews of the supply and demand perspectives on entrepreneurial origins.

perspective, which assumes that entrepreneurs are fundamentally different from the rest of us and that they appear relatively rarely, the rates of entrepreneurial activity in society depend principally on the number of individuals in a society who have such traits. Unfortunately, since the literature pays little attention to factors in a society or economy that may more likely generate such personalities, it gives little help in predicting rates of organizational founding.[2]

Entrepreneurial demand theorists, in contrast, especially economists, sociologists, and organization theorists, have emphasized mainly environmental conditions as influences on the rise of new organizations. These include culture (Geertz 1963; Light 1972; Weber 1958), competition and technological innovation (Astley 1985; Hannan and Freeman 1989; Schumpeter; Tushman and Anderson 1986), and the availability of critical economic resources (e.g., Pennings 1982). While such factors may shed light on why some cultures, some nations, or some industries, during some times, may be more or less likely to generate organizational foundings, most theories have been exceptionally broad in their characterizations of environments and their explanations about how environments generate new organizations. Consideration of the individual entrepreneur, or the information and resources that may attract the entrepreneur's attention, is almost entirely absent in this literature. For the most part, it is simply assumed in this literature that whenever any opportunity for entrepreneurial activity, such as technological innovation, arises, entrepreneurs will appear to take advantage of the opportunity.

Recent theory suggests, however, that information about opportunities and resources for building new organizations arise predominantly in the local environments of individuals' work and professional activity (Aldrich and Wiedenmayer 1993; Brittain and Freeman 1986; Freeman 1982; Jacobs 1969; Romanelli 1989b), especially the organizations and communities in which they live and work prior to founding a new organization. Founders discover ideas for new products and services or learn about demand for existing products or services primarily from the work they do in existing organizations

---

2. Although McClelland (1961), who was one of the first to give attention to the psychology of the entrepreneurial personality, explicitly considered culture, especially as it was taught to children via stories, as the medium of entrepreneurial development, the vast literature that followed McClelland's work sought mainly to prove the existence of an entrepreneurial personality, paying scant attention to factors that might produce it.

(Freeman 1982; Romanelli 1989b). They obtain resources for building the new business primarily from local banks or venture capitalists (Freeman 1986), and they find other people to join them in the founding activity from prior workplaces and through local contacts in their business, civic, and residential environments (Aldrich 1999; Aldrich and Zimmer 1986). Liabilities of newness, which Stinchcombe (1965) described as the inefficiencies of learning and the problems of inadequately established social relations, are primarily overcome in the local environment. Thus, recent theory suggests that existing organizations are the primary contexts within which individuals learn about opportunities for new organizations and that local regions are the primary arenas within which individuals obtain resources for building a new organization.

The advantage of this perspective lies in its potential for bridging the gap between very broad theories of entrepreneurial environments, which largely ignore the entrepreneur as an important agent of the process, and theories about entrepreneurial personality, which ignore the environment. In particular, this perspective locates the sources of ideas for new organizations primarily within existing organizations. Individuals develop expertise about such things as products, technologies and logistics through their work and experiences in existing organizations. Just as important, they develop expertise about markets and competition for the products and services of the existing organizations. Finally, as a consequence of their organizations' interactions with other organizations, for example, suppliers, distributors, and government agencies, individuals learn about opportunities for new products and services (Burt 1992). Thus, existing organizations direct their employees' attention to particular kinds of information in the environment and influence the salience and interpretation of different kinds of information. Although this argument remains largely untested empirically, if accurate, it sets the stage for developing theory about the characteristics of organizations and their surrounding environments that will be more and less likely to generate new organizations.

Figure 3.1 shows an existing organization as the center of a nested hierarchy of locations that may provide information and resources for entrepreneurial activity. As shown, organizations exist in two informational and resource arenas, one focusing on membership within a technological community (see Astley and Fombrun 1983; Hunt and Aldrich 1998; Wade 1995) and the other focusing on membership within a regional community (see

Romanelli 1989b; Suchman, this volume), each of which may influence an individual's likelihood of forming a new organization. Most studies of organizational founding and new population development, in organizational ecology in particular (e.g., Hannan and Freeman 1987; 1989; but cf. Hannan et al. 1995), have focused on population dynamics with little regard for any effects of geographic boundary. While these studies provide the best empirical explanation to date for rates of founding within organizational populations, they do not address either the origins of the populations in the first place (Astley 1985) or the geographic dispersion of the foundings.

In this chapter, we explicitly restrict our consideration to dynamics that develop within relatively small geographic areas, specifically, metropolitan regions. We use the rough outline of Figure 3.1 to explore how the characteristics of existing organizations, the local organizational populations in which they compete, and the regional communities of organizational populations condition the rise of new organizations, especially in large numbers.

Organizational Origins of New Organizations

No study, to our knowledge, has directly explored the sources of entrepreneurs' ideas for new organizations. Mainly, it is only anecdote, common sense, and a few threads of evidence from studies exploring other phenomena that support the idea that founders discover and act on opportunities for organizational founding primarily as a result of expertise developed through prior work in other organizations. Here, we review the bits of evidence, principally from the literature on industry clusters, to support our key proposition that, as noted by Freeman (1982, 16), "People who start Catholic convents do not do so after toying with the notion of beginning cement plants, advertising agencies, or universities."

A growing body of literature from both economics and organization theory has begun to examine how clusters of similar organizations come to inhabit relatively small and relatively few geographic regions. Information, labor, and supply externalities (Jaffe, Trajtenberg, and Henderson 1993; Marshall 1919; Rauch 1993), which tend to appear when organizations locate in close geographic proximity to one another, both reduce organizations' costs for organizational resources and increase chances for early access to information about

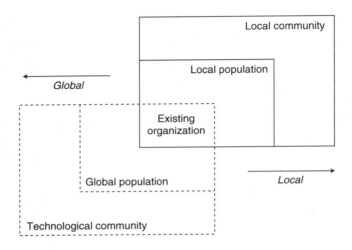

Figure 3.1 A nested hierarchy of locations for sources of entrepreneurial activity

innovations and markets. At the same time, competition for available resources may increase the innovativeness of the local population (Glaeser et al. 1992; Porter 1998), thus improving its advantages over other regions with less concentrated populations.[3] Although these studies do not directly document any link between the origins of founders' ideas for new organizations and prior work organizations they clearly suggest the development of localized knowledge. Individuals who work in organizations that are clustered should have more access to particularized information about products, services, technology, and competition than do other individuals. It is reasonable to suppose that any organizations these individuals found will be linked to the specialized information.

A related body of literature has begun to explore more directly the localization of intellectual capital. Several studies of clusters in the biotechnology community (e.g., Audretsch and Stephan 1996; Zucker, Darby, and Armstrong 1998; Zucker, Darby, and Brewer 1998) show a general co-location of

---

3. With these few references we have only scratched the surface of a vast literature, and theoretical controversy exists about whether local monopoly (Arrow 1962; Romer 1986) or local competition (Porter 1998; Glaeser et al. 1992) better stimulates innovation in regions. Our purpose here is merely to document substantial research attention to agglomeration phenomena that suggest the likelihood of local origins for new organizations.

specialized university scientists and biotechnology organizations, especially new biotechnology organizations. Audretsch and Stephan (1996) showed that distances between the scientists and the organizations were smallest when the scientists were either part of the founding teams or chairs of the organization's advisory boards. These studies, too, suggest a relationship between existing organizations and sources of ideas for new ventures, especially from expertise, but they are also inconclusive.

Principally, however, it is anecdote that supports the central thesis. Nearly every history of organizational start-ups describes an entrepreneur's discovery of an idea for a new business as developing from work in a prior organization. Leonard Bosack and Sandra Lerner, for example, who were both computer technicians at Stanford University, founded Cisco Systems as a result of their work in the early 1980s to link Stanford's incompatible computing systems. William Shockley founded Shockley Semiconductor Lab in the San Francisco Bay Area, where he was raised, as a result of his invention of the transistor at Bell Labs in the late 1940s (Kaplan 1999). Shockley put together the team whose work (and dissatisfaction with Shockley's management style) later led several of them to leave Shockley to create first Fairchild Semiconductor and then Intel. And pick up any almost issue of *Inc.* magazine to find a story of a start-up that developed an idea hatched in the founder's prior work organization.

To test the basic validity of the argument that founders discover ideas for new businesses from their work and experience in prior organizations, we investigated the backgrounds of 17 founders whose relatively young organizations appeared at the top of the *Inc.* 500 listing of high-growth companies over the years 1982 to 1999. Table 3.1 presents a list of the companies, along with information about the primary work of the young organizations and the work backgrounds of the founders who created the organizations.

Even a quick glance at the information in Table 3.1 reveals a very close association between the expertise and experience of the founders and the kinds of organizations they created. In 16 out of 17 cases, the entrepreneurs formed new businesses in the same or very closely related industries as those of their prior organizations. The sole exception, David Glickman of Justice Technology, managed the purchasing of long-distance telecommunications for American Express before leaving to found his own business as a telecommunications

Table 3.1

Backgrounds of *Inc.* 500 Founders

Year	Company	Founder
1982	Altos Computer Sysytems Manufacturer of multi-user computers, San Jose, California	David Jackson Salesperson, personal computers, Digital Equipment Corporation, California offices
1983	Sigal Construction Corporation General construction contracting, Washington, D.C.	Gerald Sigal Construction contracting agent, Tishman Real Estate, Washington, D.C.
1984	Pedus Services Security and janitorial services, Los Angeles, California	Dick Dotts 31 years experience in the cleaning business, Los Angeles, California
1985	Herbalife, Inc. Health and personal care products, Los Angeles, California	Mark Hughes Salesperson, herbal weight control products, Golden Youth, Los Angeles, California
1986	ABC Supply Company Roofing and siding contractor, Beloit, Wisconsin	Ken Hendricks Family business in roofing and remodeling, Wisconsin
1987	American Photo Group Corporation Film processing, Atlanta, Georgia	Steve Bostic Marketing executive, Berkey Photo, Atlanta, Georgia
1988	American Central Gas Natural gas services, Tulsa, Oklahoma	Kevin Sullivan Consultant, natural gas industry, Houston, Texas
1989, 1990	Cogentrix Energy Independent power producer, Charlotte, North Carolina	George Lewis Utilities executive, Boston and New York
1991	Gateway 2000 Personal computers, direct marketing, North Sioux City, South Dakota	Ted Waitt Retail computer sales, Des Moines family cattle business, South Dakota

(continued)

reseller. It is also interesting to note that 12 out of 17 of the entrepreneurs established their new organizations in the same city or region as that of their prior organizations, and three out of the five entrepreneurs who moved, moved back to regions where they grew up. Though we can and should question the representativeness of this small demonstration sample—all of these companies achieved very fast growth very early in their lives—the results are nonetheless striking in both their overwhelming consistency as well as the range of indus-

Table 3.1 (continued)

Year	Company	Founder
1992	Kingston Technology Manufacturer, computer memory upgrades, Fountain Valley, California	John Tu and David Sun AST Research, personal computers, Irvine, California
1993	Drypers Corporation Disposable diapers, Houston, Texas	Dave Pitassi Procter & Gamble (diapers division), Oregon
1994	Object Design Inc. Database management systems, Burlington, Massachusetts	Thomas Atwood Computer engineer, Digital Equipment Corporation Boston, Massachusetts
1995	The Furst Group Reseller, long-distance telephone services, Shamong, New Jersey	John Streep Independent consultant, telecommunications, Shamong, New Jersey
1996	Equinox International Multilevel marketing, Las Vegas, Nevada	Bill Gouldd Multilevel marketing, Los Angeles, California
1997	Optiva Corporation Sonic toothbrushes, Bellevue, Washington	David Giuliani Engineer, medical ultrasound devices, Seattle, Washington
1998	Justice Technology Telecommunications reseller, Culver City, California	David Glickman American Express, Buenos Aires, Argentina
1999	Roth Staffing Staffing services, Brea, California	Ben Roth Talent Tree Staffing Services, Houston, Texas

tries and geographic regions considered. The relationship between the prior work of the organizational founder and the kind of work that he or she organizes in a new organization seems strong and general.

Thus, though this first basic premise of our theory of local organizational origins awaits systematic empirical investigation, we propose that most organizational founders identify opportunities for creating new organizations from expertise and experience gained in previous work organizations.

Proposition 1: *The majority of new organizations will be founded to exploit opportunities identified on the basis of a founder's work and expertise in a previous organization.*

Most individuals, of course, will probably not establish new organizations, whatever expertise or knowledge their work may generate about opportunities for founding. We cannot conclude that organizations are the essential incubators of ideas for new ventures based only on information that founders use knowledge and expertise from prior work to identify and act on entrepreneurial activities. Perhaps these individuals, as the psychologists suggest, would have discovered ideas for new businesses whatever line of work they pursued. Nonetheless, the close association between founders' prior work and their entrepreneurial work suggests that it is expertise and experience, gained in existing organizations, that fuels the formation of new organizations. Existing organizations can be investigated both for their internal processes that generate a greater diversity of work and for the conditions that motivate individuals to leave for entrepreneurial activity.

What characteristics of organizations might increase the likelihood that some employees will be motivated to found new organizations? Following Schumpeter (1934) and Stinchcombe (1965), we assume that individuals will be motivated to accept the risks of organizational founding when they perceive that the benefits from founding, either for themselves or for some group that they care for, will be greater than can be obtained from remaining in the existing organization or career. Two characteristics of organizations may promote this condition.

First, an individual may be motivated to leave a current organization to start a new business when he or she perceives that senior managers no longer value the particular expertise or strategic outlook that the individual has developed (Brittain and Freeman 1986). Although difficult to measure directly, the value placed on developed expertise and outlook serves as an indicator of future benefits that an individual might gain from continued employment in the current organization and as a basis for comparison with potential benefits that may be obtained from alternatives. Especially when an organization moves in a major new strategic direction, perhaps when an outsider takes over as chief executive officer, or when there is a substantial change in the governance of an organization, for example, following mergers or acquisitions, competent executives may be motivated to create new businesses that will capitalize on their old expertise. For example, the formation of Intel in Silicon Valley was directly related to changes in the governance of Fairchild's California subsidiary, and many of the businesses listed in Table 3.1 were formed in the wake of mergers or acquisitions of the prior organizations of the founders. Brittain and Freeman (1986) found direct evidence for this argument, showing that organizations in a population of semiconductor producers were more likely to generate new organizations following a change in leadership or strategy.

> **Proposition 2:** *Major changes in the strategy or governance of an organization will be positively related to the organization's production of entrepreneurs who will found new organizations.*

Second, individuals may be motivated to found a new organization when the growth of their current organization indicates substantial demand for its products or services. Organizational growth, especially very fast growth, can signal the presence of unmet demand and thus opportunity for additional competitors. Growth may also legitimate the value of the organization's strategies for meeting market demand. People who are employed in growing organizations may be more knowledgeable about strategies for supplying demand successfully. Moreover, as a consequence of employment in growing organizations and the legitimacy that growth may confer, individuals in growing organizations may be better able to attract important financial and human resources for creating a new organization.

For these reasons, we also expect that the majority of new organizations produced by entrepreneurs from growing organizations will replicate the primary work of the organizations they came from. For example, web-site design organizations that are growing will tend to produce entrepreneurs who found web-site design organizations. Since substantial risk attends the founding of any organization, simple replication, when the existing organization is growing, probably presents the least risk of early failure. Moreover, a founder's greatest claim to legitimate expertise, and thus potential access to critical resources, probably also attaches to simple replication. Thus, we expect that organizational growth will positively influence an organization's production of new organizations, especially in the same population.

Proposition 3: *The growth of an existing organization will be positively related to its rate of production of entrepreneurs who found new organizations, especially new organizations that replicate the primary work of the existing organization.*

Not all organizations are founded simply to replicate the primary work of an existing organization, however, and growth alone cannot explain how expertise and experience may lead entrepreneurs to create an organization that produces a product or service that is different from the primary work of the existing organization. Jacobs (1969) explored the formation of non-replicating new organizations as a function of the tendency of *existing* organizations to generate new work and, thus, the foundations for new information and expertise. Many factors, including normal outgrowths of research and development within the organization (e.g., 3M's discovery of an adhesive, making Post-It notes possible) and technological developments appearing outside of the organization (e.g., advanced telecommunications and the Internet as the basis for new, distance-learning forms of education), may induce an organization to develop new forms of work. Organizational growth by itself may promote the splitting apart of old forms of work into specialized new forms of work (e.g., Adam Smith's pin-making factory). Finally, organizations might copy a form of work developed in another organization (Miner et al. 1999).

Work that is new in an organization is not necessarily new or innovative in the world. We are interested here in characteristics of organizations that might increase the likelihood that an individual will leave to form a new organization that differs in its primary work from the existing organization. In some cases, the work of the new organization will be broadly innovative, that is, it will introduce a new form of product or service to the world. For example, credit-reporting agencies, though they arose as a direct outgrowth of work already developed in the large retailing organizations of the northeastern United States (Aldrich 1979), introduced a fundamentally new form of service to retailers, banks, and insurance companies during the early part of the twentieth century.

In other cases, the work of the new organization will be different from that of the founder's prior organization but similar to that of other organizations that already exist. For example, the recent scarcity of technical workers in regions such as Silicon Valley and northern Virginia has prompted many professionals from the human resources departments of existing organizations to found their own high-tech personnel search organizations.[4] In both of these cases, the experience of the founders in organizations of one form provided information about product or service opportunities outside of the primary work of the existing organizations.

If entrepreneurs identify opportunities for organizational founding based on experience gained in existing organizations, a question must be asked about why the opportunities were not exploited by the existing organizations whose resources had both helped to identify the opportunities in the first place and supported the development of expertise that was eventually transferred to new organizations. Tushman and Anderson (1986) showed that existing organizations will tend to exploit an innovation that is related to their primary forms of work when the innovation is competence enhancing; when an innovation is competence destroying, new organizations will typically emerge to capitalize on the innovation. Although Tushman and Anderson did not consider the origins of the new organizations' founders (or of the innovations themselves for that matter), it seems likely that many of the founders would emerge from the established organizations. For example, in the early days of the minicomputer industry, which was one of the industries studied by Tushman and Anderson, most of the founders had been employees of mainframe computer manufacturers that had declined to exploit the minicomputer opportunity (Romanelli 1985).

We think there may also be a third, competence-related condition that may dissuade an existing organization from exploiting an entrepreneurial opportunity that was identified out of the organization's own resources. Organizations, whether single-product organizations or business units of multi-prod-

---

4. In general, we think that the literature on innovation and organizational foundings may be confounded. It may be, as Schumpeter (1934) argued, that new organizations will predominantly exploit the commercial promise of technological or organizational innovations, but this does not mean that new organizations will necessarily be the predominant sources of the innovations themselves.

uct organizations, derive competitive advantage from focus on one or a few forms of expertise, for example, engine design at Honda, merchandising and logistics at WalMart, customer service at Nordstrom's. While new forms of expertise, or capabilities, may routinely arise in organizations to support or extend the core competence, there is a limit to the number of different kinds of work that can be supported by an organization. Organizational resources, including both financial and managerial resources, are finite, and the allocation of substantial resources to a new form of work, even new work that shows substantial market opportunity, may excessively drain resources away from the organization's primary work. Internet organizations in Silicon Valley and northern Virginia, for example, had only limited resources to allocate to recruiting activities despite their great need for scarce technical personnel. Thus, the human resources personnel who had invested in the specialized recruiting expertise were free to explore the entrepreneurial opportunity. In many such cases, the first client or customer of the entrepreneurial firm may be the founder's prior organization.

Organizations likely vary in their capacities for generating new forms of work. For example, Kidder (1981) traced the roots of Data General's underground—literally in the basement of its headquarters—operation that developed the company's first 32-bit minicomputer to Edson de Castro's own renegade activities in the formation of Data General. Similar stories are told about the entrepreneurial and cultural roots of ongoing innovative capacity at Hewlett-Packard (Kaplan 1999). Organizations that were innovative in their origins may institutionalize a tolerance for work that is outside of the organizations' primary work (Jelinek and Schoonhoven 1993).[5] Organizational growth, to the extent that it produces slack resources in the organization, may also permit the development of new forms of work. Although the innovative capacity of existing organizations—which may mean simply their tolerance for work outside the primary line of work—is a subject needing much investigation, we argue for the moment that diversity in an organization's forms of work

---

5. See Jelinek and Schoonhoven, *The Innovation Marathon: Lessons from High Technology Companies*, pp. 300–306, for evidence that the managers of persistently innovative firms like Intel and National Semiconductor have a high tolerance for work outside their engineers' primary assignments, which the engineers call "finageling time" and "bootlegging," referring to the use of organizational resources to pursue their own work.

will increase its likelihood of producing entrepreneurs who will found non-replicating organizations.

Proposition 4: *The number of different kinds of work in an existing organization will be positively related to its rate of production of entrepreneurs who found new organizations, especially organizations that do not replicate the primary work of the existing organizations.*

The three characteristics of existing organizations we have described—major change in strategic direction or governance, growth, and work-form diversity—surely only scratch the surface of organizational factors that may motivate employees to found new businesses. At present, we have little more than stories to guide our theory development. Much research may be needed simply to describe the conditions of founders' prior organizations that might have influenced the founding activity. Nonetheless, these characteristics do fit the theoretical criterion of signaling future benefits in excess of benefits that can be obtained in an existing work path. At least conceptually, we can understand how these characteristics carry information, and perhaps access to resources, that should influence founding activity. Finally, the characteristics are easily observable by actors both inside and outside the organization. Thus, we think these characteristics are attractive starting points for initiating research into the organizational origins of new organizations.

Entrepreneurs, of course, do not decide to found a new organization based solely on information and incentives embodied in characteristics of their previous organizations. Information about markets, competitors, and local availabilities of human and financial capital will also certainly influence founding decisions. While most of this information may develop through the work that individuals do in existing organizations, characteristics of local environments may also significantly influence motivations and opportunities for founding.

Local Population Origins

Proposition 1 argued that founders will typically identify opportunities for new organization creation based on expertise and experience gained in existing organizations. Founders will have greatest knowledge about demand for the product or service, and they will have the most access to resources, due to reputation and relationships, in the organizational population of their experience. Founding rates in existing populations will depend, then, primarily on the ability of the environment to support more new organizations in the population.

Organizational ecologists have established population density, the number of organizations in a population relative to the environment's carrying capacity, as a basic factor influencing founding rates in organizational populations. Studies of populations of labor unions and semiconductor producers (Hannan and Freeman 1987; 1989) have shown that rates of founding in a population are curvilinearly related (in an inverted U-shape) to population density. When density is low relative to the carrying capacity, increases in the number of organizations in the population will tend to signal the legitimacy of the organizational form in terms of its ability to produce valuable goods or services and to attract needed human and financial resources; thus, foundings should increase with density. When density is high relative to the carrying capacity, however, increases in density signal an intensifying competition for resources, and foundings should decrease with density under these conditions.

It seems straightforward to assume that the same dynamics of population growth exhibited over the entire population will govern local population growth as well. Assuming that local resources are not perfectly mobile and that local regions impose their own carrying capacities for particular populations, legitimacy and competition should operate similarly to produce the same curvilinear relationship shown for national populations. Hannan et al. (1995), who examined the effects of density on founding rates in the automobile manufacturer populations of five European countries, found precisely this result, though when other-country densities were included as influences on country founding rates, legitimacy was found to have a stronger cross-local effect, while competition operated principally at the local, country level. Thus, the same curvilinear relationship between local population density and local founding rates should exist as has been shown many times for national or international populations.

Proposition 5: *Rates of founding in local organizational populations will be curvilinearly related (in an inverted U-shape) to the density of the local population.*

Ecological research into the founding of new organizations has been concerned explicitly and exclusively with effects of population dynamics on rates of founding in the same organizational population, with newly founded organizations producing the same basic product or service as that produced by other members of a population. Essentially, this research addresses the dynamics of replication. Not all new organizations, however, are founded in the same population as the parent producer. Thus, we ask, what characteristics of local organizational populations should influence the rise of innovative new organizations?

In proposition 4, we argued that nonreplicating new organizations tend to be produced by existing organizations when the existing organizations do not wish to or cannot support the new work as a separate commercial enterprise. Most new forms of work, however, will typically be related in some way to the existing organization's primary work. For example, Lerner and Bosack's work on the routing systems that eventually formed the basis of Cisco Systems, improved the efficiency of Stanford's educational work by making it easier for the university's many computing systems to communicate with one another. Stanford was in essence the first market for the new routing system. Similarly, the retailing organizations that supported the development of credit-evaluation expertise and the Internet companies that sponsored specialized technical recruiting expertise were the markets for these internal activities. The extrapolation of a larger market, outside of the existing organization, should be straightforward for the employees who developed the new forms of work. The size or attractiveness of the opportunity might be measured simply as the size of the existing organization's organizational population.

As Adam Smith (1994 [1776]) argued long ago, specialization proceeds from a fragmentation of skills born of increases in market size. Larger markets allow producers to achieve efficiencies from specialization, especially through the splitting off of work that is not competitively germane to the particular organization and that can be sold to many other organizations, often the existing organization's own competitors. Hawley (1986) also argued that higher levels of density in a human population should give rise to greater degrees of functional differentiation among individuals and organizations in the community. "Specialization of function begins whenever the number of units utilizing a service or a production becomes large enough to support the full-time conduct of the given activity" (Hawley 1986, 85). Thus, we propose the following:

Proposition 6: *The density of an existing organization's organizational population will be positively related to its production of nonreplicating new organizations.*

Although this argument is not restricted by the geographic dispersion of the existing organization's organizational population, we expect that the rate of a population's production of nonreplicating new organizations will be positively related to the density of the *local* organizational population. The founders of nonreplicating new organizations will have limited knowledge of the general market or competitive conditions for their product or service since they will be entering, by definition, a different population from that of the existing organization. Typically, a founder will be relatively more aware of local organizations that perform work that is similar to that of the existing organization in which the nonreplicating ideas for work were developed. Thus, the greater the density of the existing organization's local population, the more likely the existing organization will be to produce nonreplicating new organizations.

Local Community Origins

Local organizational populations, of course, do not exist in isolation in regions. Like organizations themselves, organizational populations exist, compete, cooperate, grow, succeed, and fail in the presence of other populations. All populations that live together in some region (Carroll 1984) constitute the local organizational community. To round off our arguments about the local origins of new organizations, we consider how community characteristics influence the rise of new organizations.

Generally speaking, we expect that the greater the number of organizational populations in a community, the greater the number of innovative new organizations that will be produced in the community. As argued above, one of the easiest opportunities that an entrepreneur can perceive is to commercialize work developed in one organization to other organizations in the same population. Often, such work may also be useful to other organizational populations. For example, the credit-evaluation and reporting work that developed in large retailers and that formed the basis for new organizations to service the population of retailers could also be used by banks, by real estate agencies, or any other organization whose profits depend on the extension of credit and collection of debt. Though not all forms of work will be able to address a multi-population market, in general we expect that the greater the number of populations in an organizational community the larger the potential market for an innovation. Thus, we propose the following:

Proposition 7: *The number of populations in a local organizational community will be positively related to the number of organizational foundings in the community.*

The diversity of populations in a local organizational community should also positively influence the community's rate of organizational foundings. The cluster of medical engineering organizations in the Boston area, for example, is larger than the cluster in the Research Triangle of North Carolina (Porter 1998) although the latter hosts some of the country's most prominent schools of medical engineering. As Porter discussed, the number of related populations—for example, major research hospitals, biotechnology firms, and medical equipment manufacturers—is larger in the Boston area. These populations serve both as incubators for new work in medical engineering and as markets for the work when new organizations are founded to commercialize the work. Burt (1992) argued that entrepreneurial opportunity develops in the "structural holes" of interorganizational exchange; the greater the diversity of populations in a local organizational community, the more likely that individuals in some organizations will identify new forms of work in the interstices of the populations. Thus, we propose the following:

Proposition 8: *The diversity of populations in a local organizational community will be positively related to the number of organizational foundings in a community.*

NEW POPULATION FORMATION

To this point, our theory has concentrated on identifying conditions of organizations, organizational populations, and organizational communities that may give rise to large numbers of new organizations. We are also concerned with factors that lead to the formation of new organizational populations. Many different arguments about the formation of organizational populations have recently emerged, including organizational speciation (Lumsden and Singh 1990), technological innovation and open environmental spaces (Astley 1985), organizational blending and segregating processes (Hannan and Freeman 1986), and the social construction of technological domains (Van de Ven and Garud 1989). Although these perspectives capture many important aspects of how populations likely evolve, no theory has gained dominance and little empirical work supports or distinguishes the arguments of any of the theories (Romanelli 1991). And almost entirely missing from the theories is consideration of the role of new organizations.

Although not all populations will develop from the activities of new organizations—Hannan and Freeman (1986) discussed organizational segregating and blending processes that can include, in addition to the processes of independent founding that we emphasize here, processes of spin-off, joint venture creation, and mergers and acquisitions, among many other forms of organizational interaction—new organizations, and the processes that generate them, surely stand as central to the origins of many populations, especially those that form around major technological innovations (Tushman and Anderson 1986). Regardless, the actions and interactions of existing organizations must be explored as the principal, socially constructing agents of new population formation.

The local-origins approach to new organization formation supports this idea in emphasizing characteristics of contexts and processes that produce new organizations, whether as replications or innovations. No hypothetical open space (Astley 1985), created by random technological innovation or otherwise, is required to posit or predict the formation of new organizational populations. All that is necessary is that conditions exist in organizations for the development of new work and in the population and community to support the commercialization of new work. New organizations, if they do not become members of existing populations, will form the nucleus of new populations to the extent that their founders can mobilize resources and create the cognitive and sociopolitical legitimacy (Aldrich and Fiol 1994; Swaminathan and Wade, this volume) that is necessary to overcome liabilities of newness.

Several of the chapters in this volume describe strategies that entrepreneurs use to create the legitimacy that will support the formation of a new population. Aldrich and Baker, for example, describe Internet retailers' use of established symbols from traditional retailing settings—for example, shopping carts, check-out processes, and electronic wallets—to signify that purchases made through this new medium are both familiar and normal. Rao describes how early automobile manufacturers developed certification contests officially to distinguish the different benefits that consumers could obtain from the products of different manufacturers, but also more generally to educate consumers about the nature of benefits that could be obtained from automobiles. The education provided by the contests was more important to the legitimacy of the automobile manufacturing population than the distinctions between the different automobiles were to the individual manufacturers. Rindova and Fombrun describe how key firms in the U.S. specialty coffee industry (1) developed and disseminated techniques for selecting, blending, and roasting coffee that guaranteed quality, and (2) created coffee bars that associated specialty coffee with a distinctive lifestyle that identified specialty coffee as both different from and better than the myriad other forms of coffee that were proliferating in the marketplace. Swaminathan and Wade, in their study of the emergence of the specialty beer brewing industry in the U.S., describe numerous ways in which the brewing entrepreneurs exploited resources and structures of the existing brewing industry at the same time as they attacked the quality of the mass-market beer.

It would be difficult to identify, in the histories of any of these industries, the existence of some prior, open environmental space that the entrepreneurs were drawn to exploit. Indeed, the point of these studies is that market space needed to be actively and collectively created by the industry entrepreneurs. If open environmental space is not the attractor, then, of entrepreneurial activity, it is reasonable to wonder about the origins of the entrepreneurs' perceptions that a market might be created.

As some entrepreneurs pioneer the commercialization of a new form of work, other entrepreneurs, including some who emerge from the pioneer organizations, will more easily perceive the attractive opportunity and be able to acquire resources to imitate the newly legitimate form. Suchman (this volume) describes the pollinating and institutionalizing influences of law firms and venture capitalists in the formation of the new organizational populations. Actors in these organizations observe the numerous forms of work and organization that are proliferating around a particular product or service, and share information about forms and activities they consider effective over many of the competing organizations. Eventually, a new organization's ability to obtain capital and other important resources for start-up depends on its conforming to the established practices and forms.

Entrepreneurs may not consciously frame any particular activity as being for the purpose of legitimating their organizations' forms. Entrepreneurs are typically intent on acquiring the resources necessary to create their organizations and on developing products and services to promote profitability. Although in retrospect it may be relatively easy to see how the activities of particular entrepreneurs were important to establishing the legitimacy of a population, legitimacy likely develops through the interaction of many new organizations testing, sharing, and adopting certain activities and practices. The greater the number of new organizations that are experimenting with variations on an organizational form, the greater the opportunity for certain elements of the form to be revealed as effective. As many new organizations come to adopt a particular form, perhaps with the help of venture capitalists' requirements, one or a few forms will emerge as legitimate.

It is difficult to imagine this process occurring within the boundaries of a single organization, especially a new organization with limited resources for experimentation. Thus, we expect that both the likelihood of new populations being formed in a local organizational community, as well as the rate of new population formation, will depend principally on the number of new organizations being founded in the community.

Proposition 9: *The number of organizational foundings in a local organizational community will be positively related to the number of new populations established in the community.*

LOCAL COMMUNITY BOUNDARIES

As developed thus far, our arguments do not necessarily imply that new organizations will be founded in close proximity to the existing organizations that produced their founders. Certainly there are examples of founders who scout multiple geographic regions in search of a location that either provides a large market for the new product or service or where the founder believes that he or she will be able to attract the best resources. For example, Jeff Bezos selected Seattle as the best location for founding Amazon.com in 1995 because of the high concentration of local technical talent (due in large part to Seattle's also being the home of Microsoft and its growing number of spin-offs) and proximity to the world's largest book warehouse in Roseburg, Oregon.

It is also difficult, in this modern age, to argue that potential founders will have information about entrepreneurial opportunities only in their local environments. National and international news media, professional associations, and of course the Internet will disseminate information about organizational innovations, and thus opportunities for founding, over very broad geographic spaces. Resources for organizational founding, especially venture capital, are unevenly distributed over geographic regions, and modern populations, especially in developed economies, are highly mobile. Thus, we might expect that clusters of new organizations of a particular form will quickly develop somewhat as an accident of the location of the first few innovative organizations in a place where resources are abundantly available (Arthur 1990a). Some potential founders will then migrate to the location of the cluster. Many, and probably most founders, however, do not.

The oft-told story of spin-offs from Fairchild and Intel, itself a spin-off from Fairchild, reveals that the majority of the new organizations were established in Silicon Valley where technical expertise was already abundant, founders had contacts to recruit talented employees, and venture capitalists were ready and able to provide the critical resource of cash. In biotechnology, dozens of scientists from the Scripps Institute and the National Institutes of Health, both of which are not-for-profit research institutes focusing on human health, and from Pfizer, a major agrochemicals organization, emerged to found new organizations that would capitalize on their research in the existing organizations. With very few exceptions (fewer than 10 out of nearly 200 new organizations), the new organizations were created in San Diego, Gaithersburg, Maryland, and Detroit, which were also home to the organizations that produced the founders. Orlando, home to Disney World, Epcott, and a growing number of theme parks owned by major motion-picture studios, has become a center for multi-media event and software companies. While a few entrepreneurs were attracted to these regions because of available technical and market expertise, more typically the available expertise in the local environment produced the entrepreneurs locally. Thus, to bring our arguments full circle, we formally propose that most new organizations will be founded in the same geographic region, or very close to it, as that of the organization that produced the entrepreneurs.

> **Proposition 10:** *Founders will most often establish a new organization in the same geographic region as that of the existing organization from which the founder came.*

DISCUSSION AND DIRECTIONS FOR RESEARCH

The ideas presented in this chapter suggest using a regional community ecology to investigate organizational origins and the development of new organizational populations. Although community ecology (e.g., Astley 1985; Baum and Singh 1994a; Hunt and Aldrich 1998) has recently emerged as an important field of inquiry in organizational studies, both for studying the origins of new organizational populations and for examining inter-population dynamics, theory has thus far largely ignored any potential effects of geographic boundary. Although many important questions may be addressed by exploring interdependencies among populations connected by technological links (Wade 1995; Hunt and Aldrich 1998), the investigation of population origins, we think, requires specification of a geographic boundary.

People found new organizations, and identify opportunities and acquire resources for founding, primarily in their local environments. We think it makes little sense, then, to ignore the local-ness of founding in theories of the origins of organizations and populations. The propositions developed in this chapter not only ground theories of organizational origins in what we think is a better representation of the empirical phenomena, they also point to regions, with their geographic boundaries, as an important arena for organizational research.

To begin, research is needed simply to document and to describe in detail the nature of regional community differences. How many populations exist in a region? Which are growing? How many new organizations are being founded within existing populations and outside of existing populations as potential instigators of new populations? How is the regional community—the number and kinds of populations that exist together in the region—changing? In other words, before ever investigating the origins or causes of any regional community development, we need to know the lay of the land. Aldrich (1999) has called this one of the glaring, ignored issues in current organizational studies. With thick description in hand and, thus, with a better understanding of how regional communities differ from one another, we can next directly investigate the propositions developed in this chapter, as well as many others that will likely arise through the work of description.

In the meantime, however, nothing prevents an investigation of at least our first propositions on the organizational origins of new organizations. Whether by survey or archival methods, it is a simple enough matter to discover the organizational backgrounds of founders and to investigate whether the work they performed in their prior organizations is the same or different from the work of their new organizations. It is also straightforward to learn whether the cities or regions of the old and the new organizations are the same or different. Such data, perhaps on a population-by-population basis, would give a very rich picture of some of the patterns in organizational origins. Patterns alone could tell us much about the development of regional industry clusters or agglomerations (Arthur 1990a; Marshall 1919; Porter 1998), which have occupied the attention of researchers for about 100 years now.

Next, if research could show a link between characteristics of existing organizations and their rates of producing entrepreneurs who found new organizations, imagine the new research areas that would open. Not only could we explore whether and where such organizations exist in regions, and thus begin to predict directly where new organizations will arise in large numbers, a new line of inquiry into the structure and development of organizations themselves would arise. It would be possible to explore how organizations fare over time if they are prolific producers of organizational founders. New questions about how to invest resources for regional development would arise for regional policy makers. Perhaps, while most investment today focuses on attracting new organizations, policy makers might consider the growth of existing organizations as the engines of organizational founding.

Finally, we think that attention to regional organizational origins and regional population and community dynamics raises a host of new questions about regional development. Saxenian (1994) offered the intriguing observation that where employees live in a region, both in relation to their work sites and in relation to one another, substantively affects both the amount and kind of information that flows in a region and, thus also, entrepreneurial activity. Regions throughout the world are today building new roads and new industrial parks to attract entrepreneurial businesses, and they are planning to build new residential areas close to the new work spaces. If it matters to the economic vitality of an organization what the geographic characteristics of the surrounding region are, then geography should matter to organization theory.

CONCLUSION

Perhaps the most important challenge facing entrepreneurship researchers today involves explaining why some local communities promote the founding of large numbers of organizations while others do not. In the United States, our fascination with the Silicon Valley phenomenon, for its effects both on the development of new industry in the U.S. and the region and on the general economic conditions of that region, underscores this challenge. Where entrepreneurship research once focused on the personality and socioeconomic conditions of individuals as the key to explaining their tendencies to form new organizations, today we are concerned with the mass effects of entrepreneurial activity on technological innovation, regional development, the revitalization of inner cities, and even national competitiveness. To explain the emergence and vitality of new industries or the growth of regions or countries, a much broader understanding of how contexts promote or impede high rates of organizational founding is necessary.

This chapter has explored the local origins of new organizations as developing jointly from the work of existing organizations and opportunities presented in the local environment. In emphasizing the importance of local conditions and processes, our theory addresses a critical and, we think, surprising omission in entrepreneurship and organization theory: the specific origins of ideas for new organizations and the location of organizational foundings as these may be related to sources of ideas. New organizations are critical to the vitality of economies, both regional and national. We need to understand the organizational and environmental conditions that produce entrepreneurs, not merely assume that some spaces will open, randomly, in the environment to elicit entrepreneurial activity.

4

The Role of Immigrant Entrepreneurs in New Venture Creation

ANNALEE SAXENIAN

Debates over the immigration of scientists and engineers to the United States focus primarily on the extent to which foreign-born professionals displace native workers or on the existence of invisible barriers to mobility, or glass ceilings, experienced by non-native professionals. Both approaches assume that the primary economic contribution of immigrants is as a source of relatively low-cost labor, even in the most technologically advanced sectors of the economy (McCarthy and Vernez 1997). The view of countries from which immigrants come, by contrast, has historically been that the emigration of highly skilled personnel to the United States represents a significant economic loss, or brain drain, that deprives their economies of their best and brightest.

Neither of these views adequately characterizes the effect of immigration in today's increasingly global economy. Debates over the extent to which immigrants displace native workers overlook evidence that foreign-born scientists and engineers are starting new businesses and generating jobs and wealth for the state economy at least as fast as their native counterparts (Borjas 1994, 1995; Smith and Edmondston 1997). Similarly, the dynamism of emerging regions in Asia and elsewhere means that it is no longer valid to assume that skilled immigrants will stay permanently in the United States. Recent research suggests that the brain drain may be giving way to a process of "brain circulation," as talented immigrants who study and work in the United States return to their home countries to take advantage of promising opportunities there (Johnson and Regrets 1998). And advances in transportation and communications technologies mean that even when these skilled immigrants choose not to return home, they still play a critical role as intermediaries linking businesses in the U.S. to those in geographically distant regions.

There is widespread recognition of the significance of immigrant entrepreneurship in traditional industries ranging from small-scale retail to garment manufacturing (Waldinger et al. 1990), yet we have only anecdotal evidence of a parallel process in the newer, knowledge-based sectors of the economy (Hing and Lee 1996). It is in these dynamic new industries that immigrants with technical skills and strong connections to fast-growing overseas markets have the potential to make significant economic contributions. Not only are skilled immigrants highly mobile, but the technology industries in which they are concentrated are the largest and fastest-growing exporters and the leading contributors to the nation's economic growth.

To provide a more informed understanding of the role of immigration in entrepreneurship, this study examines the entrepreneurial contribution of highly skilled immigrant scientists and engineers to the Silicon Valley economy. It has four goals. First, it quantifies immigrant engineers' and entrepreneurs' presence in and contribution to the Silicon Valley economy. Second, it examines the extent to which foreign-born engineers are organizing ethnic networks in the region like those found in traditional immigrant enterprises to support the often risky process of starting new technology businesses. Third, it analyzes how these skilled immigrants build long-distance social and economic network connections to their home countries that further enhance entrepreneurial opportunities within Silicon Valley. Finally, it explores the implications of this new model of immigrant-led globalization for public policy.

This is a descriptive and exploratory study that employs a mix of research methods and strategies. It relies on three primary sources. Data on immigrants' education, occupations, and earnings are drawn from the Public Use Microdata Sample (PUMS) of the 1990 census. The decennial census provides the only comprehensive data on immigrants by industry and occupation in the United States. Ample evidence suggests that the Asian presence in Silicon Valley increased significantly during the 1990s, but industrial and occupational detail is not available. As a result, the data on immigrant engineers presented here almost certainly represent a significant undercount, which can only be corrected with data from the 2000 census.

In the absence of direct data on firm founders, this study relies on immigrant-run businesses as a proxy for immigrant-founded businesses. Data on immigrant-run businesses were drawn from a customized Dun & Bradstreet database of 11,443 high-technology firms founded in Silicon Valley between 1980 and 1998. Immigrant-run businesses are defined as companies with chief executive officers (CEOs) with Chinese and Indian surnames.[1] This sample may underestimate immigrant entrepreneurship in the region because firms that were started by Chinese or Indians but have hired non-Asian outsiders as CEOs are not counted. Though the sample also includes Chinese and Indians born in the United States, it appears unlikely that this is a large source of bias, because the great majority of Asian engineers in the region are foreign-born. The Appendix lists 59 public technology firms in Silicon Valley that were founded by or were run by Chinese or Indians at the end of 1998.

The findings reported in the balance of this study are based on original data from more than 100 in-depth interviews with engineers, entrepreneurs, venture capitalists, policymakers, and other key actors in Silicon Valley. These interviews typically lasted at least one hour and were conducted between January 1997 and January 1998. An additional 67 interviews were conducted in the Taipei and Hsinchu regions of Taiwan (25) during May 1997 and the Bangalore, Bombay, and Delhi regions of India (42) during December 1997. The interviewees in Asia included national and local policymakers as well as representatives of technology businesses. Although all the interviews were conducted in English, a Mandarin- or Hindi-speaking research assistant participated in the Chinese and Indian interviews, respectively, to assist with language and cultural clarification or translation.

IMMIGRATION AND ENTREPRENEURSHIP IN SILICON VALLEY

Skilled immigrants are a growing presence in Silicon Valley, accounting for one-third of the engineering workforce in most technology firms and emerg-

---

1. Although this study focuses on Chinese and Indians, the phenomenon of ethnic networking and mutual support among skilled immigrants in Silicon Valley now extends to the region's Iranian, Korean, Japanese, Israeli, French, Filipino, and Singaporean immigrant engineers.

ing as visible entrepreneurs in the 1980s and 1990s. This study documents the growing contribution of skilled Chinese and Indians to the Silicon Valley economy as entrepreneurs as well as engineers. The data presented here suggest that well-known technology companies like Yahoo! and Hotmail, which have immigrant founders, represent the tip of a significantly larger iceberg.

The New Asian Immigrants

Asian immigration to California began in the eighteenth century, but its modern history can be dated to the Immigration Act of 1965, often referred to as the Hart-Celler Act. Before 1965, the U.S. immigration system limited foreign entry by mandating extremely small quotas according to nation of origin. Hart-Celler, by contrast, allowed immigration based on both the possession of scarce skills and on family ties to citizens or permanent residents. It also significantly increased the total number of immigrants allowed into the United States. For example, Taiwan, like most other Asian countries, was historically limited to a maximum of 100 immigrant visas per year. As a result, only 47 scientists and engineers emigrated to the United States from Taiwan in 1965. Two years later, the number had increased to 1,321 (Chang 1992).

The Hart-Celler Act thus created significant new opportunities for foreign-born engineers and other highly educated professionals whose skills were in short supply, as well as for their families and relatives. The great majority of these new skilled immigrants were of Asian origin, and they settled disproportionately on the West Coast of the United States. By 1990, one-quarter of the engineers and scientists employed in California's technology industries were foreign-born—more than twice that of other highly industrialized states such as Massachusetts and Texas (Alarcon 1999). The Immigration and Nationality Act of 1990 further favored the immigration of engineers by almost tripling the number of visas granted on the basis of occupational skills from 54,000 to 140,000 annually.

These changes in the immigration system coincided with the growth of a new generation of high-technology industries in Silicon Valley and, in turn, transformed the regional workforce. As the demand for skilled labor in the region's emerging electronics industry exploded during the 1970s and 1980s, so, too, did immigration to the region. Between 1975 and 1990, Silicon Valley's technology companies created more than 150,000 jobs, and the foreign-born population in the region more than doubled, to almost 350,000 (Saxenian 1994). By 1990, 23% of the population of Santa Clara County (at the heart of Silicon Valley) was foreign-born, surpassing San Francisco County as the largest absolute concentration of immigrants in the Bay Area.

Census data confirm the presence of a large technically skilled, foreign-born workforce in Silicon Valley. Although one-quarter of the total Silicon Valley workforce in 1990 was foreign-born, 30% of the high-technology workforce was foreign-born. These immigrants were concentrated in professional occupations: One-third of all scientists and engineers in Silicon Valley's technology industries in 1990 were foreign-born. Of those, almost two-thirds were Asians, and the majority were of Chinese and Indian descent. In fact, according to the 1990 census PUMS, more than half of the Asian-born engineers in the region were of Chinese (51%) or Indian (23%) origin, and the balance included relatively small numbers of Vietnamese (13%), Filipinos (6%), Japanese (4%), and Koreans (3%).

The disproportionate representation of Chinese and Indian engineers in Silicon Valley's technology workforce explains the focus on these two groups in the balance of this study. This reflects broader national trends: foreign-born engineers and computer scientists in the United States are significantly more likely to come from India, Taiwan, or China than from other Asian nations. The presence of large numbers of Chinese and Indians in Silicon Valley is a recent phenomenon, mirroring the timing of the changes in U.S. immigration legislation: 71% of the Chinese and 87% of the Indians working in Silicon Valley's high-technology industries in 1990 arrived in the United States after 1970, and 41% of the Chinese and 60% of the Indians arrived after 1980. Although we must await the 2000 census data for confirmation, Asian immigration to the region almost certainly accelerated during the 1990s, particularly among highly educated professionals, as a result of the higher limits established by the Immigration Act of 1990.

The Chinese engineering workforce in Silicon Valley was dominated by Taiwanese immigrants in the 1970s and 1980s. Although there were very few Chinese technology workers in the region prior to 1970, in the two subsequent decades, more than one-third of the region's Chinese immigrant engineers were from Taiwan. Immigrants from Mainland China are now a growing presence in the regional workforce. The University of California at Berkeley, for example, granted graduate degrees in science and engineering to a fast-growing proportion of students from Mainland China between 1980 and 1997, whereas the proportion granted to students from Taiwan declined correspondingly during the same period. By the mid-1990s, over half of the degrees (53%) were granted to students from China, compared with 35% in the late 1980s and only 10% in the early 1980s. The number of graduate degrees granted can be seen as a leading indicator of labor supply in Silicon Valley, as most graduates find jobs in the region's technology companies.

National trends in graduate science and engineering education mirror the above trends closely and provide insights into the changing composition of the Silicon Valley workforce. Between 1990 and 1996, the number of doctorates in science and engineering granted annually by U.S. universities to immigrants from China more than tripled (from 477 to 1,680), and those to Indian immigrants doubled (to 692) whereas those to Taiwanese remained stable (at about 300). These three immigrant groups alone accounted for 81% of the doctorates granted to Asians and 62% of all foreign doctorates in science and engineering granted in the United States between 1985 and 1996 (Johnson 1998). Moreover, California's universities granted engineering degrees to Asian students at more than twice the rate of universities in the rest of the nation (American Association of Engineering Societies 1995). In short, we can expect the 2000 census to show a dramatic increase in the number of Mainland Chinese and Indian engineers in the Silicon Valley workforce.

Not surprisingly, Silicon Valley's Indian and Chinese workforce is highly educated. In 1990, they earned graduate degrees at significantly greater rates than their White counterparts: 32% of the Indian and 23% of the Chinese employed in Silicon Valley in 1990 had advanced degrees, compared with only 11% for the White population. Their superior educational attainment is even more pronounced in technology industries: 55% of Indian and 40% of Chinese technology workers held graduate degrees, compared with 18% of Whites.

This educational attainment is only partially reflected in occupational status. Indians and Chinese working in the region's technology sector were better represented in professional and managerial occupations than their White counterparts, with 60% of Indians and 57% of Chinese employed as professionals and managers, compared with 53% of Whites. But these groups were significantly more concentrated in professional than managerial occupations: 45% of the Indians, 41% of the Chinese, and 27% of the Whites were in professional occupations, but only 15% of the Indians and 16% of the Chinese were managers, compared with 26% of the Whites. In other words, although Indians and Chinese accounted for 2% and 6% of Silicon Valley's technology professionals, respectively, they represented less than 1% and 4% of the managers.[2]

The relatively lower representation of Chinese and Indians in managerial positions could be due to several factors: biases favoring technical over business education or the linguistic and cultural difficulties of many new immigrants. It could also be a reflection of more subtle forms of discrimination or institutional barriers to mobility based on race, or the glass ceiling, although income data provide little support for the glass ceiling hypothesis. Analysis documents that there is no statistically significant difference between the earnings of Chinese and Indians in managerial, professional, and technical occupations and their White counterparts (Saxenian 1999). This is consistent with the findings of other researchers, who have documented greater disparities in managerial representation and upward mobility than in wage levels between Asian and White engineers with comparable skills and education (Fernandez 1998; Tang 1993).

Whatever the data show, many Chinese and Indians in Silicon Valley believe that there is a glass ceiling inhibiting their professional advancement. A 1991 survey of Asian professionals in the region found that two-thirds of those working in the private sector believed that advancement to managerial positions was limited by race. Moreover, these concerns increased significantly with the age and experience of the respondents. This perception is consistent with the finding that, in technology industries at least, Chinese and Indians remain concentrated in professional rather than managerial positions, despite superior levels of educational attainment. It is notable, however, that those surveyed attributed these limitations less to "racial prejudice and stereotypes" than to the

---

2. The *CorpTech Directory* lists the names and titles of all the executives in public technology firms in the region. These data show Chinese and Indians in significantly greater numbers in R&D than other functions such as CEO, finance, marketing, or sales.

perception of an "old boys' network that excludes Asians" and the "lack of role models" (AACI 1993, 22).

Lester Lee, a native of Szechwan, China, who moved to Silicon Valley in 1958, described the feeling of being an outsider that was common for Asian immigrants in that period. "When I first came to Silicon Valley," he remembered, "there were so few of us that if I saw another Chinese on the street I'd go over and shake his hand." This sense of being an outsider was reinforced in many ways. Lee noted, for example, that "nobody wanted to sell us [Chinese] houses in the 1960s." Although immigrants like Lee typically held graduate degrees in engineering from U.S. universities and worked for mainstream technology companies, they often felt personally and professionally isolated in a world dominated by White men.

Immigrant engineers like Lester Lee responded to the sense of exclusion from established business and social structures in two ways. Many responded individually by starting their own businesses. Lee became the region's first Chinese entrepreneur when he left Ampex in 1970 to start a company called Recortec. Other early Chinese engineers reported that they felt as if they were seen as "good work horses, and not race horses" or "good technicians, rather than managers." David Lee, for example, left Xerox in 1973 to start Qume after a less-experienced outsider was hired as his boss. Lee was able to raise start-up capital from the mainstream venture capital community, but only on the condition that he hire a non-Asian president for his company. David Lam similarly left Hewlett-Packard in 1979 after being passed over for a promotion and started a semiconductor equipment manufacturing business called Lam Research, which is now a publicly traded company with $1.3 billion in sales. Not surprisingly, these three have become community leaders and role models for subsequent generations of Chinese entrepreneurs.

The New Immigrant Entrepreneurs

During the 1980s and 1990s, Silicon Valley's immigrant engineers increasingly followed the career trajectories of native engineers by starting technology businesses. In contrast to traditional immigrant entrepreneurs, who are concentrated in low-technology services and manufacturing sectors, these new immigrant entrepreneurs are a growing presence in the most technologically dynamic and globally competitive sectors of the Silicon Valley economy. At least 37 public technology companies in the region were started by Chinese immigrants; another 22 were started by Indians (see Appendix). The existence of so many immigrant-run publicly traded companies suggests that there is a significant population of private, immigrant-founded companies. Unfortunately, it is difficult to get accurate estimates of ethnic or immigrant entrepreneurship in technology industries. The standard way to measure immigrant entrepreneurship is by examining the "self-employed" category in the U.S. census. Although this may be a good approximation for owner-run businesses in traditional industries, it almost certainly leads to a significant undercount in technology sectors because so many companies are funded with outside funds or venture capital, and hence are not owned by the founding entrepreneur.

A higher and probably more accurate estimate of ethnic entrepreneurship in Silicon Valley was obtained by identifying all businesses with CEOs having Chinese and Indian surnames in a Dun & Bradstreet database of technology firms founded since 1980. According to this count, close to one-quarter (24%) of Silicon Valley's technology firms in 1998 had Chinese or Indian executives, and they created both jobs and wealth in the region. Of the 11,443 high-technology firms started during this period, 2,001 (17%) were run by Chinese and 774 (7%) by Indians. In 1998, these companies collectively accounted for over $16.8 billion in sales and 58,282 jobs. These numbers may still understate the scale of immigrant entrepreneurship in the region because firms started by Chinese or Indians with non-Asian CEOs were not counted. Interviews for this study suggest that firms with this arrangement are not uncommon in Silicon Valley, where venture capital financing has often been tied to the requirement that non-Asian senior executives be hired.

The data in Table 4.1 indicate that the rate of Chinese and Indian entrepreneurship in Silicon Valley increased significantly over time. Chinese and Indians were at the helm of 13% of Silicon Valley's technology companies between 1980 and 1984, but they were running 29% of the region's high-technology companies started between 1995 and 1998. In the following sections, I develop the idea that this growth has been fueled both by the emergence of role models and by supportive networks within the ethnic communities in the

Table 4.1
Chinese- and Indian-Run Companies as Share of
Total Silicon Valley High-Technology Start-ups, 1980–1998

	1980–1984		1985–1989		1990–1994		1995–1998	
	NO.	%	NO.	%	NO.	%	NO.	%
Indian	47	3	90	4	252	7	385	9
Chinese	121	9	347	15	724	19	809	20
White	1,181	88	1,827	81	2,787	74	2,869	71
TOTAL	1,349	100	2,264	100	3,763	100	4,063	100

SOURCE: Dun & Bradstreet database, 1998

region, as well as by growing ties to Asian markets and sources of capital and manufacturing capabilities.

Chinese and Indian firms remain small relative to the technology sector as a whole, with an average of 21 employees per firm, compared with 37 employees per firm for all firms. Although these immigrant-run firms employ fewer people, they appear to be at least as productive: Chinese-run firms had sales of $317,555 per employee and Indian-run firms had sales of $216,110 per employee, compared with $242,105 in sales per employee for all technology firms in the Dun & Bradstreet database. It is impossible to precisely track the progress of the technology companies founded by immigrants, in part because so many have passed managerial responsibility to their native counterparts. But the technology companies listed in the Appendix, which were either founded by or are currently run by Chinese or Indians and are publicly traded, have average sales and employment that are much closer to the regional average.

There is an interesting sectoral division among these businesses. Chinese-run firms are more concentrated than Indian-run firms in computer and electronic hardware manufacturing and trade, whereas Indian-run companies are disproportionately in software and business services. This difference is likely due to the differences in language skills between the two groups. Indian immigrants tend to be proficient in English, but most first-generation Chinese immigrants are not. This means that Indians can move more easily into software development, whereas Chinese immigrants gravitate toward

sectors where language skills are less important. But this appears to be changing. Two well-known public technology companies started by Taiwanese
immigrants—Broadvision and AboveNet—are in the software and Internet
sectors, respectively. Moreover, in absolute terms, there are more Chinese-run
than Indian-run software and service companies.

A large number of Chinese firms also operate in the wholesale sector,
reflecting a distinctive, lower-skill segment of the Taiwanese technology
community. These firms, which are on average quite small, specialize in selling computers and computer components that are manufactured in Taiwan.
They appear to have some ties to the more technically sophisticated sector of
the Chinese community through their association, the Chinese American
Computer Corporation, as well as through personal and alumni networks.
These ties allow the wholesale and retail communities to learn quickly about
technology trends as well as to provide market feedback.

THE ORIGINS OF SILICON VALLEY'S ETHNIC NETWORKS

To this point, I have portrayed Chinese and Indian entrepreneurs as individuals or as collections of unrelated individuals, which conforms to the popular
image of the entrepreneur as a lone pioneer. In reality, however, Silicon Valley's immigrant entrepreneurs, like their mainstream counterparts, rely on a
diverse range of informal social structures and institutions to support their
entrepreneurial activities.

Unlike traditional ethnic entrepreneurs who remain isolated in low-wage,
low-skill industries (Waldinger et al. 1990), Silicon Valley's new immigrant
entrepreneurs are professionals who are active in dynamic and technologically sophisticated industries. Yet like their less-educated predecessors, the
region's Chinese and Indian engineering communities rely on ethnic strategies to enhance their own entrepreneurial opportunities. Seeing themselves
as outsiders to the mainstream technology community, Silicon Valley's immigrant engineers have created local social and professional networks to mobilize the information, know-how, skill, and capital needed to start technology firms. This is reflected in a proliferation of ethnic professional
associations.

Table 4.2 lists the professional and technical associations organized by Silicon Valley's Chinese and Indian immigrant engineers.[3] These organizations are among the vibrant and active professional associations in the region, with memberships ranging from several hundred in the newer associations to over one thousand in the established organizations.

The organizations combine elements of traditional immigrant culture with distinctly high-technology practices: they simultaneously create ethnic identities within the region and facilitate the professional networking and information exchange that aid success in the highly mobile Silicon Valley economy. They are not traditional political or lobbying organizations. With the exception of the Asian American Manufacturers Association (AAMA), the activities of these groups are oriented exclusively toward fostering the professional and technical advancement of their members.

It is notable that the region's Chinese and Indian immigrants have organized separately from one another—as well as from Silicon Valley's mainstream professional and technical associations, such as the American Electronics Association, the Institute of Electrical and Electronic Engineers, or the Software Entrepreneurs Forum. They also join the mainstream organizations, to be sure, but most are less active in these than they are in the ethnic associations. There is virtually no overlap in the membership of Indian and Chinese professional associations, although there appears to be considerable overlap in association membership within the separate communities, particularly the Chinese, with its multiplicity of differently specialized associations. There are also ethnic distinctions within the Chinese technology community. The Monte Jade Science and Technology Association and the North American Taiwanese Engineers Association, for example, use Mandarin (Chinese) at many meetings and social events, which excludes not only non-Chinese members but even Chinese from Hong Kong or Southeast Asia who speak Cantonese.

In spite of the distinct ethnic subcultures and the greater number and specialization of the Chinese associations, these associations share important functions as well. All mix socializing—over Chinese banquets, Indian dinners,

---

3. This list includes only professional associations whose focus is the technology industry and whose primary membership base is in Silicon Valley. It does not include the numerous Chinese and Indian political, social, and cultural organizations in the region, nor does it include ethnic business or trade associations for traditional, nontechnology industries.

Table 4.2

Indian and Chinese Professional Associations in Silicon Valley

	Year Founded	Membership	Brief Description
Indian			
Silicon Valley Indian Professionals Association (SIPA) Web site: *www.sipa.org*	1991	1,000	Forum for expatriate Indians to contribute to cooperation between the U.S. and India
The Indus Entrepreneur (TiE) Web site: *www.tie.org*	1992	560	Fosters entrepreneurship by providing mentorship and resources
Chinese			
Chinese Institute of Engineers (CIE/USA) Web site: *www.cie-sf.org*	1979	1,000	Promotes communication and interchange of information among Chinese engineers and scientists
Asian American Manufacturers Association (AAMA) Web site: *www.aamasv.com*	1980	> 700	Promotes the growth and success of U.S. technology enterprises throughout the Pacific Rim
Chinese Software Professionals Association (CSPA) Web site: *www.cspa.com*	1988	1,400	Promotes technology collaboration and facilitates information exchange in the software profession
Chinese American Computer Corporation (NBI) Web site: *www.killerapp.com/nbi*	1988	270[a]	Mid-technology cluster of PC clone system sellers, the majority of them from Taiwan
Monte Jade Science and Technology Association (MJSTA) Web site: *www.montejade.org*	1989	150[a] 300[b]	Promotes the cooperation and mutual flow of technology and investment between Taiwan and the U.S.

(continued)

or family-centered social events—with support for professional and technical advancement. Each organization, either explicitly or informally, provides first-generation immigrants with a source of professional contacts and networks within the local technology community. They serve as important sources of labor market information and recruitment channels, and they provide role models of successful immigrant entrepreneurs and managers. In addition, the associations sponsor regular speakers and conferences that provide forums for sharing specialized technical and market information, as well as basic information about the nuts and bolts of entrepreneurship and management for

Table 4.2 *(continued)*

	Year Founded	Membership	Brief Description
Silicon Valley Chinese Engineers Association (SCEA) Web site: *www.scea.org*	1989	400	Network of Mainland Chinese engineers founded to promote entrepreneurship and professionalism among members and establish ties to China
Chinese American Semiconductor Professionals Association (CASPA) Web site: *www.caspa.com*	1991	40[a] 1,600	Promotes technical, communication, information exchange, and collaboration among semiconductor professionals
North America Taiwanese Engineers Association (NATEA) Web site: *www://natea.org*	1991	400	Promotes exchange of scientific and technical information
Chinese Information and Networking Association (CINA) Web site: *www.cina.org*	1992	700	Chinese professionals who advocate technologies and business opportunities in information industries
Chinese Internet Technology Association (CITA) Web site: *www.cita.net*	1996	600	Forum and network for Chinese Internet professionals and entrepreneurs to incubate ideas, learn from one another, and form potential partnerships
North America Chinese Semiconductor Association (NACSA) Web site: *www.nacsa.com*	1996	600	Professional advancement in semiconductor sector, interaction between the U.S. and China

SOURCE: Interviews.
[a]corporations
[b]West Coast only

engineers with limited business experience. In addition to providing sessions on how to write a business plan or manage a business, some of the Chinese associations give seminars on English communication, negotiation skills, and stress management.

Many of these associations have become important forums for cross-generational investment and mentoring as well. An older generation of successful immigrant engineers and entrepreneurs in both the Chinese and the Indian communities now plays an active role in financing and mentoring younger generations of co-ethnic entrepreneurs. Individuals within these networks often invest individually or jointly in promising new ventures, acting as "angel" investors who are more accessible to immigrants than the mainstream venture capital community and who are also willing to invest smaller amounts of money. The goal of the Indus Entrepreneur (TiE), for example, is to "foster entrepreneurship by providing mentorship and resources" within the South Asian technology community. Similarly, both the AAMA and the Monte Jade Science and Technology Association sponsor annual investment conferences aimed at matching potential investors (often from Asia as well as Silicon Valley) with promising Chinese entrepreneurs.

This is not to suggest that these associations create self-contained ethnic businesses or communities. Many Chinese and Indian immigrants socialize primarily within the ethnic networks, but they routinely work with native engineers and native-run businesses. In fact, there is growing recognition within these communities that although a start-up might be spawned with the support of the ethnic networks, it needs to become part of the mainstream to grow. It appears that the most successful immigrant entrepreneurs in Silicon Valley today are those who have drawn on ethnic resources while simultaneously integrating into mainstream technology and business networks.[4] Below, I trace the evolution of some of the region's leading Chinese and Indian professional associations to illuminate their origins and activities in more detail.

The Chinese Institute of Engineers:
The "Grandfather" of the Chinese Associations

A handful of Chinese engineers—including Lester Lee, David Lee, and David Lam—started a local branch of the Chinese Institute of Engineers (CIE) in 1979 to promote better communication and organization among the region's Chinese engineers. The Bay Area chapter of the CIE quickly became the largest in the country. Today the CIE has some 1,000 members in the Bay Area and is regarded by oldtimers as the "grandfather" of Silicon Valley's Chinese organizations.

The organization was dominated initially by Taiwanese immigrants, reflect-

---

4. This parallels Granovetter's (1995) notion of balancing coupling and decoupling among overseas Chinese entrepreneurs.

ing the composition of the Chinese technology community in Silicon Valley at the time. Its early dynamism built on preexisting professional and social ties among these engineers, a majority of whom were graduates of Taiwan's elite engineering universities. Most Taiwanese engineers reported that by the mid-1980s they had dozens of classmates in Silicon Valley. The National Taiwan University Alumni Association, for example, has 1,500 members in the Bay Area alone. These alumni relations—which seemed more important to many Taiwanese immigrants when living abroad than when they were at home—have become an important basis for the solidarity within the Chinese engineering community in Silicon Valley.

Although the CIE is primarily a technical organization, the initial meetings of the Bay Area chapter focused heavily on teaching members the mechanics of starting a business, getting legal and financial help, and providing basic management training to engineers who had only technical education. Over time, the CIE became an important source of role models and mentors for recently arrived immigrants. Gerry Liu, who co-founded Knights Technology in 1987 with four Chinese friends, reported:

> When I was thinking of starting my own business, I went around to call on a few senior, established Chinese businessmen to seek their advice. I called David Lee . . . I contacted David Lam and Winston Chen. I called up Ta-ling Hsu. They did not know me, but they took my calls. I went to their offices or their homes, they spent time with me telling me what I should or shouldn't be doing.

Not surprisingly, immigrants like Liu began starting businesses at an increasing rate in the late 1980s and 1990s.

The CIE remains the most technical of the region's ethnic associations, and its goal is "to foster friendship, provide a forum for technical exchange and promote cooperation among Chinese-American engineers to enhance their image and influence." It also plays a central role in promoting collaboration between Chinese-American engineers and their counterparts in Asia. In 1989, the CIE initiated an annual week-long technical seminar with the parallel organization in Taiwan, and this was extended to include engineers from Mainland China during 1990s. In addition, when the Taiwanese government initiates major engineering projects, from a transit system to a power station, they consult the

Silicon Valley chapter of the CIE. These forums not only transfer technical know-how but also create professional and social ties among Chinese engineers living on both sides of the Pacific.

Although the CIE was the first organization of Chinese engineers in the Bay Area, there was already a well-developed infrastructure of Chinese associations in the region. San Francisco's Chinatown—historically the center of Chinese immigration to the area—was the home of hundreds of traditional Chinese ethnic associations, including regional and district hometown associations, kinship (clan, family, or multifamily), and dialect associations. There were also business and trade associations that supported the thousands of traditional ethnic businesses located in the city, including apparel contractors, jewelry and gift shops, neighborhood grocers, Chinese laundries, and restaurants (Wong 1998).

The CIE was distinguished from these established ethnic associations by both the social and economic background of its members and by geography. CIE members were highly educated professionals who had immigrated in recent decades from Taiwan or China and who lived and worked in the South Bay. They had little in common with the older generations of less-skilled farmers and manual workers who had immigrated from Hong Kong and southern China (Guangdong and Fujian provinces) and who lived and worked in San Francisco. The early gatherings of Silicon Valley's Chinese engineers centered in the city because of its concentration of Chinese restaurants. By the mid-1980s, as the area's Chinese population increased significantly—and, with it, the number of Chinese restaurants suitable for holding meetings—the center of gravity for socializing had shifted decisively to the Peninsula. Interviews confirm that these two communities of Chinese immigrants coexist today in the Bay Area with limited social or professional interaction.

Into the Mainstream: The Asian American Manufacturers Association

The Asian American Manufacturers Association (AAMA) was founded in 1980 by a group of eight Chinese engineers at Lester Lee's company, Recortec. Motivated by the desire to be seen as professionals rather than simply as good engineers and to participate more directly in the political process, the founding members envisioned an institution that would help Asians join mainstream

American society. There were only 21 members at the founding meeting, but they quickly achieved their vision of positioning the AAMA as a high-profile, high-caliber association with broad appeal to Asian professionals in the area.

The goals of the AAMA were broader and more political than those of CIE. The original objectives were: "(1) To obtain resources from federal, state, and local governments, and private sectors to assist in the development, growth, and success of the organization; (2) To benefit individual members of the association through mutual support and sharing of resources, information, and individual talents; and (3) To address issues that affect the welfare of the members of the association and the Asian Pacific American business community" (Gong 1996, 1).

In spite of a significantly broader agenda, the early AAMA meetings, like those of the CIE, focused primarily on teaching first-time entrepreneurs the nuts and bolts of starting and managing a technology business. These meetings also showcased role models of successful Asian Americans in the industry and provided a mutual support and networking forum for members. Such forums were intended to help their members advance professionally, but they also helped promote the adoption of American management models—rather than traditional Chinese business models based on family ties and obligations—in immigrant-run technology companies.

The AAMA now has more than 700 members and is the most visible representative of the Asian community in Silicon Valley. Its goal is now more global, to "promote the growth and success of U.S. technology enterprises throughout the Pacific Rim." But the organization's objectives still include fostering business growth and networking, facilitating management and leadership development—including providing "management development training, opportunities, and managerial/executive role models and contacts that will help members break through the glass ceiling"—recognizing and publicizing the achievements of Asian Americans, and supporting equal opportunity.

The AAMA has the broadest potential membership base and agenda of the ethnic associations in Silicon Valley. All of its meetings are conducted in English and its membership, which is open to all professionals, includes large numbers of investment bankers, consultants, lawyers, and accountants, as well as engineers. In spite of this umbrella-like character, three-quarters of AAMA members are Chinese.

These early professional associations had overlapping memberships and boards reflecting in part the small scale of the Chinese technology community in Silicon Valley. Members describe both the CIE and the AAMA—and the social networks they support—as providing helpful job-search networks and as sources of reliable information, advice and mentoring, seed capital, and trusted business partners. A former president of the AAMA described these advantages: "Doing business is about building relationships, it's people betting on people, so you still want to trust the people you're dealing with. A lot of trust is developed through friendship and professional networks like school alumni relations, business associations, and industry ties." David Lam similarly described the advantages of the ethnic networks:

> If there is someone that I know . . . if we have some mutual business interest, then the deal can come together rather fast. And if we have known each other for some years and a certain level of mutual trust has already been established, it is much easier to go forward from there. In other situations I may not have known the person directly, but through some introduction I talked to them, and things also went along very well. So I think the connections play a very important role.

The Proliferation of Chinese Professional and Technical Associations

The growing scale and diversity of the Chinese engineering community in Silicon Valley during the 1980s and early 1990s generated a proliferation of professional and technical associations. As Table 4.2 shows, at least nine more Chinese technology-related associations—or more than one per year—were started in Silicon Valley between 1988 and 1996. The new generation of Mainland Chinese have created still more associations since that time, often parallel to comparable Taiwanese organizations. All of these associations bring together the Chinese members of a given industry, and all are dedicated broadly to promoting the professional advancement of individuals and member firms. Collectively, the Chinese associations represent nearly 6,000 members in Silicon Valley—although this number undoubtedly double-counts individuals who belong to multiple associations.

Breaking the Glass Ceiling:
The Silicon Valley Indian Professionals Association

A young Intel engineer and his three Indian roommates started the Silicon Valley Indian Professionals Association (SIPA) in 1987 to provide a meeting place for Indian professionals to share their common concerns. In spite of their superior mastery of the English language, which distinguished them from most of their Chinese counterparts, they, too, were concerned about limits on the opportunities for professional advancement in the technology industry. According to the founder of SIPA, Prakash Chandra, "many Indians didn't see a career path beyond what they were doing." Many of the early SIPA meetings were thus focused on individual career strategies as well as on the nuts and bolts of the technology industry.

Silicon Valley's Indian immigrants did not mobilize collectively until a decade later than their Chinese counterparts, in part because they were later in achieving a critical mass in the region. Many Indian engineers complained about a glass ceiling in the region's established companies and responded by starting their own businesses. As one told me, "Why do you think there are so many Indian entrepreneurs in Silicon Valley? Because they know that sooner or later they will be held back." When they organized collectively, however, they created new associations such as the SIPA rather than joining existing groups such as the AAMA. This no doubt reflects the greater comfort they felt in being with other Indians, in spite of the fact that they were often from different regions of India and spoke different dialects. In fact, a sizable subset of these engineers grew up in Africa and had never lived in India. But, like their Chinese counterparts, their backgrounds were often similar—many were graduates of the prestigious Indian Institutes of Technology (IITs) or Indian Institutes of Science (IISs)—and hence were unified by common professional identities along with the pull of shared ethnic ties.

Like its Chinese counterparts, the SIPA's vision gradually expanded beyond the focus on individual professional advancement. Largely in response to visits by Indian government delegations in the early 1990s seeking to build business ties in the United States, the SIPA redefined its role to include attempting to "fill the information gap" between the United States and India. The association began sponsoring regular seminars and workshops that would allow U.S.-based Indian professionals to help their employers gain a better understanding of the recently opened Indian market and business environment and simultaneously to explore professional opportunities for themselves in India. Today, the SIPA has about 1,000 members, virtually all Indians, and holds regular seminars to disseminate information of interest and strengthen ties with business and government officials in India.

Cross-Generational Mentoring: The Indus Entrepreneur

The SIPA lost some of its momentum when its founder returned to India in 1992, but in the same year, an older generation of Indian immigrants started The Indus Entrepreneur (TiE). TiE's goal was to nurture entrepreneurs from South Asia. Its founding members included three of the region's most successful Indian entrepreneurs: Suhas Patil, former MIT professor and founder of Cirrus Logic; Prabhu Goel, founder of Gateway Design Automation; and Kanwal Rekhi, who started and ran Excelan until it merged with Novell. This core group came together in response to a visit from India's Secretary of Electronics to Silicon Valley in 1992, but when the minister's flight was delayed, they began informally to share complaints about the difficulties of running a business. In the words of another local entrepreneur who subsequently organized the first meeting of TiE, "I realized that we all had the same problems, but that we don't work together. That as individuals we are brilliant, but collectively we amounted to nothing." TiE began its monthly meetings with the intent of creating a forum for networking among its members as well as for assisting younger South Asians to start their own businesses.

Like the first generation of Chinese immigrant entrepreneurs, Indians such as Patil and Goel had succeeded in spite of their lack of contacts or community support. In the words of another early TiE member, Satish Gupta:

> When some of us started our businesses we had nobody we could turn to for help. We literally had to scrounge and do it on our own. What we see in Silicon Valley, especially with the new start-up businesses, is that contacts are everything. All of us have struggled through developing contacts, so our business is to give the new person a little bit of a better start than we had.

This goal of mentoring and assisting entrepreneurs remains central to TiE's agenda and is achieved through monthly meetings and presentations, the annual conference, and extensive informal networking and mentoring. Even TiE founders were amazed by the popularity of the first annual conference in 1994, which attracted over 500 people. Today it draws close to 1,000.

TiE founders call themselves Indus (rather than Indian) entrepreneurs, to include other South Asians such as Pakistanis, Bangladeshis, and Nepalese, but the organization's Bay Area members are almost all Indian. Forty charter members form the core of the organization. Charter membership is by invitation only and includes successful entrepreneurs, corporate executives, and senior professionals with roots in or an interest in the Indus region who support the organization with annual dues of $1,000. TiE has U.S. chapters in Southern California, Boston, and Austin as well, but the center of gravity remains in Silicon Valley. In 1999, TiE chapters were established in Bangalore, Bombay, and Delhi, India.

TiE's most distinctive contribution is its model of cross-generational investing and mentoring. Because of their earlier business successes, TiE's founders are able to provide start-up capital, business and financial advice, and professional contacts to a younger generation of Indian entrepreneurs. These engineers claim that one of the biggest obstacles to their own advancement has been bias on the part of mainstream financial organizations and, in particular, the difficulties faced by non-native applicants in raising venture capital. Like their Chinese counterparts, they felt like outsiders to the mainstream, primarily White and native, venture capital community.

TiE members often take on the roles of mentors, advisors, board members, and angel investors in new Indian companies. One early recipient of TiE funding, Naren Bakshi, presented the business plan for a company called Vision Software in 1995. Within months, TiE members had raised $1.7 million for Bakshi's company. Today, Vision Software has 60 employees and has raised additional funding—in fact, Bakshi was approached by more venture capitalists than he could use. This fits the vision of TiE's founders of supporting "diamonds in the rough" and encouraging them to expand by diversifying their funding and integrating into the mainstream technology community.

Chandra Shekar, founder of Exodus Corporation, reports that the help from TiE members extends beyond providing capital and sitting on the board of directors to serving as a "trusted friend" or even the "brain behind moving the company where it is today." One of the most important contributions these experienced entrepreneurs and executives provide is access to "entry points" with potential customers or business alliances. According to Shekar:

> The Indian network works well, especially because the larger companies like Sun, Oracle and HP have a large number of Indians. . . . You gain credibility through your association with a TiE member. . . . For example, if HP wants to do business with you, they see that you are a credible party to do business with. This is very important.

Vinod Khosla, a co-founder of Sun Microsystems and now a partner at the venture capital firm Kleiner, Perkins summarized: "The ethnic networks clearly play a role here: people talk to each other, they test their ideas, they suggest other people they know, who are likely to be of the same ethnicity. There is more trust because the language and cultural approach are so similar." Of course, once successful Indian entrepreneurs invest in a company, they provide the legitimacy that allows the entrepreneur to get a hearing from the region's more established venture capital funds. Satish Gupta of Cirrus Logic similarly noted that

> networks work primarily with trust. . . . Elements of trust are not something that people develop in any kind of formal manner. . . . Trust has to do with the believability of the person, body language, mannerisms, behavior, cultural background, . . . all these things become important for building trust. . . . Caste may play a role, financial status may play a role.

But he added that although organizations like TiE are instrumental in creating trust in the community, they also create a set of duties and sanctions:

> If you don't fulfill your obligations, you could be an outcast. . . . The pressure of, hey, you better not do this because I'm going to see you at the temple or sitting around the same coffee table at the TiE meeting . . . and I know another five guys that you have to work with, so you better not do anything wrong.

Groups like the SIPA and TiE create common identities among an otherwise fragmented nationality. Indians historically are deeply divided and typically segregate themselves by regional and linguistic differences: the Bengalis, Punjabis, Tamil, and Gujaratis tend to stick together. But in Silicon Valley it seems that the Indian identity has become more powerful than these regional distinctions. As the author V. S. Naipaul wrote of his own upbringing in Trinidad, "In these special circumstances overseas Indians developed something they would have never known in India: a sense of belonging to an Indian community. This feeling of community could override religion and caste." As with the overseas Chinese community, there are, of course, subgroups with varied amounts of familiarity and trust, but the shared experience of immigration appears to strengthen rather than undermine ethnic identities.

There is always a danger of insularity in these ethnic communities. Some suggest that the TiE network remains so closed that it prevents outsiders from participating. According to a charter member of TiE, there is little desire in the organization to connect to the outside: "This network just does not connect to the mainstream. If you look at the social gatherings that the TiE members go to, it's all Indians. There's nothing wrong with it . . . but I think if you don't integrate as much, you don't leverage the benefit that much." The challenge for Silicon Valley's immigrant entrepreneurs will continue to be to balance reliance on ethnic networks with integration into the mainstream technology community.

The Benefits of Local Ethnic Networks

Although I cannot definitively demonstrate the economic benefits of these immigrant networks, the proliferation of ethnic professional associations in Silicon Valley during the 1980s and 1990s corresponded with the growing visibility and success of Chinese- and Indian-run businesses. The entrepreneurs themselves give the networks much credit. According to Mohan Trika, CEO of an internal Xerox venture called inXight:

> Organizations like TiE create self-confidence in the community. This confidence is very important . . . it provides a safety net around you, the feeling that you can approach somebody to get some help. It's all about managing risk. Your ability to manage risk is improved by these networks. If there are no role models, confidence builders to look at, then the chances of taking risk are not there.

That's what we are saying: "come on with me, I'll help you." This quickly becomes a self-reinforcing process: you create 5 or 10 entrepreneurs and those 10 create another 10. . . . I can approach literally any big company, or any company in the Bay Area, and find two or three contacts . . . through the TiE network I know so-and-so in Oracle, etc.

This networking creates value, he says:

because we are a technology selling company for the next generation of user interface, every major software company or any software company must have at least two or three Indians or Chinese in there. . . . And because they are there, it is very easy for me, or my technical officer, to create that bond, to pick up the phone and say: Swaminathan, can you help me, can you tell me what's going on . . . he'll say don't quote me but the decision is because of this, this and this. Based on this you can reformulate your strategy, your pricing, or your offer. . . . Such contacts are critical for start-ups.

The increased visibility of successful Chinese and Indian entrepreneurs and executives in Silicon Valley in the 1990s has transformed their image in the mainstream community as well. Some Asians today suggest that although the glass ceiling may remain a problem in traditional industries, or in old-line technology companies, it is diminishing as a problem in Silicon Valley.

Sources of capital for Asian entrepreneurs are proliferating, in part because of growing flows of capital from Taiwan, Hong Kong, and Singapore in the 1990s. Several new venture capital firms dedicated primarily to funding Asian immigrants were started in the region as well during the 1990s: Alpine Technology Ventures, for example, has focused on Chinese companies, whereas the Draper International Fund specializes in financing Indian technology ventures. Other firms, such as Walden International Investment Group and Advent International, explicitly link Silicon Valley–based entrepreneurs to Asian sources of funding. Some of the major venture capital firms are even said to be hiring Asian American partners to avoid losing out on deals going to foreign-born entrepreneurs. In addition, Silicon Valley's immigrant entrepreneurs may now be advantaged relative to their mainstream counterparts by their privileged ties to Asian sources of capital, markets, and manufacturing capabilities.

GLOBALIZATION OF SILICON VALLEY'S ETHNIC NETWORKS: TWO CASES

While Silicon Valley's immigrant entrepreneurs were organizing local professional networks, they were also building ties to their home countries. The region's Chinese engineers constructed a vibrant two-way bridge connecting the technology communities in Silicon Valley and Taiwan; their Indian counterparts became key intermediaries linking U.S. businesses to low-cost software expertise in India. These cross-Pacific networks represent more than an additional ethnic resource that supports entrepreneurial success; rather, they provide the region's skilled immigrants with an important advantage over their mainstream competitors, who often lack the language skills, cultural know-how, and contacts to build business relationships in Asia.

The traditional image of the immigrant economy is the isolated Chinatown or ethnic enclave with limited ties to the outside economy. Silicon Valley's new immigrant entrepreneurs, by contrast, are increasingly building professional and social networks that span national boundaries and facilitate flows of capital, skill, and technology. In so doing, they are creating transnational communities that provide the shared information, contacts, and trust that allow local producers to participate in an increasingly global economy (Portes 1995).

As recently as the 1970s, only very large corporations had the resources and capabilities to grow internationally, and they did so primarily by establishing marketing offices or manufacturing plants overseas. Today, by contrast, new transportation and communications technologies allow even the smallest firms to build partnerships with foreign producers to tap overseas expertise, cost-savings, and markets. Start-ups in Silicon Valley today are often global actors from the day they begin operations. Many raise capital from Asian sources, others subcontract manufacturing to Taiwan or rely on software development in India, and virtually all sell their products in Asian markets.

The scarce resource in this new environment is the ability to locate foreign partners quickly and to manage complex business relationships across cultural and linguistic boundaries. This is particularly a challenge in high-technology industries, in which products, markets, and technologies are continually being redefined and product cycles are routinely shorter than nine months. First-generation immigrants, like the Chinese and Indian engineers of Silicon Valley, who have the language, cultural, and technical skills to function well in both the United States and foreign markets are distinctly positioned to play a central role in this environment. They are creating social structures that enable even the smallest producers to locate and maintain mutually beneficial collaborations across long distances and that facilitate access to Asian sources of capital, manufacturing capabilities, skills, and markets.

These ties have measurable economic benefits. Barkhan and Howe (1998) have documented a significant correlation between the presence of first-generation immigrants from a given country and exports from California. For example, for every 1% increase in the number of first-generation immigrants from a given country, exports from California go up nearly 0.5%. Moreover, this effect is especially pronounced in the Asia-Pacific region where, all other things being equal, California exports nearly four times more than it exports to comparable countries in other parts of the world.

To provide a fuller understanding of how such benefits result, I present here cases of some of the immigrant entrepreneurs in Silicon Valley who have helped to construct the new transnational (and typically translocal) networks. The region's Taiwanese engineers have forged close social and economic ties to their counterparts in the Hsinchu region of Taiwan, the area, comparable in size to Silicon Valley, that extends from Taipei to the Hsinchu Science-Based Industrial Park. They have created a rich fabric of professional and business relationships that supports a two-way process of reciprocal industrial upgrading. Silicon Valley's Indian engineers, by contrast, play a more arm's-length role as intermediaries linking U.S.-based companies with low-cost software expertise in localities like Bangalore and Hyderabad. In both cases, the immigrant engineers provide the critical contacts, information, and cultural know-how that link dynamic, but distant, regions in the global economy.

The Hsinchu, Taiwan, Region and Silicon Valley

In the 1960s and 1970s, the relationship between Taiwan and the United States was a textbook First- to Third-World relationship. American businesses invested in Taiwan primarily to take advantage of its low-wage manufacturing labor. Meanwhile, Taiwan's best and brightest engineering students came to the

United States for graduate education and created a classic brain drain when they remained in the U.S. for professional opportunities. Many ended up in Silicon Valley.

This relationship has changed significantly during the past decade. By the late 1980s, engineers began returning to Taiwan in large numbers, drawn by active government recruitment and the opportunities created by rapid economic development (Lin 1998). At the same time, a growing cohort of highly mobile engineers began to work in both the United States and Taiwan, commuting across the Pacific regularly. Typical Taiwan-born, U.S.-educated engineers have the professional contacts and language skills to function fluently in both the Silicon Valley and Taiwanese business cultures and to draw on the complementary strengths of the two regional economies.

K. Y. Han is typical. After graduating from National Taiwan University in the 1970s, Han completed a master's in solid state physics at the University of California, Santa Barbara. Like many Taiwanese engineers, Han was drawn to Silicon Valley in the early 1980s and worked for nearly a decade at a series of semiconductor companies before joining his college classmate and friend, Jimmy Lee, to found Integrated Silicon Solutions, Inc. (ISSI). After bootstrapping the initial start-up with their own funds and those of other Taiwanese colleagues, they raised more than $9 million in venture capital. Because of their lack of managerial experience, however, Lee and Han were unable to raise funds from Silicon Valley's mainstream venture capital community. The early rounds of funding were thus exclusively from Asian sources, including the Walden International Investment Group, a San Francisco–based venture fund that specializes in Asian investments, as well as from large industrial conglomerates based in Singapore and Taiwan.

Han and Lee mobilized their professional and personal networks in both Taiwan and the United States to expand ISSI. They recruited engineers (many of whom were Chinese) in their Silicon Valley headquarters to focus on R&D, product design, development, and sales of their high-speed static random access memory chips (SRAMs). They targeted the personal computer market for their products, and many of their initial customers were Taiwanese motherboard producers, which allowed them to grow very rapidly in the first several years. And, with the assistance of the Taiwanese government, they established manufacturing partnerships with Taiwan's state-of-the-art semiconductor foundries and incorporated in the Hsinchu Science-Based Industrial Park to oversee assembly, packaging, and testing.

By 1995, when ISSI was listed on NASDAQ, Han was visiting Taiwan at least monthly to monitor the firm's manufacturing operations and to work with newly formed subsidiaries in Hong Kong and Mainland China. Finally, he joined thousands of other Silicon Valley "returnees" and moved his family back to Taiwan. This allowed Han to strengthen the already close relationship with ISSI's main foundry, the Taiwan Semiconductor Manufacturing Corporation, as well as to coordinate the logistics and production control process on a daily basis. The presence of a senior manager like Han also turned out to be an advantage for developing local customers. Han still spends an hour each day on the phone with Jimmy Lee, and he returns to Silicon Valley as often as ten times a year. Today, ISSI has $110 million in sales and 500 employees worldwide, including 350 in Silicon Valley.

A closely knit community of Taiwanese returnees and U.S.-based engineers and entrepreneurs, like Jimmy Lee and K. Y. Han, has become the bridge between Silicon Valley and Hsinchu. These social ties, which often build on preexisting alumni relationships among graduates of Taiwan's elite engineering universities, were institutionalized in 1989 with the formation of the Monte Jade Science and Technology Association. Monte Jade's goal is the promotion of business cooperation, investment, and technology transfer between Chinese engineers in the Bay Area and Taiwan. Although the organization remains private, it works closely with local representatives of the Taiwanese government to encourage mutually beneficial investments and business collaborations. Like Silicon Valley's other ethnic associations, Monte Jade's social activities are often as important as its professional activities. In spite of the fact that the organization's official language is Mandarin (Chinese), the annual conference typically draws over 1,000 attendees for a day of technical and business analysis, as well as a gala banquet.

This transnational community has accelerated the upgrading of Taiwan's technological infrastructure by transferring technical know-how and organizational models, as well as by forging closer ties with Silicon Valley. Observers note, for example, that management practices in Hsinchu companies are more like those of Silicon Valley than of the traditional family-firm model that dominates older industries in Taiwan. As a result, Taiwan is now the world's largest producer of notebook computers and a range of related PC components including motherboards, monitors, scanners, power supplies, and keyboards (Institute for Information Industry 1997). In addition, Taiwan's semiconductor and integrated circuit manufacturing capabilities are said to be on a par with the leading Japanese and U.S. producers, and its flexible and efficient networks of specialized small and medium-sized enterprises coordinate the diverse components of this sophisticated infrastructure (Hsu 1997; Mathews 1997).

Taiwan has also become an important source of capital for Silicon Valley start-ups, particularly those founded by immigrant entrepreneurs. It is impossible to accurately estimate the total flow of capital from Taiwan to Silicon Valley because so much of it is invested informally by individual angel investors, but there is no doubt that it increased dramatically in the 1990s. Formal investments from Asia (not including Japan) were more than $500 million in 1997 (Miller 1997). This includes investments by funds based in Taiwan, Hong Kong, and Singapore, as well as U.S.-based venture groups such as Walden International and Advent International that raise capital primarily from Asian sources. These investors often provide more than capital. According to Ken Tai, a founder of Acer and now head of the venture fund, InveStar Capital, "When we invest we are also helping bring entrepreneurs back to Taiwan. It is relationship building . . . we help them get high level introductions to foundries [for manufacturing] and we help establish strategic opportunities and relationships with customers."

The growing integration of the technological communities of Silicon Valley and Hsinchu offers substantial benefits to both economies. Silicon Valley remains the center of new product definition and design and development of leading-edge technologies, whereas Taiwan offers world-class manufacturing, flexible development and integration, and access to key customers and markets in China and Southeast Asia (Naughton 1997). This appears to be a classic case of the economic benefits of comparative advantage. These economic gains from specialization and trade would not be possible, however, without the underlying social structures and institutions provided by the community of Taiwanese engineers, which ensures continuous flows of information between the two regions. Some say that Taiwan is like an extension of Silicon Valley or that there is a "very small world" between Silicon Valley and Taiwan.

The reciprocal and decentralized nature of these relationships is distinctive.

The ties between Japan and the United States in the 1980s were typically arm's length, and technology transfers between large firms were managed from the top down. The Silicon Valley–Hsinchu relationship, by contrast, consists of formal and informal collaborations between individual investors and entrepreneurs, and small and medium-sized firms, as well as divisions of larger companies located on both sides of the Pacific. In this complex mix, the rich social and professional ties among Taiwanese engineers and their U.S. counterparts are as important as the more formal corporate alliances and partnerships.

The Bangalore, India, Region and Silicon Valley

Radha Basu left her conservative South Indian family to pursue graduate studies in computer science at the University of Southern California in the early 1970s. Like many other skilled immigrants, she was subsequently drawn into the fast-growing Silicon Valley labor market, where she began a long career at Hewlett-Packard (HP). When Basu returned to India to participate in an electronics industry task force in the mid-1980s, the government invited her to set up one of the country's first foreign subsidiaries. She spent four years establishing HP's software center in Bangalore, pioneering the trend among foreign companies of tapping India's highly skilled but relatively low-cost software talent. When Basu returned to Silicon Valley in 1989, the HP office in India employed 400 people, and it has since grown to become one of HP's most successful foreign subsidiaries.

Radha Basu was uniquely positioned to negotiate the complex and often bewildering bureaucracy and the backward infrastructure of her home country. She explained that it takes both patience and cultural understanding to do business in India: "You can't just fly in and out and stay in a five-star hotel and expect to get things done like you can elsewhere. You have to understand India and its development needs and adapt to them." Many Indian engineers followed Basu's lead in the early 1990s. They exploited their cultural and linguistic capabilities and their contacts to help build software operations in their home country. Indians educated in the United States have been pivotal in setting up the Indian software facilities for Oracle, Novell, Bay Networks, and other Silicon Valley companies.

Few Indian engineers, however, choose to live and work permanently in

India. Unlike the Taiwanese immigrants who have increasingly returned home to start businesses or to work in established companies, Indian engineers—if they return at all—typically do so on a temporary basis. This is due in part to the difference in standards of living, but most observers agree that the frustrations associated with doing business in India are equally important. Radha Basu explained that the first HP office in India consisted of a telex machine on her dining room table and that for many years she had to produce physical evidence of software exports for customs officials who did not understand how the satellite datalink worked. She added that when the Indian government talked about a "single window of clearance" to facilitate foreign trade, she would joke, "Where is the window?"

Business conditions have improved dramatically in India since Basu first returned there. The establishment of the Software Technology Parks (STPs) scheme in the late 1980s gave export-oriented software firms in designated zones tax exemptions for five years and guaranteed access to high-speed satellite links and reliable electricity. The national economic liberalization that began in 1991 greatly improved the climate for the software industry as well. Yet even today, expatriates complain bitterly about complex bureaucratic restrictions, corrupt and unresponsive officials, and an infrastructure that causes massive daily frustrations, from unreliable power supplies, water shortages, and backward and extremely costly telecommunications facilities to dangerous and congested highways.

Moreover, many overseas Indians, often referred to as nonresident Indians (NRIs), feel out of place in India. NRIs often face resentment when they return to India—a resentment that is not unrelated to India's long-standing hostility to foreign corporations. In contrast to the close collaboration between Taiwan's policymakers and U.S.-based engineers, there has been almost no communication at all between the Silicon Valley engineering community and India's policymakers, even those concerned directly with technology policy. Moreover, young engineers in India prefer to work for U.S. multinationals, which they see as a ticket to Silicon Valley. Software companies in Bangalore report turnovers of 20% to 30% per year, primarily because so many workers jump at the first opportunity to emigrate. Of course, some U.S.-educated Indians return home and stay, but, on balance, the brain drain of skilled Indian workers to the United States continued unabated throughout the 1990s.

Silicon Valley's Indian engineers thus play an important but largely arm's-length role in connecting U.S. firms with India's low-cost, high-quality skill. Although some, like Basu, have returned to establish subsidiaries, most do little more than promote India as a viable location for software development. As they became more visible in U.S. companies during the 1990s, NRIs were increasingly instrumental in convincing senior management in their firms to source software or establish operations in India. The cost differential remains a motivating factor for such moves: wages for software programmers and systems analysts are ten times lower in India, and the cost of an engineer is 35% to 40% of what it is in the United States. The availability of skill is, of course, the essential precondition for considering India, and it is of growing importance for Silicon Valley firms facing shortages of skilled labor. The low wages provide a viable trade-off to working in an environment plagued by chronic infrastructural problems.

The Indian software industry has boomed in recent years, but most of the growth is still driven by low-value-added services (Heeks 1996; Parthasarathy 1999). Throughout the 1980s and early 1990s, India was confined almost exclusively to low-value segments of software production such as coding, testing, and maintenance. A majority of this activity was in the form of on-site services overseas—or "body-shopping"—which proved to be extremely lucrative, given the size of the wage gap.[5] Although more of the work is now being done offshore (in India), and a handful of large Indian firms and American multinationals have started to provide higher value-added design services, much of the software development in India today differs little from body-shopping. The time difference makes it possible to work around the clock, with programmers in India logging on to a customer's computers to perform relatively routine testing, coding, or programming tasks once a U.S.-based team has left for the day.

The climate for entrepreneurship in India is not hospitable, and it remained one of the main constraints on the upgrading of the Indian software industry in the 1990s. India lacks a venture capital industry, and the domestic market

---

5. Body-shopping is defined narrowly: it refers to offering on-site programming services (in the U.S., for example) on the basis of time-and-material contracts. On-site services accounted for approximately 90% of the value of Indian software exports in 1990 and for 61% in 1995.

for information technology is very small. As a result, the software industry is dominated by a small number of large export-oriented domestic and foreign corporations that have minimal ties with each other, local entrepreneurs, or the Indian engineering community in Silicon Valley. These companies have been so profitable exploiting the wage gap that they have had few incentives to address higher value-added segments of the market, or to nurture entrepreneurial companies that might do so.

As a result, most economic relations between Silicon Valley and regions like Bangalore are still conducted primarily by individuals within the large American or Indian corporations. There are few U.S.-educated engineers who have their feet sufficiently in both worlds to transfer the information and know-how about new markets and technologies or to build the long-term relationships that would contribute to the upgrading of India's technological infrastructure. And there are no institutionalized mechanisms—either public or private—that would both facilitate and reinforce the creation of more broad-based interactions between the two regions.

Communications between the engineering communities in India and the United States are growing fast, however, especially among the younger generation. Alumni associations from the elite Indian Institutes of Technology (which have many graduates in Silicon Valley) are starting to play a bridging role by organizing seminars and social events. A new journal, *siliconindia* (www.siliconindia.com), provides up-to-date information on technology businesses in the United States and India and has recruited several of Silicon Valley's most successful engineers onto its editorial board. And a growing number of U.S.-educated Indians report a desire to return home, whereas others have left the large Indian companies to try their hand at entrepreneurship in Silicon Valley. In short, there is a small but growing technical community linking Silicon Valley and Bangalore, one that could play an important role in the upgrading of the Indian software industry in the future.

Taiwan and India Meet in Silicon Valley

Silicon Valley–based firms are now well positioned to exploit both India's software talent and Taiwan's manufacturing capabilities. Mahesh Veerina founded Ramp Networks (initially named Trancell Systems) in 1993 with several Indian friends, relatives, and colleagues. Their vision was to develop low-cost devices that speed Internet access for small businesses. By 1994, they were short on money and decided to hire programmers in India for one-quarter of the Silicon Valley rate. One founder spent two years setting up and managing their software development center in the southern city of Hyderabad, which was seen as "a big sacrifice." They followed the current trend of choosing Hyderabad over the increasingly congested Bangalore because business costs and labor turnover were lower. Ramp obtained funding to expand the Indian operation from Draper International, a San Francisco–based venture fund dedicated to financing technology activity in India.

Veerina did not discover Taiwan until 1997, when he was introduced to the principals at the Taiwanese investment fund, InveStar Capital. After investing in Ramp, InveStar partners Ken Tai and Herbert Chang convinced Veerina to visit Taiwan. They set up two days of appointments with high-level executives in Taiwanese technology companies. Veerina, who travels regularly to India but had never visited East Asia, was amazed: "the Taiwanese are a tight community and very receptive to and knowledgeable about new technologies and companies over here. They also do deals very quickly. . . . It is incredible the way they operate, the speed with which they move, and the dynamism of the place." He told Tai and Chang that he wanted to return to Taiwan immediately.

In less than three months, Veerina established original equipment manufacturing (OEM) relationships for high-volume manufacture of Ramp's routers with three Taiwanese manufacturers, six months less than it took for them to establish a similar partnership with a U.S. manufacturer. The price per unit quoted by the Taiwanese was almost half what Ramp was paying for manufacturing in the United States, and the Taiwanese were able to increase its output one-hundred-fold because of the relationships that Veerina subsequently built with key customers in the Taiwanese PC industry. Ramp also decided to use the worldwide distribution channels of its Taiwanese partners. Moreover, when Ramp designed a new model, the Taiwanese manufacturer was prepared to ship product in two weeks, compared with the six months it would have taken in the United States.

Veerina says he could never have built these business relationships without the help of InveStar's partners and their network of high-level contacts in Taiwan. In a business where product cycles are often shorter than nine months, the speed as well as cost savings provided by these relationships provides critical competitive advantages to a firm like Ramp. InveStar's Tai and Chang see this as one of their key assets: intimate knowledge of the ins and outs of the business infrastructure in Taiwan's decentralized industrial system. By helping outsiders (Chinese as well as non-Chinese) negotiate these complicated social and business networks to tap into Taiwan's cost-effective and high-quality infrastructure and capability for speedy and flexible integration, they provide their clients with far more than access to capital. In 1999, when Ramp went public on NASDAQ, its software development was in India, its manufacturing in Taiwan, and new product definition and headquarters remained in Silicon Valley.

As Silicon Valley's skilled Chinese and Indian immigrants create social and economic links to their home countries, they simultaneously open foreign markets and identify manufacturing options and technical skills in growing regions of Asia for the broader business community in California. Firms in traditional as well as technology sectors, for example, now increasingly turn to India for software programming talent. Meanwhile, California's complex of technology-related sectors increasingly relies on Taiwan's fast and flexible infrastructure for manufacturing semiconductors and PCs, as well as their growing markets for advanced technology components (Dedrick and Kraemer 1998). It is particularly striking that these advantages are now equally accessible to entrepreneurs like Ramp's Veerina as well as to more established corporations. In short, although these new international linkages are being forged by a relatively small community of highly skilled immigrants, they are strengthening the economic infrastructure of Silicon Valley as well.

CONCLUSION

This research underscores important changes in the relationships among immigration, trade, and economic development in the 1990s. In the past, the primary economic linkages created by immigrants to their countries of origin were remittances sent to families left behind. Today, however, a growing number of skilled immigrants return to their home countries after studying and working abroad. Those who stay often become part of transnational communities that link the United States to the economies of distant regions. The new immigrant entrepreneurs thus foster economic development directly, by creating new jobs and wealth, as well as indirectly, by coordinating the information flows and providing the linguistic and cultural know-how that promotes trade and investment flows with their home countries.

Scholars and policymakers need to recognize the growing interrelationships among immigration, trade, and economic development policy. The economic effect of skilled immigrants, in particular, is not limited to labor supply and wage effects. Some of their economic contributions, such as enhanced trade and investment flows, are difficult to quantify, but they must figure into our debates. The national debate over the increase of H1-B visas for high-skilled immigrants, for example, focused primarily on the extent to which immigrants displace native workers. Yet we have seen here that these immigrants also create new jobs and economic linkages in their role as entrepreneurs. Economic openness has its costs, to be sure, but the strength of the California economy has historically derived from its openness and diversity, and this will be increasingly true as the economy becomes more global. The experience of Silicon Valley's new immigrant entrepreneurs suggests that California should resist the view that immigration and trade are zero-sum processes. We need to encourage the immigration of skilled workers, while simultaneously devoting resources to improving the education of native workers.

The fastest-growing groups of immigrant engineers in Silicon Valley today are from Mainland China and India. Chinese, in particular, are increasingly visible in the computer science and engineering departments of local universities as well as in the workforces of the region's established companies. Although still relative newcomers to Silicon Valley, they appear poised to follow the trajectory of their Taiwanese predecessors. Several have started their own companies. And they are already building ties to their home country, encouraged by the active efforts of Chinese bureaucrats and universities, and by the powerful incentive provided by the promise of the China market. Ties between Silicon Valley and India will almost certainly continue to expand as well. Whether the emerging connections between Silicon Valley and regions in China and India generate broader ties that contribute to industrial upgrading in these nations—as well as creating new markets and partners for Silicon

Valley producers—will depend largely on political and economic developments within those nations. Whatever the outcome, the task for policymakers remains to maintain open boundaries so that regions like Silicon Valley continue both to build and to benefit from their growing ties to the Asian economy.

Appendix

Public Immigrant-Founded or Immigrant-Run Technology Companies Based in Silicon Valley in 1998

Company	Immigrant Name	Position	Sales ($000)	Number of Employees	Year Founded
Indian (total Indian public firms = 22)					
Accom, Inc.	Junaid Sheikh	Chairman of the Board	17,627	64	1987
Alliance Semiconductor Corporation	N. D. Reddy	Chairman of the Board	118,400	168	1985
Aspect Development, Inc.	Romesh Wadhwani	Chairman of the Board	49,929	536	1991
Asyst Technologies, Inc.	Mihir Parikh	Chairman of the Board	165,463	606	1984
Celeritek, Inc.	Tamer Husseini	Chairman of the Board	56,317	422	1984
Cirrus Logic Corporation	Suhas Patil	Founder	1,146,945	1,857	1984
Digital Link Corporation	Vinita Gupta	Chairman of the Board	66,008	281	1985
Excelan	Kanwal Rekhi	Founder	sold to Novell		1981
Exodus Communications	K. B. Chandrashekar	Founder	12,408	93	1992
Gateway Automation Design	Prabhu Goel	Founder	sold to Cadence		1982
Integrated Device Technology	Norman Godinho	Founder	587,136	4,979	1980
Integrated Process Equipment Corporation	Sanjeev Chitre	Chairman of the Board	189,012	1,100	1989
Integrated Systems	Naren Gupta	Founder	120,469	584	1980
Micronics Computers, Inc.	Shanker Munshani	President	99,276	122	1986
NeoMagic Corporation	Prakash Agarwal	President	124,654	162	1993
Nuko Information Systems, Inc.	Pratap K. Kondamoori	Chairman of the Board	11,082	96	1994

(continued)

Company	Immigrant Name	Position	Sales ($000)	Number of Employees	Year Founded
Oryx Technology Corporation	Arvind Patel	President	16,000	17	1990
Pinnacle Systems	Ajay Chopra	Founder	105,296	323	1986
Quality Semiconductor, Inc.	R. P. Gupta	President	62,691	206	1988
Raster Graphics, Inc.	Rak Kumar	President	48,928	140	1987
SMART Modular Technologies	Ajay Shah	Chairman of the Board	694,675	636	1988
Sun Microsystems, Inc.	Vinod Khosla	Founder	9,791,000	26,300	1982
Chinese (total Chinese public firms = 36)					
Above Net Communications, Inc.	Sherman Tuan	CEO, founder	3,436	71	1995
Asante Technologies, Inc.	Jeff Y. Lin	Chairman of the Board	83,279	190	1988
Avant Corporation	Gerald C. Hsu	Chairman of the Board	38,004	701	1986
Award Software International	George Huang	President	23,367	163	1993
Broadvision, Inc.	Pehong Chen	President	27,105	188	1993
C Cube Microsystems, Inc.	Yen-Sheng Sun	Founder	33,712	750	1988
Communication Intelligence Corporation	James Dao	Chairman of the Board	5,516	88	1981
Compression Labs	Wen Chen	Founder	87,882	317	1976
Digital Video Systems, Inc.	Edmund Y. Sun	Chairman of the Board	3,521	563	1992
Documentum	Howard Shao	Founder	75,635	388	1990
ECAD	Paul Huang	Founder	sold to Cadence		1982
Epic Technology Group	Sang S. Wang	Chairman of the Board	sold to Synopsis		1986
ESS Technology, Inc.	Fred S. Chen	Chairman of the Board	249,517	447	1992
E-Tek Dynamics	Ming Shih	Founder	106,924	657	1983
Everex Systems, Inc.	Cher Wang	Chairman of the Board	125,000	190	1993

(continued)

Company	Immigrant Name	Position	Sales ($000)	Number of Employees	Year Founded
Genelabs Technologies, Inc.	Frank Kung	Founder	12,790	147	1984
Infinity Financial Technology	Roger Lang	President	sold to SunGuard		1989
Insignia Solutions, Inc.	Robert P. Lee	Chairman of the Board	55,095	167	1987
Integrated Device Technology	Chun Chiu Tsu-Wei Lee Fu Huang	Founder Founder Founder	587,136	4,979	1980
Integrated Silicon Solution, Inc.	Jimmy Lee	President	108,261	450	1988
Komag, Inc.	Tu Chen	Founder	631,082	4,738	1983
Lam Research Corporation	David Lam	Founder	1,052,586	3,300	1980
NVidia Corporation	Jen-Hsun Huang	CEO	32,421	115	1993
Oak Technology, Inc.	David D. Tsang	Chairman of the Board	157,106	511	1987
Opti, Inc.	Jerry Chang Kenny Liu Fong-Lu Lin	Chairman Founder Founder	67,842	133	1989
Pericom Semiconductor Corporation	Alex C. Hui	President	49,198	172	1990
Premisys Communications, Inc.	Raymond C. Lin	President	102,298	331	1990
Quality Semiconductor, Inc.	Chun P. Chiu	Chairman of the Board	62,691	206	1988
Qume Corporation	David Lee	Founder	sold to Wyse		1973
Sigma Designs, Inc.	Jimmy Chan Jason Chen	Founder Founder	36,982	71	1982
Silicon Storage Technology	Bing Yeh	President	75,322	184	1989
Solectron Corporation	Winston Chen	Founder	3,694,385	18,215	1977
Trident Microsystems, Inc.	Frank Lin	President	113,002	439	1987
Vitelic Corporation	Alex Au	Founder	merged with Mosel (TW)		1982
Weitek	Chi-Shin Wang Edmund Sun Godfrey Fang	Founder Founder Founder	7,972	27	1981
Yahoo! Inc.	Jerry Yang	Founder	67,411	386	1995

5

The Magic Beanstalk Vision

Commercializing University Inventions and Research

ANNE S. MINER, DALE T. EESLEY, MICHAEL
DEVAUGHN, AND THEKLA RURA-POLLEY

Think how great her Jack's surprise was,
when, on getting up next morn,
he perceived the beans had sprouted,
grown so very tall and high,
that the topmost of their branches
seemed to lose itself in sky . . .

. . . Quite inclined for greater riches,
as he knew an easy road;
up he climbed the beanstalk ladder, and
returned with such a load!

—"Jack and the Bean-stalk,"
The Blue Beard Picture Book
(London: George Routledge
and Sons, n.d. [c. 1875])

Scholars have long considered the contextual factors that influence the rate of new venture creation (Carroll, Delacroix, and Goodstein 1988; Cooper 1973; Pennings 1982). These include such factors as culture, natural resources, the presence of economic barriers to employment, solidarity within ethnic groups, or the presence of potential funding institutions (Aldrich and Waldinger 1990; Bonacich and Modell 1980; Carlton 1983; Light and Bonacich 1988; Reynolds 1991; Siegal, Siegal, and MacMillan 1993). In addition to individual factors such as life situation, aspirations, skills, and alternatives, these factors presumably shape the possibility that new ventures will arise. In some situations, governments and other institutions deliberately try to influence new venture creation rates by intentionally adjusting incentives, laws, institutional constraints, cultural values, and capabilities (Auster and Aldrich 1984; Weiss 1987; 1988). Increasingly, universities have come to see one of their roles as fostering the creation of new ventures that stem from research and innovations by their faculty members. This chapter reports on an exploratory study of the assumptions about university-based new ventures among university officers in eight different countries, conducted to reveal how universities in different parts of the world view university-linked new ventures. We then examine the available literature to assess whether the assumptions that underlie their views seem to be valid.

THE STUDY CONTEXT:
COMMERCIALIZING UNIVERSITY INVENTIONS

Major universities have traditionally engaged in knowledge creation and dissemination through research and teaching. One common twentieth-century view of universities is that they can and should also enhance economic prosperity through educating students. Scholars in several different disciplines have tried to examine the impact of universities on economic development, with a recent renewed emphasis on the notion of technology transfer between universities and industry (Nelson 1993). For example, recent research has

---

We thank Howard Aldrich, Ted Baker, John Bollinger, Lawrence Casper, Richard Leazer, Robert Pricer, Elaine Romanelli, Scott Shane, Kaye Schoonhoven, and Philip Sobocinski for feedback on earlier drafts of this paper. Margaret Wilkins provided valuable editorial assistance.

considered links to economic growth through knowledge spillovers (Audretsch and Stephan 1996; Dasgupta and David 1994), structured faculty-industry interaction (Cantlon and Koenig 1991; Mowery 1990), and technology licensing (Mitchell 1989). There are four basic ways in which university knowledge may influence economic growth: (1) by training students who carry knowledge to organizations; (2) through broad dissemination of knowledge by such means as conferences and publications; (3) knowledge transfer through programs deliberately facilitating technology transfer to existing organizations, such as research consortia, invention licensing, contract research; and (4) knowledge transfer through programs designed to encourage new businesses based on university knowledge, which may be facilitated by incubators, science research parks, and faculty coaching.

Many informed observers conclude that the greatest impact arises through the first two pathways, educated students and broad knowledge transfer (Nelson 1993; Wiley 1999). In the past two decades, however, some governments and universities have increasingly devoted attention to the last two avenues. These efforts are embodied in the creation of university-industry liaison offices, technology licensing offices, research consortia, science parks, venture funds, and other efforts to create knowledge transfer bridges between universities and commercial activity (Brett, Gibson, and Smilor 1991). Research on this major social trend has focused largely on the impact of universities and technology-transfer processes indicated by the first three ways in which universities influence economic growth. In this chapter, we focus specifically on the fourth channel of knowledge use: the creation of new ventures based on university knowledge.

Figure 5.1 shows that there are several distinct ways that new ventures may be linked to universities. Segment A indicates ventures initiated by faculty or students that also involve inventions made at the university (people and inventions). Segment B indicates ventures that formally license university inventions but do not necessarily employ any students or faculty (inventions only). Segment C indicates outside ventures that employ students or previous university employees who bring their personal skills and acquired knowledge but not necessarily university inventions (people only).

We will use the term university-linked venture to refer to any new firm that exploits a university invention, whether it is founded by faculty or students or

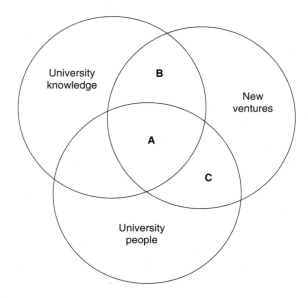

A—Faculty, staff, or students start new venture based on university knowledge
B—University knowledge licensed to new venture not founded or owned by university people
C—Faculty, staff, or students work for new venture not based on university knowledge

Figure 5.1 Types of links between universities and new ventures

by others using an invention made in the university. The focal invention may or may not be formally licensed from the university. Much contemporary discussion has focused on segments A and B, especially on whether universities should hold equity in such firms. While we consider any firm grounded in university-created knowledge to be a university-linked new venture, we focus here mainly on segments A and B.

Recent debates and media reports have put the spotlight on university-linked new ventures, frequently highlighting the powerful phenomenon of Silicon Valley's growth in California. As part of a larger study of university technology-transfer practices, we were especially interested in beliefs about such practices and their potential impact. We define such beliefs as taken-for-granted causal loops, which consist of an assumption that the presence of some entity predictably causes an expected outcome. Taken-for-granted causal loops link a set of conditions to a set of relatively automatic outcomes. The view that keeping all firm intellectual property secret will produce better firm performance exemplifies a causal loop among general managers. Experienced managers observe, in contrast, that when a firm seeks to create a technology standard, keeping certain intellectual property secret may actually reduce performance.

THE MAGIC BEANSTALK VISION OF UNIVERSITY-LINKED NEW VENTURE

For our exploratory study on perceptions of and assumptions underlying university technology-transfer practices in general, we conducted a total of 35 semi-structured interviews in seven countries between March 1997 and September 1998. These countries included Canada (two interviews), France (eight interviews), Germany (two interviews), Japan (four interviews), Singapore (seven interviews), Thailand (six interviews), and the United States (six interviews). We also collated archival data from additional sources such as university publications and web sites. The latter were also available from Australia, where we were unable to do interviews.

The informants were primarily senior university officers, technology-transfer administrators located in their university's technology licensing/patenting office, or individuals outside the office who were knowledgeable about the university's technology-transfer practices. For most countries, we interviewed informants from several different universities, located in different geographic regions of the country when possible (Strauss and Corbin 1998). We used a semi-structured interview protocol in each setting (Denzin and Lincoln 1999; Fetterman 1989; Miles and Huberman 1984), with a total of five interviewers conducting the sessions over the study period. In most cases, two members of the team were present, and one investigator participated in the majority of interviews.

We followed an inductive strategy in our analysis of the interviews with respect to assumptions or beliefs about university-linked new ventures. We used an iterative process to assess the interview data (Denzin and Lincoln 1999; Ragin 1987; Strauss and Corbin 1998). After one member of the research team reviewed notes on 30 interviews, two other team members reviewed the interview notes independently looking for patterns in beliefs or assumptions. One of these reviewers had not attended any of the interviews, providing a check on the tendency of the reviewers to see all interviews through the lens of those in which they had participated (Denzin and Lincoln 1999; Strauss and Corbin 1998). These two reviewers independently noted statements and actions by university officials, along with organizational, structural changes that explicitly or implicitly revealed beliefs or assumptions about university-linked new ventures. After completing these tasks, the two reviewers and the initial reviewer discussed patterns observed in the separate reviews and pooled observations to yield the patterns described here (Denzin and Lincoln 1999; Strauss and Corbin 1998).

In addition, we collected and examined pamphlets, publications, web sites, and government documents to assess (1) whether they mentioned the issue of university efforts to stimulate related new ventures and (2) if so, what explicit and implicit statements were made regarding institutional beliefs or assumptions. This part of the project did not represent an independent archival investigation using formal text analysis (Denzin and Lincoln 1999). Instead, we checked these data to see if factual reports or the language were consistent with the patterns found in the interview data and noted where written reports tended to corroborate or conflict with our interpretation of the interviews. The pooled analysis of our field interview data and the supplementary review of archival information appeared consistent with each other, with the latter providing corroborating evidence for our findings from the interview data.

The analyses revealed that three assumptions and beliefs among informants were strikingly similar across all or most countries. More specifically, they revealed a taken-for-granted causal loop linking universities to economic growth through the new ventures. We call this causal loop the Magic Beanstalk Vision because descriptions of this process often resemble the image of the fairy-tale hero tossing seeds onto the ground, which then result in a magic beanstalk leading to unimagined riches. In this vision, the role of universities is seen as generating local or regional or national economic growth through facilitating the creation of university-linked start-ups. Moreover, the Magic Beanstalk Vision involves the belief that it is the new ventures in particular that will lead to economic prosperity.

Many university officers believed that their universities could and should increase the number of such ventures, that this would generate economic growth, and that the impact of this economic growth would help solve pressing local or regional economic problems. Without intending to trivialize the powerful issues involved, we named this bundle of beliefs the Magic Beanstalk Vision to capture the powerful sense of optimism and the image that planting a set of seeds will produce a self-generating highway to radically new levels of wealth or well-being. This Magic Beanstalk Vision involves three main beliefs: (1) any university can generate university-linked ventures; (2) facilitating such ventures will create economic growth through new jobs; and (3) such ventures will help solve local social problems by creating jobs.

Shared Belief #1: "Any university can generate new ventures." Many of our informants assumed that while there were obstacles to generating new ventures in their own settings, any university could generate them in natural or unproblematic ways. In addition, most discussions of new ventures treated them as an undifferentiated phenomenon: universities either generated science-based firms or they did not. Many informants took it for granted that in other parts of the world, especially the United States, universities were already generating many new ventures that were having a positive impact. The discussions often also implied that if such start-ups were not occurring naturally, a university could take deliberate steps to increase the chances they would arise. Informants typically did not distinguish between different types of such start-ups or suggest that different universities or practices might produce different types. In short, most of our conversations revealed a taken-for-granted assumption of homogeneous university-based start-up firms and a universal process by which they arise.

According to many informants, it is the proper alignment of university practices, government policies, and financial incentives that produces a pattern of new ventures. The crucial processes believed to influence the production of university-linked new ventures included changing policies, providing motivating incentives, and changing norms. The programs to encourage such ventures were often imaginative and thoughtful. For example, one university-linked science park established a patent application fund to help founders defray patent filing expenses (a presumed barrier to faculty-initiated start-ups). Several institutions tried to encourage researchers to set up new ventures by providing incentives and funding programs, in some cases at the level of millions of dollars.

University officials specifically raised the topic of incentives in many interviews. Some advocated reform in equity ownership rules for university faculty inventors, others pushed for changes in patent ownership rights. Although there was wide variation in the types of incentives cited, officials from many countries believed that incentives were needed to stimulate the commercialization of university inventions through start-ups. Officials in three countries argued that cultural changes would also be needed to encourage university faculty to commercialize their inventions at all. One official commented that motivating inventors is key, because they know the best applications and potential users, but that culture is a problem: "Asians [are] very humble [they] never think [their invention] is valued. There will be loss of face if [the innovation is] disclosed and not licensed." An official of a European scientific research institute expressed similar feelings:

> If you don't succeed, it's okay in the U.S., but not in France. If you are not successful [here], you risk losing your reputation. This can lead to a loss of resources ... research assistants, labs, etc. This makes it difficult to try again. Thus, scientists are not motivated to commercialize their research.

What is important to note in these comments on the obstacles to the creation of university-linked new ventures in specific settings is that the informants often assumed that without the specific barrier they described, the underlying patterns involved in the formation of such ventures are transportable across locales, there is no distinction between types of new ventures, any university can produce new ventures, and the resulting patterns would be similar wherever this occurred. In some cases, the barriers were often perceived to be minor—given the right incentives, they could be easily surmounted.

Many university officials held the implicit conviction that there is a recipe for combining the essential ingredients that will lead to success stories in their own countries or regions. The key, they often reasoned, was to find and follow the right recipe. A few officials expressed frustration that although they had put in place parts of the recipe, this had not yet produced a critical mass of new ventures, and they presented nuanced analyses of specific obstacles hindering them. Typically, these analyses focused on the university not implementing all the steps of the recipe, rather than on doubts about the recipe itself. A university technology-transfer officer, in talking about the university's potential to generate new ventures and related economic value, masterfully articulated the essence of the belief in the recipe's power: "It is like a big salad bowl. We now have all of the necessary ingredients. All that is left to do is to toss the salad."

Archival data supported these observations. Pamphlets, internal reports, curriculum designs, and formal policies all revealed specific actions or measures by the university, government, and/or research policy officials that provide corroborating evidence for the assumption that, with proper steps, any university can and will produce new ventures. The archival evidence also made clear that the commitments based on these assumptions were not just symbolic. We found considerable evidence that many universities have committed substantial resources to this issue and have adjusted existing policies and practices in many cases. In some regions, prior attention allocated to technology transfer between universities and existing industries was specifically redirected to the issue of new ventures, with shifts in budgets to reflect this new emphasis.

Shared Belief #2: "Facilitating university-linked new ventures will generate economic growth through new jobs." Although some university missions are regarded as having intrinsic merit, nearly every informant also took it for granted that the creation of new ventures would generate some form of economic growth. Many if not most of our interviewees pointed to Silicon Valley's experience as the "brass ring," which was within the grasp of any university that followed a correct recipe to encourage new ventures. The link between the new ventures and economic growth was taken for granted: if university science-based new ventures arise, growth will follow relatively automatically. Silicon Valley was the dominant image of the outcome of this process, although many observers also referred to Route 128 in Massachusetts and to more recent university-linked growth in North Carolina. These oft-cited examples seemed to represent a shared aspiration on the part of officials across countries. Comments to the government by an influential research policy consultant illustrate this claim:

During the last two years incubators have been mushrooming in Europe. Every university wants its incubator. However, many people think, and so do I, that only incubation structures with a critical mass can create conditions for a sustainable highly creative system, like the famous Silicon Valley, the ultimate objective.

This informant did not take it for granted that once any start-ups occurred, economic growth would automatically occur, but he did assume that with a *critical mass,* such growth would unfold naturally from the new ventures. In many instances, the informants did not postulate the need for a critical mass or special conditions but assumed that the presence of start-ups would naturally produce economic growth. In one country, officials emphasized that they were in need of a single success story such as Yahoo! (founded by two former Stanford graduate students and located in Silicon Valley) to increase the perceived effectiveness of their efforts.

University leaders often implied or stated that their respective universities, regions, or countries could replicate what they observed in Silicon Valley if they just could "live up to their potential." In some cases, interviewees were confident that they already had the requisite intellectual resources to make their own "Silicon Valley" a reality. One high-level university technology-transfer officer remarked that the quality of researchers in his country was very high. The same official, who had previously visited the United States to study business incubators, emphatically concluded: "this country has the knowledge and the resources," implying the creation of prosperity through university-linked new ventures was not just possible but very likely. Together, the examples above suggest that officers and professionals in several countries, by virtue of their references to Stanford University/Silicon Valley, MIT/Route 128, or the United States in general, share an implicit belief that the occurrence of university science-based new ventures will generate economic growth.

Archival data such as brochures, web sites, and policy documents explaining efforts to enhance the creation of such new ventures nearly uniformly took it for granted that they would produce economic growth. This also appeared in government documents advocating more funding to encourage universities to foster start-ups and in rationales for new curricula emphasizing entrepreneurship in some universities. Even opponents of university efforts to encourage these new ventures, who believed their creation would undermine important university values, routinely assumed the new ventures would generate economic growth.

Shared Belief #3: "University science-based new ventures will help solve local social (job creation) problems." Logically one could imagine that even if universities successfully encouraged new ventures, and these firms produced wealth creation, the benefits might not accrue to local regions and might even exacerbate other economic or social problems. In our interviews, these possibilities rarely came up. Instead, the universities often assumed that an important virtue of promoting new ventures was to encourage *local* economic growth. The vision was often one in which new technology-based start-ups would be formed reasonably close to the university or to related research park facilities in which university scientists would have ongoing links to firms so that there would be some form of regional synergy. The vision often assumed that firm-university linkages would continue over time, through students working for the new firms, new inventions, and personal interaction fueling additional start-ups and spin-offs, and informal interactions continuing in a stable, regional pattern. The desired image of an energized regional or local culture of start-ups and science was broadly shared.

Many of our informants also believed that the creation of such regional economic growth would solve very specific local or regional social problems. For example, officials in one country intimated that entrepreneurship could help ease some of the social problems with the various local ethnic groups by promoting growth. An executive officer at a prestigious European research institute strongly suggested that there was a causal link between the country's innovation (or, rather, lack thereof) and the contemporary socioeconomic problems in this particular country, especially unemployment. In discussing start-ups, this administrator offered the following opinion: "Everything is linked. Commercialized inventions create jobs. Jobs lead to a decrease in social problems because unemployment creates disorder. We need to do this to maintain a social equilibrium."

In several regions of the United States, university officials saw this type of economic growth as a way to overcome specific local contemporary challenges. In one region, the university was concerned with the loss of jobs in heavy manufacturing over the past two decades; in another, the concern was with the decline in government contracts with local defense contractors. In some U.S. regions, the informants implied that they felt their regions have traditionally been "knowledge importers" with large U.S. firms coming only to establish low-cost manufacturing in their areas. They saw university-linked new ventures as a way for their region to become knowledge exporters, selling expertise to U.S. and worldwide markets. This perspective was also voiced by interviewees in some countries outside the United States who saw such new ventures as a path to becoming knowledge exporters. In some small countries, this growth engine was seen as a way to compensate for a low level of physical resources. In some U.S. regions with no unemployment problems, these new ventures were seen as the way to create growth that would endure despite competitive threats in the next century.

The archival data also supported the existence of the belief that university-linked new ventures help solve idiosyncratic regional problems. One web page stated that facilitating the establishment of such ventures "will help reverse [our country's] science and technology 'Brain Drain.'" An executive of one of the high-tech parks in the same country expressed a similar sentiment: "Currently there are 5,500 people and 100 companies at the [science park] and two million people within 100 kilometers of [the city]. We have the critical mass to solve the development problems within the region and to start businesses." Although the perceived key local problem varied, the common perception was that university-linked new ventures would solve the problem. We examined the possible grounding for this shared belief and the other two by reviewing informal and formal literature on university start-ups.

EVIDENCE ON THE IMPACT OF
UNIVERSITY-LINKED NEW VENTURES

Despite substantial research on university technology transfer, systematic research specifically related to university-linked new ventures is scarce. For this reason, we reviewed selected journalistic, university, government, and descriptive reports along with scholarly research related to the widely shared beliefs listed above.

Shared Belief #1

The core of the first shared belief is that if obstacles are removed and proper policies are added, universities can and do naturally generate spin-offs based on university inventions. Important additional tacit assumptions are that such new ventures themselves are homogeneous and that some underlying uniform process generates successful new ventures. Our interviews rarely touched on the possibility of different types of start-ups or important distinctions in processes through which they would be created. To explore this cluster of assumptions and beliefs, we looked at descriptive information on the tendency for university start-ups to arise. First, we looked at the number of new ventures with a university connection, at patterns in the nature of these new ventures, and at the processes that link universities to new ventures. We then compared the creation of university-linked new ventures with non-linked new ventures, looking for differences between these types of start-ups. Our first goal was to see if university-linked new ventures are common events.

In 1991, the Association of University Technology Managers (AUTM) started to conduct annual licensing surveys of its member institutions. AUTM's membership consists mainly of university technology licensing officers—individuals charged with facilitating technology transfer—who represent more than 200 U.S. and Canadian universities and research institutes. In the 1993 survey, AUTM began querying its members on new ventures. In 1996, AUTM surveyed a convenience sample of 89 of the top 100 U.S. research universities, asking them for retrospective information on new ventures founded since 1980. According to this survey 1,881 new ventures were formed as a result of licensing an invention from these universities between 1980 and 1996 as shown in Table 5.1. AUTM reported that 1,143 (75%) of the university-linked new ventures founded between 1980 and 1995 were still operational in 1996.

While this evidence clearly indicates that universities are creating new ventures, the numbers are not large—an average of less than 100 per year—although Table 5.1 clearly indicates an upward trend, as shown by an average of 237 new firms founded annually from 1994 to 1996. For several reasons, the actual number of university-linked new ventures is higher than the totals the AUTM reports. First, the data were collected retrospectively in 1996 from

Table 5.1
Number of New Ventures Reported
by AUTM Members

Fiscal Year	U.S. Universities	Total*
1980–1993	n/a	1,169
1994	n/a	241
1995	69	223
1996	184	248
TOTAL	n/a	1,881

SOURCE: AUTM 1998.
*Total includes institutions in Canada and other research institutes.

only a small number of universities. One might expect that earlier records are less complete and more new ventures than reported might have been created in the early 1980s. Furthermore, new ventures that were built on university inventions but did not involve a formal licensing agreement with the university were not counted in this particular survey.

Reports by individual university and popular press articles also provide suggestive data on the creation of new ventures. For example, Chalmers University (Gothenburg, Sweden) reported 38 new ventures between 1964 and 1981 and a total of 98 by 1985 (McQueen and Wallmark 1982; 1985). Chrisman, Hynes, and Fraser (1995) reported that faculty inputs helped to create 100 new ventures at the University of Calgary (Canada). Farley (1992) reported that MIT influenced the creation of 636 businesses in Massachusetts between 1967 and 1988, and a recent study at the University of Wisconsin-Madison counted 172 new firms linked to university inventions over a forty-year period (Sobocinski 1999). Thus, even with few formal efforts to stimulate new ventures, university inventions have been associated with new firms for a long time. What are changing are the deliberate, active role of universities and the increased rate of creation.

Patterns by scientific field. Varied data sources suggest that some scientific fields are more likely than others to generate new ventures and that these patterns may also change over time. Studies from the 1980s using self-reported data on Chalmers University (McQueen and Wallmark 1985) and Cambridge

Table 5.2

Spin-off Companies from Chalmers and Cambridge Universities by Industry, 1984

Chalmers Spin-offs				*Cambridge Spin-offs*		
INDUSTRY	NO	%		INDUSTRY	NO	%
Consulting*	50	44%		Computer software	60	23%
Electronics /computers	31	27%		Electronics capital goods	57	22%
Instruments	15	13%		Instrument engineering	44	17%
Electrical equipment	5	4%		Computer hardware	29	11%
Machinery/equipment	4	4%		Other electronics	26	10%
Transport equipment	3	3%		Consultancy/R&D	16	6%
Metal products	3	3%		Chemicals/biotechnology	10	4%
Chemicals	2	2%		Other	10	4%
Pharmaceuticals	0	0%		Electrical equipment	8	3%
Rubber products	0	0%				

SOURCES: McQueen and Wallmark 1985; Wicksteed 1985.

*If categorized similarly to those at Cambridge, firms classified as consulting at Chalmers would spread across other categories proportionately.

University (Wicksteed 1985) yielded surprisingly similar rates of new venture creation among similar industries. As can be seen in Table 5.2, computers and electronics dominated these new ventures, while new firms in the chemical industry had the lowest frequency. The more recent AUTM data indicate, however, that of the surviving new ventures in 1996 in one sample, 647 (57%) were in the life sciences (biology, medicine, chemistry, medical devices, etc.), a category virtually absent from Table 5.2, and 496 (43%) were in the physical sciences (engineering, software, business systems, etc.). Sobocinski (1999) reported that 68% of new ventures at the University of Wisconsin in the past ten years occurred in the life sciences. While regional differences or even simple reporting inconsistencies may explain these differences, another possibility is that the intrinsic nature of some sciences alters the likelihood of university-linked new ventures (Zucker, Darby, and Armstrong 1998; Argyres and Liebeskind 1998). Specifically, some researchers argue that biotechnology has a "collapsed" discovery process, in which basic research is more likely than yield directly commercializable discoveries than the traditional sciences. Argyres and Liebeskind (1998) argued that the work at the frontier of biotechnology can move more quickly than other sciences to commercially valuable knowledge. By their logic, increases in activity in the life sciences will produce more new ventures than increases in activity in other sciences.

Processes of new venture creation. Research on processes by which university-linked new ventures arise remains rare. Several types of studies do provide suggestive evidence on whether and how universities influence the creation of new ventures, however, and there is a growing body of systematic work on this issue. This work suggests that these processes may be more complex than often assumed and begins to delineate the contours shaping the creation of university-linked new ventures. For example, a descriptive study by Roberts and Peters (1981) reported that a large percentage of a university faculty at MIT generated ideas with perceived commercial value, but only a small fraction of those faculty members took steps to exploit these ideas in any way. Surveying 66 faculty members from three different departments (Mechanical Engineering, Electrical Engineering, and Physics) at MIT, they recorded not only the ideas that faculty had for commercially oriented products and processes but also the degree of actual commercial exploitation of those ideas. Out of 68 ideas reported in the survey, 47% were not pursued at all, 38% were commercially exploited, and 15% received some follow-up attention but were not deemed exploited by the authors' criteria.

While the MIT study relied on self-reported claims by faculty members and lacked an acceptable criterion to determine if an idea had been exploited, it was among the first studies to attempt to estimate systematically the proportion of faculty-generated ideas that members might act to exploit commercially. On one hand, if one assumes all faculty members can and do naturally generate ideas with commercial potential, the percentage of commercially exploited ideas may seem low in this study. The study has been cited as evidence of the university's relatively small influence (Malecki 1991, 343) in the debate on the role of universities in cultivating new ventures. On the other hand, if one assumes that most faculty members do not produce commercially valuable ideas and that faculty culture discourages a focus on commercialization, these percentages are surprisingly high. It may be useful to take into account the institutional setting in which they appeared. MIT has traditionally maintained a strong research faculty and a culture that does not stigmatize commercialization of science. Two well-crafted surveys of U.S. faculty and administrators in 1985 confirmed substantial differences among universities in faculty participation in the commercialization of technology. Faculty members holding equity in firms related to their own research were concentrated in a few universities (Louis et al. 1989).

In a later descriptive study, Roberts (1991) provided evidence that the links to university knowledge may be complex. He found that the majority of all new ventures linked to eight MIT units probably would not have been founded without the university link, but there were varied types of connections. Twenty-six percent of the new ventures relied on university knowledge to found their firm, while 27% relied partly on university knowledge and partly on other experiences. Another 34% made use of the general technical background in which the university knowledge was embedded but did not transfer any specific technology, while only 13% reported no relation to research performed at MIT at that time. This work underscores that individual university-linked new ventures may vary substantially in terms of whether they develop specific inventions created by university researchers while carrying out their university research or whether they embody other forms of university related knowledge or participants.

Other research has tried to infer the role of the university more indirectly by comparing patterns of start-ups in different contexts. Bania, Eberts, and Fogarty (1993) found mixed results for the relationship between university research and new venture creation. They studied six manufacturing industries within the electrical and electronic equipment industry and the "instruments and related product" industry located in 25 metropolitan areas. Although the authors found a statistically significant positive relationship between university research and firm births in the electrical and electronic equipment industry, the relationship in the "instruments and related products" industry was not statistically significant. They suggested that this might be due in part to differences in the nature and maturity of that industry compared with others. They argued that the role of the university may vary, depending both on the basic scientific basis for the industry and on dynamic patterns in industry formation.

A major study by Zucker, Darby, and Brewer (1998) provides some of the first systematic evidence about specific processes that link university research to new ventures. They collected 14 years of panel data for 183 economic regions in the United States, consisting of 751 firms, 511 of them new ventures. They also gathered data on 327 "star" scientists who were exceptionally productive in their field of biotechnology and linked new firm births in the biotech industry to these star scientists. Zucker and her colleagues found that the actual number of new biotech ventures exceeded the expected number and concluded that the growth and location of intellectual human capital was the principal determinant in the growth and location of the biotech industry. They also found that star scientists tended not to leave their university appointments, so that any of their commercial pursuits almost always produced university-linked industrial benefits. Because the data were not simply anecdotal reports of individual surviving new ventures, this study provides important evidence of widespread new venture founding processes. It contradicts a vision in which knowledge diffuses in a broad way through general spillover and underscores the role of a select group of individual scientists who play a key role in the process of generating university-linked new ventures.

Additional insight has been provided by an investigation of the effect of inventors' prior patenting, financing experience, and faculty rank on the chances that a given invention generated a firm founding at MIT. Shane (1999a) found that the chances of a new firm arising from university invention were influenced by the nature of the inventions themselves, with more important and radical technologies more likely to generate a firm, as well as by the prior experience of the faculty member who generated the invention. The technology field also mattered: mechanical and drug inventions were more likely to lead to new firms than were chemical or electrical inventions, which the author suggested may occur because drug and mechanical inventions are easier to evaluate than the others. In a fine-grained study of eight sets of entrepreneurs who exploited a single MIT invention, Shane (1999b) provided even more powerful evidence that the processes through which university-linked new ventures arise can vary immensely, even with a single invention.

Comparing university-linked ventures with other new ventures. Although observers draw on extensive anecdotal evidence, we still have little systematic research comparing university-linked ventures with other new ventures. Perhaps surprisingly, the traditional entrepreneurship literature has not considered universities as important drivers of economic growth through the creation of new ventures. Birch (1987, 140), for example, conceded that a university is the "wellspring of the high-innovation economy" but argued that it is still only one of the elements that enhances entrepreneurship, a claim his work does not test formally. In a largely anecdotal investigation, Rogers (1986, 178) also concluded that "the presence of an outstanding research university in a locale does not necessarily cause the development of a high technology center." Instead, Birch and Rogers assert that the university contributes most directly to entrepreneurship and resulting growth by producing a pool of trained graduates from which both future entrepreneurs and technical workers can be drawn. In a similar vein, Mian (1996) compared three university-sponsored technology incubators with publicly sponsored incubators and found no meaningful differences, implying that the influence of the university on the type of business founded was not important in these cases.

Shared Belief #2

The second shared belief presumes that new ventures are in general the primary source of new jobs, and that university-linked new ventures in particular will create new jobs. Our review of the literature showed that the widespread broad assumption that small firms account for most new job creation is not supported. Recent work indicates that only certain types of new firms create high levels of job creation and that large firms also play a key role in job creation. David Birch is often credited with first arguing for the potential impact of small businesses as job generators in the U.S. (Birch 1989; Gendron 1995; Harrison 1994). Birch's early work (1979) reported that a large percentage of new jobs came from companies with fewer than 500 employees and from young companies (zero to four years). But Birch's data were collected at different points in time in an economic cycle, which may have may created spurious results. Both of Birch's main studies began in recessionary times and ended in periods of expansion (1969–1976, 1981–1985). Over longer periods of time, job creation through new ventures appears to be proportionate to the ventures' total employment (Reynolds, Miller, and Maki 1995) rather than exceeding the expansion of existing firms.

More precisely, recent research indicates that it is crucial to consider both the creation and persistence of jobs in assessing the impact of different types of firms (Davis and Haltiwanger 1994). Davis, Haltiwanger, and Schuh

(1996), who presented data on the creation and destruction of U.S. jobs in manufacturing plants over a fifteen-year period, show that during that period large mature plants accounted both for most newly created and for most newly destroyed jobs. Smaller manufacturing plants showed much higher gross job creation rates, but not higher net job creation rates, than larger ones. They also found that young plants had a higher job creation rate, but also a higher job destruction rate, than older plants, although they still show net job growth. While these data apply to manufacturing plants in a specific time period, this study highlights that new ventures may or may not have a greater tendency to create new jobs and that is important to look both at job creation and job destruction rates in assessing the impact of venture creation.

Contemporary evidence suggests that the key potentially positive link between new ventures and job creation comes from a very small number of high-growth firms that do grow and expand over time. Harrison (1994) cited a Dun & Bradstreet study of 245,000 businesses founded in 1985, which revealed that 75% of the employment gain made by 1988 occurred in just 735 (0.3%) fast-growing firms. Of these firms, all were created with over 100 employees. This would be consistent with a pattern in which many start-ups fail or remain small, but a few exceptionally high-growth firms have an impact on job creation. These findings imply that it is not the creation of hundreds of new firms that is the source of new jobs but, rather, the founding of a select group of high-growth firms. This, in turn, implies that simply creating a large number of new firms of any sort may or may not generate economic growth in terms of the net number of new jobs.

Effect of university-linked ventures on prosperity and job creation. University-linked new ventures represent a special case of new firms. In our review of the literature, we found no study that gave direct evidence on whether such a new venture is more likely to produce high growth in jobs than any other type of firm. The vivid image of Silicon Valley is often taken as evidence that these ventures automatically create high growth compared with other firms, but the fact that some university-linked new ventures have generated high growth does not imply that such new ventures do so in general or that high-tech firms without university links do not generate comparable growth.

There is some work that tries to compare university-linked new ventures themselves by region. These may provide insight into relationships between universities and high-growth firms. Saxenian (1994), who conducted a qualitative study of Silicon Valley and the Route 128 corridor, argued that while both had access to quality institutions, firms in Silicon Valley had a greater ability to bounce back from market missteps that influenced their relative economic growth. She attributed this to a general culture in each region. Although criticized for its anecdotal nature, her work implies that a strong science base and university-linked new ventures alone may not guarantee a critical mass of start-ups and rapidly growing firms.

Other work indicates that similar high-tech start-ups can vary enormously in the degree to which they create job growth. Carlsson and Braunerhjelm's (1998) study of biotechnology/medicine and polymer ventures in Ohio and Sweden showed different patterns in growth by country and by industry. For example, 94 new Ohio polymer firms created as many jobs and 50% more sales than 242 Swedish polymer start-ups. The same pattern held in biotechnology/medicine: 108 Ohio firms generated 1,792 jobs and $1,700 million in sales compared with 982 jobs and $100 million by a larger number of Swedish firms. These data indicate that even when high-tech firms do generate new jobs, there can be tremendous variation in how substantial this effect will be.

Research also indicates that in some cases university-linked new ventures may generate lower job creation than other types of new ventures. Descriptive studies of university-linked new ventures in England and Western Europe claimed that such firms were small and grew slowly (Reitan 1997; Segal 1986). In a longitudinal survey of more than 200 firms from 1986 to 1992, Westhead (1995) found that ventures established by key founders who had last been employed in a higher education institution recorded markedly lower levels of employment growth than other firms. One plausible factor that may help produce this pattern is that some university-linked new ventures are not created to become high-growth firms at all. Instead, they are created by faculty members as places to do interesting research that is not part of their regular university agenda or to do small contract-research work. Other potential factors include founders' lack of management skills in some university-linked new ventures or weak technological bases.

The overall effect of universities in producing economic growth more broadly has been explored in multiple literatures and is beyond the scope of this paper (Nelson 1993; Henderson and Cockburn 1996). One could argue, however, that university-linked new ventures, like other university activities, create valuable multiplier effects, even if their direct, immediate economic impact is not easily observed. For example, Segal (1986) asserted that the direct effect of European firms in his study may be trivial but that university-linked new ventures have an unmeasured multiplier effect, as evidenced by the growth of the region. Unfortunately, systematic research to test this notion has not been conducted.

Shared Belief #3

If universities facilitate the creation of new ventures, which, in turn, generate economic prosperity in the form of job growth, will the growth occur in the region of the university itself, thus solving local social problems? To explore this question, we start with the more general issue of regional growth. Economic geographers and economists have long argued that agglomeration effects can enhance the local impact of new firms in a particular area (Appold 1995; Krugman 1995; Martin and Sunley 1995). Interactions between firms close to each other create positive growth patterns that would not occur if the same firms operated independently in separate regions. This line of work implies that we might expect that university-linked new ventures will have a positive local effect because it is their clustering together that promotes growth. But research on regional and national innovation systems implies that such agglomeration effects are not automatic and may require subtle combinations of deliberate and accidental factors for sustained growth to occur, even in the presence of some strong individual firms (Nelson 1993).

Beeson and Montgomery (1993) investigated the effects of colleges and universities on local labor markets, although their work did not focus on university-linked new ventures in particular. Using the Public Use Microdata Sample (PUMS) of the 1980 Census, Beeson and Montgomery correlated four measures of university activity with local labor market indicators in 218 Standard Metropolitan Statistical Areas (SMSAs). They found that universities had measurable effects on local labor markets but that the effect varied with specific features of the universities. They found that area employment growth rates were positively related to changes in R&D funding and to the number of nationally rated science and engineering programs. This study does not separate out how much of these effects come from university-linked new ventures versus other channels. The results are consistent, however, with the view that different universities face different constraints in making use of science in pursuit of economic growth. This study found only weak evidence for a university effect on income, the employment rate, or the mix of high-tech and other industries in the area, which would occur if there were varied processes through which technology transfer in general and university-linked new ventures in particular influence job creation.

A number of studies provide some evidence that universities have a specifically local economic impact by showing that firms choose to locate in proximity to a university. In a longitudinal survey of over 100 firms located in or near a science park, Westhead (1995) found that many entrepreneurs had established their companies in close proximity to the university. Interviews with managers in the companies revealed that they expected easier access to human and technological resources. This was especially true for firms located in science parks. Interestingly, companies that located outside the science parks initially had lower levels of university contact, yet over time they developed links with the university like those of the other firms. The links for companies within and outside the science parks were mostly informal. If we assume that some of these firms involved university inventions or faculty, this process means these university-linked new ventures will be local and, presumably, have local impact. A case study of a small number of Swedish firms by Klofsten and Jones-Evans (1996) produced similar results.

Similarly, Acs (1996) reported that R&D managers used the proximity of university R&D as a factor in location decisions because they expected spillovers from neighboring university research to influence commercial innovation. Also supportive of the possible local, rather than more general university impact, Acs, Audretsch, and Feldman (1994) found a significant positive effect of geographic proximity on innovation, especially for small firms, although we cannot be sure this was directly linked to new ventures involving university inventions. Moreover, states with higher rates of university R&D had significantly higher rates of innovation within small firms, including several new ventures.

Although prior studies do not show definitively that university-linked new ventures, rather than other university links, lead to local job growth in particular, they are consistent with that idea. Some other studies, however, don't support a simple causal link between university-linked new ventures and local job creation as distinct from other forms of job creation. Noting that the majority of universities are located in capital cities, Jones-Evans et al. (1998) looked at the capital cities of Hungary and Bulgaria and identified approximately 50 firms as university-linked new ventures. While over 40% of the Hungarian firms were still located at their founding institutions, over half of the firms were situated at a distance from the center that had acted as an incubator. Mixed results were also found by Carlsson and Braunerhjelm (1998), who found that start-ups were clustered around relevant universities and research centers for biotechnology in Ohio and Sweden, while new polymer firms were clustered around research centers in Ohio but not in Sweden. These studies imply that in some circumstances university-linked new ventures, if they provide growth, do not necessarily affect the area close to the university.

Results from other surveys have directly repudiated the idea that universities influence new venture location in some cases. Galbraith and De Noble (1988) found that the proximity of prestigious research universities and venture capital was not an important consideration in location decisions of 226 high-technology firms. Instead, the firms' greatest concerns were the supply of highly qualified workers, culture (ambience), cost, expansion, and security. Vedovello (1997) came to the same conclusion in a study of a British science park. He found that the geographical proximity of the partners was not an important influence for those firms that were directly connected to university research. Links to distant universities were as common and strong as links to the local science-park firms. These studies indicate that encouraging the creation of university-linked new ventures can produce growth in areas not close to the focal university.

The most probative evidence on patterns in the local versus nonlocal impact of university-linked new ventures comes from a series of studies involving the U.S. biotechnology industry. Zucker, Darby, and Brewer (1998) found that the presence of star scientists was the main determinant of where and when the U.S. biotechnology industry developed. They suggested that this finding provides an example of localized spillovers as envisioned in the agglomeration literatures. In a subsequent study, Zucker, Darby, and Armstrong (1998) looked at relationships between particular individuals and new ventures comparing them with general dissemination processes. Using a sample of 110 biotech firms and 55 star scientists in California, they examined the link between the star scientists' involvement and the number of products in development or on the market, as well as changes in employment. The results indicated that the knowledge transferred to these relatively new firms did not result from generalized spillovers but from identifiable market exchanges between scientists and firms.

Audretsch and Stephan (1996) took issue with the findings that Zucker, Darby and Brewer (1998) presented in an earlier working paper and proposed a more complex model based on their analyses. They expected that the presence of star scientists would affect early decisions to locate near universities but that this effect would diminish as an industry matured. They used the population of biotechnology firms that prepared an initial public offering (IPO) in the early 1990s to study their links to university-based scientists. While the data collection did not specifically focus on new ventures, the data appear to offer a reasonable proxy, considering that most firms were very young at the time of their IPO. While a substantial number of university-based scientists participated in geographically bounded networks, over 70% of the links between biotechnology companies and university-based scientists were nonlocal. Thus, Audretsch and Stephan (1996) argued, the university impact on the location decisions quickly diminishes as an industry grows, and agglomeration effects account for location decisions more than the proximity of university-based star scientists. This study implies that even if university-linked new ventures create local growth initially, the effect may rapidly disappear over time in some areas.

Bania, Eberts, and Fogarty (1993) made a similar argument in their study of the electronics and instrument industries. While noting that studies by Jaffe (1989) and Jaffe, Trajtenberg, and Henderson (1993) had found a strong geographic association between university research and corporate patenting activity, they concluded that "the pipeline between university research and *local* commercialization as measured by a higher start-up rate of new firms, has substantial leaks" (Bania, Eberts, and Fogarty 1993, 765 [emphasis added]).

Summary

Overall the evidence indicates that although the creation rate of university-linked new ventures has increased in the past decade, it is currently still small in terms of absolute numbers—in contrast to images in the popular press and imagination—with the exception of a handful of U.S. universities. Nonetheless, it is also clear that the creation rate is increasing in countries around the world. It is not possible to assess now whether low rates in some settings represent an inevitable early period of "priming the pump" or a sign that a high rate cannot be achieved in some contexts.

More important, data suggest that rather than representing an undifferentiated outcome driven by a universal process, there are varied types of university-linked new ventures and different processes or fields that give rise to them. The rate of creation is probably influenced by the scientific field as well as by many previously identified contextual features, such as national laws, regulations on faculty and permissible roles, intellectual property systems, physical infrastructure, the availability of capital, and national and local culture (Nelson 1993). Research also indicates that the processes by which a university's presence affects new venture creations are more complex than a broad diffusion of inventions into start-ups. Star scientists who provide not only specific inventions but also legitimacy and ongoing insight into ground-breaking scientific areas may be a key factor in university-linked new venture creation (Zucker, Darby, and Armstrong 1998).

Although there is support for the general claim that university-linked new ventures can have an economic impact, research highlights that such new ventures will not necessarily produce economic growth. Many new ventures fail or do not provide much growth, implying that the growth impact typically comes from a few exceptionally successful firms or from multiplier effects. There is a "survivor bias" in the public's perception that university-linked new ventures generally have a positive effect: the public does not see the many failed or struggling university new ventures. Further, data on the area affected by university-linked new ventures underscores that in some cases these new ventures do not arise close to the university whose inventions are most crucial and have little or no impact on the university's local region. This distancing can occur when star scientists become involved as scientific advisors or officers of new ventures in other regions or even other countries when a new venture resulting from licensing a university invention locates outside the university's region, or when local ventures move to other regions after creation. Research also indicates that the degree of local impact may vary with industry maturity, with university-linked new ventures in mature industries being less likely to provide local growth.

THE MAGIC BEANSTALK VISION:
FASHION, SOCIAL MOVEMENT, VICARIOUS LEARNING?

Overall, the evidence supports the idea that university-linked new ventures are potentially important but also points to the possibilities that they vary in their nature and creation processes and may create local growth only under specialized conditions. Prior to the 1980s, most universities did little to encourage commercialization of inventions, or encouraged only licensing, not new ventures. Given its recent appearance and the ambiguous empirical support for a simple formulaic version of the Magic Beanstalk Vision, we wondered, first, whether the shared basic beliefs might reflect a tendency of the professionals we interviewed to rationalize whatever program responsibilities they have been assigned. A review of our interview notes and experiences, however, convinced us this was not the source of the shared beliefs found in our qualitative work. In our judgment, most of the university officials genuinely believed that fostering new ventures was absolutely necessary to improve the social welfare of their respective regions or countries. Although there were interesting and important distinct aspects of each university's view of these new ventures, the degree of commonality in aspirations, assumptions, and even language used in the interviews raised the question of why these views were so similar. Theory points to three important social processes that produce similarity across organizations: fads, social movements, and vicarious learning.

Abrahamson (1996a, 257) defined a management fashion as "a relatively transitory collective belief, disseminated by management fashion setters, that a management technique leads to rational management progress." He and others have argued that industries experiencing uncertainty tend to follow practices of fashion-setting organizations such as consulting firms, companies with admirable practices, seemingly successful companies, or companies that receive favorable mention in the relevant media (Abrahamson 1991; 1997; DiMaggio and Powell 1983; Haunschild and Miner 1997; Haveman 1993).

The Magic Beanstalk Vision has some elements of a fashion that is attractive to university officials and entices them to follow it. First, there are highly visible, high-prestige institutions that have facilitated new ventures. The majority of our interviewees invoked the image of Stanford University, and in some cases MIT, or the Research Triangle in North Carolina as representing the goal of their activities. Many observers seem to take Stanford as an icon whose practices can provide a template that, if followed, will generate economic growth.[1] Second, few interviewees discussed the potential for failure or made contingency plans in case following the template did not work in their specific situation. We considered whether this might simply be the result of normal professional behavior in an interview with strangers: why focus on concerns or the possibility of failure of an important initiative? Most of the officers, however, genuinely appeared to believe that encouraging new ventures represented a crucial new strategy for sustainable success that did not need contingency planning. Third, in the archival evidence we found many phrases that were exactly the same or very similar in pamphlets from very diverse institutions. Fourth, in a few places senior administrators appeared to be pursuing new ventures because it was what other people in their professional peer groups were doing.

Though these features of the Magic Beanstalk Vision resemble the characteristics of a current fad that may go out of fashion in the future when a new practice becomes fashionable, the officers whom we interviewed often manifested deep conviction and internalization of the vision. Such behaviors are normally not associated with a fashion, but more with a social movement. A social movement is defined as "a purposive and collective attempt of a number of people to change individuals or societal institutions and structures" (Zald and Ash 1966, 329). Social movements mobilize resources for a specific cause or action. More recently, Zald and Berger (1990) have suggested that social movements not only exist within nation-states but also within organizations. In both cases, social movements represent the cause and effect of emerging change outside sanctioned channels.

---

1. Katherine Ku, Stanford University Office of Technology Licensing, personal communication, 1998.

Social movements often start their life in periods of unrest and derive their continuing energy from dissatisfaction with the status quo, together with hopes for a different and better future (Zald and Ash 1966). Reflecting on the language used by our interviewees and their strong belief in the Magic Beanstalk Vision, which bordered on an ideology, we conclude that the actions and beliefs expressed by many university officers committed to creating more new ventures are consistent with features of a social movement. In many cases the advocates were very aware that others in their universities saw their goal as challenging deep, prevailing university norms about the appropriate role of basic research scientists, open sharing of research findings, ethical use of graduate students' efforts, and the role of universities themselves. Many specifically advocated changes in university norms, especially in terms of the value of solving local economic problems. Some informants had worked to encourage technology transfer from universities for decades and experienced current efforts to encourage new ventures as gratifying, since their values were finally being enacted. Some saw their activity as part of a more general reformation of education to a more applied mode.

Furthermore, the goals and aspirations were perceived as, and in fact did represent, substantive challenges to the traditional goals of the universities in some instances. Some informants (but not all) saw themselves as locked in a struggle with mainstream members of their institutions, some had sacrificed prior career opportunities for many years before such ventures became popular, and several interviews revealed an unmistakable sense of mission and optimism far beyond a simple acceptance of professional trends. This sense of being part of a determined effort to refocus major social institutions to achieve a new social good characterizes social movements (Zald and Berger 1990).

The pursuit of their vision was not solely a matter of passion and local hope. Our interviews also suggested that some of the specific shared beliefs result from deliberate vicarious learning by universities studying other universities. The vicarious learning often involved learning about both goals and tactics. The general goal of encouraging new ventures was often learned through media or professional associations that emphasize the Silicon Valley vision. Our informants often had acquired their views of the recipe to achieve new-venture-driven growth through attending professional meetings, reading related policy and university documents, and actively visiting universities they perceived as having made headway (Miner and Holzinger 1998). Although many officers invoked the icon of Silicon Valley, many also reported having actually visited a broader range of potential models not only in the United States but in other countries as well.

Some officials had given very careful thought to what parts of the recipe would be easy or hard to replicate in their settings. These activities and reflection on their mission indicated that university officials and the institutions they represented were not only following an ideology but were also seeking to learn from the experience of others. One small country had already implemented some of the standard recipes to encourage high-tech venturing but did not observe the assumed automatic rapid growth. They concluded that their country was not large enough to generate the same form of self-sustaining economic activity observed in Silicon Valley and that their country had distinct constraints as well as strengths. They devised a strategy for a different type of university-linked venture formation for their context.

Further supporting the notion that vicarious learning was occurring, many ideas about certain specific practices, such as science parks, faculty incentives, and consulting policies, arose in part from deliberate visits made to other universities (e.g., Tornatzky, Waugaman, and Casson 1995; Turner 1995). Interestingly, the most careful observers seemed to come from very high-quality research institutions outside the United States and were less cavalier than those in weak U.S. schools. In contrast, university officials in some U.S. regions seemed to take it for granted that a standard formula would automatically produce growth.

IMPLICATIONS

Selected Implications for Policy and Practice

Taken as a whole, the empirical evidence suggests that in many cases universities are overly optimistic in assuming they can automatically contribute to local economic prosperity through following standard recipes for stimulating new firms based on university inventions. It is clear that universities can increase the odds of new ventures forming around university inventions and that the founding rate of such new ventures is growing. It is also clear, how-ever, that such ventures can take many different forms and arise through var-ied processes. In addition, there is no guarantee they will create jobs or have a local or regional impact without attention to the specific setting in which they occur.

The empirical evidence to date points to three straightforward ways in which a university pursuing the Magic Beanstalk Vision may experience unan-ticipated outcomes. First, efforts to generate university-linked new firms may succeed in generating new firms, but this outcome may not lead to economic prosperity. Several studies revealed cases in which university-linked firms were founded but did not lead to economic growth (Reitan 1997; Segal 1986; Westhead 1995). Contemporary evidence and professionals in the field emphasize that this comes only from the "home run" firms that achieve dra-matic growth, and such firms may or may not arise from a given cluster of uni-versity-linked new ventures. This means that universities pursuing this strat-egy would need to pay close attention not just to firm creation but also to their own efforts and local factors that will make high growth likely.

At the same time, active management of university-linked new ventures goes against university charters in some cases, does not typically match uni-versities' strengths, and raises substantial issues of conflicting interests and val-ues (BenDanile et al. 1997). These tensions have long been discussed in pol-icy settings. They have also generated important experiments in new organizational forms designed to deal with the "development gap" generally and university-linked new ventures in particular. These include affiliated but separate development corporations or venture funds to foster high-growth firms without depending on the universities themselves to play too close a role in that process. Although these efforts have involved nontrivial amounts of capital, assessment of these new forms is difficult and perhaps premature. Some professional assessments indicate that seeking to link such ventures too tightly to local economic objectives may overburden such funds with multi-ple and conflicting objectives (Atkinson 1994), highlighting the importance of carefully designing such organizations.

Second, economic growth from university-linked new firms may not pro-duce local growth but may actually enhance regions other than the area or nation of a given university. Both descriptive data and more complex studies underscore this possibility (Audretsch and Stephan 1996; Bania, Eberts, and Fogarty 1993). Anecdotal evidence indicates that some new ventures remain near their university of origin in their early stages but then migrate to regions with richer infrastructures of capital, expertise, or employees. The ease with which some new ventures migrate away from their university of origin, and evidence that universities have less impact as industries mature (and often generate higher returns), underscores the importance of thinking ahead about factors that will help universities harvest the value of the new ventures they help create. Our interview data also indicate that university-linked new ventures increasingly include e-commerce and web-based ventures whose geographical impact may be highly diffuse. This implies that universities may need to consider carefully the incentives and structural factors that will affect whether these new ventures influence both local wealth creation and local jobs. This will include close attention to trade-offs between encouraging new ventures versus other commercialization processes.

Our informants often had very thoughtful views on the local constraints on their universities successfully facilitating new ventures. Scholars in organizational strategy have argued that to gain a sustainable competitive advantage, a firm needs to identify capabilities and resources that (1) provide a distinct advantage over time and (2) cannot easily be imitated by others. Efforts to spawn new ventures at multiple universities create a competitive landscape of university and regions. Simply removing local constraints and following a standard recipe seems unlikely to provide a sustainable strategy (Wiley 1999). From this perspective, the most important activity each university can undertake is to look for specific, local, sustainable features that can inform its efforts to create new ventures. This might include specific areas of scientific strength, regional culture, values or constituencies, or areas of legal flexibility.

Third, and perhaps most important, universities' efforts to facilitate new ventures may have major unintended outcomes for universities themselves or society as a whole. As has often been observed, efforts to stimulate new ventures may generate short-term prosperity but may ultimately harm the university. For example, a university may set up incentives that lead productive faculty who previously generated streams of inventions to leave the university to create new firms. Over time, this process could ultimately destroy the university's underlying capacity to generate new knowledge and could leave the university with the faculty members least likely to produce sustained inventions (Miner and Holzinger 1998). For a resource-rich university that can afford to replenish its top researchers, this danger may be slight. It is hard to see, however, how resource-poor universities would remain productive in research.

University leaders, faculty members, government officials, and thoughtful media observers have long highlighted even deeper concerns about the erosion of university values and integrity through the movement to increase university-linked new ventures (Louis et al. 1989; Press and Washburn 2000). On one hand, close observers point out that such ventures may revitalize a region in unanticipated ways beyond the simple creation of new jobs (Sobocinski 1999). They may reinvigorate key research areas, help attract new faculty and students, or set in motion unexpected pathways of scientific discovery. Interactions among scientists' work on research tools for industry and academia, commercial products, and basic science can lead to discoveries that might not arise in any of the three domains on their own. On the other hand, efforts to generate new ventures may not only use up major resources but may also erode the deepest values of university life. Explicating these specific dangers is beyond the scope of this review, but they include such well-known issues as conflicts of interest and the integrity of journal review processes when investigators hold equity in related firms, conflicts of interest and abuse of power in directing doctoral research, and failure to address scientific areas with little commercial potential, such as diseases common to underdeveloped countries. Issues receiving increasing attention include problems of faculty members using insider trading for litigation between students and their universities over intellectual property, and struggles over copyrights and intellectual property linked to software start-ups. The ultimate danger envisioned by those most concerned is that without careful design, the increasing creation of new ventures will limit the ultimate contribution of science to society.

Theoretical Implications

Theories of entrepreneurial processes. The factors we have emphasized as influencing the creation or impact of new ventures can be seen as interacting with the individual life choices of university participants—whether these be specific life events such as failure to be promoted, individual capabilities, prior experience or life circumstances (Aldrich and Waldinger 1990; Robert Pricer, personal communication, 1998; Shane and Khurana 1999). To some degree, our findings seem consistent with traditional entrepreneurship research in which universities have been viewed as potential but not decisive factors in the creation of new ventures. At the same time, our findings indicate a sharp increase in the numbers of university-linked new ventures and certainly in deliberate efforts to jump-start regional economic growth through such ventures around the world. Exploring these trends can be important in developing a more fundamental understanding of firm creation and links between technological evolution and economic growth.

Research has already shown that simple theories of knowledge creation and spillover leading to organizational foundings and increased prosperity are inadequate. Further investigation of the impact of scientific networks (Powell, Koput, and Smith-Doerr 1996), the role of social and financial intermediaries, and the hidden impacts of social structures on firm and industry formation seem especially promising. In addition, research on university-linked new ventures offers a promising avenue for refining and testing current theories about how technological innovation relates to firm creation.

Our findings of shared beliefs across universities and especially across countries were somewhat unexpected. They brought to our attention the importance of continuing to work on shared ideologies about entrepreneurship in general and within institutions in particular. The shared vision of the feasibility and desirability of university-linked new ventures masked several different origins of beliefs about entrepreneurship and of recipes for how to enhance it. Further research could use this interesting situation to examine the processes through which shared strategic maps and industry recipes unfold over time. These investigations would advance theoretical development of cognitive theories of strategy.

Industry evolution and population-level learning. We suspect that the pursuit of the Magic Beanstalk Vision by universities around the world will have an unexpected impact on patterns of industry formation. Although our informants often perceived the same basic recipe for success, they also described distinct obstacles to following the recipes in their countries or regions. The perceived obstacles were often outside the universities themselves but sometimes were within. These considerations imply that universities' efforts to sustain successful venture formation will likely fail in some areas, despite intelligent efforts to encourage them. Different obstacles and constellations of legal, cultural, and scientific resources may also create different types of new ventures. This, in turn, may mean that new industries and regional prosperity will not unfold uniformly by country or region but, rather, as a "lumpy" structure of some regions whose growth reaches a critical mass and many more that do not.

The findings also suggest that university-linked new ventures do not occur with equal probability in different scientific fields. This may be because of different features within the knowledge discovery process itself or because of differing periods of development of science in different areas. If the feasibility and growth of these new ventures differ by scientific area, it implies that regional or national economic development grounded in university-based ventures will have a bias toward those fields most likely to produce such ventures, unless there is external intervention to compensate for such a bias. Thus, a region with a university strong in one scientific area may show much greater growth than one with a university emphasizing a different science domain.

The data also suggest that local factors may powerfully influence *who* tends to form university-related firms, which may in turn affect the success of industry formation in different regions. In some countries it is illegal for faculty to hold ownership in new firms or for government employees to do so in some places where the very top scientists typically are employed by the government. In these settings, university-related start-ups now tend to be formed by doctoral students or by part-time faculty. These participants bring different expertise to the process than do traditional full-time research faculty members, including those who have generated inventions over long periods of time. This will create different national patterns in the level of experience and scientific expertise typically represented in the new firms, even when they arise at equal rates. Under these circumstances, a university might see a steady rate of formation of university-related ventures, but the result might not include a highly competitive cluster. The cluster might not be able to compete internationally with other clusters that include star scientists who provide legitimacy and access to crucial frontiers. The importance of this potential effect seems likely to vary by industry. In software development, for example, one might expect a weaker effect because of less separation between university and industry scientific activities and between top scientists in universities and their students and industry scientists.

A less obvious outcome of local constraints and university properties will be the way different universities influence the *rate* of formation of entire new industries. Prior research has shown that large firms often pace their development of new products to allow them to harvest the value of existing technology. For example, if they hold patents for a breakthrough technology in a certain area, they may put off moving into that area until they have gained full value from their existing technology. This strategy is particularly likely if product life spans are shortened such that the previous investment cannot be recaptured (von Braun 1997).

Universities that strongly encourage faculty involvement in new firms—in contrast to licensing arrangements—may unwittingly speed up the pace of industry formation around some breakthrough technologies. This would happen if an invention that would have been delayed for introduction if held by an existing firm were developed instead by faculty in new ventures. The new firm would not face the same disincentive to move ahead with the new product group, which would accelerate the university development of this type of firm and product. Thus, the nature and type of new ventures could influence the timing of new industry formation around breakthrough technologies, so that an industry might develop in one country or region before it developed in another. This would then produce first-mover advantages (and disadvantages) for the focal region.

An additional, nonobvious way in which pursuit of the Magic Beanstalk Vision may generate unexpected national or other patterns of industry development is suggested by Powell, Koput, and Smith-Doerr's (1996) work, along with more general research on models of cooperative games (Dasgupta and David 1994). Powell, Koput, and Smith-Doerr (1996) presented some evidence that the growth of the U.S. biotechnology industry has depended on networks of relationships over time. These networks, rather than individual firms, have acted both as the engine for discovery and as the collective memory in which prior knowledge was held. We speculate that universities may sometimes play a key role in industry formation precisely because they create a neutral ground for relationships between scientists. Universities may not facilitate the creation of specific firms but may serve as a neutral territory in which scientists form and sustain relationships outside the proprietary, competitive world of direct competition between firms. Such neutral university space permits cooperative behavior that in turn generates more productive networks, permitting more rapid or more fruitful knowledge creation. This implies that differences among universities in rules concerning faculty involvement in consulting and new ventures will generate unintended variation in the levels of industry evolution in different countries or regions through their impact on the types of relationships faculty can sustain.

Population-level learning. Miner and Haunschild (1995) introduced the idea that groups of organizations such as industries or regional clusters could be seen as learning over time. They defined one important learning outcome as change in the nature and mix of routines enacted in these populations of organizations. Recent work using this emerging framework emphasizes how recurrent interorganizational learning and collective learning processes can shape whether a whole population of organizations changes, survives, or prospers (Miner and Anderson 1999).

Although our evidence on this point is anecdotal, our interviews suggested that some universities outside the United States and Europe may be creating more radical programs and combinations of activities to encourage new ventures. This is consistent with prior research underscoring the innovative role of organizations outside the current dominant segment of an industry or organizational population. These more radical experiments may serve as an engine of learning for the international community of universities, with even the failures of some efforts providing important information to the population as a whole (Miner et al. 1999).

Shared mental models, such as this taken-for-granted causal loop, can be an important factor in population learning (Lant and Phelps 1999; Spender 1989; Strang and Macy 1999). The Magic Beanstalk Vision represents such a cognitive routine. Some prior theorists have argued that the pursuit of such a widespread shared cognitive routine will produce homogeneity in the population, with organizations or organizational communities looking alike. The reasoning above implies, in contrast, that the pursuit of the Magic Beanstalk Vision by many universities within different local landscapes will actually produce heterogeneous patterns of practices and outcomes, including both failed and successful new industries, varied participants, and altered time sequences of industry evolution.

Further research will be important to test our intuitions about how pursuit of a common aspiration based on a taken-for-granted causal loop under different local conditions will generate structural variation in industries and regions. An important component of such work will be examining whether universities that share taken-for-granted assumptions, aspirations, and information over time find it possible to learn useful rules of thumb from one another and accurately assess the value of specific programs and routines enacted by others. These processes could increase the chances that collections of universities might prosper while enhancing regional prosperity. At the same time, if the pursuit of the Magic Beanstalk Vision actually generates powerful economic growth in some but not all regions, competitive dynamics may decrease the traditional willingness of universities to share practices with each other. This may generate new distributions of practices in populations of universities around the world, which may or may not prove valuable for the long-term prosperity of universities. For researchers who themselves work in universities, the examination of these phenomena and related theoretical questions may have special poignancy because they will shape the nature and role of universities themselves.

6

Knowledge Industries and Idea Entrepreneurs

New Dimensions of Innovative Products, Services, and Organizations

ERIC ABRAHAMSON AND GREGORY FAIRCHILD

It has become a cliché to declare that we live in a world in which the production of new and improved technical knowledge is rapidly outpacing the production of both products and services. But what do we know about the producers of such progressive technical knowledge? Perhaps justifiably little when it comes to the knowledge industries and idea entrepreneurs who supply individual idea consumers with techniques for making better pasta or romantic choices, for achieving instant wealth or sexual ecstasy, or for reading astrological charts or the stock market. But also perhaps *unjustifiably* little when it comes to the knowledge industries and idea entrepreneurs who supply vitally important organizational consumers in the business, military, educational, and governmental sectors with important technical knowledge (Aldag 1997). Such knowledge can vary from knowledge about techniques for producing machines, products, or services to techniques to found, lead, or manage organizations, to techniques for winning battles or educating our youth. More concretely, the knowledge produced can range from how to design napalm canisters, to how to launch an airline, or to how to teach writing with the invented spelling method.

This chapter examines knowledge industries, knowledge communities, and the knowledge entrepreneurs that supply technical knowledge. Therefore, at the outset, we need to be very clear about what we mean by these terms. We call industries sets of organizations that supply substitute products or services. This chapter is about knowledge industries, that is, the set of organizations that produce substitutable knowledge products: books in the book publishing–knowledge industry, classes in the education-knowledge industry, advice in the consulting-knowledge industry, and articles in the mass media–knowledge industry, for example. We call sets of interdependent industries communities (Abrahamson and Fombrun 1994). Knowledge industries depend on each other, as when consultants in the consulting industry market their knowledge via the book publishing industry. Therefore, this chapter is also about knowledge communities, sets of interdependent knowledge industries that supply knowledge consumers on the demand side of management markets.

Most important, this chapter is about so-called idea entrepreneurs—consultants, journalists, scholars, technical experts—the individuals and organizations that populate knowledge communities, making it their business to satiate the turbulent demand for progressive technical knowledge. By using the term "idea entrepreneur," rather than the more general term "knowledge worker," which might be defined as any individual employed in a knowledge-producing industry, we have in mind only those knowledge workers who participate in the creation, elaboration, and marketing of new ideas and knowledge products. These individuals are entrepreneurs, not so much in the sense that they found new organizations, although they often do, but more so in that they create new ideas and knowledge products, new segments in a knowledge market, or even entirely new knowledge markets (Low and Abrahamson 1997). Frederick Taylor, for instance, theorized and marketed general techniques of management and became the founder of a management knowledge market that continues, to this day, to sell knowledge about management techniques (Abrahamson 1997).

Virtually nothing is known about such idea entrepreneurs. What are their backgrounds? What do they do? And how do they create, articulate, and disseminate progressive ideas for mass consumption by often-global idea customers? This chapter addresses these questions. It has the structure of an hourglass. The first part considers very broadly, and therefore necessarily superficially, the structure and dynamics of industries and communities that supply technical knowledge products, as well as the idea entrepreneurs in the organizations constituting these industries and communities. Because the topic is so broad, the second part focuses more narrowly on the management-knowledge community, which supplies technical management knowledge, as well as on the management-idea entrepreneurs who found, populate, and animate organizations across this community. The third part narrows the focus even more precisely to an empirical analysis of how management-idea entrepreneurs interacted and competed in launching one management technique: quality circles, small groups of employees who meet regularly, without managerial supervision, to improve products or services. The study of knowledge communities and industries is in its infancy, and so we use our case study more as a way of raising questions deserving further investigation than as a way of rigorously testing clearly specified hypotheses. The final part broadens out the chapter's hourglass structure again to some general ideas about knowledge communities and idea entrepreneurs that are inspired by the quality circle case study.

KNOWLEDGE COMMUNITIES AND IDEA ENTREPRENEURSHIP

Figure 6.1 presents an orienting framework for conceptualizing knowledge industries and communities that supply technical knowledge, as well as the demand side of the market that consumes this technical knowledge.[1] The top of Figure 6.1 depicts cultural norms that engender knowledge markets. Rational norms are expectations that knowledge be about rational techniques (i.e., techniques that provide efficient means to important ends). Rational norms create the expectation that knowledge of rational techniques exists and, therefore, demand for such knowledge. Progressive norms are expectations that knowledge about rational techniques will progress over time (i.e., knowledge about existing techniques will be replaced repeatedly by knowledge about new and improved techniques) (Abrahamson 1996a; Abrahamson and Fairchild 1999). Progressive norms create demand for a continuous stream of new and improved rational-technical knowledge.

The middle of Figure 6.1 depicts the knowledge market. On the supply side

---

1. The discussion of this figure is abridged, as these ideas have been presented elsewhere (Abrahamson 1996a; 1996b; Abrahamson and Fairchild 1999).

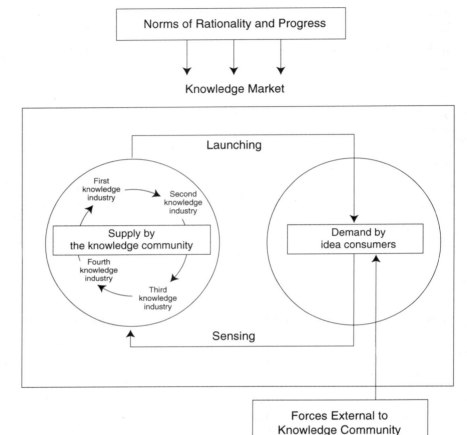

Figure 6.1 General framework

of the market is a variety of interacting knowledge industries that constitute the knowledge communities. Knowledge entrepreneurs populating these industries and communities supply rational and progressive technical knowledge. Knowledge consumers on the market's demand side consume it. Demand for technical knowledge is shaped by the supply of new knowledge, but, as Figure 6.1 suggests, forces emanating from outside the management knowledge market also shape demand. The demand for a new military tech-

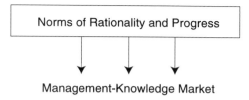

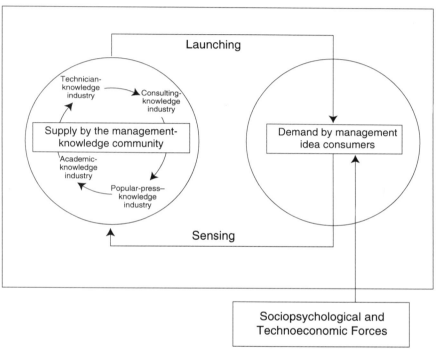

Figure 6.2 The management-knowledge community

nique (guerrilla warfare, for example) might occur in response to a new kind of enemy (rich and poor post-colonial powers, for instance). Thus, the bottom of Figure 6.1 portrays the impact of such exogenous forces on the demand for technical knowledge and on the need for idea entrepreneurs to be responsive to such exogenous forces. We turn to one such market for greater concreteness—the market for progressive management techniques—that we believe is typical of knowledge markets in general.

The Management-Knowledge Market

Figure 6.2 depicts the structure of the management-knowledge community. The bottom part depicts the techno-economic and socio-psychological forces emanating from outside the management-knowledge market that shape the demand for ideas about progressive management techniques. A number of authors have shown that macroeconomic and macropolitical forces shaped demand for particular types of management techniques over the last century (Abrahamson 1990; 1996a; 1996b; Barley and Kunda 1992; Guillen 1994; Shenhav 1995). An earlier study of ours suggests that such forces may shape the demand for particular progressive management techniques by engendering collective anxiety among idea consumers and increasing their susceptibility to purportedly simple management techniques that promise to alleviate the sources of this anxiety (Abrahamson and Fairchild 1999). Managers populate the demand side of the management-knowledge market. Managers can use progressive management techniques for pragmatic ends, such as achieving particular organizational goals. They can also use these techniques, as well as the content that management-idea entrepreneurs use to promote them, for symbolic ends: (1) to demonstrate to stakeholders that these managers are at the cutting edge of rational management progress or (2) to appease these managers' and stakeholders' anxieties (Abrahamson 1991).

At least four types of interdependent industries make up the management-knowledge industry that supplies management knowledge to consumers: the popular-press management–knowledge industry (e.g., business magazines), the business education–knowledge industry (e.g., business schools), the technical management–knowledge industry (e.g., associations of quality-control technicians), and the consulting management–knowledge industry (e.g., management consulting firms). Different types of knowledge entrepreneurs populate organizations in each of these industries.

Management-Knowledge Entrepreneurs

Virtually nothing is known about knowledge entrepreneurs' backgrounds, what they do, and how they interact. The management literature, however, has pointed to a great variety of such entrepreneurs. Therefore, before we can address questions about their backgrounds, actions, and interactions, we must distinguish different types of knowledge entrepreneurs. Three dimensions are useful in classifying management-knowledge entrepreneurs. First, management-knowledge entrepreneurs can belong to four different industries in the management-knowledge community: journalists belong to the popular-press management–knowledge industry, scholars to the business-education management–knowledge industry, technicians to the technical management–knowledge industry, and consultants to the consulting management-knowledge industry. Second, idea entrepreneurs supply the consumers of rational technical ideas. They not only conceive such ideas but also produce content—discourse, computer programs, sounds, and images to disseminate these ideas to knowledge consumers and stakeholders on the demand side and to enable these knowledge consumers to retransmit this content to stakeholders in order to appear legitimate in their eyes. This content carries labels denoting particular techniques, specifies important performance goals, and explains persuasively why this rational technique is the means of attaining these goals most efficiently. We can distinguish, therefore, the idea entrepreneurs in each industry who originate and produce content (e.g., scholars) from the content-publishing organizations and their managers that disseminate such content (e.g., academic journals and their editors). Third, certain idea entrepreneurs may lead other idea entrepreneurs, who imitate these leaders. These people who are usually called "gurus," for example, may be the first to create new content promoting a management technique, first to disseminate it, and first to migrate to promoting the next progressive management technique (Gill and Whittle 1993).

The two-by-two matrix in Figure 6.3 captures these three distinctions. The horizontal dimension distinguishes idea entrepreneurs who produce the content promoting progressive management techniques from the organizations that disseminate it. The vertical dimension distinguishes idea entrepreneurs and organizations that lead in the creation and dissemination of content promoting progressive management techniques (leaders) from the idea entrepreneurs and organizations that imitate them (laggards). Each of the four boxes distinguishes entrepreneurs who belong to the popular, scholarly, technical, and consulting management–knowledge industries. This classification allows us to begin posing questions about how different idea entrepreneurs interact in the process of creating and disseminating content in management knowledge.

	Authors	Publications
Leaders	Gurus Consultants, journalists, technicians, scholars	Leading-edge publications Consultant press, journalistic press, technical press, scholarly press
Laggards	Disciples Consultants, journalists, technicians, scholars	Lagging-Edge publications Consultant press, journalistic press, technical press, scholarly press

Figure 6.3 Various types of knowledge entrepreneurs

The Dynamics of Knowledge Entrepreneurship

Having distinguished different types of knowledge entrepreneurs, we can begin speculating about their background, what they do, and how they interact. We distinguish two analytically distinct stages in the management-knowledge creation and content dissemination process. First is an introduction stage, during which a progressive management technique is introduced into one industry in the management-knowledge community and then, sequentially, into the other three industries that make up this community. Second is a diffusion stage, in which the amount of content produced by each industry, publication, or idea entrepreneur may change as the idea's popularity changes.

Introduction stage. Two questions about the introduction stage matter particularly. First, do management-idea entrepreneurs introduce ideas about a progressive management technique on the management-knowledge market's supply side, or are they introduced on its demand side, flowing to the supply side only subsequently? Second, when a progressive management technique is introduced on the supply side, in which supply-side industry do idea entrepreneurs introduce it first, and in what order do entrepreneurs introduce it into the other three supply-side industries making up the management-knowledge community?

Some have argued that most ideas about progressive management techniques are introduced on the demand side by managers. Galbraith (1980, 162), for example, asserted, "I know of no new form of organization that was invented by organization theorists while advancing the theory. I have seen no new form emerge from the test tubes of organization theory. Instead, the researchers record what the inventive practitioner creates and give it labels like grids, system 4, or matrix organization." Others have considered the possibility that certain idea entrepreneurs may invent, rediscover, or reinvent the management techniques they disseminate through their content (e.g., Abrahamson 1996a). These two possibilities raise the first research question:

Question 1: *Do management-idea entrepreneurs introduce progressive management techniques on the supply side of the management-knowledge market, or are they introduced on its demand side?*

We distinguished four analytically distinct knowledge industries belonging to the knowledge community that makes up the management-knowledge market's supply side (the popular press, scholarly, technical, and consulting industries). This raises the following question:

Question 2: *In which industry of the management-knowledge community do management-idea entrepreneurs introduce progressive management techniques, and, after introduction, in what sequences do idea entrepreneurs introduce these techniques into the other industries that make up this community?*

A priori, we can give different, equally plausible answers to question 2. We might reason either that (1) the technical sector would tend to introduce ideas because technicians, such as quality-control technicians, are first to come into contact with management inventions; (2) the consulting industry would, in view of the potential gains to first-movers; (3) the popular-press industry would, because of journalists' extensive industry contacts; or (4) the scholarly sector would, because of the expertise provided by careful scholarship (Barley, Meyer, and Gash 1988).

Diffusion stage. A number of scholars have noted that progressive techniques have a characteristic life cycle. After ideas about a progressive technique are introduced into supply-side–knowledge industries, they tend to enter a latency phase, during which idea entrepreneurs produce very little content promoting them (Abrahamson and Fairchild 1999). At a later time, however, the amount of content promoting that idea can grow very rapidly, crest briefly, and decline suddenly until it disappears. The term "fad" or "fashion" is frequently used to describe such a wave in a progressive idea's popularity (Abrahamson 1991). Likewise, the amount of content produced by each supply-side industry, publication, or idea entrepreneur may grow, plateau, or decline as the idea wave flows, crests, and ebbs. We consider this process at a knowledge-industry level of analysis first and then at the level of idea entrepreneurs and publications.

Each of the four supply-side industries could proceed, in unison, through the latency, growth, and decline phases of an idea wave. If they do not, however, then it may be that the growth or decline of the idea wave in one industry antedates the growth and decline of this wave in other industries in the knowledge community. Such a possibility raises the following question:

Question 3: *Which knowledge industries in the management-knowledge community lead and lag in publishing content about progressive management techniques during the latency, growth, and decline phases of idea waves?*

Gurus and Disciples

For the four analytically distinct management-knowledge industries there are four corresponding, analytically distinct types of management-idea entrepreneurs: journalists, scholars, consultants, and technicians. Management-idea entrepreneurs belonging to each type may or may not deserve the label "guru," a term that has been defined as an individual who has "developed and popularized his or her ideas on some aspect of management" (Huczynski 1993, 46) or, more succinctly, as popular management thinkers (Jackson 1996). It is the charisma of gurus that distinguishes them from other idea entrepreneurs and allows them to become leaders among idea entrepreneurs (Huczynski 1993; Clark and Salaman 1996; Jackson 1996). Gill and Whittle (1993), for example, described a life cycle in which charismatic gurus launch progressive management ideas that provide the concepts that are mass marketed by means of the content produced by other types of idea entrepreneurs who imitate these gurus. Thus, the term "management guru" should be defined as a management-idea entrepreneur who is an opinion leader among idea entrepreneurs. The term "management-idea disciple" should then be reserved for those management-idea entrepreneurs who imitate the content disseminated by gurus.

If such gurus exist, and there is little hard evidence that they do, we would expect that they would lead idea entrepreneurs in two ways: (1) by being among the first to produce content in the growth phase of a wave of interest in an idea about a progressive management technique, causing disciples to surf the wave also and (2) by being among the first to abandon this wave of content as it crashes, to get onto the next wave ahead of others. Our definitions, unlike some others, expressly do not attach pejorative connotations to the terms "guru" or "disciple." They do, however, raise the next question addressed in this study:

Question 4: *Are there gurus among management-idea entrepreneurs?*

Our definitions also do not imply that gurus generally come from the same knowledge industry, although they might. Micklethwait and Wooldridge (1996) argued that most gurus are from the academic sector, whereas Huczynski (1993) argued that there are three types of gurus: academic gurus, consultant gurus, and hero managers. Thus, we ask:

Question 5: *What is the background of management gurus?*

Leading- and lagging-edge publications. We also explored whether knowledge organizations produce in unison the content promoting a management technique, or whether there are leading-edge publications whose decision makers, like gurus, tend to (1) in the growth phase of an idea wave, publish a lot of content on an idea before lagging-edge publications and (2) in the decline phase, stop producing content and migrate to content promoting the next progressive technique before these lagging-edge publications. These possibilities raise the following question:

Question 6: *Are there leading-edge publications among knowledge-disseminating publications?*

METHODS

There are many waves of content promoting ideas about progressive management techniques. This creates a problem of deciding which progressive management technique to begin studying. In making this decision, we were guided by a mixture of historical, analytical, and practical considerations. As Figure 6.4 indicates, four major waves of content promoting ideas about progressive employee-management techniques have flowed and ebbed since the 1970s: job enrichment, quality circles, total quality management, and business process reengineering (Abrahamson and Fairchild 1999). We focused on the second major employee-management wave in this period, quality circles, so that we could examine both this wave and whether the gurus and leading journals that were first to produce content promoting quality circles were also first to migrate to producing content in the next idea wave, total quality management.

Practical considerations also drove us to focus on quality circles because we could obtain data on a moderately sized, full wave of written content, as well as on the beginning of the next wave, total quality management. This would not have been possible had we focused on an earlier wave, such as the job enrichment wave, which antedates the computerization of articles' texts, or later waves, such as business process reengineering that have not yet undergone a full cycle.

To detect the invention and diffusion of written content about quality circles in and across the management-knowledge community, we relied on both historical data and treatments of this wave (Cole 1979; 1985; 1989), as well as on counts of articles and books from publications in the journalistic, scholarly, technical, and consulting knowledge industries. An important caveat is in order, however, about what these publication data can tell us. We used the year of publication of articles, books, and dissertations to understand when idea entrepreneurs began *publishing* content conveying these ideas, when this publishing activity began to spread to other knowledge industries, how long it persisted, and when it began to decline. Therefore, these data do not reveal when

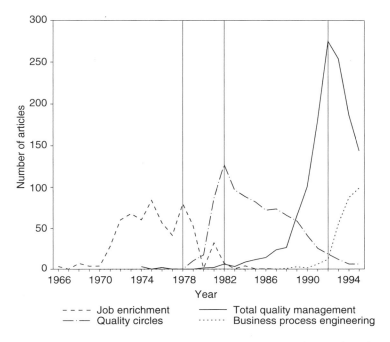

Figure 6.4 Adjusted number of job enrichment, quality circles, total quality management, and business process reengineering articles

these ideas came into being, when they were first articulated, nor even when they were first scripted. Nor do these data reveal the quality of the knowledge published or the breadth or depth of its impact on various audiences. The strength of these data is, rather, their capacity to reveal accurately when an idea became available in print to a greater or smaller number of knowledge consumers and idea entrepreneurs willing to read them in published form. They can reveal, therefore, which idea entrepreneurs or knowledge industries got their ideas to the knowledge market faster than others. These data provide insights, therefore, on the dynamics of knowledge competition between idea entrepreneurs spanning knowledge organizations, industries, and even entire communities.

In addition, the speed with which idea entrepreneurs can get their ideas to the knowledge market, as well as the segments of this market that they can reach, is influenced by idiosyncrasies of the publishing outlets they use to disseminate the content conveying their ideas. This chapter, for example, took months to be written, carefully edited, and submitted. Moreover, chapters like this one may take years to appear, if ever, in a widely available format, and will most likely be read by a small number of cognoscentes, although in rare instances, they can have an influence beyond these cognoscentes, spanning decades or even centuries. A journalist, by comparison, can decide to research and write an article on this topic today that would be published tonight, read tomorrow morning, and forgotten by nightfall. The idiosyncrasies of publishing outlets, therefore, may play an important role in explaining why certain idea entrepreneurs consistently beat others in the speed with which they get ideas to the knowledge market and with what impact.

In short, our publication data cannot tell us who had an idea first, only who published it first. In this chapter, therefore, we supplemented these publishing data with historical data and treatments of this period to ascertain not only who published an idea first but also how and when the knowledge-producing activity of one sector of the management-knowledge market might have influenced this activity in another sector.

Technical journals. Cole (1985; 1989) pointed to one organization of idea entrepreneurs whose media arm disseminated content about quality circles: The American Society for Quality Control (ASQC). The ASQC, founded in 1946, brings together primarily quality-control technicians. It publishes a journal called *Quality Progress.* We used Cole's (1989) data for the number of articles on quality circles published in *Quality Progress* between 1977 and 1987 to measure the written content produced by these idea entrepreneurs.

Consulting journals. Cole (1985; 1989) pointed to a second association of idea entrepreneurs who publicized quality circles, the International Association of Quality Circles (IAQC). The IAQC was founded in 1978 by two consultants, Donald Dewar and Jeff Beardsley, and, over time, became increasingly dominated by consultants and quality circle facilitators. The IAQC began publishing the *Quality Circle Quarterly* in 1978 and the proceedings of its yearly meetings between 1979 and 1986. The articles in the *IAQC proceedings* vary widely in length, and we measured therefore the volume of written content in these proceedings by measuring their thickness in millimeters (*IAQC proceedings,* 1977–1986).

Academic and popular-press journals. To measure the volume of quality circle discourse produced by academic- and popular-press idea entrepreneurs, we counted the number of articles in the ABI Inform database with subject headings such as "quality circle" or "quality control circles." ABI Inform's assignment of articles to subject headings, like the "Quality Circle" heading, is accomplished and checked by trained and experienced content analysts, working in industry- and function-specific teams.[2] To check whether these assignments reliably captured the number of articles pertaining to quality circles, we also electronically searched the titles and abstracts of all ABI Inform articles for word strings denoting quality circles: "QC(s)," "QCC(s)," "Quality Control Circle(s)," and "Quality Circles(s)." There was an 88.7% overlap between the set of articles identified by the two search methods, and examination of the remaining 11.3% of articles revealed that they usually pertained to different subjects altogether.

The total number of articles indexed in ABI Inform increased markedly from 1974 to 1995. To adjust for this growth, we multiplied the number of quality circle articles in any one year by the ratio between the total number of articles indexed in 1984 and the total number of articles indexed that year. This adjustment technique is analogous to the technique used by economists to transform nominal into real currency amounts, thereby factoring out the effect of inflation. We used a similar adjustment for every other article count in this study.

A characteristic that distinguished academic journals, in which academics publish, from popular-press journals, in which journalists and other idea entrepreneurs (e.g., consultants) publish, is that the former publish articles that cite references to previous articles on the topic, whereas the latter do not. We distinguished three classes of journals: (1) academic journals (e.g., *Academy of Management Review*), which publish articles that always contain references; (2) popular-press journals (e.g., *Business Week*), which never contain references; and (3) semi-academic journals (e.g., *Harvard Business Review*), which sometimes contain references.

Books and dissertations. We examined two other types of content. First, to measure the number of books on quality circles, we used the Eureka RLIN database and counted the number of books listed under the "Quality Circle"

2. Conversations with several ABI Inform content analysts.

and "Quality Control Circle" subheadings, excluding non-English language books (Research Libraries Group, Inc.). Second, to measure the prevalence of doctoral dissertation content on quality circles, we counted the number of U.S. doctoral theses listed under "Quality Circle" and "Quality Control Circle" headings in the Dissertation Abstracts International database.

Gurus and leading-edge publications. We defined gurus and editors of leading-edge publications as opinion leaders among management-idea entrepreneurs. Thus, we reasoned that if there were such gurus and leading-edge publications, then they should (a) produce a lot of written content about quality circles, (b) do so before other idea entrepreneurs who wrote less about this idea, and (c) migrate before these other idea entrepreneurs to producing written content about the next related progressive technical idea, total quality management.

We operationalized producing a lot of written content about quality circles as belonging to the top 5% of authors or journals in terms of the number of articles written about this technique. This 5% cutoff corresponds to definitions of opinion leadership in the innovation diffusion literature (Rogers 1995). We then examined whether the idea entrepreneurs or publications in this top 5% wrote or published relatively early about quality circles by measuring the yearly percentage of articles that they wrote or published during each year of the quality-circle idea wave. We also measured whether these idea entrepreneurs and publications migrated first to the next idea, total quality management (TQM), by measuring the yearly percentage of articles about both quality circles and TQM that they wrote. Our expectation was that they would write or publish the majority of article content on quality circle/TQM around the time the TQM wave began growing in 1991.

To identify the backgrounds of gurus, we searched for databases of idea entrepreneurs that would reveal membership in one of the four supply-side industries of the management-knowledge community. We were only able to find out whether idea entrepreneurs belonged to either the scholarly or consulting knowledge industry. To determine membership in the scholarly sector, we examined (a) if individual gurus had completed doctorates by searching for their names in the Dissertation Abstracts International database, (b) if they were members of the Academy of Management using the Academy of Management Membership Directory, and (c) if they were faculty members at academic institutions, using the *McGraw-Hill Directory of Management Faculty.* To determine whether gurus had engaged in consultancy, we searched the *Directory of Consultants.*

RESULTS

Introduction of Quality Circles

We searched both the published and historical record for the first use of the term "quality circle," and its variants, in each of the four industries of the management-knowledge community: technical, consultant, scholarly, and popular press. Figure 6.5 summarizes the results. As the figure indicates, a Japanese association of quality-control idea entrepreneurs, the Union of Japanese Scientists and Engineers (JUSE), coined the term "quality control circle" and used its publication *QC Sakura Koryo* (General Principles of the QC Circle) to disseminate quality-circle content throughout Japan beginning in 1962 (Ishikawa 1968; Cole 1979). A quality-control idea entrepreneur, Joseph Juran, had extensive contacts with JUSE dating back to the 1950s (Cole 1989). He belonged to the ASQC and therefore became the conduit for quality-circle content between the Japanese and the U.S. quality-control technical-knowledge industry. He published the first U.S. article disseminating quality-circle content in the ASQC journal (Juran 1967).

The second flow of quality-circle content occurred between Japan's quality-control technical-knowledge industry and the demand side of the U.S. management-knowledge market. As a result of a study trip to Japan and contact with JUSE, three employees at the Missile System Division of the Lockheed Aerospace Corporation—Jeff Beardsley, Donald Dewar, and Wayne Rieker—brought JUSE quality-circle content to Lockheed.

The third flow of quality-circle content occurred from Lockheed (management-knowledge market-demand side) into the consulting industry (management-knowledge market-supply side). This occurred when Beardsley, Dewar, and Rieker left Lockheed to become idea entrepreneurs and founded their own consulting firms disseminating quality-circle content. Our data indicate that Beardsley and Dewar led in introducing quality-circle content

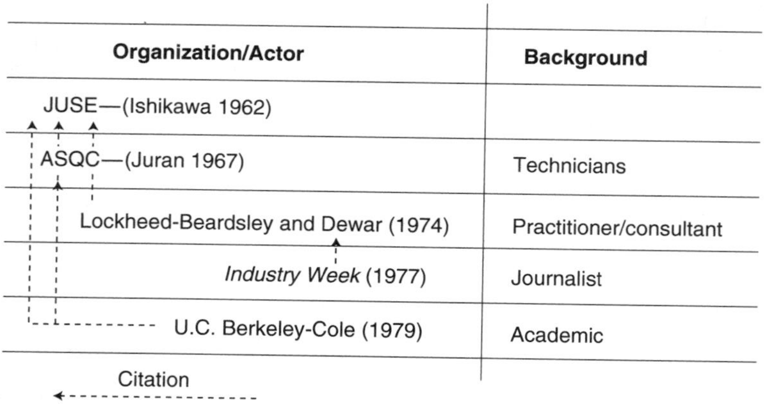

Organization/Actor	Background
JUSE—(Ishikawa 1962)	
ASQC—(Juran 1967)	Technicians
Lockheed-Beardsley and Dewar (1974)	Practitioner/consultant
Industry Week (1977)	Journalist
U.C. Berkeley-Cole (1979)	Academic
Citation	

Figure 6.5 Introduction of the quality circle label in the management knowledge producing community

into published management-consulting discourse in 1977 in a co-authored book titled *Quality Circles* (Beardsley and Dewar 1977). Dewar and Beardsley also founded the International Association of Quality Circles (IAQC), the first association comprising only idea entrepreneurs dedicated to producing quality-circle content: training manuals, speeches, articles, and books about quality circles. The introduction of quality-circle content into the publications of the journalistic sector did not occur until 1977, however, when *Industry Week* published the first of many articles popularizing quality circles (*Industry Week* 1977). In the scholarly knowledge industry, Robert Cole, a member of both the ASQC and IAQC, was among the first of the idea entrepreneurs to disseminate quality-circle content into the sector through a book about Japanese management (Cole 1979). Cole referenced both Juran (1967) and earlier JUSE discourse, evidencing a content flow from the quality-control technicians' knowledge industry of Japan and the U.S. to the U.S. scholarly sector.

Research question 1 asked if ideas about progressive management techniques are introduced on the supply or demand side of the management-knowledge market. The data reveal the sequential introduction of the quality-circle idea into the supply side of the U.S. management-knowledge market and, only then, into its demand side. Research question 2 concerned the management-knowledge market's supply-side industries. Specifically, we asked in which industry were progressive management techniques introduced, and after introduction, what was the sequence of introduction into the other three knowledge industries? The quality-circle idea flowed through knowledge industries of the U.S. management-knowledge market in the following sequence: (1) from the technical sector (Juran 1967) to (2) the demand side of the knowledge market (e.g., Lockheed 1974), to (3) the consulting industry (Beardsley and Dewar 1977), to (4) the business-press industry (*Industry Week* 1977), and, finally, to (5) the academic sector (Cole 1979).

Growth and Decline in Publishing

We examined first the flow and ebb of the published quality-circle content wave in each of three different content types (articles, books, and dissertations). We then examined waves of content publishing, by knowledge industry, by looking at the articles about quality circles published in each of the four industries that make up the knowledge community supplying the management-knowledge market.

Articles, books, and dissertations. Figure 6.6 reveals a surge of four books on quality circles in 1977. With this one exception, which we return to below, the figure reveals a clear pattern in which the article wave antedates slightly the book wave, which, in turn, leads the dissertation wave. We cannot tell whether this pattern reveals idea leadership by article writers or the shorter publication lead time of article content as opposed to book content and of book content as opposed to dissertation content. To understand which sectors in the management-knowledge market led and lagged in publishing article content promoting quality circles, we focused on the articles published in each industry's knowledge publications.

Waves of content publishing. Figure 6.7 shows the growth and decline in the number of articles published in technical and consulting publications, which were the first two industries to start producing content promoting the quality-circle idea. Three pieces of evidence indicate that quality-circle idea entrepreneurs in the technical and consulting industries published a small stream of article content publicizing quality circles well before the other three indus-

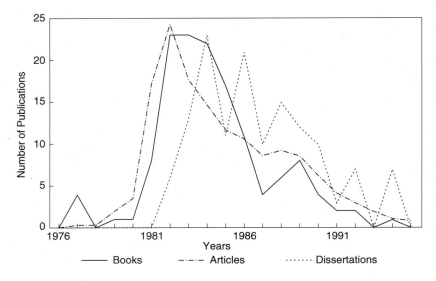

Figure 6.6 Number of articles, books, and dissertations about quality circles

tries of the management-knowledge community. First, Juran wrote an article on quality circles in 1967. Second, Cole (1989) indicated that *Quality Progress,* the publication of the key association of quality-control idea entrepreneurs, published five articles on quality circles before 1975. Third, Figure 6.7 reveals a rapid increase in the number of articles in 1979. Interestingly, the figure also indicates that quality-control idea entrepreneurs were among the *first* to stop producing content promoting quality circles around 1982 because, as Cole (1989), a member of the ASQC indicated, quality circles were perceived as yet another management fad. Lockheed Aerospace, another early user of quality circles and producer of quality-circle content, also stopped using quality circles in this period. By 1979, quality circles had all but died out at Lockheed, as the three idea entrepreneurs that launched the Lockheed quality-circle initiative had founded their own consulting firms producing quality-circle content.

Consulting sector publications were next to disseminate quality-circle content. Between 1977 and 1979, the Lockheed idea entrepreneurs published two books promoting quality circles. In 1978, two of them founded the IAQC and

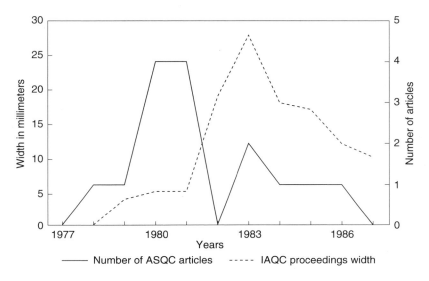

Figure 6.7 Number of ASQC and IAQC articles about quality circles

launched the journal *Quality Circle*. Figure 6.7 also indicates a surge of qual-ity-circle article content in the *IAQC Proceedings* beginning in 1979.

Figure 6.8 reports counts of popular, semi-academic, and academic articles and dissertations. The figure reveals a clear pattern in which popular-knowl-edge publishing leads semi-academic–knowledge publishing, which in turn leads academic-knowledge publishing.

Similarly, Figure 6.9 indicates that the lag in academic-knowledge pub-lishing characterizes both articles and dissertations. Once again, speed of pub-lication may provide the most parsimonious explanation.

How sustained was the production of article content about quality circles by these different knowledge publications? The production of popular-press article content peaked at 78 articles and stayed above the mode in the 0- to 78-article range (39 or more articles) for only four years (1980–1983). By con-trast, semi-academic article content production stayed above its mode for eight years (1982–1989), and academic article content production stayed above its mode for all but one year in an eleven-year period (1983–1993). These results suggest that the popular-press content wave was both earlier and

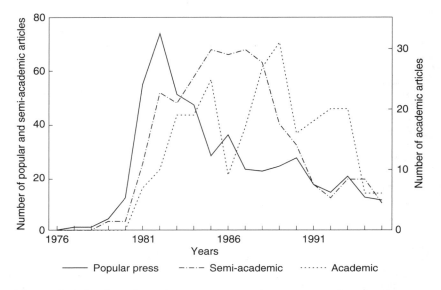

Figure 6.8 Number of popular press, semi-academic press, and academic press articles about quality circles

shorter than the semi-academic content wave, which in turn was earlier and shorter than the academic content wave.

In response to question 3, we examined the leadership and laggardship in the growth and decline phases of the production of content promoting ideas about progressive management techniques. We found a pattern identical to the sequence in which progressive technical ideas were introduced across the four management-knowledge industries. Technicians showed leadership as idea entrepreneurs in both the increase and decline phases of the idea wave, followed by consultants and journalists, and then by academics. Conversely, academics were the most persistent in producing quality-circle content, followed by journalists and consultants, and then by technicians.

Gurus and Leading-Edge Knowledge Publications

Research question 4 concerned opinion leadership among idea entrepreneurs. Figure 6.10 graphically compares the date and frequency of publication among those who produced extensive content about quality circles and those who did

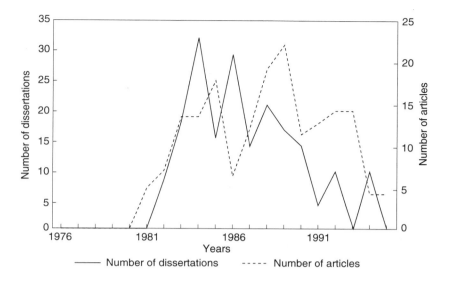

Figure 6.9 Number of articles and dissertations about quality circles

not. The bar chart in the background illustrates the total number of quality-circle articles over the study period, whereas the dashed line illustrates the yearly percentage of all articles on quality circles published by gurus. Results suggest that the 5% of idea entrepreneurs who wrote the most articles about quality circles also began writing earlier than the 95% of idea entrepreneurs who wrote fewer articles about quality circles. Thus, in response to research question 4, our results are consistent with the proposition that there is a small set of idea entrepreneurs, who we call gurus, who both produced more written content about quality circles and did so earlier than the remainder of the idea entrepreneurs, who we call disciples.

Another question about idea entrepreneurs is whether gurus, so defined, would also be among the first idea entrepreneurs to stop producing content promoting one progressive management technique (e.g., quality circles) and start producing content championing the next, replacement progressive technique (e.g., TQM). Figure 6.10 compares the proportion of articles by gurus and disciples discussing both quality circles and total quality management simultaneously. The solid line in the figure illustrates the percentage of articles

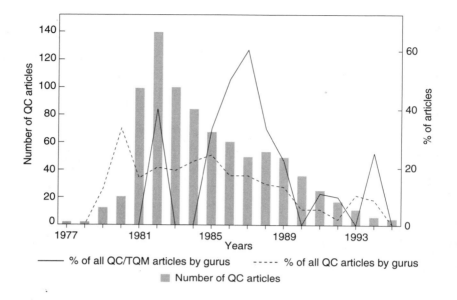

Figure 6.10 Percentage of quality-circle–related articles written by gurus

about both quality circles and TQM written by gurus. Figure 6.10 suggests that not only were gurus more likely to produce more content promoting a progressive management technique earlier, but they were also likely to be among the first idea entrepreneurs to produce content promoting the next, replacement progressive management technique.

The final research question involved the behavior of idea entrepreneurs guiding leading-edge versus lagging-edge knowledge publications. The results are virtually indistinguishable from those in Figure 6.10. They suggest that there are what we call leading-edge publications (analogous to gurus) that are more likely to produce more content promoting a progressive-management technique earlier than lagging-edge publications (analogous to disciples) and to migrate to producing content about the next, replacement progressive technique before the lagging-edge–knowledge publications.

Backgrounds of gurus. Question 5 involved the background of gurus and what sectors they tend to come from. Our list of gurus, defined as the top 5% of idea entrepreneurs in terms of the number of articles on quality circles reads as a *Who's Who* list of the quality-circle movement. Three types of idea-entrepreneur gurus stand out particularly. First are quality-control gurus, such as Juran, who channeled quality-circle content from the association of Japanese quality-control idea entrepreneurs (JUSE) to the association of U.S. quality-control idea entrepreneurs (ASQC). Second are scholarly gurus, such as Robert Cole, who was among the first to introduce quality-circle content into the academic sector in 1979 (Cole 1979), or Edward Lawler and Susan Mohrman, who were among the first to call quality circles a fad (Lawler and Mohrman 1985). Third are the practitioner/consultant gurus, such as Beardsley, Dewar, and Rieker, who launched quality circles at Lockheed and went on to found their own quality-circle consulting firms, as well as the IAQC.

The face validity of our list of idea-entrepreneur gurus encouraged us to examine their backgrounds. We found that (1) 50.9% of the idea entrepreneurs on the guru list had completed a dissertation listed on the Dissertation Abstracts International database, (2) 27.3% were listed as members in the Academy of Management Membership Directory, and (3) 21.8% of the frequent writers were listed in the *McGraw-Hill Directory of Management Faculty*. Finally, the names of 38.7% of our gurus appeared in the directory of consultants. Our results indicate, in response to research question 5, that gurus tend to come from the technical, scholarly, and consulting sectors.

DISCUSSION

There are at least two key patterns across our results that increase our understanding of the role of idea entrepreneurs in the management-idea creation and knowledge-dissemination processes. The first involves patterns of leadership and laggardship across the four management-knowledge industries in producing content that promotes ideas about progressive management techniques. The second involves the existence of idea-entrepreneur gurus and leaders of leading-edge publications.

Our results suggest that, in the case of quality circles, the technical sector led in the production of content about a progressive management technique. It was followed by the consulting, journalistic, and scholarly knowledge industries respectively. We found this pattern three times across our results. First we found it in the historical record, in the introduction of the idea about a progressive management technique in the four sectors. Quality-circle technical idea entrepreneurs invented the quality-circle label and idea, which were then introduced into the consulting, journalistic, and scholarly sectors, respectively. Second, we found this pattern in the initiation and abandonment of publishing content about quality circles across each sector. Technical idea entrepreneurs both started and abandoned publishing first, followed by consultants and journalists, and then by academic idea entrepreneurs. Third, we found this pattern in the persistence with which this content was produced by each industry. Technicians were the least persistent idea entrepreneurs, followed by journalists and consultants and, finally, by academics who were the most persistent. This laggardship of academic idea entrepreneurs is consistent with a prior study by Barley, Meyer, and Gash (1988) and is cause for greater attention by researchers, if not greater concern.

We also found that though invention occurred first on the supply side of the management-knowledge market, the demand side was also involved early in the management-knowledge creation process, when former managers from an influential, early adopting firm (Lockheed) became idea entrepreneurs and founded three consulting firms and an association (IAQC) dominated by consultant idea entrepreneurs, who produced content promoting quality circles widely.

Our results also suggest a pattern of leadership and laggardship among idea entrepreneurs. The results suggest the existence among management-idea entrepreneurs of gurus who lead disciples. We also found evidence suggesting the existence among management-knowledge publications of what we call leading-edge publications that lead lagging-edge publications. We found generally that leaders (gurus and leading-edge publications as well as their editors) tend to produce more content earlier than laggards (disciples and lagging-edge publications) and tend to migrate to content promoting replacement progressive management techniques ahead of these laggards.

CONCLUSION

In closing, consistent with the hourglass structure of this chapter, we focus on two interrelated points bearing on the dynamics of knowledge communities and idea entrepreneurship in general. First, we focus on three dynamic aspects of knowledge communities: the dynamics of circular knowledge flows in knowledge markets, as well as the resultant coevolution of a body of knowledge with both the supply side and demand side of knowledge markets in which this knowledge is produced, transacted, and consumed. We focus second, and relatedly, on some of the unique challenges of idea entrepreneurship, as opposed to product or service entrepreneurship. We describe the hypercompetitive environment of idea entrepreneurship and some of the challenges, tactics, and strategies that idea entrepreneurs must employ to thrive and survive in the face of such knowledge hypercompetition.

The Dynamics of Knowledge Communities

The first noteworthy dimension of the dynamics of knowledge communities and idea entrepreneurship is the continuous, circular flow of ideas through various idea channels in knowledge markets. This circular flow of ideas spreads ideas from supply side to demand side and from demand side back to supply side, as in the case of quality circles. It also spreads them across various knowledge industries—from academics, to technical specialists, to consultants, and back to academics, in the case of quality circles. The flow of ideas moves across different knowledge markets in one country, or across the same knowledge market in different countries—from the U.S. to the Japanese knowledge market in the case of knowledge about quality control and from Japan back to the U.S. knowledge market in the case of knowledge about quality circles and total quality management. Other flows might characterize other knowledge products and fields, and they deserve further study.

The second noteworthy dimension of the dynamics of knowledge communities and idea entrepreneurship is the coevolution of a body of knowledge and the organizational communities that supply such knowledge. When idea entrepreneurs cause a body of knowledge to evolve, they also create a fertile soil in which new types of idea entrepreneurship and new knowledge organizations can mushroom and old ones will wither. The quality-circle idea, for example, made for a rich environment for a new class of idea entrepreneurs (quality-circle experts) and for the founding of new knowledge organizations (professional organizations, management consulting firms, and journals), many of which failed as the quality-circle fashion collapsed and this knowledge-creation segment disappeared. What may be at work here is another causal loop wherein (a) communities produce knowledge and ideas, which (b) creates new knowledge market niches that can (c) be filled by new knowledge organizations and idea entrepreneurs, and thereby (d) altering the boundaries and composition of knowledge communities, with a subsequent impact on (e) knowledge and ideas that these communities can produce.

The third noteworthy dimension of the dynamics of knowledge communities and idea entrepreneurship is the coevolution of a body of knowledge and the organizational communities that consume it. Stinchcombe (1965) was among the first to note that organizations were imprinted for decades with the organizational designs that idea entrepreneurs had made fashionable at the time these organizations were founded. What Stinchcombe did not discuss, however, was the origins of these organizational templates. He did not consider that the organizational designs that were imprinted might have been discovered initially by idea entrepreneurs in organizations populating the very communities of organizations that were subsequently imprinted with this knowledge. Put differently, organizing templates may emerge on the demand side of management-knowledge markets and flow back to these markets, where they create opportunities for entrepreneurs, as well as new organizational templates for entrepreneurial activity. An example is the notion of virtual organizations, network-like amalgams of various outsourced activities, which are typically exemplified by organizations like Nike that have outsourced all but a few core activities. Organizations like Nike (demand side of the knowledge market) engendered ideas and knowledge about new templates for organizing that, when disseminated by idea entrepreneurs (supply side of the knowledge market), gave birth to entrepreneurial possibilities engendering the founding of network organizations (demand side of the knowledge market).

Hypercompetition in Idea Entrepreneurship

The need for nearly continuous innovation in idea entrepreneurship occurs because the supply of many ideas tends to create an almost instantaneous demand for a new idea. This is because progressive knowledge is unlike products and services in one important respect. When people like a candy bar, they consume bars like it again and again. By contrast, they consume most ideas only once, a few times at the most. This is because at an individual level of analysis, a consumed idea, that is, an idea that has been understood, need not be re-understood repeatedly. It suffices, for example, to be exposed to a limited amount of content promoting most management techniques to understand their use, at least at a superficial level. Because most ideas are consumed only once, idea entrepreneurs must continuously invent, reinvent, or repackage ideas to stay in the knowledge business.

At a social level of analysis, the widespread diffusion and consumption of a new and improved idea across individuals in a knowledge-market segment renders this idea known and passé in that segment and creates demand and supply for the next progressive replacement idea in that segment. As a result, there have been frequent waves in the popularity of progressive ideas. The job-enrichment idea, for example, gave way to the quality-circle idea, which in turn gave way to the total-quality-management and business-process-reengineering ideas, respectively. Succinctly, the supply of a progressive idea creates demand for the next progressive idea because progress can never stop progressing. Idea entrepreneurs must continuously ride the flow and ebb of waves of demand for progressive ideas (Abrahamson and Fairchild 1999).

Intense competition in knowledge industries also tends to result from three conditions. The first is low entry barriers into the industry. Indeed, a brain, a personal computer, and a web page are becoming the only entry barriers to many knowledge industries. Second is the general ease of imitation of knowledge products. Even copyright or patent infringement barriers can be circumvented using tactics ranging from modifying the idea slightly to relabeling it. Third is the consequent difficulty in sustaining competitive advantage in knowledge products resulting from their easy imitability.

The simultaneous rapid pace of idea innovation and the rapid obsolescence of such ideas, combined with intense rivalry in knowledge industries, create hypercompetitive conditions in these industries. The challenge of hypercompetition for idea entrepreneurs appears to be twofold: effectively surfing knowledge waves and not appearing like a knowledge surfer.

In an earlier study of the quality-circle knowledge wave, we found evidence that knowledge entrepreneurs use very different tactics in different stages of knowledge waves (Abrahamson and Fairchild 1999). In their upswings, they use emotional content to stress dangerous and vitally important organizational performance gaps, as well as particular techniques that will purportedly and infallibly narrow such gaps, as evidenced by a few high-reputation early adopters of the technique or by the rapidly growing number of later adopters. As the wave crests and begins to decline, however, idea entrepreneurs' strategies become much more differentiated. We recognized at least three distinct strategies. First, idea entrepreneurs following debunking strategies advocate a complete rejection of the technique and offer no substitutes. Entrepreneurs debunk ideas because debunkers can gain notoriety. Second, idea entrepreneurs following surfing strategies advocate a complete rejection of the technique in favor of a substitute technique. These idea entrepreneurs are then in a position to launch a new and purportedly improved replacement technique. Books by gurus promoting these techniques can become best sellers (Jackson 1996; Clark and Salaman 1996). Articles championing them can bring consulting opportunities to consultants, speaking honoraria to gurus, and readership as well as advertising revenue to popular-business publications.

Not every idea entrepreneur, however, abandons a technique in its downswing phase. We also found a rich variety of sustaining strategies, discourse advocating the continued use of the technique despite acknowledged problems with it. This strategy employs at least three analytically distinct rhetorical tactics. First, content contains what might be called narrowing tactics: the technique works only under certain specifiable conditions—when it is well implemented, for instance. Relatedly, the discourse employs what might be called escalation tactics: users of the technique must increase the involvement of idea entrepreneurs (consultants or facilitators) for the technique to work. Third, idea entrepreneurs use what might be called broadening tactics, wherein the technique is cast as part of a larger toolkit of techniques that the idea entrepreneur begins to promote (not quality circles but TQM, for example).

The uses of these various tactics illustrate the challenges that idea entrepreneurs face in surviving in highly dynamic, transitory, or hypercompetitive knowledge markets. In these markets the shelf life of an idea is short, and idea entrepreneurs must sow the seeds of new ideas in their field, harvest them as long as they are being consumed, and be ever prepared to sow the next crop of progressive ideas. One danger, as idea entrepreneurs surf from idea to idea, is to ride an idea too long and thereby risk being associated with an outdated idea. Another danger is to be perceived as a surfer—an idea entrepreneur associated with each passing fad—and, therefore, risk losing the credibility necessary to disseminate any new idea. How certain idea entrepreneurs surf succeeding idea waves is a delicate challenge that needs to be further studied and understood.

This has only scratched the surface in the study of knowledge industries and communities and idea entrepreneurship. This type of study commends itself, however, because of the large number of idea consumers and organizational stakeholders whose thoughts and actions are shaped by such ideas, sometimes with beneficial consequences, but sometimes with devastating results as well. An understanding of the knowledge market can only help us understand how to improve their functioning.

7

From the Technology Cycle to the Entrepreneurship Dynamic

The Social Context of Entrepreneurial Innovation

JOHANN PETER MURMANN AND
MICHAEL L. TUSHMAN

Entrepreneurship often involves the development and application of new technology. Technological breakthroughs are a key force in opening up opportunities for entrepreneurial activity (Schumpeter 1950). Organization theorists, strategy scholars, economists, and historians of technology have all highlighted the powerful role of technology in shaping organizational outcomes. It is by now a well-established observation that technological change is one of the prime movers of industrial, strategic, and organizational change (e.g., Barley 1990; Henderson and Clark 1990; Tripsas 1997a; Tushman and Anderson 1986). Starting with the pioneering work by Abernathy (1978) and Abernathy and Utterback (1978), scholars in the management disciplines have developed the concept of a dominant design and the technology cycle model to explain how technological change shapes organizational outcomes (Anderson and Tushman 1990).

Entrepreneurs—whether founders of independent new ventures or operating within established organizations—need to understand the opportunities and threats posed by new technologies. Previous research has made clear that

We would like to thank Elaine Romanelli, Kaye Schoonhoven, and the participants of the Balboa Bay Conference in Newport Beach for their helpful suggestions.

the emergence of dominant designs is an important juncture in the evolution of a technology and its associated industries. We argue in this chapter that during eras of ferment, before one design becomes dominant, entrepreneurial opportunities are the greatest and that eras of incremental change, after a dominant design is adopted, also offer many entrepreneurial opportunities (Hunt and Aldrich 1998; Miner and Haunschild 1995; Van de Ven and Garud 1994). Entrepreneurs and researchers on entrepreneurship need to have a firm intellectual understanding of how technologies change. In a previous article (Tushman and Murmann 1998), we reviewed the writings on dominant designs and proposed a hierarchical model to clear up some of the persisting confusions in the literature. We argued that to understand technological dynamics it is necessary to analyze technologies as systems that are made up of components, linkages, and multiple levels of subsystems. This refined model of dominant designs offers a useful tool for analyzing entrepreneurial opportunities at different levels of the system.

Although the concept of a dominant design has played such a prominent role in the management literature over the last two decades, empirical research on dominant designs has for the most part not paid attention to possible national differences in the way technologies come about and evolve over time. The implicit assumption in most writings on dominant designs and the technology cycle (including our 1998 paper) is that their dynamics play out in the same manner in all social contexts. Given what we already know about the histories of a number of industries, this may not be a very plausible scenario. It leaves a number of questions unanswered. Are radical innovations in a product class as likely to originate in one country as the next? Do all countries provide the same number of design variants during eras of ferment? Do dominant designs emerge in every country at the same time? Are the selection processes that give rise to a dominant design the same across different nations?

National differences are evident, however, in some of the prominent technologies featured in the literature on corporate and industrial change. For many decades until the early 1970s, Swiss watch firms were responsible for introducing the vast majority of innovations (Landes 1983). Based on this technical and entrepreneurial prowess, Swiss firms dominated the industry for more than 100 years, until a number of Japanese firms seized the opportunities offered by quartz technology and captured a large market share, destroying many of the Swiss watch firms as well as their subsystems suppliers. The first video recorders produced for commercial TV stations were invented in the U.S. But a number of Japanese firms developed the technology to the point at which video recorders for home use became viable. Not a single format for home video recorders was put on the market by American firms. The battle for a dominant design was waged between the Japanese VHS and Betamax and the European Video 2000 formats (Cusumano, Mylonadis, and Rosenbloom 1992). In computers, by contrast, American firms have been the sources of radical innovations and dominant designs at every level in the design hierarchy. All serious contenders for dominant designs in operating systems came from the U.S.: DOS and Windows from Microsoft; OS/2 from IBM; the Mac OS from Apple; UNIX initially from Bell Laboratories, then from SUN, HP, and IBM. As these examples show, populations of firms centered in a particular nation often account for a much larger share of the design variants than would be predicted by chance. The examples suggest that higher rates of entrepreneurial activity in a particular country make it more likely that firms from that particular country will develop the global dominant design.

Similarly, if one examines the same technology in different national contexts, the mechanisms selecting a dominant design frequently vary across nations. Chesbrough (1998) found that, because of institutional differences, entrepreneurial activities drove the disk-drive industry in the United States, while, at the same time, incumbent firms drove generational transitions in Japan. Similarly, in mobile telephony, while in European countries the GMS standard was negotiated among firms and regulatory authorities before installing the networks, in the U.S. no such order was negotiated. As a result, a number of incompatible designs (CDMA, TDMA, GMS) are currently battling for market share. The disk-drive and mobile telephony examples suggest that, independent of technological complexity, social context has a strong influence over how dominant designs are selected.

We argue in this chapter that research on dominant designs needs to introduce social context into its analytical framework. Sociologists of technology have emphasized for over a decade that technologies are socially constructed (Bijker, Hughes, and Pinch 1987); that is, the timing of their appearance, their use, and their diffusion through a society is to a significant extent determined by social factors. By adopting a sociological view, we can ask such questions as why do technological discontinuities appear first in a particular country? Why does the era of ferment last longer in one country than another? Why is the era of incremental innovation shorter in one country than the next? All these questions invite the researcher on dominant designs to investigate the matrix of institutions that constitute the innovative capabilities of a nation (Nelson 1993). Universities, government research institutions, research consortia, patent laws, tax incentives for research, and so on, are likely to have a strong impact on entrepreneurial behaviors and technology cycles. To highlight the importance of social context, we present a case study of the synthetic dye industry to illustrate two important phenomena, namely, (1) that new technologies open up entrepreneurial opportunities and (2) that social context determines to a considerable extent the level of entrepreneurial activity. Our goal is to provide some evidence that a macro-sociological approach to entrepreneurship promises to put entrepreneurship research on a more solid conceptual footing.

THE SYNTHETIC DYE INDUSTRY AND NATIONAL DIFFERENCES IN PATTERNS OF ENTREPRENEURIAL ACTIVITY

The first synthetic dye, a product created by chemical synthesis rather than extraction of naturally appearing coloring materials, was put on the market in 1857 by the British start-up firm Perkin & Sons.[1] This innovation broke with the 2,000-year-old practice of dyeing textiles with naturally occurring coloring materials. For the first decade, British and French firms were the clear leaders in the world market for synthetic dyes. Perkin & Sons and the firm Simpson, Maule and Nicholson (both British) and La Fuchsine (French) were quick to put bright purple, red, and blue synthetic dyes on the market and dominate the field of entrants. Much like the computer industry in current times, the synthetic dye industry was a very dynamic one from 1857 until 1914. A few thousand dyes were introduced in this period, and growth was rapid (3,800% in terms of value from 1862 until 1913). Around 1870, German firms such as

---

1. This case study is based on the dissertation *Knowledge and Competitive Advantage in the Synthetic Dye Industry, 1850–1914: The Coevolution of Firms, Technology, and National Institutions in Great Britain, Germany and the United States* written by Johann Peter Murmann.

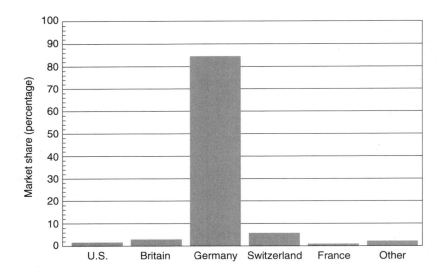

Figure 7.1 Synthetic dye market share by country in 1913

BASF, Bayer, and Hoechst took over the lead in the global synthetic dye industry as these novel synthetic dyes replaced more and more natural dyes, reducing them to small niches by 1914. The German synthetic dye industry steadily expanded its global market share from about 50% in 1870 to 85% in 1885. For the next three decades before the outbreak of World War I, German firms kept this dominant position, accounting for the vast share of the large number of new synthetic dyes that were put on the market each year.

Figure 7.1 depicts the distribution of market shares among countries in 1913. The French and British synthetic dye industries fell so far behind that even Switzerland (with 6.2% market share) had a larger synthetic dye industry in 1914 than France (1.2%) and Britain (3.1%). Domestic production in the U.S. accounted for 1.9% of the global output. Given that Britain not only represented the largest market for dyestuffs in the world in 1857 but also had the most abundant supply of coal-tar[2] from which all synthetic dyes

---

2. Coal-tar was a waste product of making illuminating gas that was used to light cities in Great Britain until the turn of the twentieth century.

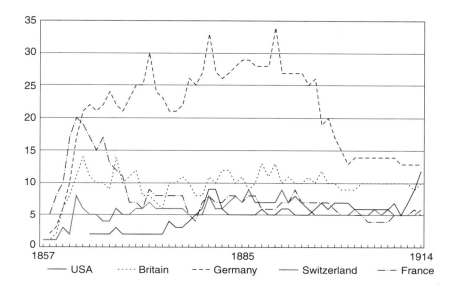

Figure 7.2 Number of synthetic dye firms in different countries per calendar year

were produced, we are left with the puzzle of why German entrepreneurs became so much more successful than their British counterparts as the industry developed. And how could Switzerland with no domestic raw materials and a very small home market for dyes overtake the British and French industries?

If one examines Figure 7.2, charting the number of firms that existed in a particular country in each year, part of the answer becomes apparent. By 1862, more dye firms existed in Germany than in any other country. Already in the second year of the industry, more entrepreneurs entered the industry in Germany and France than in Great Britain. Although Figure 7.2 gives some indication that many German firms were pushed out of the market, it does not adequately reveal the large amount of turnover among firms. Between 1857 and 1914, approximately 91 of the 116 firms that had entered the industry in Germany had exited again. The corresponding figures for Britain are approximately 47 entries and 36 exits, for France, 63 entries and 55 exits, for the United States, 35 entries and 25 exits, and for Switzerland, 23 entries and 19 exits. As these numbers demonstrate, the German leadership position in this industry was based on a much higher level of entrepreneurial activity. The vast majority of entrepreneurial ventures failed, but the few that had stumbled on the right business formula for the industry outcompeted all other ventures, both at home and abroad.

But why did many more entrepreneurs open up a dye business in Germany than in other countries? The numbers of start-ups in the different countries are too different to be explained by chance. Since we have no reason to believe that German entrepreneurs by nature were very different from their counterparts in Britain, France, or the United States, it is necessary to move the analysis one step backward in the causal chain. The moment we focus not only on individual entrepreneurs but also look at the larger social environment, we discover striking differences across countries that go a long way toward explaining the very different national frequencies of entrepreneurial activity in the early synthetic dye industry.

The most obvious difference between Germany and Switzerland, on the one hand, and France and Britain, on the other, concerns the national patent practices at the beginning of the synthetic dye industry in 1857. Britain and France had patent laws on the books while Switzerland and Germany did not.[3] Henry Perkin, the British inventor of the first synthetic dye, successfully obtained a patent for his purple dye, which allowed him to prevent other firms from making this dye in Great Britain. Similarly, the French firm La Fuchsine obtained, after a court battle, such a sweeping patent grant in France that it was able to force most competitors out of the market. The steep decline in the number of dye firms in France after 1863 was directly linked to La Fuchsine's broad patent grant. German and Swiss entrepreneurs, in contrast, did not face any patent restrictions in entering the synthetic dye industry. Hence many German and Swiss entrepreneurs simply copied the innovative British and French synthetic dyes and produced them without any threat that the police would shut down their operations. By 1870 the number of German producers had grown to 25, while the number of French producers had plunged to eight from a high of 21 in 1862.

---

3. Germany before 1871 was fragmented into 39 independent states. Although some states had patent laws on the books, the German custom union agreement (Zollverein) undermined patent protection such that for practical purposes patent protection did not exist in the territory of the 39 German states.

The second striking difference between the two German-speaking countries, Germany and Switzerland, on the one hand, and Britain, France, and the United States, on the other hand, concerns the quality and quantity of the national science capability in organic chemistry. Before the rise of the synthetic dye industry, Swiss and particularly German universities were the world centers of organic chemistry, attracting students from the world over. Germany trained many more chemists than any other country. Because there was often an oversupply of chemists in Germany, many of them had to find employment abroad or start their own entrepreneurial ventures. The first significant effect of the German educational environment was to produce many more individuals who would have the necessary chemical training and thereby could recognize the opportunities offered by the synthetic dye industry. In an important way, entrepreneurial opportunities were not uniformly distributed across countries because of the differences in educational systems.

Until the middle 1880s, academic researchers invented the most important synthetic dyes. Consistent with this pattern, Perkin was a student at the Royal College of Chemistry under C. A. Hofmann in London when he invented the first synthetic dye. Firms that developed strong ties to leading university chemists such as C. A. Hofmann (who moved from London to Berlin in 1865) and Adolf von Baeyer (Berlin and, later, Munich) would gain earlier and sometimes even exclusive access to the leading synthetic dye technology. As a result, those German entrepreneurs with close ties to the leading academic researchers, who happened to be predominantly in Germany, then enjoyed a significant competitive advantage over entrepreneurs who did not develop such relations.

The differences in national scientific capabilities had another profound effect on success in the synthetic dye industry, particularly after Friedrich August Kekulé developed his benzene ring theory, in 1866, which provided a new tool for systematically searching for new dyes. Until this time, new synthetic dyes were based mainly on trial-and-error mixing of chemicals, a method that did not provide leading scientists with a significant advantage over self-taught chemists in finding new dyes. But Kekulé's idea that a 6-atom carbon ring formed the building block of organic colors gave great impetus to the science of how structure leads to the color properties of a particular dye. From then on, the scientifically educated chemist would become the only source of novel synthetic dyes. If firms wanted to develop new dyes, they had to recruit academically trained chemists. Because it was easier, on average, for German firms to recruit German trained academic chemists, German entrepreneurs had a significant advantage over their foreign competitors. Hence, forging close ties with the leading organic chemists was also important for the purpose of recruiting talented students from a professor's laboratory.

Tracing the connections between the key players both in academia and in industry provides a powerful insight into why German entrepreneurial firms came to dominate the industry. Figure 7.3 is a simplified representation of the early dye network. It does not contain all relationships and is meant to be suggestive rather than exhaustive. Circles represent individuals in industry (the words in small letters identify the firm the individual is affiliated with, if not evident from his name); rectangles (or the benzene ring in the case of Kekulé) represent academics. Lines with arrows on one end represent student-teacher relationships. Graebe, for example, was a student of von Baeyer. Individuals on the right side of the figure are Germans; individuals in the southwest corner are British; individuals in the northwest corner are French; and Clavel and Muller-Pack in the upper middle are Swiss. Thicker lines indicate that the individual is relatively more important. Professor Hofmann is positioned in the middle of the figure because he assumed the central role in the early period of the industrial-academic network. Professor Hofmann taught in London, while his students discovered the first synthetic dyes, and then moved to Berlin in the mid-1860s. He and von Baeyer trained a very large number of students who subsequently became leading dye chemists in German and foreign firms. Individuals who had access to this knowledge network of synthetic organic chemistry would be in a much better position to find out about new products and technologies that could transform the industry. Martius, as one example, had such a close tie to Hofmann that Martius received not only Hofmann's best students after 1867 but also the professor's commercially promising discoveries.

The usefulness of analyzing a product in terms of system, subsystems, components, and linkage mechanisms becomes evident in the case of the synthetic dye industry. Dominant designs for synthetic dyes did not emerge at the system level. Rather, chemists devised a dominant method for linking atoms in the form of the so-called diazo bridge. With the advent of Kekulé's benzene ring theory, academic chemists developed much more precise models of the

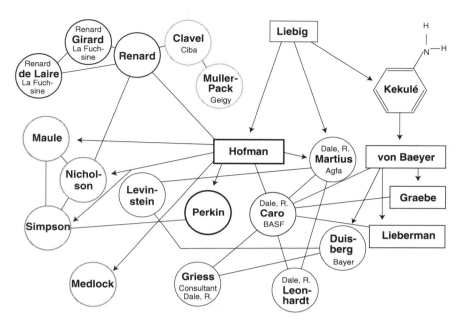

Note: Circles represent individuals in industry, and rectangles represent academics. Arrows show teacher-student relationships.

Figure 7.3 The early academic industrial dye network

molecular structure of a particular synthetic dye. Often, a molecule would change its coloring properties simply by adding an atom at a particular position in the molecule. Just as in the case of airplanes, radios, or computers, innovations took place at many different levels of the design hierarchy. Only academic chemists would be able to understand that a virtually unlimited number of different organic compounds could be created by using the diazo reaction as a linking mechanism of molecules that, when joined together, would give rise to new coloring properties. The vast majority of new dyes after 1880 were created by this dominant diazo-linking mechanism, which is diagrammed in Figure 7.4. Only those firms that had scientists on the payroll who knew how to create new molecules from existing molecules via the diazo bridge were capable of competing in this era of the synthetic dye industry. Thus, the diazo bridge became the strategically crucial link between subsystems.

The case of the early synthetic dye industry demonstrates that entrepre-

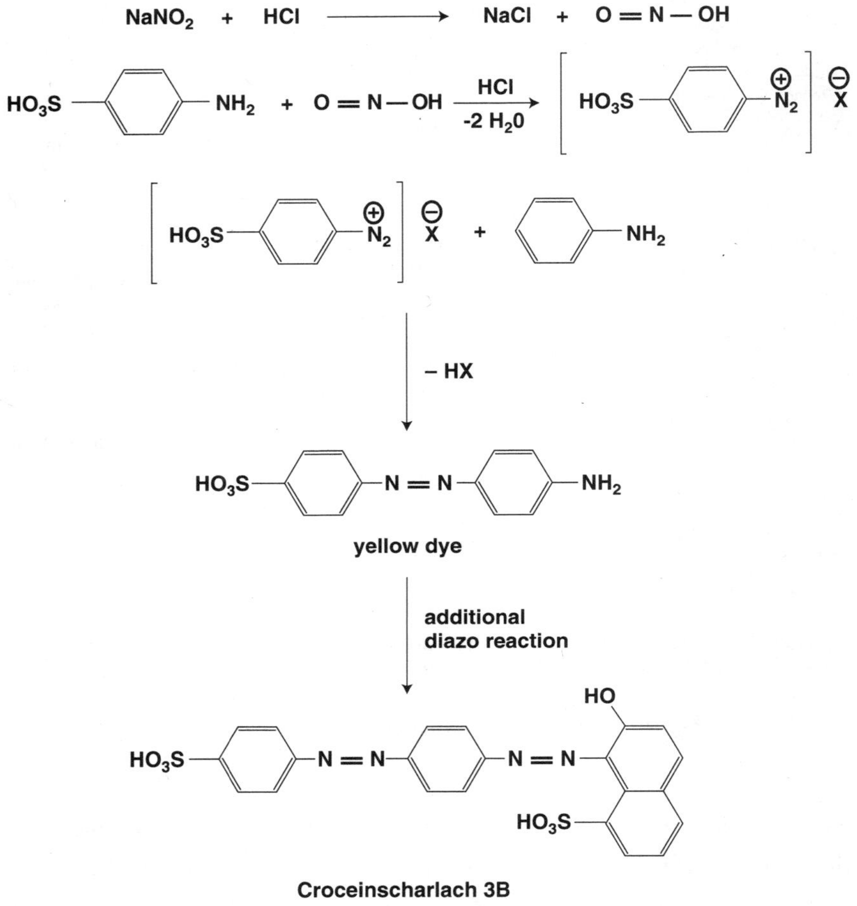

Figure 7.4 A dominant linking mechanism for synthesizing dyes: the diazo reaction

neurial activity is determined in large part by the social environment of would-be entrepreneurs. Individuals in Germany faced very different opportunities because the educational systems in the different countries created knowledge and information asymmetries. An academically educated German chemist faced much lower risk than a British or American would-be entrepreneur, who knew nothing about organic chemistry and could not judge what molecules and reactions would offer the best opportunities for developing new synthetic dyes. Those firms with an understanding of how to add atoms at precise locations in the hierarchical structure of molecules and how to create new molecules by combining existing ones in novel ways had significant advantages over their competitors. Patent laws also played a significant role in leading to many more start-ups in Germany than in Britain, the U.S., and France, by either erecting barriers or facilitating the formation of new dye firms.[4] A key observation from this case study is that entrepreneurial opportunities were more numerous before firms such as BASF, Bayer, and Hoechst created large laboratories staffed with research chemists who would systematically use the diazo-linking mechanism to create thousands of new molecules to obtain a few commercially viable dyes. Before the emergence of a dominant design for linking molecules to form new dyes, entrepreneurs had a much greater chance of starting a viable firm. In contrast, after the emergence of the dominant linking mechanism, entrepreneurial opportunities were much more constrained, because incumbent firms used a large cadre of scientists to systematically exploit the dominant linking mechanism. In this era of incremental innovation, entrepreneurs would have to enter the industry on a much larger scale and with more up-front investment, making such a move much riskier than in earlier periods. The varying opportunities for entrepreneurs become clearer if we look more closely at research on dominant designs and pay more attention to social context.

RESEARCH ON DOMINANT DESIGNS: STATE OF THE ART

The concept of a dominant design, pioneered by Abernathy and Utterback (1978), has stimulated a large amount of research on the evolution of industries. Dominant designs have been reported in typewriters, TVs, electronic calculators (Suarez and Utterback 1995), automobiles (Abernathy 1978), VCRs (Cusumano, Mylonadis, and Rosenbloom 1992), flight simulators (Rosenkopf and Tushman 1998; Miller et al. 1995), cochlear implants (Van de Ven and Garud 1994), fax transmission services (Baum, Korn, and Kotha 1995), main-

---

4. For a much more detailed treatment of the development of the global synthetic dye industry, see Murmann 1998.

frame computers (Iansiti and Khanna 1995), photolithography (Henderson 1995), personal mobile stereos (Sanderson and Uzumeri 1995), microprocessors (Wade 1995; 1996), disk drives (Christensen, Suarez, and Utterback 1998), in the glass, cement, and minicomputer product classes (Anderson and Tushman 1990), and cardiac pacemakers (Hidefjall 1997). In an earlier paper (Tushman and Murmann 1998), we developed a model of the technology cycle and dominant designs as a nested hierarchy of technology cycles (components are nested in subsystems, and subsystems are nested in systems) to provide a conceptual resolution to many of the confusions that have plagued the literature on dominant designs about the level in the system at which dominant designs are adopted and what their effects are.

Our refined model is built on Anderson and Tushman's (1990) notion of technology cycles that alternate between periods of variation and periods of incremental change, as shown in Figure 7.5. Periods of variation (eras of ferment) are initiated by technological discontinuities and closed by the selection of a dominant design. For instance, in the early period of the automobile industry, designers created three competing motor technologies—steam, internal combustion, and electric engines (Basalla 1988). But around 1902 the internal combustion engine won this competition, and engineers subsequently focused their attention on improving the internal combustion engine for cars. After a dominant design emerges (i.e., one design variant captures over 50% of new sales), subsequent innovation extends the selected variant's technological trajectory (Dosi 1980). We saw this pattern in the synthetic dye industry before 1914: after the emergence of the diazo reaction as the dominant linking mechanism for molecules, firms concentrated on designing thousands of dye variations with the help of the diazo bridge. Eras of incremental change are, in turn, broken by subsequent technological discontinuities, and the next cycle of variation, selection, and retention processes begins. Eras of ferment are fundamentally more uncertain than eras of incremental change. Dominant designs are, then, a key transition point between eras of ferment and eras of incremental change because they signal a reduction in uncertainty about the direction of the technology.

In this model of dominant designs, technologies are conceptualized as systems (for example the entire automobile), multiple levels of subsystems (e.g., the engine, a first order subsystem, and, at a lower level, the cylinder,

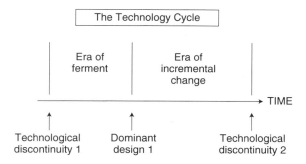

Figure 7.5 Anderson and Tushman's 1990 model of dominant designs

a second-order subsystem), linking mechanisms (e.g., the auto chassis), and basic components (e.g., the screws holding engine parts together). Often, linkage mechanisms are complex, and they should be analyzed as subsystems in their own right. Not every subsystem is equally important for the performance of the overall system. Some subsystems are core (e.g., the integrated circuit or the operating system software in personal computers), and other subsystems are peripheral. One way in which subsystems become core is if they serve as the link to many other subsystems as shown in Figure 7.6. A second, less important way in which component and subsystem technologies become core is by constituting a bottleneck in the overall performance of the system. Sometimes entire collections of subsystems are replaced, as quartz technology replaced mechanical watches, and new core subsystems may arise. Because core subsystems impose greater constraints on the development path of the overall system, firms that control core subsystems enjoy more power than firms that control peripheral ones, which can have important implications for entrepreneurial activities, since firms that control core subsystems (e.g., Microsoft and Intel) are likely to reap huge financial rewards. The ability to identify core subsystems is, therefore, a key challenge for strategy makers.

The key point to understand about the nested-hierarchy model is that while a dominant design may arise in the operational principle of a subsystem (the engine), lower-level subsystems and components may experience technological discontinuities. Strictly speaking, a dominant design for the overall system only emerges if all lower-level subsystems and components are in an era

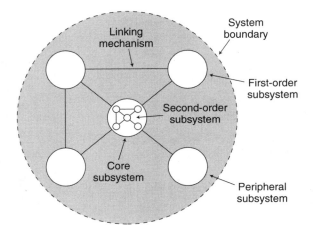

Figure 7.6 System composed of subsystems and linking mechanisms

of incremental change. This implies that dominant designs are more likely to arise in subsystems and components.

Because researchers confused these different levels of analysis, they often made the mistake of identifying a dominant design at the level of an entire product (e.g., an automobile) but of only presenting evidence at the level of several subsystems (internal combustion engine, closed steel body, etc.). Hence, we are left with a limited understanding of where the most important dominant designs reside in the system hierarchy and how they are related.

Dominant designs emerge through a variety of selection mechanisms. Except for simple, non-assembled products (e.g., cement), uncertainty about the potential of certain designs cannot be adjudicated by technology alone; rather, dominant designs emerge out of a sociopolitical, economic process of compromise and accommodation played out in the community (Rosenkopf and Tushman 1994). This means that the best technology does not necessarily win the competition between alternative designs. Coalitions of different actors, government intervention, and the power of large users all can have a decisive influence on what design variant will become the dominant one. Because the selection of a dominant design in any nonsimple technology involves sociopolitical processes, entrepreneurial activity can shape what design emerges as the dominant one.

THE TECHNOLOGY CYCLE AND
ENTREPRENEURIAL OPPORTUNITIES

Dominant designs can arise in any of several ways. In a pure market process, one technology gains market share and over time comes to dominate its rivals, as VHS came to dominate the Beta and Video 2000 formats. Dominant designs are also sometimes mandated directly by governments with little or no influence of market processes; the HDTV (high-definition TV) standard, for example, was mandated by the U.S. government as an outcome of mainly political processes. Finally, and between these two extremes, dominant design standards are sometimes negotiated, often through the agency of a voluntary standards organization; the establishment of fax transmission protocols are an example of these so-called negotiated standards. In all three kinds of processes, entrepreneurial activities can shape what design becomes dominant. In the market process, being first in the market, signing up large customers early, and forming alliances with other producers are often the decisive factors. When standards are negotiated, forming coalitions with other entrepreneurs and organizations is an important strategy for making a particular design the winner. Even when the standard is mandated by government, entrepreneurs can influence the selection of a dominant design through targeted lobbying campaigns.

The ties entrepreneurs or organizations have to other actors is key for improving the odds that a campaign for a particular design is successful. This is particularly true for complex technologies in which components and subsystems need to be integrated to form the overall product. When firms make only part of the system, coordinating the makers of other core subsystems is very important in shaping dominant designs. Entrepreneurs and organizations most effective at shaping evolving dominant designs may have diverse external linkages and capabilities (Powell and Brantley 1991; Tripsas 1997b; Wade 1995). The efficacy and importance of being tied to other actors was evident in the German dye industry. German dye firms joined forces with professors in a successful lobbying campaign for changes in the patent law. In many technologies, patent laws (or their absence) determine how many alternative designs can come on the market and compete to become the dominant design.

One important implication of the technology cycle model is that entrepreneurial opportunities are greater in the era of ferment. Levels of uncertainty vary dramatically between eras of ferment and incremental change. During the era of ferment, demand is uncertain because it is difficult to predict how many users will find a new technology sufficiently valuable to adopt it. It is also not clear how many users delay their adoption of a technology until a dominant design emerges, which reduces their risk of picking the wrong technology. This uncertainty tends to keep existing organizations that flourish on incrementally refining the dominant design of the previous technology cycle from devising radical new designs. As a result, entrepreneurs and entrepreneurial organizations have many more opportunities in the eras of ferment than in the eras of incremental change. In the eras of incremental change, incumbent firms have build up capabilities to refine the dominant design in line with the requirements of existing users. As the history of IBM during the mainframe computer era demonstrates, it is very difficult for entrepreneurial ventures to match dominant firms' capabilities. We also saw this pattern in the synthetic dye industry. Once the diazo bridge emerged as the dominant linking mechanism, existing firms such as BASF, Bayer, and Hoechst, with their large R&D laboratories, were responsible for the vast majority of new dyes and dominated the market. After a technological discontinuity, entrepreneurial ventures can exploit the fact that existing organizations often find their capabilities rendered obsolete (competence-destroying innovations), or even when their capabilities retain their value (competence-enhancing innovations), existing players are frequently more inert and cannot respond as quickly as entrepreneurs. Sull, Tedlow, and Rosenbloom (1997) found that competence-destroying technological change in the tire industry (i.e., radial ties) triggered slow and incompetent moves by incumbents. In the United States, every veteran firm but one was dominated by new players. Methé, Swaminathan, and Mitchell (1996) reported that in the telecommunications industry, veteran firms initiated competence-enhancing technological discontinuities, while new firms initiated competence-destroying technological discontinuities.

In an era of ferment, the incentives for entrepreneurial action are also greater than in an era of incremental change. If a new venture is successful in establishing its design as a dominant one, it will realize much higher financial rewards than would be possible by making an incremental innovation to an existing dominant design. Entrepreneurial opportunities are greater after a technological discontinuity precisely because the selection of a dominant design is highly susceptible to strategic action by entrepreneurs and firms. Dominant designs, then, are pivot points between alternative modes of technological change and represent fundamentally different entrepreneurial contexts (Miner and Haunschild 1995; Tushman and Rosenkopf 1992). This leads us to the general proposition that entrepreneurial activities will be significantly higher in eras of ferment than in eras of incremental change.

Our hierarchical model of dominant designs stresses that component and subsystem technologies often will not be in the same stage of the technology cycle. The model makes it possible to examine what parts of a technological system offer the greatest opportunities and the greatest threats. Displacing a well-entrenched system-level design in the market is very difficult, because it requires deep pockets and a wide variety of technological capabilities. Opportunities for substituting one particular subsystem with a radical new technology or reconfiguring the linkages between the different subsystems in a radical way (Henderson and Clark 1990) present themselves more often than opportunities for replacing an entire system. As a general rule, as one moves down in the hierarchy of technology cycles from the system level all the way to the level of individual components, it is easier for entrepreneurial ventures to create a radical new technology that has a chance of succeeding and becoming a dominant design. There is already some evidence that discontinuous subsystem innovations are frequently initiated by entrepreneurial acts by firms or innovative users (e.g., Cooper and Smith 1992; Foster 1986; Tripsas 1997a; Von Hippel 1988). Veteran firms often either ignore these technological discontinuities at the subsystem level or react incompetently. For example, although veteran firms were well aware of fundamentally new microprocessor, reprographic, and oscillation technologies, it was new firms that initiated RISC (Reduced Interaction Set Computing) and reprographic technologies and the quartz movement (Glassmeier 1991; Von Hippel 1988; Wade 1995). These considerations lead us to the general proposition that, for individual subsystems and linking technologies, technological discontinuities and subsequent eras of ferment are more frequently initiated by entrepreneurial firms than by veteran firms, especially as one moves down in the design hierarchy. New and old firms alike, however, are subject to the influence of the social context of the technology cycle.

EMBEDDING DOMINANT DESIGNS IN SOCIAL CONTEXT

As we noted earlier, for many technologies the frequencies of technological discontinuities and rival designs are not distributed equally across industrialized nations of the world. In the synthetic dye industry, innovative activity came to be dominated by German firms. German firms obtained the vast majority of all dye patents between 1900 and 1914, not only in Germany but also in Britain and the U.S. (see Murmann 1998, 19–23, for detailed statistics). A current survey of Internet search engines across the world shows that most of them are American or are powered by American technology. A survey of innovative activity around the world has convinced us that future research on dominant designs needs to investigate how social context shapes the technology cycle.

The Frequency of Radical New Designs

Radical innovations in the synthetic dye industry initially came from Britain and France, but after 1875 and until World War I, they came almost exclusively from Germany. Direct cotton diazo dyes and synthetic indigo are important cases in point. Before the late 1880s, radical dye innovations originated in organic chemistry laboratories of universities and were commercialized by a variety of German firms. Because the most important organic chemistry university laboratories were located in Germany, more radical innovations appeared in Germany than in any other country, and this had profound effects on entrepreneurial opportunities in different national environments. A tight network of university researchers and domestic firms had formed in Germany, and, as a result, firms in Germany would be more likely to get access to the knowledge of particular university laboratories. Equally important, when a firm introduced an important new dye, other German firms were more able to draw on this industrial-academic knowledge network to come up with alternative dye designs.

Just as the social context of different countries goes a long way toward explaining the frequency of radical dye designs that appeared in each country before World War I, differences in social context in more recent times explain why technological discontinuities appear more frequently in one social context than another. One reason why the vast majority of serious contenders for computer operating systems came from the U.S. has to do with the development of computer science departments in the U.S. after World War II. With the beginning of the Cold War, the Pentagon poured large resources into developing computing capabilities in the U.S. and thereby created a computer science capability that is unmatched to date around the world (Bresnahan and Malerba 1999; Mowery 1999). University computer science departments educated many people who would start entrepreneurial ventures. Silicon Valley is the most prominent social space with tight links between universities and industrial firms, and it created more entrepreneurial opportunities than other social spaces (Saxenian 1994). The biotech industry is another example of how differences in national laws and scientific capabilities in molecular biology had a profound effect on which countries would lead in creating radically new biotech products and processes. Because Germany had placed severe restrictions on genetic engineering until the early 1990s, the country's innovation rate lagged far behind the U.S. in this field. German firms such as Bayer opened up research laboratories in the U.S. to overcome the obstacles imposed on it in the German environment.

Alternative Selection Processes

If one surveys how dominant designs even in the same technology arise in different national contexts, it becomes evident that selection mechanisms often vary across social contexts. Because of the different development trajectories of individual countries, the existing social institutions and industrial infrastructures can impose quite distinct rules on how dominant designs are selected. Baumol (1993, 29) highlighted that entrepreneurial activities are directed by the incentive structure and rules of the game that are set up in the social environment. Governments differ in the extent to which they interfere in markets. The influence of governments on the selection of dominant designs ranges from providing mere tax credit for innovative activities to imposing tight regulations on what kind of technological design can be sold and operated within the boundaries of the nation. Whereas in most countries of the world public authorities selected the Global System for Mobile Communication (GSM) technology as the national standard for digital mobile telephony, in the U.S. three different designs are battling to become the dominant design.

The fragmentation of the U.S. market, according to many observers, has been the key reason why European firms such as Nokia and Ericsson became the leading assemblers of mobile phone sets in the world. The idea here is that by agreeing on a common transmission standard, firms were able to focus innovative activity on creating new features in the telephones themselves. Or in the language of our hierarchical model, because firms agreed on a dominant design for the core linkage (transmission) subsystems, many opportunities opened up for radical innovations in other subsystems of the technology, giving European firms a head start on American firms.

Governments and social institutions influence selection mechanisms in a variety of other ways. They can encourage developers of technology to make dominant designs public as opposed to proprietary. If a country decides to have a patent law granting inventors temporary monopoly on a product in exchange for disclosure of technical information, it creates a situation in which dominant designs are not selected through a market process. In the French dye industry, one company received such a wide-ranging patent that rival firms were prevented from introducing alternative designs for aniline dyes. The same thing could happen in current times with respect to the human genome. If the U.S. or other countries will allow the patenting of the genetic sequence information of the human genome, companies that own the sequences may have the power to limit the number of variants of drugs that are introduced in the market for a particular disease. At present, we know relatively little about how selection processes differ across social contexts, and as these examples are intended to illustrate, systematic research on this question is very much needed.

Social Origins of Dominant Designs

Joseph Schumpeter (1950, 132) emphasized that entrepreneurs need not necessarily invent anything. Instead, entrepreneurs and entrepreneurial ventures may bring to the market innovative technologies invented by someone else. For example, the Japanese did not invent quartz technology; rather, they were the ones who recognized in the early 1970s the opportunity of replacing the core subsystems of a watch with a new operational principle (Glassmeier 1991; Landes 1983). The new technology was so successful that the Japanese, and not the Swiss, established quartz technology as the dominant subsystem design in the mass market for watches. The Swiss watch industry was almost wiped out in the process. Employment figures tell this story very well. In 1970, the Swiss watch industry employed 89,448 people; by 1985, it employed only 32,000 people. Using our hierarchical model of dominant designs allows us to do a more precise analysis of what happened to the Swiss watch industry. By the mid 1980s, the watch-system assemblers belatedly also embraced quartz technology, and a radical redesign of the face subsystem (the Swatch Watch), along with full automation of the assembly process, allowed the Swiss to recapture market share. Before the quartz revolution many firms in the Swiss watch industry specialized in making one or a few parts that went into a watch. Over the centuries, a whole network of component and subsystem suppliers developed along with the assemblers of the entire watch system. The dominance of the Swiss watch industry was based in part on an institutional matrix of educational institutions and associations that helped pass on the skills of fine mechanical engineering from one generation to the next. Quartz technology destroyed the value of these social institutions. The establishment of quartz technology as a dominant design at the subsystem level did not kill the system assembly part of the Swiss watch industry, but it killed the vast majority of subsystem suppliers who specialized in making mechanical parts.

The lesson from this example is that technological innovations at different levels in the system hierarchy will not have the same effect in different social contexts. Quartz subsystem technology represented a great opportunity for the Japanese, who had in place a sophisticated electronics capability; for Switzerland, it meant that its leadership position in mechanical subsystems was destroyed. Given additional evidence from airplanes (Tushman and Murmann 1998) and flight simulators (Rosenkopf and Tushman 1998), we suspect that the same story holds true for a great many innovations that revolutionize subsystem technologies. Depending on the existing structure of a technology, social context can either facilitate or hinder the development of radical new designs.

Level of Uncertainty During Eras of Ferment

The literature on the technology cycle gives the impression that uncertainty created by a technological discontinuity is the same for all actors. The case of synthetic indigo illustrates that this is hardly the case. In 1870, Professor von Baeyer first synthesized indigo in the laboratory. He signed an agreement with BASF and Hoechst, allowing the two firms to develop his invention into a commercial process. BASF worked for 17 years on the problem of synthesizing indigo before it became the first company to create a chemical process that could manufacture synthetic indigo at prices that could compete with natural indigo grown largely in India. In its development activities, BASF drew on insights and help from numerous people outside the company, for example, Heumann, a German chemist working at the Federal Polytechnic in Zurich, and Rudoph Knietsch, a chemical engineer who was brought into the effort to create a highly concentrated sulfuric acid. The network of contacts that spanned German-speaking universities and industrial firms made entrepreneurial activity in the synthetic dye industry less uncertain in Germany than in Britain, France, or the U.S., where technological capabilities, firm capabilities, and market knowledge were not as widely available. For British firms importing natural indigo, the technological discontinuity triggered by BASF's synthetic indigo process created much more uncertainty than for German synthetic dye firms. The latter could draw on knowledge both in-house and in the social environment to create rival designs. In response to BASF's radical innovation, four other synthetic indigo processes were created in Germany, none in any other country. For instance, Hoechst soon developed a process that was even more efficient and rendered BASF's process obsolete. Also in response to BASF's synthetic indigo, Bayer developed a whole new set of blue dyes that could compete in the market served by indigo. These examples demonstrate clearly that the technological discontinuity ushered in by synthetic indigo created less uncertainty in the social context in Germany than in Britain.

CONCLUSION

Previous research has not addressed the question of how the technology cycle and dominant designs are influenced by the larger social context. But as our case study on the synthetic dye industry has already indicated, social context appears to have an important influence on technological dynamics. For reasons of presentational simplicity, we have focused on countries in the synthetic dye case as examples of different social contexts, though cities, regions, and states are other possible units of analysis for social contexts (see also, Aldrich and Fiol 1994; Chesbrough 1998).

Our empirical examples have shown that it is important to examine how the matrix of social institutions is responsible for facilitating or hindering the supply of new technological designs and how it influences what kind of selection mechanisms lie behind a particular dominant design. But there are many different units of analysis besides countries for examining the effects of social context. In some cases, particular industries can very well be the most important social context for understanding how a technology evolves. The recent history of consumer electronics has demonstrated that firms have learned from their costly battles over the dominant format in video recorders and now prefer to negotiate standards and avoid risky and expensive market selection processes. Players in the industry negotiated the standard for digital TV (HDTV) and the new DVD (digital versatile disk) format, for instance, rather than fighting it out in the marketplace with rival designs. Firms in a particular industry seem to be able learn from their previous dominant design-strategies, suggesting that an analysis of social context must account for cumulative, population-level learning processes that are likely to be stronger within an industry than across different industries (Miner and Haunschild 1995).

Much like the literature on dominant designs, research in entrepreneurship has neglected the role of social context (see also Stuart 1998; Stuart, Hoang, and Hybels 1999). Since there is a natural intersection between research on entrepreneurship and research on dominant designs, ideas about bringing social context in the analysis of technological dynamics can also be applied to entrepreneurship research. Venkataraman (1997) has called for a systematic analysis of where entrepreneurial opportunities come from and how such entrepreneurial opportunities get exploited. Our case of the synthetic dye industry has provided evidence that the dominance of German entrepreneurs in the synthetic dye industry was linked to much greater entrepreneurial opportunities arising in the German national context than in Britain, France, or the U.S. The case study also provided evidence that a macro-sociological approach that employs such institutional structures as universities and patent laws can offer a persuasive explanation for differences in rates of entrepreneurial activities across different social contexts (see also Murmann and Landau 1998). Such a macro-sociological approach would involve a number of analytical steps. First, one would investigate how much of the entrepreneurial activity can be explained by examining differences in social contexts rather than individual differences in people. Second, one would introduce populations of firms as a unit of analysis, to study how different social settings cause variations in the level of entrepreneurial activity (e.g., Aldrich and Fiol 1994). Third, one would conceive of individual entrepreneurs as differing not so much in their psychological properties as in their relations to other actors (Burt 1992; Tilly 1998). For example, two German dye firms, Bayer and Jäger, were located in the same town and entered the synthetic dye industry during the first six years of the industry. In trying to explain why Bayer became a global leader in the synthetic dye industry while Jäger remained a tiny player, a sociological account would examine the structural position of each firm in the network of actors that connects customers, suppliers, university researchers, and other relevant players. Bayer was much more successful than Jäger precisely because Bayer had a much more central position in the network than Jäger and developed much stronger ties to academic researchers.[5]

A sociological approach to entrepreneurship research is very likely to strengthen scholarly efforts because it will move the researcher away from the entrepreneur and bring into focus the creation and exploitation of entrepreneurial activities. Research that focuses on the single entrepreneur misses the fact that entrepreneurial activity in the present day is carried out by existing organizations. Hence, it is important to make a clear distinction between the entrepreneur and entrepreneurial activity. For the welfare of society it is not important who introduces new products and processes. In connection with economic growth, the central issue is that welfare-improving innovations are introduced and diffused throughout the economy as quickly as possible.

Once an innovation has been introduced in one segment of the economy, the key role of entrepreneurial activity is to bring the new technology to other sectors. This process of diffusion often involves much less technological innovation than the creation of organizations that have developed an understand-

---

5. For a detailed comparison of the two firms, see Murmann 1998, 99–202.

ing of how existing technologies can be applied in new social settings. In both cases, however, having a strong conceptual understanding of technological dynamics is crucial for successful entrepreneurship. Those agents, be they individuals or organizations, who have a better understanding of how social context shapes technological dynamics have an important advantage in making their ventures successful and enhancing the wealth of society.

II

Entrepreneurship in the Evolution of Industries

8

Learning and Legitimacy

Entrepreneurial Responses to Constraints on the Emergence of New Populations and Organizations

HOWARD E. ALDRICH AND TED BAKER

Pioneering founders face different conditions than founders in established populations, conditions that call for different strategies. Entrepreneurs in emerging populations must craft strategies for generating and sustaining new organizational knowledge and legitimacy. Such strategies, if successful, make it easier for member firms to organize collectively and create conditions benefiting their entire industry. The outcome of the process is not assured, however, and, thus, new populations are relatively rare. The population-level outcome of most attempts to create new firms while simultaneously building a new population is nothing at all.

The challenges facing entrepreneurial industry pioneers differ from the challenges facing new ventures that are either part of or sheltered by sponsoring organizations. They also differ from the struggles facing entrepreneurs attempting to build new businesses that will compete in established populations. Most organizational, management, and entrepreneurship research focuses on what happens in existing populations of organizations, but the processes we analyze, those that shape the struggle to create a place for a new population, come first.

Myriad factors are likely to influence whether pioneering entrepreneurs become the progenitors of new populations, including changes in the state of the overall economy. A simple credit crunch may drive otherwise promising businesses out of existence. Technological developments can place a new industry in a hot growth market or render an industry obsolete overnight. Moves by organizations in competing populations can destroy the competitive advantage shared by organizations built around new activities. More generally, however, two contextual factors in particular are likely to discourage potential founders and threaten the survival of organizations founded in the early days of an emerging population: (1) lack of effective organizational knowledge and (2) lack of internal and external legitimacy for their new activities. New ventures in what may become new populations face tremendous learning challenges. Their founders need to learn about new markets and develop the competencies to exploit new niches. At the same time, they need to establish their legitimacy with a variety of potential stakeholders, including employees, customers, regulators, vendors, and sources of finance.

In this chapter, we focus on issues of learning and legitimacy as factors influencing whether a new industry emerges around the pioneering efforts of a few early organizations or falls apart. We illustrate our argument with examples taken from a variety of industries. Many of our examples come from what is popularly known as e-commerce (short for electronic commerce) or Internet commerce. E-commerce refers to a group of industries and potential industries loosely connected by the common thread of economic transactions mediated by electronic interfaces and, in particular, the graphical user interface of the world wide web ("web"). Although there have been many historical studies of established populations, very few studies have examined processes of population emergence. Researchers have seldom examined populations that failed before establishing a niche, and only a few studies have undertaken systematic research on new populations (Miner 1993). Thus, any theoretical argument concerning the emergence and failure of new populations is necessarily speculative.

Aldrich and Fiol's (1994) evolutionary model of the legitimation of new populations focused on entrepreneurial actions embedded in multiple levels of constraints and resources. We build on their original model to examine the strategic actions that entrepreneurs, individually and in association, can take as they seek to build new industries, drawing from observations of new population emergence and failure in Internet commerce. Because Internet commerce is a very new and rapidly growing institutional field in which organizational legitimation processes are occurring at a rapid pace (Hunt and Aldrich 1998), it presents organization scholars with a rare opportunity to study ongoing processes of population emergence, and failure, in a rich environment where selection processes operate swiftly and decisively.

We draw on three types of evidence in this chapter. First, where clear parallels exist, we make use of scholarly studies of industries outside of Internet commerce. Second, because we had few scholarly studies of Internet commerce to draw upon, we illustrate our arguments with media accounts concerning this emerging institutional field. Third, we conducted field studies of several firms engaged in providing both business-to-business and business-to-consumer Internet commerce services. We were fortunate to gain access to several firms involved in creating some fundamental Internet commerce business routines and competencies. Our research included interviews, observation, and participant observation. Here, we focus on the learning and legitimacy constraints that pioneering entrepreneurs must overcome to create a niche for a new population and the cognitive and sociopolitical strategies entrepreneurs individually and collectively create in response to these constraints.

COGNITIVE AND SOCIOPOLITICAL STRATEGIES FOR NEW POPULATION CREATION

Organizational entrepreneurs in new populations face the twin problems of a lack of effective organizational knowledge and a low level of cognitive legitimacy. Pioneering entrepreneurs begin their organizing efforts without widespread knowledge and understanding of their activities. As with all new ventures, they begin at the organizational level by creating a knowledge base in their own organization, but with much more experimentation than in reproducer organizations. They must frame their activities not only around their own organizations but also within their emergent population, as they respond to inquiries and pressures from potential employees, clients and customers, suppliers, creditors, and others. As organizations in a population carve out their niche, collective action through trade associations, industry councils, and other groups brings population boundaries into sharper focus.

Learning: The Diffusion of Organizational Knowledge

In established populations, entrepreneurs can choose from a variety of existing organizational templates (Spender 1989). Joint agreement on a dominant design enables technology-based populations to push ahead with their expansion, whereas disagreement discourages potential entrepreneurs from entering. In new populations, however, beneficial templates are scarce. Instead, pioneering entrepreneurs must create their own templates for organizing the information they need for founding new ventures (Aldrich 1999, chap. 4). Without the development of a broad knowledge base for the population, low founding and high disbanding rates will hamper population growth and increase a population's vulnerability to predatory attacks from other populations. Building a knowledge base and learning vicariously from other organizations in the emerging population is therefore necessary for population growth.

A new population's growth also depends on the extent to which its potential audience learns more about it and what its expected value is to the various constituencies it affects (Suchman 1995a, 578). Customers, suppliers, creditors, employees, and others need to learn the basic facts about a new population before they can form judgments concerning their own involvement in it. A dominant design makes it easier for consumers and other potential industry participants' to learn the value of a new product. For example, the emergence of two early personal computer standards, the IBM and the Macintosh, accelerated the diffusion of knowledge about the industry to potential customers. Growing knowledge spawned many start-ups. Similarly, Internet commerce benefited from the rapid emergence of a dominant design in the fundamental enabling technology of the browser. Browsers represent part of the technological core of Internet commerce, and from a user's perspective, the Netscape and Microsoft versions were very similar. The core technology has remained fairly stable (Tushman and Murmann, this volume), whereas peripheral technical subsystems, such as audio and video Internet software, are still evolving. E-commerce populations also benefited from an extraordinary level of popular media coverage. Because the very nature of the world wide web enhances rapid diffusion of knowledge and lowers barriers to entry, the rate of new business starts—though not yet measured with any precision—appears to be both rapid and accelerating. The survival of this population, however, is likely to depend on its perceived legitimacy.

Legitimacy: Cognitive and Sociopolitical

We adopt Suchman's (1995a, 574) inclusive definition of legitimacy: "Legitimacy is a generalized perception or assumption that the actions of an entity are desirable, proper, or appropriate within some socially constructed system of norms, values, beliefs, and definitions." He proposed three types of legitimacy—pragmatic, moral, and cognitive—which we modify here, subsuming pragmatic legitimacy as part of organizational learning and adopting a two-part typology of legitimacy as either cognitive or sociopolitical. Sociopolitical legitimacy has both moral and regulatory aspects, with moral legitimacy limited to conscious assessments of right and wrong and with regulatory legitimacy referring to government approval.

Cognitive legitimacy refers to the acceptance of knowledge about a new kind of venture as a taken for granted feature of the environment. The highest form of cognitive legitimacy exists when a new product, process, or service is accepted as part of the sociocultural and organizational landscape. When an activity becomes so familiar and well known that people take it for granted, time and other organizing resources are conserved when people try to copy it, and they are more likely to succeed (Hannan and Freeman 1986, 63). From a producer's point of view, cognitive legitimacy means that new entrants to an industry are likely to copy an existing organizational form, rather than experiment with a new one. From a consumer's point of view, cognitive legitimacy means that people are knowledgeable and committed users of the product or service.

Sociopolitical legitimacy refers to the acceptance by key stakeholders, the general public, key opinion leaders, and government officials of a new venture as appropriate and right. It has two components: moral acceptance, deriving from conformity with cultural norms and values, and regulatory acceptance, deriving from conformity with governmental rules and regulations. Indicators of conformity to moral norms and values include (a) the absence of attacks by religious and civic leaders on the new form and (b) heightened public prestige of its leaders. Indicators of conformity to governmental rules and regulations include (a) laws passed to protect or monitor the industry and (b) government subsidies to the industry. For example, the Internet Tax Freedom Act, which became law in October 1998, placed a three-year moratorium on new taxes on the Internet. This act embodies the federal government's attempt to allow Internet commerce to continue its development free of attempts by states or municipalities to tax it differently from how they tax mail and phone-order purchases (Wald 1998). Protection from new taxes implicitly subsidizes firms engaging in electronic commerce. Gaining cognitive and sociopolitical legitimacy for a new industry requires both individual and collective strategies.

Individual and Collective Strategies

Founders can pursue strategies individually, but collaboration with other founders is more effective in reshaping population and community-level environments to accept a new population. First, collaborating founders may learn valuable lessons that are not yet publicly available. Second, standard designs and processes emerge more easily when collaboration enables founders to find or construct common interests. Third, the common front created through collaboration can make it more likely that outsiders will perceive the set of entrepreneurs' firms as an identifiable bounded group, a population. Fourth, collaboration provides an opportunity for organizations to pool their resources and direct their use in an organized manner, such as through trade associations.

Our use of the term strategy refers not only to conscious plans but also to any consistent stream of actions that are intended to further an entrepreneur's objectives (Mintzberg 1978). We neither claim nor believe that pioneering founders ordinarily plan out learning or legitimation strategies. Rather, the challenge of constructing and pursuing innovative opportunities typically results in a series of actions or tactics that we can describe after the fact as more or less coherent strategies (Weick 1995).

The process of learning and building legitimacy involves four levels of aggregation: organizational, within populations, between populations, and then within the entire community of populations. We treat the levels of aggregation as levels of analysis, working our way up the hierarchy. Our distinctions are analytic, not temporal. Founders' actions in building knowledge and legitimacy might involve them simultaneously in several levels, but for ease of exposition, we deal with them separately in our explanation.

COGNITIVE STRATEGIES

Every pioneering founder faces cognitive learning and legitimacy issues, whereas challenging sociopolitical issues arise less often. Thus, we devote the bulk of our attention in this chapter to cognitive rather than sociopolitical concerns. As Delacroix and Rao (1994) noted, firms in capitalist nations benefit from a diffuse belief that profit-seeking activities are valid and appropriate. Although it may be legally validated in the form of a legal charter, however, an entirely new activity often begins with low levels of knowledge, depressed cognitive legitimacy, or both. Either of these problems may be an obstacle to population growth, and founders must overcome them, or populations will grow sluggishly, if at all.

Without widespread knowledge and understanding of their activity, entrepreneurs may have difficulty maintaining the support of key constituencies. Potential customers, suppliers, and sources of financial resources may not fully comprehend the nature of the new venture. Potential employees may view jobs in the new population with a mixture of skepticism and distrust. To succeed, founders must find strategies to raise the level of public knowledge about a new activity to the point at which it is taken for granted.

Organizational-Level Strategies

The fundamental rules of organizing are widely diffused in all societies, and entrepreneurs in established populations can begin by taking such culturally defined building blocks for granted (Aldrich 1999). Knowledge about how to reproduce common forms of organization can be obtained relatively easily, such as by hiring industry veterans into a new firm. Beginning with these basic templates, founders of new ventures in established populations use feedback from their initial activities to guide their subsequent actions. The challenges of learning and establishing cognitive legitimacy are more difficult, however, when pioneering entrepreneurs must choose among disparate building blocks for new forms of activity. Relying on new and untested organizational knowledge, pioneers face critical problems of cognitive legitimacy. Without clear guidelines for assessing performance in an emerging industry, a new venture's stakeholders have difficulty weighing risk/reward trade-offs. For example, observers continue to be amazed at the valuations of Internet IPOs and wonder whether future revenue and income streams can possibly support the stock prices observed.

In an established industry, founders can justify their strategies to their employees and other stakeholders by citing tradition. Given the taken-for-granted status of such actions in an established population, few people will demand justification for them. People will recognize that much of what the firm is doing reproduces what firms in the industry have always done. In new populations however, questions and challenges from a variety of stakeholders are the order of the day, and entrepreneurs must find ways of convincing others to trust them, in spite of their risky undertaking. Trust is a critical first-level determinant of founding entrepreneurs' success because, by definition, little knowledge exists regarding their new activity. The less information people have, the more they must rely on trust. Network ties are likely to be particularly important in establishing this trust (Aldrich 1999, chap. 4). For example, founders can use the connections of third parties to certify their reliability and reputation (Podolny 1994). They can also draw on their own social skills for securing cooperation if they are adept at managing interpersonal relations (Baron and Markman 1998; Bateson 1988).

Entrepreneurs can take advantage of the inherent ambiguity in interpreting new behaviors by skillfully framing and editing their behaviors and intentions vis-à-vis the trusting parties. Pettigrew (1979, 574) argued that entrepreneurs not only create the rational and tangible aspects of organizations, but also "symbols, ideologies, languages, beliefs, rituals, and myths, aspects of the more cultural and expressive components of organizational life." Founders can emphasize those aspects of their ventures and their own backgrounds that evoke identities that others will understand as risk-oriented but responsible. For example, in the uncertain world of junk bonds, the status of third-party underwriting firms affects perceptions of quality much more than in the certain world of investment grade bonds (Podolny 1994).

To gain legitimacy, founders can emphasize the continuity between their innovative activity and those activities familiar to their customers, employees, creditors, and others. For example, some Internet customers are uncomfortable sending their credit card numbers over the Internet, and occasional news articles about hackers breaking into web sites and stealing credit card numbers out of unprotected databases has heightened public concerns about security. In response, some merchants now permit customers to place an order online and then follow up with a telephone call to provide the card account number. Potential customers thus overcome their hesitancy about shopping online because they are permitted to pay for their purchases in a familiar manner.

The generalized legitimacy of profit-seeking activities extends to the demand side of economic activities. Despite periodic waves of critical discontent with the consumerism that characterizes modern life, activities that contribute to the enhancement of consumption, for example, the construction of new malls, are assumed legitimate until proven otherwise. Accordingly, pioneering entrepreneurs in Internet commerce have adopted banal metaphors of consumption as a veneer for their radically novel ventures. Such metaphors represent strategies to gain cognitive legitimacy with consumers. Thus, we may shop online accompanied by "shopping carts," using "digital wallets" that contain "electronic cash." If we grow tired of going from store to store, we can choose to shop instead in an "online mall."

Within-Population Strategies

Within-population processes shape new populations by structuring their immediate environments. Two problems confront pioneering ventures because they are part of new populations. First, founders must create and spread useful organizational knowledge despite conditions of uncertainty and ambiguity. Under the right circumstances, founders can imitate others who have developed effective routines and competencies. Convergence on a dominant design then eases the way for new entrants. Second, founders must somehow obtain collective agreement on standards and designs so that the population becomes taken for granted by its constituents. Without accepted standards and designs, population boundaries will be ambiguous and organizational knowledge fleeting.

With startling rapidity, the web and Internet commerce have become taken-for-granted aspects of life in the United States (Hunt and Aldrich 1998). As recently as 1992, the Internet was still a tool used mainly by academics and scientists, and an anticommercial ethos prevailed. Internet participants who attempted to make commercial use of this shared tool—for example, by using e-mail and online interest groups as advertising mailing lists—were commonly "flamed" and brought into line with the cultural norms of noncommercial information sharing. The change came with the invention and dissemination of browser technology and the rapid development of commercial transaction-oriented web sites, which fomented a massive cultural revolution. New users streamed to the Internet, free of the conservative noncommercial mores of the academics and scientists who held sway in cyberspace for many years.

In addition, the essence of the Internet as an almost ubiquitous anywhere-to-anywhere connection, combined with a variety of early innovative commercial uses, led to an onslaught of media coverage (Hunt and Aldrich 1998). Even people who have never been online are unlikely to have missed the message that Internet commerce has become very important. Advertisements for online merchants have proliferated in traditional advertising venues, including television, newspapers, and billboards. Growth in retail sales over the web has continually outstripped the projections of well-informed observers. Industry associations and consulting groups reported that online sales more than tripled during the 1998 holiday season, compared with 1997 (Quick 1998), although only a doubling had been expected. Several popular sites were brought to their virtual knees by the unexpected surge in business. Symbolic milestones continue to pile up. For example, with Charles Schwab surpassing Merrill Lynch, "the biggest online brokerage firm is worth more than the biggest of all brokerage firms" (Anders, McGeehan, and Kranhold 1998). Overall, Internet commerce has rapidly emerged as an accepted and normal part of the commercial landscape of contemporary life.

Issues surrounding dominant designs. Dominant designs comprise an agreed upon architecture and a set of components constituting a product or service. During the period following a radical innovation that initiates a new population, an era of ferment may arise in which struggles occur between contending designs. The era of ferment ends when a dominant design is selected for the core subsystem. An era of incremental change follows (Anderson and Tushman 1990; Tushman and Murman, this volume). Convergence toward an accepted design is facilitated if new ventures find it easy to imitate pioneers, rather than seek further innovation.

The lack of convergence on a dominant design in new industries constrains the perceived reliability of founding firms by increasing confusion about what standards should be followed. Founders not only must convince skeptics of their organization's staying power but also must fend off organizations offering slightly different versions of their products and services, creating confusion in the minds of constituents. For example, the embryonic "electronic cash" industry seems to have suffered from the lack of a dominant design. Even with the proliferation of credit cards in the U.S., people still use cash and write millions of checks. In theory, it makes sense to have an electronic equivalent to cash for use on the Internet. An electronic wallet might then contain credit cards, debit-card check equivalents, and cash.

Several pioneering firms, headed by well-respected and well-funded entrepreneurs, have seen the perceived market for an electronic wallet as an opportunity. At these pioneering firms, managers have encountered a problem they describe as "the need for currency to be universal." They have in mind the phrase stamped on a dollar, "Legal tender for all debts, public and private." To convince consumers to accept a branded form of electronic cash, the firm providing that brand must ensure that it is widely accepted by merchants. To convince merchants to accept their particular brand of electronic cash, providers must demonstrate that it enjoys widespread acceptance by consumers. A proliferation of diverse forms of electronic cash will slow progress toward any particular form or brand achieving successful penetration. If convergence on a standard for electronic currency does not occur, the perceived need for a cash equivalent might pass, in which case the entrepreneurial opportunity would be lost.

Some populations depend more heavily than others on convergence around a dominant design. Many web sites, perhaps an increasing percentage, have adopted a "shopping cart" metaphor. Shoppers frequenting these sites are able to make purchases in more or less the same way at each site. Merchants imitating this approach are likely to benefit because consumers will take the "check-out" process for granted. Additionally, to the extent that consumers find that many sites structure purchase transactions similarly, a site adopting the common approach will seem "normal" and therefore legitimate, and convergence on a dominant design will proceed. At present, the Internet continues to support many different ways of making a purchase. Consumers may find it difficult to figure out what steps are required to make a purchase, to judge the adequacy of security provisions in place, or to determine how difficult it will be to make a return, should the need arise. Because a dominant design for Internet commerce is not fully entrenched (Ghosh 1998; Tenenbaum, Chowdhry, and Hughes 1997), Internet merchants using inconvenient ways of buying can still co-exist. If a dominant design emerges, these merchants will either adapt to it or fail.

Convergence on a dominant design occurs through the imitation and copying of vicarious learning, as followers adopt a leader's approach, perhaps with some enhancement. A new venture's ability to imitate others depends on whether knowledge is protected by legal instruments—patents, copyrights, and trade secrets—and on whether the innovation is codified (Teece 1987). If an innovation cannot be legally protected and involves a product or process whose nature is transparently obvious to outsiders, others may freely copy the innovation. By contrast, if the innovation can be protected and its nature is difficult to understand, except through learning by doing, others are unlikely to imitate it (Dosi 1988). Such conditions can exacerbate discord over a dominant design. If the design can't be protected but is hard to copy, imperfect imitations may proliferate. Finally, a design that can be protected but is easy to adopt may lead to licensing arrangements. This may be the case with the recent proliferation of Internet commerce patents. The technology for implementing fundamental metaphors is simple to copy or improve upon, but the underlying ideas seem to be generating knowledge that can be patented.

Vicarious learning about forms of Internet commerce may be easier than in other industries. For example, the parent company of retailer Victoria's Secret failed in an early venture to put The Limited Express retail operations into an online mall. Subsequently, firm representatives studied the Internet commerce web sites of 18 competitors, analyzing 75 aspects of each firm's online presence. What they learned enabled them to try again, bringing the Victoria's Secret site successfully online (Quick 1998). Vicarious learning is also enhanced if industry leaders deliberately create a de facto standard, with the expectation that lesser players will follow. For example, a consortium of major banks formed a joint venture with IBM in 1998 to "create a common industry interface for retail banking over the Internet" (Ghosh 1998, 135). Although would-be competitors attempting to get between banks and their customers may reject the standard that emerges, smaller banks are likely to adopt the standards that emerge from the banking consortium.

Web-based commerce is now going through an era of ferment in which struggles are occurring between contending designs. In some sectors, dominant designs are beginning to emerge, suggesting that convergence among firms is likely. The greater transparency of contending designs has facilitated imitability and learning. New ventures find it easier to imitate pioneers, rather than seek further innovation, but it appears that the life of dominant designs will be relatively short.

Collective action and business interest associations. Trade associations, as well as less formally organized business groups, contribute to learning and legitimacy in new populations. Initial collaborations between organizations in new populations begin informally, in networks of interfirm relations, but some later develop into more formalized strategic alliances, consortia, and trade associations (Powell 1990; Van de Ven and Garud 1991). Trade associations are associations of organizations in the same population that devise product or process standards via trade committees and publish trade journals (Aldrich and Staber 1988). They also conduct marketing campaigns to enhance the industry's standing in the eyes of the public and organize trade fairs at which customers and suppliers can gain a sense of the industry's stability.

Trade associations are minimalist organizations, able to operate on low overhead and quickly adapt to changing conditions, and are thus easier to found than, for example, production organizations (Halliday, Powell, and Granfors 1987). Large numbers of Internet and Internet commerce trade associations have already emerged, as documented in Hunt and Aldrich (1998), although the role of industry associations in Internet commerce has not yet emerged as fully distinct from the role of less formalized associations. Because the industry is so new, formal studies of e-commerce trade associations do not yet exist but the culture of technical cooperation in the development of Internet technologies seems to have eased the way to a rapid proliferation of slightly more formalized trade groups.

A typical Internet commerce company is involved in very large numbers of collaborative alliances, joint ventures, and licensing deals with other industry players. Welles (1999, 25) noted that "there are competitors who sit on each other's boards, invest in each other's companies, and ask each other's advice. E-commerce has been changing all the rules." He suggested that because the industry is so young and unstable, formal organizations and interorganizational relations are less important than in other populations. Instead, peer groups and networks among individuals continue to be more important and more stable than formalized ties between organizations.

Trade associations and other interfirm entities play a critical role in helping founders promote an industry's cognitive legitimacy because they can raise its standards to a taken-for-granted status (Aldrich and Staber 1988). Trade associations can also increase the rate of population-level learning. For example, trade associations in Japan have played a very active role in linking their members to developments overseas. They have created libraries of foreign language publications and established databases of patents and scientific reference manuals. Japanese trade associations have also sent delegations overseas to study research programs in firms, laboratories, and public agencies (Lynn and McKeown 1988).

Industry associations can play multiple roles, supporting both stability and change. Evidence presented by Rindova and Fombrun (this volume) supports the important point that a dominant industry participant can use an industry association to help define and legitimate industry boundaries but simultaneously use the legitimacy of its own position to challenge those same industry boundaries. For example, "rather than looking for further alignment with the industry through the administrative body of the association, Starbucks has created alliances and partnerships outside the industry. . . . Other industry players are also increasingly pursuing distribution alliances, co-branding agreements, and acquisitions to keep up with industry growth."

Internet commerce has not yet benefited from all the advantages that effective trade associations can bring. From the beginning, however, the high degree of technological collaboration and informal alliances characterizing the industry have provided functional substitutes for formal associations. If the industry evolves to a more competitive than cooperative set of populations, informal ties and alliances are likely to be replaced by industry associations taking a much stronger role. In the application service provider industry, such a strong association has already emerged. The ASP Industry Consortium was formed in May 1999 and quickly enrolled the largest firms in the industry (Aldrich and Fortune 2000). By the end of the year, it had over 250 members.

Between-Population Cognitive Strategies

Interindustry processes—the nature of relations between industries, whether competing or cooperating—affect the distribution of resources in the environment and the terms on which they are available to entrepreneurs. New populations are, in a sense, surrounded by established populations and are thus vulnerable to attack. Organizations in established populations that feel threatened sometimes attempt to alter the terms on which resources are available to emerging industries by questioning their efficacy or conformity to the established order. Even after a new population grows into a recognized entity, organizations in other populations may withhold recognition or acceptance of it. Cognitive legitimacy can be achieved if a critical mass of founders discovers a way to unite and build a reputation for their new industry as a visible and taken-for-granted entrant into the larger community. Business interest associations and political action groups that organize across industry boundaries also facilitate population-level learning and cognitive legitimacy (Aldrich 1999).

Because Internet commerce spawns so many new potential populations of organizations, it is difficult to separate between-population versus within-population cognitive strategies. The process through which cognitive legitimacy develops is simultaneously implicated in the processes of boundary formation around a new population. Groups of organizations that achieve legitimacy as a group are consequently more likely to emerge and be sustained as an identifiable population. The lack of clear boundaries between emergent Internet commerce populations stands out in the amorphous character of the value chain. Where in the process of bringing goods and services to online purchasers is value added? Where will profits eventually accrue? Internet commerce entrepreneurs have difficulty determining which services will become commodities and which represent opportunities to develop rare and hard to imitate competencies. Companies such as OrderTrust, which bills itself as "The Leading Order Processing Network," have been built on the idea that it makes no sense for most firms to develop competencies in the logistics involved in turning Internet orders into delivered goods. From this perspective, order management and logistics should be commodity services, purchased by most Internet merchants rather than handled in-house. Other service providers, such as major systems integration and information technology consulting firms, are nonetheless trying to sell merchants their own customized order-processing systems. They argue that order processing and logistics capabilities will enable some Internet merchants to stand out from the pack.

Given the ease with which companies can create a presence on the web, and the possibility of creating a successful merchant presence independent of any physical infrastructure, it seems likely that logistics and order processing will be important business services complementing Internet sales and marketing activities. Many thousands of companies whose core competencies are in sales and marketing will need to acquire the ability to manage networks of suppliers and turn orders into completed transactions. It is unclear, however, whether order-processing networks will emerge and thrive as a population of organizations. This struggle is much like traditional make-or-buy decisions, except that in the Internet environment, the outcome will determine whether a new industry will exist five years from now.

Organizational and population boundaries appear to be very fluid and unclear in Internet commerce, taken as a whole, and rather than becoming clearer, boundaries are less clear from month to month. Boundaries between emerging populations within Internet commerce were unclear throughout 1999: will a single population of organizations provide Internet access, search capabilities, and content, or will these activities be carried out by distinct industries? Ongoing consolidations and mergers between well-known industry players muddy population boundaries further.

Blurred boundaries also characterize the relation between Internet and traditional merchants. Traditionally, organizations in established populations that felt threatened by newcomers have attempted to undermine a new venture's cognitive legitimacy through rumors and information suppression or inaccurate dissemination. For example, early mail- and phone-order computer supply stores in the United States were highly specialized, selling mainly to people who were very knowledgeable about electronics and were building or modifying their own equipment. When the industry began to grow rapidly in the 1980s, selling to amateurs, traditional walk-in stores argued that mail- and phone-order firms did not provide after-sales service and thus were an inferior form. But traditional merchandisers have made only a few serious attempts to undermine the cognitive legitimacy of Internet merchants. Some small traditional booksellers, adopting a defensive posture, have emphasized the unique pleasures of intimate local bookstores. In contrast, some of the larger national bookstore chains have adopted a more aggressive posture by creating their own web presence. Far from attacking Amazon.com as in any way illegitimate, Barnes and Noble engaged in a struggle to beat Amazon at its own game.

Companies involved in electronic data interchange (EDI)—a more traditional means by which firms exchange data over public or dedicated telephone lines—are using their industry associations in an attempt to improve their position over more generic Internet solutions. In general, existing populations seem to view the Internet more as an opportunity than as a threat. Many other populations, however, such as travel agents and insurance brokers, have only recently begun to show an awareness of the serious threat posed to their livelihood by online commerce. Pressure from online travel service firms has already pushed many smaller conventional firms out of business.

Industry associations have made fairly weak responses to the threat posed to their members by e-commerce, perhaps because of the lack of clear boundaries around Internet commerce populations. Many trade associations straddle the boundaries of several industries, narrowly defined. Dealing with external relations requires attention to domain definition and various forms of interorganizational relations, and a heterogeneous membership complicates such matters, making collective rationality difficult (Olson 1965). Adding another industrial sector to an already heterogeneous association severely complicates governance (Aldrich and Staber 1988). The more diversity within an association, the greater the problem of governance. Problematic internal governance might cause potential members to create a new association instead of joining an existing one. The amorphous boundaries and extreme heterogeneity of Internet commerce organizations are thus likely to undermine any attempt by any one industry association to assert leadership.

Community-Level Cognitive Strategies

Community-level conditions affect the rate at which an industry grows by affecting the diffusion of knowledge about a new activity and the extent to which it is publicly or officially accepted. If founders have pursued effective trust-building and reliability-enhancing strategies within their emerging industry and have established a positive reputation vis-à-vis other industries, they have laid the groundwork for attaining legitimacy at the community level. If not, then population survival becomes much more problematic. At this level, founders are no longer working as isolated individuals. Instead, many vehicles for collective action are involved: industry councils, cooperative alliances, trade associations, and other organizations. At the community or societal level, three sets of organizations and institutions play an important role in population legitimacy: the media, educational institutions, and certifying agencies.

First, established industries enjoy an enormous benefit from the institutionalized diffusion of knowledge about their activities. The social space (Delacroix and Rao 1994) an industry has achieved in a society is sustained, in part, by widespread understanding of how it fits into the community. In the beginning, organizations in the new industry are too rare to create the critical mass needed to raise the public's level of understanding of a new population. Reporters, newspaper and magazine editors, and other mass media gatekeepers create inaccurate descriptions because they are unfamiliar with the set of terms for describing the activity. Thus, potential entrepreneurs may be grievously misled if they rely on such reports, and mistakes in imitating the new activity will be common (Phillips 1960). As media gatekeepers become more familiar with new populations, their accounts become more accurate and persuasive.

Second, educational institutions create and spread knowledge about dominant competencies (Romanelli 1989b), thus putting resources in the hands of potential founders. To the extent that specific competencies underlie particular populations, the activities of educational institutions may increase the diversity of organizational communities. Universities, research institutes, and associated programs not only conduct research but also train persons who are able to exploit the latest research products. Dean Frederick Terman of Stanford University's Engineering School promoted close and reciprocal ties between Stanford and local industry in the 1940s, helping to build an interdependent network of technical scholars. Educational institutions also "formalize and centralize information by establishing courses and degree programs that train students in basic competencies. Once technologies are understood, and stabilized and identifiable jobs (e.g., computer engineer) emerge in industry, colleges and universities take over much of the training of skilled personnel" (Romanelli 1989b, 230). Historically, the growth of national educational systems has spurred founding rates by spreading generalized competencies that give entrepreneurs the necessary skills to succeed (Nelson 1994).

New populations must either build on the competencies already supported by educational institutions or find ways to encourage the provision of new ones. In technology-based industries, the basic research on which firms draw has often been generated in university laboratories a decade or more before it was commercialized (Link and Bauer 1989). For example, the basic ideas for cochlear implant devices were developed in the late 1950s and early 1960s, almost two decades before the ideas were fully commercialized. Thus, firms such as Nucleus and 3M had an already developed pool of scientific expertise from which they could draw consultants and employees (Van de Ven and Garud 1991). The growth of the Internet and the world wide web will increase the amount of information available to nascent entrepreneurs who are diligent in their search for new opportunities. Accordingly, the founding rate of information-technology based firms will probably increase in the early decades of this century.

Third, new populations can achieve legitimacy through the actions of certifying institutions. In the first few decades of the industrial revolution in the United States, fledgling industries were disadvantaged by the lack of independent agencies and institutions that could certify their legitimacy (Zucker 1986). The population of organizations that could certify trust and reputation grew slowly, spurred on by trade associations, a growing consumer movement, occasional government commissions, and the rise of a commercial market for independent assessment of firms and products. The growth of independent consumer watchdog organizations was a result of battles between organizational entrepreneurs with very different cultural conceptions of how consumers could be protected from inferior and unsafe products. In addition to nonprofit groups such as Consumers Union, commercial firms evaluating products and services have also flourished (Rao 1999, this volume). Among these are certified public accounting (CPA) firms, which play an important role in certifying the financial soundness of corporations (Han 1994). Web sites now commonly provide evidence of third party certification of the security of information sent to the site. A quick search turned up a large number of different certifying agents, and it appears that no dominant set of third parties has yet emerged. Perhaps CPA firms will enter this market space aggressively over the next several years.

Interaction with key constituents helps define a population's boundaries. Recognition by public agencies and vocational training programs and certification by private and nonprofit organizations lends an aura of legitimacy and credibility to a new population. In time, if the population survives, it gains a taken-for-granted status in the organizational community. For many populations, however, issues of moral acceptance and regulatory approval impede their growth, and dealing with those issues requires different strategies to gain legitimacy.

SOCIOPOLITICAL LEGITIMACY STRATEGIES

Sociopolitical legitimacy is the acceptance by key stakeholders—the general public, opinion leaders, and government officials—of a new venture as appropriate and right. Sociopolitical legitimacy has two components: the moral value of an activity according to cultural norms and acceptance of an activity by political and regulatory authorities. Founders must find ways either of adapting to existing norms and laws or of changing them. In the process, they may have to fend off attacks from religious and civic leaders and find ways of raising the public's image of the population. Through strategic social action, entrepreneurs construct new meanings that may eventually alter community norms and values. Social contexts, from this perspective, not only represent patterns of taken-for-granted meaning, but also sites within which the construction of new meaning takes place. Founding entrepreneurs of innovative ventures—the first stage in creating new populations—are initiators in this process of reconstruction.

Organization-Level Strategies

At the organizational level, few founders face serious moral legitimacy issues in established capitalist societies, because entrepreneurs have a presumptive right to create new ventures. For founders involved in struggles over the morality of their organizations, however, severe challenges can arise. For example, organizations providing abortion services are involved in a very public and sometimes violent struggle that has continued for decades. Purveyors of online pornography are embroiled in controversies in which supporters of family values are in pitched battles with advocates of free speech. By themselves, individual founders can do little to overcome the moral deficiencies attributed to them. Gaining moral legitimacy often requires collective rather than individual action.

Organizations seeking moral legitimacy must be wary of appearing cynical or self-interested, because the public's moral calculus rests on communal rather than interest-based foundations. Nonetheless, Suchman's (1995a, 580–82) proposed typology of four forms of moral legitimacy does suggest the general outlines of a strategy for new populations.

Consequential legitimacy rests on a claim that what an organization produces is good for the public, such as better health care or a cleaner environment. For example, what might otherwise be attacked as the crass commercialism of many web sites has been successfully legitimated because it results in the provision of myriad free services and sources of information online. For the price of being subjected to nonstop banner advertising, users can access millions of web sites without paying any fee. Free Internet access and free email are available under the same terms.

Procedural legitimacy depends on an organization using socially accepted techniques to generate its products or services. In situations in which outputs are difficult to evaluate, procedures might be the only observable activities. Many pornographic web sites now take users through a series of steps asking for verification that the consumer is an adult. Some sites advertise products such as the "Net Nanny," designed to allow parents to keep children from accessing adult sites. Such procedural steps generate an aura of concern for children, regardless of whether they actually stop inappropriate access.

Entrepreneurs typically pay as little attention as possible to the web of government rules and agencies that shape commerce in the U.S. (Reynolds and White 1997). With the exception of highly regulated fields such as biotechnology, technology entrepreneurs have generally been portrayed as treating government and politics as, at worst, a hindrance to innovation and growth and, at best, an annoyance to be ignored for as long as possible. "The Valley guys generally start out with the view that politics doesn't have any meaning, and that politicians are bumper stickers traveling as human beings" (Miles 1998, 182).

Structural legitimacy stems from organizations displaying the proper form expected of organizations in their population. Clearly, for new populations, the form itself is still in flux. Thus, mimetic isomorphism—copying the most common or highly valued structure in the population—is not an option. Instead, founders have an opportunity to create the structures that will come to be perceived as legitimate. On the web, particular ways of structuring economic transactions appear to be emerging as legitimate. We may already be approaching a time when online consumers ask, "Does this site offer an online shopping cart and a guarantee against credit card theft like those I'm accustomed to seeing at Amazon.com? Will it be easy to make a return if I don't like the product or service I receive?" Online auction services are currently growing very rapidly, but currently no clearinghouse certifies the promises of buyers or sellers who trade through the web. We expect that simple mechanisms will develop quickly that lead buyers and sellers to trust their trading partners. Already, escrow services—third parties that hold buyers' funds until product or service delivery is made—are becoming available.

Finally, *personal legitimacy* depends on the charisma of organizational leaders. The mass media periodically promotes an Internet entrepreneur as the next charismatic business leader, such as Jeff Bezos of Amazon.com or James Barksdale of Netscape. Because charisma is unstable and difficult to institutionalize, its long-run value to an organization is questionable. For new ventures, however, charisma plays an important role in mobilizing resources in the absence of personal assets or experience (Aldrich 1999, chap. 4).

Within-Population Strategies

Collective action constitutes the foundation of sociopolitical strategies for population-level action. As we argued in discussing cognitive strategies, the formation of other types of organizations can strongly affect the emergence of new populations as stable entities. Gaining moral legitimacy for a new population sometimes involves altering existing norms and values, something individual organizations usually lack the resources to accomplish. Similarly, winning legal and regulatory acceptance generally requires campaign contributions, political action committees, lobbying, and other costly activities beyond the reach of most individual organizations. Thus, early in a new population's growth, sociopolitical issues are often addressed by interorganizational action.

One traditional interorganizational strategy for avoiding entanglement with government regulators is to develop structures and routines of self-regulation (Aldrich 1999). The online pornography industry, perhaps the oldest and most firmly established industry doing business on the Internet, is actively engaged in attempts at self-regulation as it works to avoid additional government-imposed controls. As in most public debates over pornography, strong coalitions emerged quickly in support of free speech. For example, the Citizens Internet Empowerment Coalition (CIEC) web site describes its organization as "a large and diverse group of Internet users, businesses, nonprofit groups, and civil liberties advocates, who share the common goal of protecting the First Amendment and the viability of the Internet as a means of free expression, education, and commerce. CIEC members believe that parents, not the United States Government, are the best and most appropriate judges of what material is appropriate for themselves and their children" (CIEC web site 1998). The CIEC web page lists an impressive membership roster and delivers sophisticated ideological arguments in favor of extending unfettered rights of free speech to the Internet.

The online pornography industry benefits directly from the concerted political and ideological actions of groups such as the CIEC. One victory was claimed when the U.S. Supreme Court declared the Communications Decency Act unconstitutional in June 1997. Whether free speech arguments and attempts to establish legitimacy for online pornography will succeed is beyond our ability to predict, but success may hinge partly on the ability of the industry to find a way to enforce a consistent self-regulatory discipline across a surging population of pornography vendors facing minimal barriers to entry.

Sociopolitical approval, especially regulatory approval from governmental agencies, may be jeopardized if collective action fails. Failure to agree on common standards leaves a new population vulnerable to illegal and unethical acts by some of its members. Such actions may bring the entire population into moral disrepute and jeopardize its legitimacy. For example, purveyors of child pornography on the Internet—an activity lacking a strong political constituency—might seriously damage any claims to effective self-regulation made by other online adult-entertainment businesses. In contrast, mobilization around a collective goal may enable new populations to shape the course of government regulation and perhaps even win favorable treatment. As Edelman and Suchman (1997, 489) noted, organizations and associations are not only subjects of the law but also builders of it. If early founders succeed in creating an interpretive frame that links a new population to established norms and values, later founders will marshal support much more easily.

Internet commerce pioneers have been relatively slow to form effective political action organizations. Eventually, the evolving Internet community involved large numbers of not-for-profit technology alliances involving the government and private organizations, user groups, open platform proponents, and other structured forms of cooperation. Nonetheless, until the late 1990s, information technology and Internet entrepreneurs did not seek active engagement in the political process that shapes government regulations. In 1998 and 1999, however, a surge of government activism drove Internet competitors from their political isolationism.

The U.S. Justice Department, now a primary participant in the "browser wars," began arguing in a very public way in 1998 about whether the federal government should be interfering in the competitive battle taking place between Microsoft and AOL's Netscape operations (Wolffe 1998). Leading Internet competitors were drawn into a struggle over the sociopolitical legitimacy of their industry. The heads of various software companies received wide media coverage as they traveled to Washington D.C. to present their arguments and complaints before congressional committees. The congressional hearings were something of an epiphany as people watched "the billionaire geek who couldn't believe that guys who failed high school physics were judging his software getting slapped down hard by politicians who couldn't believe that a guy who didn't grasp high school civics was giving them backtalk" (Miles 1998, 182).

Having overcome their political reticence, the heads of Silicon Valley firms seem to be demonstrating an eagerness to have the government do their bidding. Powerful political consultants and lobbyists—for example Tony Podesta, brother of former White House Chief of Staff John Podesta—are eager to help bridge the cultural divide separating Silicon Valley power brokers from those in Washington, D.C. (Miles 1998). Almost every week in 1998 brought another pronouncement from a major player regarding how the antitrust suits involving participants in the browser wars should be resolved.

Between-Population and Community-Level Strategies

The emergence and growth of new populations may be threatened by sociopolitical attacks by other populations that depend on the same resources exploited by the emerging industry. In defending against such attacks, industry associations are often useful tools, both for established and emerging industries. In general, however, Internet commerce has faced few effective attacks on its sociopolitical legitimacy from other industries. Rather, the wide variety of alliances that has characterized the industry since the beginning has been able to draw in participants from many different industries (Hunt and Aldrich 1998). To a large extent, the industries that might have been expected to attack Internet commerce—for example, commercial banks, which might fear further erosion of influence over the U.S. payment system—have instead become participants in the new forms of commerce. They have treated the Internet as an opportunity rather than a threat.

In contrast, in the biotechnology industry, lack of support at the community level by government officials responding to citizens' concerns has undercut efforts by the industry to secure sociopolitical approval in Europe. Popular disapproval has been a big problem for the biotechnology industry in Germany. In addition to federal regulatory barriers, local elected officials in Germany were hostile to biotechnology laboratories in their communities. Environmentalists, such as the politically powerful Green movement, spearheaded public opposition to genetic technology research and production. Sociopolitical opposition, combined with the traditional conservatism of the

German business community, resulted in only 17 biotechnology companies in Germany in 1994, compared with about 1,200 in the United States. "Public suspicion of biotechnology in Europe has led many European chemical and pharmaceutical firms to establish research laboratories in the United States and to develop research, development, and other alliances with American firms" (Ryan, Freeman, and Hybels 1995, 346–47).

Nor has the U.S. been immune to the suppression of promising industries. In the 1980s, the removal of federal regulations in many industries made us aware of how many populations—for example, cellular telephony—were suppressed by implicit governmental strictures against their activities. But it is unlikely that Internet commerce will meet this fate. The high degree of cross-population cooperation in Internet commerce—outside of the browser wars and a few other big issues—is likely to enhance the overall political influence of Internet commerce industry groups and minimize problems of gaining community-level sociopolitical legitimacy. Two pieces of evidence mentioned above—passage of the Internet Tax Freedom Act, and the Supreme Court's finding that the Communication Decency Act is unconstitutional—also suggest that Internet commerce industry associations will not face a major struggle over issues of community level sociopolitical legitimacy.

We have argued that issues of cognitive legitimacy are more salient than are sociopolitical issues for organizations in most new populations. Accordingly, we have devoted most of this chapter to cognitive issues. Nonetheless, issues of moral and regulatory legitimacy require strategies at the organizational, intraindustry, interindustry, and community levels. Participants in Internet commerce have formed large numbers of alliances, largely around technological development, since the early days of the industry. Recently, in response to political activism by the government and family-values coalitions, these alliances have become more highly politicized. Moreover, because of the extraordinary growth and popularity of the Internet, there has been very little opposition from any particular quarter to the growth of Internet commerce. Rather than joining the battle against emerging populations, most industries have jumped on the bandwagon. We will be interested in seeing whether sociopolitical struggles become more important when, eventually, resource growth slows and processes of competition begin to play a stronger role relative to forces of legitimation.

CONCLUSION: NEW POPULATIONS AND THE WEB

Given the organizational, intraindustry, interindustry, and community conditions facing pioneering founders in new populations, different strategies are called for than those used by founders in established populations. Gaining the trust of stakeholders within and around the firm provides a foundation on which to build a knowledge base through cooperative exchange with similar organizations. Such strategies, in turn, make it easier for member firms to organize collectively and to build a positive reputation of their industry as an enduring reality. After a dominant design and standards are set within a population, its boundaries come into sharper focus. New entrants are then judged on their conformity to the institutionalized order. An established reputation also facilitates the co-optation of institutional actors, ultimately improving a population's chances of achieving effective collective action and legitimacy.

The period during which a new industry emerges deserves more attention from entrepreneurship researchers because the struggle to carve out a niche for a new industry involves such strong forces that the events of that period may be forever imprinted on the organizations that persist (Stinchcombe 1965). Indeed, our model of population emergence suggests a new activity pattern in which new populations eventually become integrated into their interorganizational and community-level environments. As settled members of the community, new populations take their place as defenders of the status quo. Many promising new activities clearly never realize their potential because founders fail to develop trusting relations with stakeholders, are unable to cope with opposing industries, and never win external support.

What forms will Internet commerce and associated populations take in the future? Many different entrepreneurs are pushing their own visions of Internet commerce, and they have created a variety of organizations pursuing distinct goals. Many observers are excited that the Internet provides an opportunity for small and thinly capitalized new ventures to achieve global reach overnight. Others—for example, Internet commerce pioneer Shikhar Ghosh—predict that because the Internet reduces the importance of physical distance, makes rapid growth easier, and allows targeted and differentiated services, "a small number of companies can meet the diverse needs of large segments of the global market" (Ghosh 1998, 133). In this rapidly evolving environment, we cannot predict which industries will become more or less concentrated in response to Internet-based innovations.

Taken-for-granted assumptions among some groups of Internet commerce participants are sometimes heavily contested by the visions and experiments of other participants. For example, the "portal wars" are competitive attempts to attract customers to web sites like Yahoo.com that serve as portals that consumers use as regular routes to access Internet resources. The larger the number of users a portal can attract, the more money it can charge for the right to place advertising on its web site. Many companies are paying millions of dollars to successful portal sites to put advertising banners in front of the portals' users. The implicit business model is very traditional: attract customers through advertising and pull them into your (usually virtual) store.

At the same time, a new business model is being constructed around the use of "intelligent agents" or "shopbots" and "electronic shoppers," which is software that runs on the Internet and searches for information fitting a profile selected by a consumer (Kalakota and Whinston 1996). These agents are expected to be able to act as highly intelligent personal shoppers, coursing through the Internet, looking for good deals on products and services a consumer or a business wants to buy. The irony is that in the face of an effective "bot," pull-style advertising on Internet portals could become much less valuable. Merchants can advertise heavily, but if Internet consumers use intelligent agents to compare available deals, all that matters is price, terms, and conditions. The importance of brand and image might erode very rapidly. If a merchant offers goods and services, the bot will find them, subject their offerings to cold, hard comparisons with other merchants, and help the consumer to make an informed purchase decision. Pull-style advertising becomes largely moot.

Overall, the point we want to make is very simple. Internet commerce has arrived. With spectacular speed, it has become part of our lives. But it has arrived as a proliferation of experiments with products, services, technologies, and organizational forms. In the true spirit of evolutionary arguments, we find ourselves fascinated by the open-ended nature of the emerging populations of organizations being born on the Internet today. No one knows which entrepreneurial visions will become the foundations for new industries and which will disappear. Potentially spectacular new industries seem to emerge weekly, built on the taken-for-granted infrastructure of the Internet. The Internet and Internet commerce provide primordial organizational soup from which we may expect a tantalizing variety of incipient populations to emerge very quickly. Organization scholars face a forward looking opportunity, and challenge, to study the dynamics of entrepreneurship and the social construction of organizational, population, interpopulation, and community-level dynamics.

We have outlined a model that helps us to understand the processes through which the individual and concerted efforts of entrepreneurs sometimes result in the founding of new industries. More often, however, the result is nothing at all, leaving little trace of what was once dreamed and attempted. Our model remains evolutionary—the future is open-ended and uncertain, and every entrepreneurial thrust and parry faces a challenging selection environment. However, some entrepreneurs *do* found new populations, and our argument has attempted to give the role of entrepreneurial strategy its due.

9

Entrepreneurial Action in the
Creation of the Specialty Coffee Niche

VIOLINA P. RINDOVA AND CHARLES J. FOMBRUN

Entrepreneurship research has been traditionally concerned with the role of the entrepreneur—the person who creates an organization to pursue an opportunity (Gartner 1985; Stevenson, Roberts, and Grousbeck 1989). Economists, who set the agenda for the field of entrepreneurship, highlighted the role of the entrepreneur as a bearer of risk and uncertainty (Knight 1921), as an innovator who transforms industries (Schumpeter 1950), and as an alert actor who discovers opportunities in the form of unfilled market niches (Kirzner 1973). The discovery of opportunity requires awareness of demographic, industry, and sociocultural changes, of new knowledge development, and of the existence of system incongruities (Drucker 1993). In addition to discovering an opportunity, however, an entrepreneur can create one through the process of creative destruction (Schumpeter 1950). Creative destruction refers to the innovation process through which entrepreneurs invent not just new products, but new methods of production and distribution, and strike at the heart, not just at the margins of existing competitors.

Whereas innovation has received the greatest amount of attention as a means for creating opportunities for industry change and transformation (Romanelli 1991), more recently researchers have drawn attention to entrepreneurs' capacities to generate cognitive and institutional change (Rao

The authors would like to acknowledge the support of the Berkeley Center for Entrepreneurial Studies at the Leonard Stern School of Business, New York University.

1994). The macro-cognitive approach to entrepreneurship emphasizes that an entrepreneur can pursue changes in the marketplace by promoting changes in the patterns of meaning that govern the exchanges between the venture and key stakeholders (Aldrich and Fiol 1994). These new theoretical ideas need further development with regard to the specific activities and strategies that entrepreneurs use to shape their market and institutional contexts.

The purpose of the study reported here was to examine the specific activities through which entrepreneurs seek to create a change in both their market and their institutional environments. The study uses the empirical setting of the specialty coffee niche, which emerged as a rapidly growing niche in the context of the declining U.S. coffee industry in the 1980s and 1990s. Past research has treated the emergence of such niches as opportunities created by exogenous industry changes, including deregulation, technological discontinuities, or changes in consumer preferences (Delacroix and Solt 1988; Drucker 1993). In contrast, our study focuses on the endogenous entrepreneurial activities that create opportune changes in firms' environments. We show that rather than discovering an open environmental space created by an exogenous change, entrepreneurs in the specialty coffee industry created their own environment by restructuring the social space of the coffee industry, through their specialty products, as well as through their efforts to educate consumers. Rather then being pulled by preexisting demand or pushed by technological change, specialty coffee retailers developed specialized product knowledge in a community of roasters and retailers and then communicated this knowledge to a gradually expanding niche of consumers.

From a traditional entrepreneurship perspective specialty coffee retailers were better able to satisfy latent consumer needs by modifying the methods of coffee production and improving the product quality. From a traditional population ecology perspective, the specialty coffee retailers are specialists that partitioned the resources available to the industry with the traditional commercial roasters, which are coffee generalists (Carroll 1988). Although both of these approaches capture important aspects of the change, they do not explain how an old and familiar commodity like coffee became a trendy, life-style beverage; how one small roaster became the dominant player in the industry and one of the most visible brands of the 1990s; or how an industry consisting of small scattered ventures captured 30% of the coffee market, for which large commercial roasters competed vigorously (Andrews 1992).

To understand these profound changes in the industry, we trace the actions of key players over time and show how they cumulatively led to changing perceptions of coffee, to changes in consumer lifestyles, and, ultimately, to higher levels of industry growth. In studying the construction of the market for specialty coffee, we were interested in the effects of entrepreneurial activities on the overall niche, as well as on the relative competitive positions of the players. The construction of the market resulted from the interactions of multiple actors in the organizational field (DiMaggio and Powell 1983), including coffee brokers, roasters, retailers, roaster-retailers, design firms, industry media, general business media, leaders and imitators, chains and independent single stores and cart operators. Yet within this community of firms, some accumulated a disproportionate share of resources and achieved dominant positions. For example, in the early 1980s the current industry leader, the Starbucks Coffee Company, had only six to seven stores, while a now relatively unknown coffee outfit from Berkeley, Café Espresso Roma, had more than 30 stores operating in different college towns under different Italian names. By 1990, Starbucks and Gloria Jean's Coffee Bean both had around 100 stores and were contending the leadership position. Today, Starbucks is a multinational corporation with close to 2,000 stores, Gloria Jean's has been bought and sold several times, and Café Espresso Roma is one of the many specialty coffee retailers struggling for survival in an increasingly populated niche. If the entrepreneurs of these firms discovered and acted on a similar opportunity to sell higher-grade coffee at a premium price, through what strategic activities did some improve and others lose their positions? What activities contributed to their differential access to resources over time? In this chapter, we argue that to understand the evolution of the industry and the positions of firms in it, we need to understand how firms managed the interactions through which different domains of the social space were created and sustained.

Using in-depth case analysis of the actions of the four leading specialty coffee chains, we examined how these firms restructured the social space to create the favorable market and institutional conditions defining the niche. To dimensionalize the social space, we use Fombrun's (1986) framework, which describes changes of social structure as unfolding simultaneously at infrastructural, sociostructural, and superstructural levels. At the industry level of analysis, the infrastructure is "the resource base that the population draws on in terms of technology, personnel and other material inputs and the product markets to which it sells" (Fombrun 1986, 405). Thus, infrastructure describes the flow of resources to and from the industry, as well as the use of resources through which the firms in an industry create consumer value and investor wealth.

The patterns of resource exchanges create a set of social interactions among competing firms and between competing firms and exchange partners, interactions that constitute the sociostructure of a given social space. The sociostructure comprises both the administrative organization of the industry and the social context of exchange relationships (Fombrun 1986). It spans both the population of competing firms and the community of resource providers with whom they exchange resources.

Finally, through the practices of resource exchanges and social interactions, firms in an industry develop common ideas about how to compete (Abrahamson and Fombrun 1992; 1994; Porac, Thomas, and Baden-Fuller 1989; Spender 1989). According to Fombrun (1986, 406) "the symbolic representations and interpretations of collective life that come to be widely shared by participants" comprise the superstructure of the industry.

RESEARCH APPROACH

The ideas in this chapter derive from a field study of specialty coffee chains conducted by the first author (Rindova 1998). The study focused on tracing the activities of the top four specialty coffee chains but also included interviews with founders and managers from multiple firms to capture the bigger picture of the evolution of the industry. A total of 29 interviews were conducted with founders, managers, and expert observers of specialty coffee chains. Summary information about the interviews is presented in Table 9.1. The interview data were supplemented with reports on the industry and the four focal companies. Media reports, industry analyses by marketing research firms, consulting firms, and financial analysts were examined. Finally, reports prepared by the industry association, the Specialty Coffee Association of America, as

Table 9.1

Description of Informants and Interview Topics

Interviewees	Interview Topic	Illustrative Questions
Informants from the Focal Firms		
5 founders/CEOs, 2 VPs Operations, 2 district managers, 4 VPs Marketing	Industry growth and firm strategy	What was the idea behind founding the firm? What is distinctive about it? Who are your competitors? How are they similar to or different from you? How did specialty coffee chains emerge?
	Communication strategy	How do you communicate about your firm? What about it? In what form? For what purposes?
Informants from Other Specialty Coffee Chains		
5 founders/CEOs, 2 VPs Operations, 2 VPs Marketing	Industry growth and firm strategy	How did specialty coffee chains emerge? What is important to successful competition in this industry? Who are the key players?
	Communication strategy	How do you communicate about your firm? In what form? Are there exemplary companies in terms of communication?
Industry and Communication Experts		
1 historian, 1 investment banker, 1 consultant, 2 advertising consultants, 2 PR consultants	Industry evolution and competitor profiles	How did specialty coffee chains emerge? Who are the key players? On what basis do they compete?
	Communication strategy	What kind of information do specialty coffee chains seek to convey? In what form? For what purposes?

well as the industry association of the larger coffee industry, the National Coffee Association, were collected and examined. Table 9.2 provides information about the archival sources used.

The analysis followed the methods of grounded theory building (Glaser and Strauss 1967) and case analysis (Eisenhardt 1989; Miles and Huberman 1984) to identify key activities, categorize them, and combine these categories into an overall theoretical framework. The method is based on theoretical sampling,

Table 9.2

Additional Sources of Evidence About the Specialty Coffee Industry, 1970–1997

Source	Evidence
Company documents	
Product brochures	Product characteristics
Product catalogues	Product variety
Customer newsletters	Product- and company-related topics
Employee newsletters	Company-related topics
Employee training guides	Company practices, missions
Press releases	Key strategy actions, financial performance
Annual reports	Financial performance, strategic actions
Company histories	Missions, goals, distinctive company characteristics
Industry documents	
Industry newsletters	Current issues, product characteristics
Industry standards	Product characteristics
Industry directories	Industry size, growth, and strategic groups
Expert reports	
Financial analysts reports	Competitive categorizations, strategic actions
Company credit reports	Performance, strategic actions
Marketing research reports	Industry size
Industry growth reports	Industry evolution and growth
Media industry-overview articles	Industry evolution and growth
Company feature articles	Company characteristics, competitive categorizations

that is, the choice of empirical context and the data collection are driven by the research question. Since we were interested in the role that entrepreneurial activities play in the process of restructuring a social space, we chose the specialty coffee industry as a setting in which resources had shifted from established players to new ventures and established patterns of meaning were challenged and replaced. The specialty coffee niche emerged in an environment of declining coffee consumption and unfavorable public perception of the product. During the period of study, from the late 1960s to 1996, however, the specialty coffee niche grew rapidly, and the status of coffee changed from a commodity to a differentiated branded product. The growth of the niche in terms of demand, variety of participants, and the change in perceptions indicate restructuring of that social space on several levels.

The method requires iteration between theory and data (Eisenhardt 1989). We made several revisions to the theory. Our early theoretical focus was on the different business models entrepreneurs had, an approach consistent with more traditional entrepreneurship theory (Carland et al. 1984). Although entrepreneurs' business models were important, their impact on the industry can be understood only if their mutual influence on each other and differential imitation by other firms were accounted for. Thus, we sought to develop a framework that would capture the initiatives of entrepreneurs to establish not only market share but also industry influence. Fombrun's (1986) theoretical analysis of the structuring of organizational collectives provided a set of orienting constructs that guided the empirical inquiry (Miles and Huberman 1984).

THE EMERGENCE OF THE SPECIALTY COFFEE NICHE FROM THE U.S. COFFEE INDUSTRY

In the late 1960s, the U.S. coffee industry was caught in a vicious cycle. Three big commercial roasters dominated the industry: Maxwell House (a division of General Foods), Folgers (a division of Procter & Gamble), and Nestle. They competed on price to take market share from each other. To keep costs low they developed coffee blends with a high percentage of robusta beans, which are relatively cheap, but yield coffee with flavor. These sourcing practices lowered product quality and decreased demand, which triggered more intense competition for a larger share of the shrinking market. According to the National Coffee Association, between 1962 and 1991, coffee consumption per person declined from 3.1 cups a day to 1.75. John Naranjo, commercial policy chief for the Federacion Nacional de Cafeteros (FNC), Colombia's powerful coffee growers association, blamed it on the industry's poor product quality:

> If one industry has been handled very lousy, it is the coffee industry by the roasters of the U.S. The coffee you drink in the U.S. is very bad. Not because of the raw material—you can buy good raw material—but because of the blends. The way they have prepared coffee, it is not a good product. The rest is a simple mar-

ket fact: If consumers don't like the product, they change from coffee to other beverages. . . . After many years what they have been doing is killing an industry. . . . They have destroyed consumption. (McGuire 1993, 1)

Technological developments also allowed the big roasters to roast, grind, and package coffee on a large scale, which further reduced their costs but also lowered the quality of their product. The big commercial roasters' focus on price competition converted coffee into a packaged consumer good sold through the supermarket channel and consumed as a morning pick-up beverage. New generations of consumers grew up experiencing coffee as a canned product with little difference in flavor and characteristics from one company to another. These properties of the product increased the propensity of consumers to focus on the price attribute, which in turn further led the big three to compete on price.

In this impoverished market, a few small coffee roasters began to target a small number of consumers interested in higher-quality, freshly roasted coffee. They offered a wide selection of unblended coffees from different regions and roasted to different degrees to magnify flavor differences. They charged premium prices for a premium product and operated on very small scale. By the mid-1990s many of these small roasters had become multi-store chains of specialty coffee bars. The industry as a whole had grown explosively. Between 1983 and 1995 the sales of gourmet coffee grew 578%, from $295 million to an estimated $2 billion. The estimated $2 billion constitutes 31% of the total coffee market in terms of dollar value and 12% in terms of sales volume. Current growth is estimated at 7% to 10% (Anderson 1996).

Creating the Industry

Industry players trace the beginning of the industry to the founding of Peet's Coffee and Tea Company in 1966. Although specialty coffee roasters have existed in the U.S. at least since the 1890s, Peet's founder pioneered several practices, such as the dark roast, that became a part of the industry's identity. Alfred Peet was a second-generation coffee and tea broker. He had extensive firsthand experience with coffee tasting and selection from different parts of the world. According to one informant, "Peet's started with a different vision.

Alfred [Peet] had been a tea taster for the Dutch government; he had lived in Indonesia and Java and some of those places. He was part of the government, tasting tea around the world. He knows good beans, the difference in coffee." A founder of a chain of coffee houses that competed with Peet's in the Bay Area in the 1980s described the difference between the practices that Peet's initiated and the established industry practices:

> He was roasting there, and he was like the European, German-Dutch chemist type kind of guy. He knew what coffee should taste like, and he would tell people what they should drink, and he was very outspoken. . . . We were just sort of the coffee house thing, and I didn't know anything about coffee, we had a simple blend of coffee. At that point in time our coffee was Colombian and Mexican. A coffee roaster in San Francisco sold me my first espresso machine, and he said that it will be a good blend . . . a real cheap blend, and we did it.

Alfred Peet roasted the beans darker than was traditional roasting among commercial U.S. roasters. According to other specialty coffee retailers, "His trademark is the dark roast. Some people who are used to drinking light coffee may say this coffee is burnt. . . . There is a fine line in coffee tasting between burnt coffee and just being roasted to its fullest." An industry historian explained the approach of dark roasting: "Coffee ideology is what excites people about coffee. One such thing is the darkness of the roast. Alfred Peet created a certain style—it tipped the roasts toward the dark end of the spectrum, which has put pressure on traditional roasters. Others fiercely resist it. The medium roast is classic." Such conceptual differences existed particularly between specialty coffee retailers on the East Coast and on the West Coast. Several specialty coffee roasters in New York, such as Guilles Coffee Company, Dallis Brothers, and Shapiro, had existed on the fringes of the traditional coffee industry since the turn of the century. Their coffee was freshly roasted and carefully selected, but the blends and the roasts were more similar to the flavor profiles of the coffees produced by the big three. Whereas they made a high-quality product, they did not differentiate it as clearly from the mainstream coffee industry as Alfred Peet did.

Dark roasting produces a stronger flavor, but it requires higher-quality beans that can endure the high temperatures. In addition, it requires a significant amount of tacit knowledge about temperature and timing, which industry members learned from one another. (For example, at the annual convention of specialty coffee retailers, roasting discussion sessions are held, in which participants debate their experiences with discovering optimal roasting techniques). Alfred Peet had the knowledge necessary to select, define, and distinguish specialty coffee from traditional coffee. His practices became guidelines for other aspiring specialty coffee retailers. He contributed to the industry by setting his practices as standards. Informants who interacted with him and learned from him commented on his intense personality and his conviction that his practices were "the right way" of doing things. One telling example of his efforts to establish his own practices as standards is that when he trained the original founders of Starbucks, he insisted that they learn to roast, although they had requested that he supply roasted beans to their newly opened store in Seattle. Several other founders interviewed were also personally trained or employed as coffee buyers by Alfred Peet.

Several key firms in the industry were founded under the influence of Alfred Peet, most notably, the Starbucks Coffee Company (1971, Seattle) and the Coffee Connection (1974, Boston). These companies followed closely the practices of bean selection, blending, roasting, and delivery established by Alfred Peet, although the Coffee Connection adopted a lighter roast, characteristic of tastes on the East Coast.

Creating the Opportunity

The dissemination of product expertise and the growing sense of the emergence of a distinct product category gave rise to a tenfold increase in microroasters between 1979 and 1989, from 40 to 385 (Andrews 1992, 12). This exponential increase in the number of players was paralleled by some changes in technology, such as the development of decaffeinated, flavored, and organic coffees, the introduction of the one-way valve vacuum packaging, and the shift from percolators to drip coffee brewing machines. These innovations increased product variety and enabled industry players to offer their product to a wider set of consumers.

Yet, the most significant change of the 1980s was the development of the specialty coffee bar. The combination of a traditional coffee house with a coffee bar selling specialty beans may appear obvious today but this was not the case in the mid-80s. As one coffeehouse owner explained:

> They were totally separate, and the overlap is a phenomenon that has occurred in the last ten years, and that's something I don't think too many people are aware of. But we were totally separate. I didn't know Alfred then, he was coffee beans, and we were a coffeehouse. We had the seats and the place where people would hang out and play chess. I didn't know much about coffee, but we were making good cappuccino. The product we had was "making a good cappuccino." The product Alfred had was "making a good strong cup of coffee," or "having twenty-five or thirty different blends of coffee." He knew how to blend coffee, and blending coffee was something I knew nothing about.

The development of the coffee bar is associated with the growth of the Starbucks Coffee Company. The story, often told in the press, goes something like this: "A 1983 trip to Italy by Schultz [Starbuck's CEO] introduced him to some of the 200,000 coffee bars in that country. The next year Starbucks opened its first coffee bar in Seattle" (Geranios 1992, 10C).

The coffee bar offered specialty coffee retailers the opportunity to expand their product mix with higher margin products, such as beverages. It also offered a space where consumers spent a substantial amount of time in the ambiance created and largely controlled by the retailers. Nevertheless, the development of the bar generated some industry opposition. It represented a departure from the principles Alfred Peet had instilled: the focus was shifting away from beans—the sacred symbol of the industry's worldwide quest for quality, flavor, and taste—and toward beverages. Furthermore, it emphasized milk-based beverages, which diluted the pure coffee taste the industry so proudly had restored after years of dominance by commercially canned coffee. One informant complained, "Because it is becoming more and more beverages, you don't need as much sophistication anymore. It becomes more of an industry, an assembly line concept, but it's not a great product."

Not all competitors benefited to the same degree from the resource shifts occasioned by the new coffee bars. The new entrants, technologies, distribution channels, and philosophies that sprang up in the industry in the 1980s modified the infrastructure, the sociostructure, and the superstructure and created more diversity. For instance, flavored coffees were frowned upon by Peet's,

Starbucks, and the Coffee Connection, but Gloria Jean's, Barnie's, and the Coffee Beanery argued that flavored coffee is an innovation that gives consumers more choice.

As the industry infrastructure developed, there were more entrants, more products, more roasting technologies, and the superstructure became more fragmented. With growth, the diversity in viewpoints increased, industry participants began interacting more frequently, and they established a more formal organization to represent the best practices in the industry. A number of specialty coffee retailers who had met informally during trade shows for gourmet products between 1982 and 1989 initiated the formal incorporation of the Specialty Coffee Association of America (SCAA) in 1989. One of its founding members explained why the association was organized:

> Its goals were to be a forum for education within the trade and for dissemination of information outside the trade, both to the media and the public. We thought the world would be a better place if there were more people in it who produced better coffee, both as growers and as roasters and as retailers, and we thought it was very important in order to facilitate that information that was not proprietary and that was permitted by law to be exchanged between companies should be exchanged to raise the level of intelligence among the little businesses that existed then.

Evidently, the sociostructure was called upon to generate superstructural standards and principles to support the expanding infrastructure of the industry.

Full Steam Ahead in the 1990s

In the 1990s, the industry grew explosively. In 1996, there were approximately 7,000 specialty coffee outlets, including multiple stores of what had become a popular organizational form, the specialty coffee chain. Table 9.3 shows the distribution of outlets among the top four players in the industry at the end of the data collection period in 1996.

As Table 9.3 shows, the industry has expanded and a clear leader has emerged: the Starbucks Coffee Company. Starbucks alone had 38% of the multistore chain outlets by 1996, and the top four chains had 59%, indicating that the industry had become quite concentrated. Through a series of

Table 9.3
Size of the Top Four Specialty Coffee Chains (1996)

Company	Number of stores
Starbucks	860 (corporate owned)
The Second Cup / Gloria Jean's Coffee Bean	513 (franchised)
The Coffee Beanery	180 (primarily franchised)
Barnie's Coffee and Tea Company	100 (primarily corporate owned)

diversification moves and entries into international markets, however, the industry leader has moved away from the core activities of specialty coffee retailers. Its nearest competitors, especially the Second Cup, have grown into sizeable coffee chains, seeking to become distinctive and well-recognized brands. The increased interest in branding is evident in the fact that all major competitors have hired professional consultants, such as ad agencies, public relations consultants, and design experts to professionalize their communications. They represent themselves primarily as lifestyle brands, creating unique experiences for consumers. They also seek to broaden their customer base to various social groups that would be attracted by the "the 1990s" look and feel of specialty coffee bars and products, thus continuously increasing the size of the niche. Table 9.4 summarizes the key changes that took place in the industry in this period.

ENTREPRENEURIAL ACTIVITIES AS RESOURCE CLAIMS

We began our data analysis by using Fombrun's (1986) framework of restructuring of social collectives to map the activities of our focal companies over time and examine the pattern within each domain and across domains. Our goal was to understand what the drivers are of industrywide change and what the leverage points are that enable some firms to become more prominent and more successful in the industry. Going back and forth between theory and data, we recognized that the more prominent firms in the industry have either been able to define several of the structural domains at some point in time or at least have attempted to renegotiate, reinvent, or reconnect elements of the

Table 9.4

Key Changes in the Industry by Time Period and Domain

Level of Analysis	Key Variables	Birth (1970s)	Shaping (1980s)	Growth and Consolidation (1990s)
Superstructure	Identity and expertise claims through:	Focus on bean selection and roasting	Focus on espresso-based beverages and coffee bar ambiance	Focus on consumer experience
	Product and customer definition	Customer is a coffee connoisseur	Customer is a well-educated professional	Customer is anyone attracted to ambiance
	Reputation management	Reputation managed through direct contact	Starbucks seeks national recognition	All key players rely on professionally managed branding
Sociostructure	Leadership claims based on position in networks:			Starbucks' dominance
	Direct links	Low interaction among small players	Chain growth increases contact	
	Reputation	Informal centers of expertise (especially Peet's)	Formation of an industry association (1982–1989)	
Infrastructure	Resource claims based on product distinctiveness	Key foundings:	Entrants quadruple	Entrants increase tenfold
	Foundings	1966– Peet's	Emergence of chains	Expansion through capital markets
	Technological change	1969– Coffee Beanery (a wholesaler)		Innovation through diversification
	Product and distribution innovations	1971– Starbucks		
		1974– The Coffee Connection		
		1979– Gloria Jean's Coffee Bean		
		1980– Barnie's Tea and Coffee Company		

ensemble. Further, the firms that were successful at restructuring some aspect of the space at some point have effectively converted the idiosyncratic beliefs of their founders and the attributes of their strategies into "model" activities and principles. The processes entailed a normative twist: what was merely "so," had become "good," "useful," "beneficial," or a "best practice." This process is akin to legitimation in that it validates a firm's strategy, status, or vision, but it is also very different, because it is not driven by conformity with established norms, values, and beliefs (Suchman 1995a) that determines the legitimacy of new ventures. Instead, the process is driven by the essence of the entrepreneurial process on each venture and its claims with regard to value creation, social status, and identity.

To capture the essence of that process, we drew on impression management theory, which explains how people shape the perceptions of observers about their behaviors and the outcomes the behaviors generate (Hewitt 1994). Impression management research has uncovered a variety of strategies through which individuals change the valence of information about activities. In particular, Schlenker (1980) distinguished between entitling acclaimers, which highlights the contribution of an actor to outcomes, and enhancing acclaimers, which emphasizes the importance of the contribution. Borrowing from these ideas, we use the term claims to describe the activities through which a firm establishes the benefits, significance, and centrality of its contributions to a market or an industry.

Using the concept of claims to capture patterns in the data across structural domains and time periods, we reanalyzed the data on the activities in each domain to examine the manifestation of the construct in each domain. That analysis suggested the concepts of value claims that take place in the infrastructure, leadership claims that shape the sociostructure, and identity and expertise claims that play a key role in the superstructural domain.

Value claims. The infrastructural activities of specialty coffee retailers distinguished the population of the specialty coffee retailers from a larger population of coffee companies (Andrews 1992). Specialty coffee retailers distinguished themselves from commercial roasters on the basis of how they sourced coffee beans (i.e., what raw materials they used), how they roasted (i.e., what technology they relied on), and how they delivered coffee to the customer (i.e., how they entered the market). Furthermore, specialty coffee retailers varied in how they performed the activities within these categories, thus forming strategic groups within the population of specialty coffee retailers.

Restructuring of the infrastructural domain of the coffee industry took place as resources flowed to the new ventures, as demand for coffee shifted from the general coffee category toward the specialty category, or as companies gained access to previously unavailable resources, as young consumers were attracted to the product category for the first time since the 1970s. For example, the infrastructural activities of U.S. specialty coffee retailers, such as sourcing methods, contributed to their reputation with the community of coffee growers, which in turn created access to coffee types previously reserved for the European and Japanese markets (*Chicago Tribune* 1990).

Although all specialty coffee retailers differed from commercial roasters in their practices of roasting in small batches and the like, some of them relied on these distinguishing practices to a greater degree. For example, because East Coast specialty coffee roasters stayed closer to the traditional roast, they did not create distinguishable differences in their flavor profile and could not make a significant claim on the resources, such as consumer demand, that flowed to commercial roasters. In contrast, Peet's roasting practices created strong flavor differences, which really forced consumers to make choices and even reevaluate their preferences.

Being able to attract consumer demand at a premium price enabled specialty coffee retailers to engage in sourcing of better and rarer coffee varietals, which in turn made their product offerings more diverse and exotic. These new dimensions of product value became the foundation for making stronger claims to the relative share of resources that flowed to the industry. The differences that distinguished specialty coffee retailers from traditional roasters provided some measure of value created. As a result, a venture with more distinctive infrastructural practices can make stronger (and more credible) claims to value creation and, through those, to receiving the resources flowing to the industry.

Similarly, the development of the coffee bar and its difference from traditional coffeehouses gave rise to new resource claims for the industry as a whole because it broadened the target-customer segments. The coffee bar was better suited to attract not only coffee connoisseurs but also affluent educated consumers, who were drawn to it by the sophistication of the new beverages and by the coffee bar ambiance. To the degree that Starbucks was identified as the initiator and the foremost exponent of the "bar concept," it could make greater value-creation claims than other firms whose outlets did not have the same distinctiveness.

Therefore, in the infrastructural domain, specialty coffee retailers engaged in practices geared toward developing a better quality product than commercial roasters. They introduced both product and distribution channel innovations to offer products that were distinctive from those of traditional coffee companies. Yet most specialty coffee retailers did not enter the industry with a radical innovation; rather, they made adjustments in their infrastructural characteristics as they learned from each other and from customers. The more distinctive the features of the product (flavor, specialty beverages), the greater the value creation claims they represented and the more likely they were to shift demand away from existing competitors and toward the new ventures. In other words, the new ventures improved their access to resources previously channeled to others by making value creation claims based on infrastructural practices that yielded highly distinguishable product dimensions. Although this interpretation has some similarities with the Schumpeterian notion of innovation, in this case, it is not the innovativeness of the practices per se (East Coast specialty coffee retailers have existed at the margins of the traditional coffee industry since the end of the nineteenth century) but, rather, their ability to yield products with distinguishable performance on certain attributes that constitute the foundation of the value creation claims.

Leadership claims. The sociostructural activities of specialty coffee retailers entailed the formation of a social network of coffee companies that engaged in the distinctive infrastructural practices discussed above. In addition, specialty coffee retailers formed relationships with coffee brokers and coffee growers as populations whose activities they viewed as tightly linked to the well-being of their population, an aspect of their operations that was highlighted in interviews with coffee buyers from several companies. Thus, they established a social organization both at the population and the community level.

One of the important functions of sociostructure is that it outlines the social boundaries of the community and generates governance mechanisms to establish the norms of the community. The specialty coffee industry is naturally very fragmented and, in fact, some industry participants believe that the nature of the product—fresh produce—dictates that the scope of operations remain primarily local. Nevertheless, industry participants sought to foster interaction and formed an association in 1989. The informal networks were important in developing a community and an industry, especially in the 1980s, when the industry was still building critical mass. The association was created with the goals of promoting standards (i.e., to provide guidance with regard to the infrastructural practices of the industry) and promoting awareness of specialty coffee (i.e., to broadcast the value creation claims of the industry). Although the association has generated a significant number of meetings, training seminars, guided coffee buying trips, and so forth, the two main functions—of advancing standards and promoting product differences—were effectively performed by the leading firms in the industry. In the late 1960s and 1970s, the leadership role was attributed to Peet's Coffee and Tea Company and, in the 1980s and 1990s, to the Starbucks Coffee Company.

Alfred Peet trained and educated, directly or indirectly, several founders of coffee chains and a number of chief coffee buyers in the industry. As a result, he claimed a de facto leadership position for Peet's in the sociostructure of the industry. Interview data, however, suggest that neither Alfred Peet nor other early entrants envisioned the emergence of the industry back in the 1970s. Thus, although his practices enabled value creation and leadership claims that promoted the firm to a central position in the emerging industry, there is no evidence that Alfred Peet as an entrepreneur recognized that aspect of his activities.

Similarly, Starbucks' leadership claims were based primarily on the firm's value claims and established reputation. The involvement of the firm with the industry association was a lot less than that of its nearest competitors, the founders or top managers of which performed key governance and educational functions in the association. Industry participants viewed Starbucks as a leader relative to the broader institutional and market environment, rather than within the industry itself. Thus, the interesting point here is that the leadership claims in the industry were made both within the context of the sociostructure, through the formal governance mechanisms and the structure of the network, and through the activities in the infrastructural and the superstructural domains. The second path makes leadership claims more of an outcome of value creation and identity claims than an outcome of the structure of the network.

Starbucks positioned itself as superior to its rivals that "have outlets in shopping malls and carry flavored coffees." Schultz, Starbucks' CEO, said Starbucks would never sell an artificially flavored coffee. According to him, "It is a bastardization of the product" (Harrison 1993, D1). In trying to establish their practices as standards, specialty coffee retailers often called on their identities to provide authority. In the preceding example, the Starbucks' CEO also added: "We do have a bit of arrogance. We feel we deserve it." This quote exemplifies the mix of identity and leadership claims through which the key players sought to establish their right to shape the industry. These claims were validated or modified by the pattern of resource allocations consumers made. Starbucks' claims, for example, were supported by its loyal consumer following (Reese 1996). Thus, firms able to attract more resources exercised a leadership role in that their activities became watched and imitated by competitors. Explained one founder:

> And what we did was look at what Schultz [Starbucks] did. I spent hours in their stores and I'd send people there. . . . Anyone who had a clear picture of what was happening had to be aware of what they were doing, so you studied what he did. A lot of companies really imitate Starbucks. . . . A lot of companies . . . have taken their entire range of roasts and darkened it.

The fragmented nature of the industry—and the resulting relatively weak sociostructure—may explain why leadership claims rested more on infrastructural and superstructural activities than on activities specific to the sociostructural domain.

Expertise and identity claims. One of the most important dynamics we observed in the industry was the important role that superstructure played in the evolution of the industry. The superstructure determined what practices industry players deemed appropriate for their specific venture, as well as for the industry as a whole. It determined what changes they were willing to make. Finally, it affected how players positioned themselves in the industry by pursuing and configuring resources in ways consistent with their internal identity commitments.

The two central components of the industry superstructure were product-related expertise (knowledge about coffee) and organizational identity. First, the superstructural activities of specialty coffee retailers included defining the distinguishing characteristics of specialty coffee relative to traditional coffee—for themselves as well as for the marketplace. In essence, at the superstructural level, specialty coffee retailers established a set of standards for their product. A number of them attempted to dominate the definition of those standards.

Second, the organizational identities of specialty coffee retailers are strongly defined by their coffee knowledge and the strategic visions and operational principles deduced from that knowledge. Thus, in contrast with the findings of previous studies on cognitive characteristics of communities of practice (Lant and Baum 1995; Porac, Thomas, and Baden-Fuller 1989) the central elements of the superstructure in the specialty coffee industry were less related to defining competitors and more to defining what the industry does and who its customers are. The competitive definition of the industry was primarily one of difference with commercial roasters than among specialty coffee retailers per se. It is also important to note that most of the key players in the industry are both roasters and retailers, thus spanning two industry groups. Whereas specialty coffee retailers recognized the infrastructural differences between those, however, they minimized the superstructural differences. In other words, coffee ideology was widely shared among industry players with somewhat different value chains at the infrastructural level.

The beginning of the development of a superstructure in the industry is associated with the industry's founding father, Alfred Peet, who largely defined the core identity of the industry. Although many other entrepreneurs have pioneered some aspects of the industry value-chain, it is the place that Alfred Peet occupies in the industry superstructure that makes his heritage so lasting. It was also Alfred Peet who seems to have linked the concepts of identity and coffee expertise with his strong, almost moralistic attitudes toward coffee selection (as reported in the excerpts from the field interviews).

The more distinctive were the infrastructural practices that a specialty coffee retailer engaged in, the stronger the expertise and identity claims it made to define the standards of the industry. For example, specialty coffee retailers who roasted coffee more darkly were viewed as more representative of the category and as having a stronger specialty coffee identity (Albert and Whetten 1985). The retailers who engaged in these practices also made stronger identity claims that their practices exemplified the industry's superstructure. Thus, the restructuring of the superstructure of the U.S. coffee industry took place as the expectations of both coffee firms and consumers shifted toward the standards promoted by specialty coffee retailers.

Although coffeehouses have existed in different parts of the country, Starbucks made the identity claim of pioneering the Italian-type espresso bar in the U.S. It further moved to expand the concept rapidly by both proliferating the espresso-based beverages and increasing the number of stores. Starbucks thereby combined its identity claims with value creation claims and reached for broader access to new resources both geographically and in terms of consumer preferences. Gloria Jean's also moved to expand its stores; it added beverages to the product mix but claimed that "the espresso machine is primarily a decoration item." Thus, whereas all key players sought to expand their value creation claims with the expansion of the niche, they coupled those with different expertise and identity claims guided by different philosophies. In doing so, they maintained some degree of differentiation, while expanding the resource base of the niche as a whole.

Although the increased social interaction and direct market contact created isomorphic tendencies, most early entrants in the industry maintained their distinct identities as guides to their strategic choices. Thus, whereas competitors imitated the industry leaders to some extent, they also maintained their identities. Informants pointed to founders' philosophies, industry socializing influences, and product expertise as factors sustaining each firm's identity claims in the face of isomorphic pressures. Although the industry growth invited a slew of imitators, the interview data reveal that imitative strategies were employed primarily by late entrants with inferior resources. In fact, it is the distinctiveness of their identities that pushed the leading firms to innovate and to preserve the differences rather than to adopt the available models of success.

More important, specialty coffee retailers also relied on their identities to explain their strategic choices about how they made resource allocations in the infrastructural domain. In some cases, their identities were a source of cognitive inertia and prevented firms from responding to competitors' moves. The latter observation is consistent with past research on cognitive communities, which tend to form identities around what is common to the group and different for firms outside the group (Porac, Thomas, and Baden-Fuller 1989; Spender 1989). Overall, however, the superstucture of the specialty coffee niche differed from this pattern. As discussed earlier, the expertise and the coffee ideology provided the common ground and included even firms with different infrastructural arrangements. In contrast, firms' identities were used as a differentiating factor even among firms with otherwise very similar infrastructural practices.

Thus, the influence of expertise and identity claims on the construction of the niche is twofold: the expertise component formed the foundation for promoting industry standards, which many informants viewed as "elevating" the industry to a level of professionalism. In addition, they viewed standards as a mechanism for protecting the reputation of the niche at a time when the levels of growth at the infrastructural level attracted a large number of entrepreneurs who had not been socialized gradually into the evolving superstructure of the industry.

The identity claims acted as a counterbalancing force—they spoke of difference, individuality, and competing expertise claims. Thus, identity claims maintained the diversity within the niche and, as such, broadened the potential range of appeal and the size of the customer base that the industry could attract. They also enabled individual players to build individual reputations (Rindova and Fombrun 1999). Starbucks' reputation, for example, was often quoted as the primary factor that attracted a number of companies (e.g., PepsiCo) to partner with the firm and enabled it to pursue and create new opportunities. The interesting dynamic here is that whereas identity claims are initially related to product expertise claims and tightly coupled with infrastructural practices, as firms build reputations with outside observers, identity claims become the bases around which new infrastructural combinations are created.

Together, these observations demonstrate the multiple levels of links among the domains and the rippling effects that changes in one domain produced in others. One of the implications of understanding entrepreneurship as a series of claims undertaken in multiple domains is that, to be successful, entrepreneurs should, at a minimum, be aware of the consequences of their activities or inactivities across domains. Ideally, entrepreneurs should develop strategies that chart their activities in all three domains. Based on our interviews with industry informants, one of the biggest competitive differences between Starbucks and the rest of the industry, especially in the 1980s and early 1990s, was Starbucks' "marketing function," as informants described it. Indeed, Starbucks' expertise and identity claims enabled it to dominate the superstructure of the industry, which translated into numerous advantages in all domains— its pervasive reputation in the superstructural domain, its de facto leadership in the socio-structural domain, and its market share, which still exceeds that of all its nearest competitors combined.

Viewed as a series of claims, industries are comparable to courtrooms, in which claims are continuously made, modified, countered, and disclaimed. Direct competitors, producers of substitute goods, as well as third-party observers such as consumer advocates, make alternative claims to those made by any firm. The fact that social actors continuously counter each other's claims has led some authors to talk about "cognitive entrepreneurship" (Rao 1994). Therefore, the relationship between claims and desired outcomes may not be one of direct causality. Our study suggests that claims in multiple domains interact with each other in creating perceptions about market growth and the position of a given firm.

The important message for entrepreneurs is that, in contrast to the traditional individualistic focus of the majority of writing on entrepreneurship, entrepreneurship is a process of restructuring the social space at three levels of organization. Tracing the evolution of the specialty coffee industry, we found that entrepreneurs in the industry exerted and absorbed influence from other industry players to different degrees. We have used the idea of claims to understand the activities of entrepreneurs in the three structural domains through which they sought to secure differential influence, resources, and positions in their industry. Given what we have learned from the emergence and growth of this industry, we can propose a general model. Figure 9.1 presents a model of entrepreneurial activities as claims that may help us understand opportunity and industry creation in other industries.

CONCLUSION

Through an in-depth analysis of the evolution of the specialty coffee niche, in this chapter we developed a framework that represents entrepreneurial activities as a series of claims undertaken in multiple domains. During the period of the study between the late 1960s and the 1990s, the specialty coffee niche

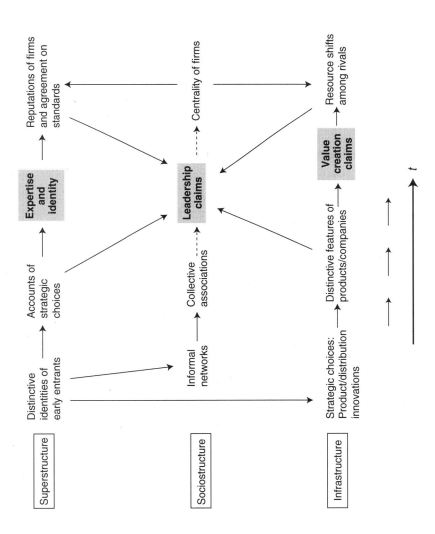

Figure 9.1 Model of entrepreneurial activities as claims

emerged as a high-growth segment amidst the stagnant U.S. coffee industry. If one examines the entrepreneurial activities in the niche from a traditional entrepreneurial perspective, the growth of industry leader, the Starbucks Coffee Company, seems to epitomize the myth of the visionary entrepreneur who perceives an opportunity and mobilizes resources to exploit it through expansion. The story of how Starbucks' CEO, Howard Schultz, perceived the opportunity of bringing to the U.S. the Italian-style coffee beverages and bars, and the atmosphere and lifestyle they expressed, has been widely circulated in the press. His relentless drive toward growth and expansion to exploit the opportunity have also been reported in the press and lauded by the investment community.

Yet a detailed analysis of the entrepreneurial activities in the niche, based on interviews with multiple industry participants, reveals that the creation of the niche and the opportunity associated with specialty coffee was a collective process, to which all industry participants contributed. Industry participants improved the product quality by buying better beans and custom-roasting them; they built local and national networks, in which they shared coffee expertise; and they conveyed their sense of mission of making a difference to their communities and local markets. In this scenario, local operators stimulated interest in specialty coffee locally.

Starbucks brought to the industry marketing sophistication, which enabled it to propagate its claims—value creation, leadership, expertise, and distinct identity—to larger numbers of consumers, as well as diverse stakeholders. Thus, Starbucks helped attract resources to the niche, while retaining a significant share of them. Starbucks' claims also expanded the opportunity for other specialty coffee retailers by creating national awareness of the product, the industry, and the firm's unorthodox practices. Its success made the opportunity highly visible and attracted a slew of imitators, as well as challengers. New firms entered the industry seeking to bring more elaborate options to consumers, and Starbucks leveraged its assets in diversified ventures. Thus, the innovations and new entries in the infrastructural domain contributed to variation in the industry, whereas the increasing organization of the industry at the socio-structural level, both through administrative mechanisms and consolidation, led to more stable patterns of resource flows. In the superstucture the various knowledge and expertise claims made by specialty coffee retailers stabilized into a set of standards, which could be reliably transferred to new entrants through the governance mechanisms of the sociostructure. The standards of the superstucture tended to reflect the expertise and identity claims of the earlier entrants, which have achieved dominant positions in the market.

The mix of individual and collective actions that create the dynamics of variation, selection, and retention in the industry suggest that researchers should seek to understand entrepreneurship activities simultaneously at multiple levels of analysis (Aldrich and Fiol 1994). Individual actions create the material, social, and cognitive structures of industries. But the process through which these structures form and reform takes place at the collective level. Specialty coffee retailers restructured the social space, thus creating an opportunity, through following and challenging, through innovation and imitation, through social influence and formal organizing, through one-on-one interaction and mass persuasion. These activities underlay their claims about the value of their products, the distinctiveness of their expertise and identity, and the centrality of their role in the industry. The more reinforcing the claims were, the more they contributed to superior access to resources. The same actions that attracted more resources to the industry also increased its stratification into winners, mere survivors, and losers. Thus, whereas specialty coffee retailers reinvented the product category of coffee collectively, the entrepreneurial firms who made the strongest and most reinforcing claims took the prize.

10

The Power of Public Competition

Promoting Cognitive Legitimacy Through Certification Contests

HAYAGREEVA RAO

A core premise of organizational theory is that new organizational forms lack taken-for-grantedness in the eyes of financial and personnel markets, governments, consumers, and other key actors in the environment (Aldrich 1999; Hannan and Freeman 1989; Stinchcombe 1965). Organizational sociologists routinely distinguish between sociopolitical legitimacy and cognitive legitimacy (Aldrich and Fiol 1994; Hannan and Carroll 1992). Put simply, sociopolitical legitimacy consists of endorsement by legal authorities, governmental bodies, and other powerful organizations. By contrast, cognitive legitimacy implies the taken-for-granted assumption that an organization is desirable, proper, and appropriate within a widely shared system of norms and values (Scott 1987).

Empirical research on new organizational forms, conducted principally by organizational ecologists, depicts sociopolitical and cognitive legitimacy as positive spillovers flowing from individual instances of an organizational form. Density dependence theorists propose that new forms become taken for granted as the number (density) of organizations embodying the form increases. Initial increases in density produce economies of scale in collective

I benefited from the helpful suggestions made by participants at the Balboa Bay Conference in Newport Beach. The editors, Kaye Schoonhoven and Elaine Romanelli, provided incisive comments.

action and collective learning, boost founding rates, and diminish death rates. Beyond a point, however, growing density unleashes competition, depresses founding rates, and increases death rates. Numerous studies reveal an inverted U-shaped relationship between density and foundings and a U-shaped relationship between density and deaths (see Baum 1996; Hannan and Carroll 1992 for reviews).[1] A parallel body of research suggests that interorganizational linkages established by individual firms confer sociopolitical legitimacy on the form. Baum and Oliver (1992) showed that relational density (links between existing firms with governmental organizations) initially increased birth rates and diminished death rates. In a similar vein, Hybels, Ryan, and Barley (1994) demonstrated that strategic alliances between firms in a population increased founding rates. Thus, a striking feature of ecological research is that, even if the legitimacy of the form is a public good, deliberate collective action is not required.

But recent versions of neo-institutionalism suggest that the creation of new organizational forms entails an institutionalization project wherein the theory and values underpinning the form are justified by institutional entrepreneurs (DiMaggio 1988, 18). Some researchers liken the institutional project to a social movement (Fligstein 1996) and imply that new organizational forms become validated through a bottom-up process of institutional entrepreneurship (Rao 1998). In this line of work, a new organizational form can become cognitively legitimate only when institutional entrepreneurs or activists succeed in framing it as valid and reliable (DiMaggio and Powell 1991; Snow and Benford 1992). Concretely, activists have to design and deploy a strategy of claimmaking to establish the new form's necessity, reliability, and usefulness. Yet there is little research that shows how actors legitimate the new form or that demonstrates the impact of these legitimating strategies on organization building (Baum and Powell 1995).

This chapter suggests that a challenge for activists in new industries is to promote cognitive legitimacy while at the same time proving the reliability of

---

1. There is disagreement about whether legitimacy should be measured directly (Zucker 1989), how density effects are to be unbundled (Delacroix and Rao 1994), and whether endorsements play a crucial role in the legitimation of new forms (Baum and Powell 1995). In response, Hannan and Carroll (1995) observed that institutional research does use indirect measures and that the density-dependent approach is simple, comparable, and replicable.

the radically new product in question. One way for activists to legitimate the form and simultaneously create a platform for claims of quality is to organize certification contests, in which producers are ranked on the basis of their performance. A study of how consumer activists organized reliability and speed races in the early American automobile industry during 1893 and 1912 is offered to show that action was essential to legitimate the automobile. In the empirical analyses, I examine how the number of certification contests influenced two entrepreneurial outcomes: incorporation and operational start-up rates. By focusing attention on whether certification contests enabled potential founders, defined as entrepreneurs possessing a prototype, to incorporate new ventures and initiate production, this chapter directs attention to how legitimation influences the selection of emerging organizations.

COLLECTIVE ACTION, COGNITIVE LEGITIMACY, AND CERTIFICATION CONTESTS

An organizational form is new if it differs from preexisting forms in terms of core features such as goals, authority relations, technology, and served markets. Since an emerging form may differ in form from its precursor on some or all of the four criteria, the newness of a form is a continuous variable (Rao and Singh 1999). Examples of new forms include new industries that differ from existing industries in terms of technology and markets (e.g., the personal computer industry) or new governance structures that differ from existing governance structures in terms of goals and authority structure (e.g., the multidivisional form).

New industries embody radically new products and face a liability of newness because knowledge about the new product in question is neither widely diffused nor codified. Taken-for-granted understandings of products are essential if distinctions are to be made among producers and if consumers are to be able to recognize quality. Sociopolitical legitimacy is also essential for new industries that jeopardize vested interests. A new form can become legitimate when institutional entrepreneurs validate the form and establish its standing. Institutional entrepreneurs are ideological activists who combine hitherto unconnected beliefs and practices to justify a form. These ideological activists may constitute informal coalitions or may be located in formal organizations. Activists overcome collective action problems because they are able to exclude others from the psychological benefit of contributing to a cause (McCarthy, Smith, and Zald 1996). Since institutional entrepreneurs are trying to convince others to go along with their view, the formation of new industries and forms resembles social movements (Fligstein 1996, 663–64).

Institutional entrepreneurs or activists can consist of executives in producing firms or trade associations, professionals located in fieldwide organizations, or enthusiastic consumers who have banded together. Executives of producing firms can play a key role in legitimating new industries, as did Steve Jobs, who played a crucial role in the development of the personal computer industry. Collective action by producers through trade associations can also build the legitimacy of the new form and protect the form from attacks (Aldrich 1999). For instance, the American Gaming Association lobbies legislators in state governments to permit the establishment of casinos. Professionals can also be important actors in legitimating new industries that advance the professional project (DiMaggio and Powell 1991). The Harry Benjamin International Gender Dysphoria Association, for example, a professional society of gender-reassignment specialists, played a significant role in establishing worldwide standards and creating the gender reassignment industry. Consumers can also organize campaigns to legitimate new forms. Bicycle clubs consisting of cycling enthusiasts have played a more important role in establishing the bicycle as a source of health and happiness than individual producers who bankrolled campaigns to advertise the bicycle as a valued product (Smith 1973).

The roles of trade associations, professionals, and consumer activists in the legitimation process can vary across new industries (Meyer 1994). In some industries, free-rider problems may impede collective action by producers, and in others, trade associations may only be formed later in the evolution of new industries. Similarly, preexisting professional infrastructures may be weak in some cases, and in others, new industries may actually promote the birth of new professions (Aldrich 1999). When collective action has failed and professional infrastructures are moribund, consumer groups can provide the infrastructure and personnel for legitimating new organizational forms through claimmaking.

Irrespective of their social location, institutional entrepreneurs garner legitimacy for a new industry by making claims about its necessity, validity, and appropriateness (Snow and Benford 1992, 150). Entrepreneurs have to be "active, and sometimes, skilled users of culture" (Swidler 1986, 287) who recombine existing cultural elements to make novel forms acceptable (Douglas 1986). When activists advance claims, they have to draw on strategies that capitalize on shared understandings and consist of defined activities within broadly sculpted scripts that link numerous actors (Tilly 1997, 11).

Impression management theorists and social movement theorists have inventoried strategies of claimmaking. In the impression management literature, claimmaking strategies are geared toward image defense, consist of verbal accounts, and subsume excuses, justifications, admissions of responsibility, apologies, and denials (see Benoit 1995). In contrast, social movement theorists describe how activists use strategies of contention consisting of demonstrations, petitions, boycotts, lawsuits, letter-writing campaigns, and op-ed campaigns to de-legitimate existing social arrangements and justify new policies and structures (see McCarthy, Smith, and Zald 1996). Yet while institutional theorists assert that legitimacy is essential for new forms, they have glossed over the specific strategies of claimmaking used by entrepreneurs to build legitimacy for new forms (DiMaggio 1988; Rao 1998).

In practice, institutional entrepreneurs use a wide variety of strategies of claimmaking to legitimate new industries: adopting accepted procedures, conferences, trade shows, report cards, and organizing certification contests. Brint and Karabel (1991) showed how the American Association of Junior Colleges, a consortium of producers, promoted the legitimacy of vocational colleges by developing legitimate recruiting, guidance, and placement programs for them. Conferences are ubiquitous strategies of claimmaking that link diverse participants together into a collective performance. For example, hedge funds gained acceptance when entrepreneurs co-opted prestigious financial newspapers organizing a series of annual conferences such as the MAR/Hedge Conference on Hedge Funds and invited a selected group of institutional investors to educate them.

Activists may also develop "report cards" to establish a new form's legitimacy. In 1991, the National Committee on Quality Assurance, a group consisting of producer and consumer representatives, defined sixty performance measures and integrated them into a report card for managed care organizations (Cerna 1993). These report cards were plausible claims of quality that allowed individual health maintenance organizations to stand out and the industry to legitimate itself as a customer-centered and cost-focused innovation. Enthusiastic consumers may also take the initiative in legitimating a new form through certification contests and product demonstrations. In the bicycle industry, clubs composed of enthusiasts organized races to establish the bicycle as a source of health and vitality (Smith 1973).

Thus, strategies of claimmaking can vary from using institutionalized programs and conferences, to report cards and contests. If adopting accepted procedures masks differences between the new form and others, contests exalt differences within the new form and bracket the new form as a discontinuity. Contests are mirrors that allow firms to observe themselves: they provide a frame of comparability and, thereby, establish a new form as a category. White (1992, 13) noted, "Burger King, MacDonald's, Wendy's and so on induce a *net category of equivalence*, the fast-food restaurant, exactly and only by striving to be better—which requires, and therefore, induces as a presupposition, being comparable" (italics mine).

Certification Contests

An important but underemphasized source of legitimacy for new organizational forms is certification contests organized by parties involved with the new form. Certification contests are yardstick competitions in which participants are ranked on socially legitimate criteria. Despite their popularity, certification contests have been overlooked as a source of cognitive validity and social standing in the literature on organizational legitimacy. In many industries, special-purpose organizations establish contests to evaluate products or firms, rank-order participants according to their performance on preset criteria, and sometimes give prizes to winners in yardstick competitions. For example, insurance companies are rated by A. M. Best or Moody's and are classified on the basis of their viability. Michelin guidebooks and the AAA tour books rank-order restaurants and determine their standing in the eyes of consumers. Consumer Reports ranks rival products in numerous product categories, ranging from exercise machines to automobiles, and influences their taken-for-grantedness. J. D. Powers ranks automobiles according to their performance on predefined criteria and shapes the image of automobile manufacturers. Similarly, business magazines such as *Forbes, Business Week, Money,* and *Smart Money* rank mutual funds on the basis of their performance in up and down markets and reduce uncertainty for prospective investors.

Such certification contests are social tests of products and organizations (Thompson 1967) wherein the technical criteria chosen to evaluate performance are themselves the outcomes of institutional processes. In new industries, certification contests structure search in crowded and confused markets and circumvent the issue of measuring capabilities. Indeed, certification contests may induce artificial distinctions between equivalent participants and foster Type II errors (false positives), such that winners in one year may have lesser capabilities than winners of other years.

Certification contests are a source of legitimacy because they simultaneously enable activists to legitimate the form and enable individual firms to build reputations. The effects of certification contests on reputations are particularly important. Victories in certification contests are small, fortuitous events that create a reputation that becomes magnified by positive feedback. Victories in certification contests legitimate organizations and validate their reputation because of the taken-for-granted axiom that winners are "better" than losers and the belief that contests embody the idea of rational and impartial testing. Thus, certification contests shape the reputations of individual organizations and influence their viability.

But certification contests also have form-level effects. By providing extrinsic criteria of fitness, certification contests reduce the ambiguity caused by the lack of standards and the absence of complete knowledge (Thompson 1967, 86–91), and improve the taken-for-grantedness of new forms. Contests explain the new form to consumers, financiers, and competitors, diffuse knowledge about the form, and justify the new form by investing it with a sheen of credibility. The very act of discriminating among members of a social order makes the social order cognitively valid and appropriate.

In turn, the macro-level legitimation of a new organizational form is likely to strengthen the beliefs of potential founders about the viability of their ventures and induce them to incorporate their ventures and commence operations. Certification contests may be seen as mechanisms that provide social proof that a product is safe, beneficial, and viable. Thus, the larger the number of certification contests in a new industry, the stronger is the taken-for-grantedness of the new form and the easier it is for prospective founders to gain access to resources, incorporate their ventures, and commence operations. Therefore:

Hypothesis 1a: *The greater the number of certification contests, the more likely are potential founders to incorporate ventures.*

Hypothesis 1b: *The greater the number of certification contests, the more likely are potential founders to commence operations.*

Start-ups already in operation are likely to incorporate themselves at a faster rate than other potential founders when a new form becomes legitimate. Since operational start-ups manufacture products and deliver services and have greater know-how and a better track record than other potential founders, they are more likely to expand when they encounter proof of the viability of the product. The larger the number of certification contests, the greater is the facticity of the new organizational form and the more likely are operational start-ups to increase their growth. The first step in the process, of course, is to incorporate themselves, because a legal identity is a prerequisite for them in obtaining financing from strangers. A legal identity is a mechanism of impersonal trust designed to enable entrepreneurs to obtain resources from strangers (Zucker 1986). Therefore:

Hypothesis 2a: *The greater the number of certification contests, the more likely are unincorporated producers to establish legal identities.*

Certification contests also enable incorporated entities to acquire resources and start operations by enhancing the legitimacy of the new organizational form. Entrepreneurship entails obtaining resources from strangers and offering goods and services to strangers (Stinchcombe 1965). The larger the number of certification contests, the greater is the taken-for-grantedness of the organizational form and the easier it is for incorporated entities to obtain resources from strangers and commence operations. Therefore:

Hypothesis 2b: *The greater the number of certification contests, the more likely are incorporated entities to commence operations.*

The American Automobile Industry

The hypotheses were tested in a study of the early American automobile industry from 1893 until 1912. The early history of any industry, as Hannan and Carroll (1992, 164) observed, is the period in which the legitimation constraints ought to be the strongest. The industry was at risk of new firms being founded since 1893 and faced a problem of legitimacy. Speed and reliability races organized by automobile clubs as certification contests were responsible for the legitimacy of the automobile. By 1913, reliability races were discontinued because of the social acceptance of the automobile. Speed races continued because they had become a sport and a source of entertainment.

The early American automobile industry was chosen as the research setting for two reasons. First, there is an implicit presumption in the literature that producers are the central actors of legitimating new forms (see Aldrich 1999). But producers may be unable to organize collective action because of free-riding problems. Enthusiastic consumers may leap into the breach and organize campaigns to legitimate new organizational forms. Second, reliability and speed contests created bridges between producers and consumers. There has been little study of the producer-consumer interface in sociological analyses of new industries. Frenzen, Hirsch, and Zerrillo (1994, 410) noted that the "processual linking of producers and consumers is a rich, though still unexplored research arena for economic sociology, with available archival and contemporary data sources waiting to be mined."

Although the origins of the automobile industry can be traced to a patent filed by George Selden in 1879 for a gasoline engine, it was only in 1893 that the Duryea brothers demonstrated that the automobile was a viable means of transportation. During the intervening period between the Selden patent and the Duryea vehicle, a few able inventors such as Roper, Olds, and Morrison explored the possibilities of developing motor cars (Flink 1988). After the demonstration of the automobile by the Duryeas in 1893, there was a flurry of inventive and commercial activity to exploit the potential of steam, electricity, and gasoline as the sources of motive power for automobiles (Rae

1959). The first successful organizing attempt to produce and market automobiles was the firm set up by the Duryeas in 1895 (Flink 1970).

As a novel technology, the automobile per se was unfamiliar to prospective consumers and putative inventors. Consumers were confused because the source of power, the number of cylinders, systems of steering and control, and the mode of stopping were topics of considerable controversy (Thomas 1977, 19). The only point of agreement about the automobile was that it could not be powered by animals. Consumers were hesitant to purchase cars because they felt that they were in no position to decide if the engineers could not agree on the best design (Epstein 1928, 89–92). Moreover, consumers were still reeling from an earlier debacle: the explosive growth and collapse of the bicycle industry (Rae 1959).

Consumers also could not evaluate the products offered by producers. In turn, producers suffered from a dearth of information about the strengths and weaknesses of rival designs. Hiram Maxim, a pioneer of the industry, wrote that he was "blissfully ignorant that others were working with might and main . . . on road vehicles" (cited in Thomas 1977, 17). Writers in automobile magazines and the local press complained about the proliferation of firms without track records and reputations (Flink 1988). Many cars were unable to complete a drive successfully and had to be hauled back by a team of horses. Quite a few vehicles were designed with whip sockets and harness hitches (Epstein 1928), and the misleading advertisements issued by some firms evoked complaints against advertising.

Additionally, since the automobile threatened to displace the horse-drawn carriage, it evoked some opposition from horse breeders, livery stable owners, and horse-drawn vehicle driver associations (Flink 1970, 64). These groups frequently presented petitions urging civil authorities to ban the automobile on public roads because it jeopardized safety and was a plaything of the rich.

The dearth of institutional standing for the automobile industry and individual firms was complicated by the fact that customers with the potential to influence the market, such as the War Department, the Post Office, and municipal governments, were late to adopt the automobile (1908–1909), and even then their policies did not give preference to any one technology or manufacturer (Flink 1988, 120–25). Trade associations and professional bodies did not exist in the first five to six years of the industry. Although the

National Association of Automobile Manufacturers was established in 1900, it failed to ensure product quality and was superseded by the Association of Licensed Automobile Manufacturers (ALAM), which was formed in 1903. The ALAM was a trade association formed to license the Selden patent and was ostensibly set up to prevent incursions by unlicensed producers. But the Selden patent right was widely disregarded and the ALAM was unable to secure quality by enforcing its threat of litigation because of its own internal divisions.

A rival association, called the American Motor Car Manufacturer's Association (AMCMA), was established in 1905 and also proved to be an ineffective mechanism of collective action. Both trade associations disintegrated between 1909 and 1911 as a result of legal battles, and their secondary functions were assumed by the Society of Automotive Engineers (SAE), which was established in 1905. The SAE was a professional body of engineers that focused on common standards for automobile components made by suppliers, but it had little ability to police the technical quality of the cars made by automobile producers (Flink 1970, 289).

It was in this context that numerous enthusiasts in the industry began to organize contests. The first contest was the *Times-Herald* race held on Thanksgiving Day in 1895. The publisher of the *Times*, H. H. Kohlsaat, wanted to organize the competition "with the desire to promote, encourage and stimulate the invention, development and perfection and general adoption of motor vehicles" (quoted in Thomas 1977, 21). Five of the eleven original entrants participated, and only two vehicles were able to complete the race. The first prize of $10,000 was won by a Duryea car powered by gasoline that had a winning speed of 8 miles an hour. The *Times-Herald* report the next day stated that the race had been run in 30-degree temperatures "through deep snow and along ruts that would have tried horses to the utmost" and implied that automobiles were practical.

Soon thereafter *Cosmopolitan Magazine* offered a prize of $3,000 and held a contest on May 30, 1896, that was won by a Duryea. Subsequently, the Rhode Island State Fair Association offered $5,000 in prize money and organized a competition that was won by an electric car. The Riker Electric car won the race, but spectators found the contest to be so dull that they originated the cry "get a horse" (Flink 1970, 42). The stage was set for numerous enthusiasts to sponsor reliability contests (hill climbing runs, endurance tours, and fuel economy contests) and speed races. Contests were organized in Trenton, Detroit, Omaha, Chicago, Empire City, Brighton Beach, Florida, and speedways such as Indianapolis and Atlanta. In 1901, the Automobile Association of America's New York City club formulated a set of racing rules and assisted promoters.

Organizers of these contests placed few restrictions on participants so as to increase the number of entries. There were strong incentives for firms to participate in these contests because they had a chance to test technical improvements and acquire publicity as innovators (Flink 1988). Manufacturers sponsored cars directly in these contests, and although a few contests, especially the Glidden tour, stipulated that cars were to be driven by their owners, firms were able to circumvent this, because any executive of an auto firm could drive the recent models himself (Flink 1970, 42). Some contests were one-shot exercises, and others, such as the Glidden reliability tour or the Vanderbilt Cup speed races, were organized by different groups of organizers each year. All competitions awarded a prize to the first-place contestant, whereas a few dispensed additional prizes to second- and third-place contestants. Moreover, organizers of the contests also sought to assure the viewing public of their integrity by allowing extensive press coverage and instituting grievance procedures (Thomas 1977). Despite the fact that these contests were free to the viewing public, there were still sufficient incentives for organizers to schedule such events. Many of the organizers were enthusiastic activists, committed to the development of the automobile; there was no incentive problem, because the organizers could exclude others from the psychological benefits of contributing to a cause or to the creation of automobile clubs (Rae 1959; Flink 1988).

As the public watched contests and learned about them through the media, knowledge of the automobile per se diffused across different sections of American society. Newspapers such as the *Chicago Times-Herald* and newsmagazines such as *Cosmopolitan Magazine* sponsored contests. Specialized trade journals arose to disseminate information about the automobile, and many of them dedicated resources to the coverage of contests such as the Glidden tour, the Vanderbilt races, Indy races, and more-local contests.

As a result, the automobile began to be considered to be more reliable than

a horse. By 1906, observers such as Frank Munsey were proclaiming the automobile to be inevitable. Although the diffusion of the automobile into rural
areas evoked hostility from farmers in some areas, the resentment did not
snowball into a large movement or a call for restrictive legislation (Flink
1970). By 1909, industry insiders such as Duryea were of the view that the
novelty of the automobile had worn off. By 1912, organizers of reliability races
stopped organizing them because the automobile was accepted as a safe and
dependable product. Races such as the Glidden tour were discontinued, and
firms such as Ford even decided to stop entering cars in races. Speed races,
however, continued to be organized because they had become a sport.

DATA AND METHODS

Data on founders were collected from the *Standard Catalogue of American Cars,
1805–1942* (Kimes 1985; Kimes and Clark 1989). The two editions of the
Standard Catalogue of American Cars provided valuable information: the year
in which the prototype was completed, the year in which a venture was incorporated, the year of operational start-up, and the year in which developers terminated their efforts. Data on races were obtained from numerous issues of the
premier automobile journal in the industry, *Horseless Age.*

During the period between 1893 and 1912, there was considerable organizational ferment in the automobile industry. Preexisting firms established in
other industries entered the automobile industry. The risk set consisted of all
firms in industries such as bicycle making, carriage manufacture, engine manufacture, and boat making. From this risk set, some firms developed prototypes, but only a few succeeded in producing automobiles and in reaching the
destination state (Epstein 1928; Rae 1959). Lateral entries were not analyzed
as a dependent variable because they did not entail the creation of a new
organization but, instead, involved an adaptive change (diversification) by
existing organizations.

The construction of new organizations was an important source of organizational diversity. Figure 10.1 depicts the state transitions involved in the formation of new organizations in the American automobile industry. It identi-
fies developers of prototypes as potential founders. A prototype was defined as

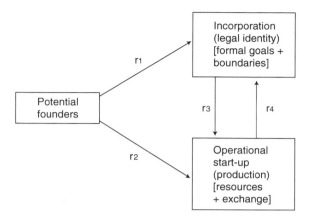

Figure 10.1 Founding subprocesses in the early American auto industry

a four-wheeled powered entity that was built as an example, experiment, or backyard creation by an individual or group of individuals.

The universe of potential founders without prototypes was enormous and the risk set comprised entrepreneurs in a wide range of industries, ranging from boat making to sewing machine manufacture. Some of these businessmen succeeded in building incorporated entities and eventually producing automobiles, but many were unsuccessful (Flink 1970; Rae 1959). Because this group was potentially boundless, it was not included in the analyses. The number of potential founders with prototypes was tightly delimited, however, so the analysis was restricted to individuals or groups who had completed the development of automobile prototypes.

After the Duryeas demonstrated their car in 1893, numerous individuals began developing prototypes of the automobile. Hundreds of people experimented with the automobile and developed prototypes relying on different sources of power. They invested significant amounts of time, effort, and emotion in the development of prototypes. Some of the developers of prototypes succeeded in reaching the destination state of incorporation. For example, the Duryea brothers demonstrated their prototype in 1893 and went on to establish a firm in 1895. Others also commenced operations by starting to produce and sell cars. Only the potential founders with prototypes were included in the analysis.

Figure 10.1 shows that potential founders with prototypes could incorporate (r1) or start operations (r2), incorporate and then commence operations (r3), or, finally, start operations and then establish their legal identity (r4). The figure highlights three striking characteristics of the founding process in the American automobile industry. It suggests that the creation of new organizations was a heterogeneous process rather than a fixed sequence. Moreover, it also shows that potential founders could fail to complete any of the possible transitions, thereby reducing organizational diversity. Finally, Figure 10.1 indicates that the operational start-up rate was a composite of r2 and r3 whereas the incorporation rate was a function of r1 and r4.

Dependent Variables

There were two dependent variables in the analysis. *Incorporation* was defined as the acquisition of a legal identity, that is, a firm or company was organized or incorporated, according to Kimes and Clark (1989). *Operational start-up* was defined as the initiation of manufacture of cars for the purpose of selling them. Both of these variables were coded as binary variables with the year of incorporation/start-up being coded 1. In other years, these variables were coded 0.

Observations on entrepreneurs ended when they disavowed their intention to manufacture, changed their line of business, sold their prototype to other manufacturers, became bankrupt, lost their identity by absorption, or disappeared from sight and their continuation became doubtful. Some potential founders disavowed their intention to manufacture because they judged their venture to be imprudent, and the year in which they declared their intention not to manufacture was treated as the year of termination. In a few other cases, potential founders built prototypes as a hobby; such founders were presumed to have built a prototype at the beginning of the year and disavowed the intention to manufacture at the end of the same year. When potential founders decided to become an engine maker, a car dealer, or a garage instead of an automobile producer, they were deemed to have changed their line of business. A prototype developer's sale of an experimental automobile and rights to its manufacture was also treated as the termination of a founding attempt. Bankruptcy and the loss of identity because of absorption by other producers were also viewed as terminations of founding attempts.

Potential founders were deemed to have terminated their founding attempts when their continuation became doubtful. In several cases, Kimes and Clark (1989) did not provide a termination date for several potential founders, but, for some of these cases, Kimes and Clark provided the year in which a founder was observed and then noted that there was no further record of the founder in city directories, or they indicated that subsequent continuation was doubted. In other cases in which Kimes and Clark (1989) did not provide such information but merely indicated the last observed date, potential founders were deemed to have terminated their founding efforts if there was no subsequent mention of them in the authoritative periodical of the day, the *Horseless Age*. This procedure was analogous to the one followed in the Baum and Mezias (1992) study of the Manhattan hotel industry in which hotels were deemed to have ceased operations when they were delisted by the *Red Book* and other archival sources.

Independent Variables

Certification contests were defined as the sum of the number of the speed and reliability races organized in a year. The number of speed and reliability races was cumulated and updated each year and combined to construct a time-varying measure of certification contests.

Several control variables were created. *Duration* was defined as the natural logarithm of elapsed time from the completion of prototype development and the event of interest (incorporation or operational start-up). It was included because long gestation periods can reduce the success of founding attempts. *Spinout* was defined as firms started by individuals who had co-developed a prototype in a given firm and then left that firm to start their own organization. It was coded as a dummy variable. *Founding status* was constructed to assess if incorporated entities commenced operations faster than others and if operational start-ups incorporated at a greater rate than others. In the analyses of incorporation, it was set equal to 1 after unincorporated entrepreneurs commenced operations. Similarly, in the analyses of operational start-ups, it was set equal to 1 after potential entrepreneurs incorporated their ventures. *Gasoline-powered car* was created to distinguish experimenters who chose to work on the gasoline-powered car. *Density*, or the number of existing organizations, was included to control for competition from lateral entries and new operational start-ups already in existence. Since the data did not span the complete history of the industry, curvilinear density effects could not be modeled. *Sales* was treated as a control, following Carroll and Swaminathan (1991), who used the log of sales as a control in their studies of foundings in the brewing industry. Density and sales were lagged by a year.

Tables 10.1 and 10.2 provide the descriptive statistics for the data used to analyze incorporations and operational start-ups. An inspection of the tables indicates that the correlations are in the expected directions, although the log of sales is highly correlated with cumulative contests.

Methods and Models

Incorporation and operational start-up were the two dependent variables of interest. They were estimated using logit models. The logit function takes the following form:

Table 10.1

Correlations Among the Variables Used to Study
Incorporation Rate Among Prototype Developers in the
American Automobile Industry, 1893–1912

	1	2	3	4	5	6	7
1. Gasoline power		.07[a]	.03[a]	.03[a]	.03[a]	.06	.06
2. Spinout status			.01[a]	.02[a]	.08[a]	.17[a]	.20[a]
3. Founding status				.02[a]	−.03[a]	−.02[a]	−.03[a]
4. Log of duration					.06[a]	−.05[a]	.07[a]
5. Density						.31[a]	.60[a]
6. Log of sales							.81[a]
7. Cumulative contests							

NOTE: [a]p < .05

$$\log(P(t)/[1-P(t)]) = a + b_i x_i + c_j x_j(t),$$

where $P(t)$ is the probability of incorporation or start-up, bi is the set of coefficients for explanatory variables xi that do not change over time, cj is the set of coefficients for explanatory variables xj(t) that do change with time, and a is a constant. The hazard rates of incorporation and start-up were modeled separately (Tuma and Hannan 1984). To use time-varying independent variables, the history of all potential founders was split into one-year records or spells, with all spells except the year of incorporation/start-up being coded as right-censored.

When the data structure contains multiple observations per potential founder, the observations are not independent. In such cases, a well-recognized option in the literature is to calculate the standard errors of estimates of the beta coefficients using a robust estimation procedure rather than a standard estimation procedure (White 1980). The use of robust estimation has no effect on coefficient estimation, but it does tend to increase the standard errors of the estimates of the coefficients. The net effect is to *increase* p values and to provide a more conservative test of the hypotheses by accounting for the clustering of observations per firm.

Table 10.2

Correlations Among the Variables Used to Study
Operational Start-up Rate Among Prototype Developers
in the American Automobile Industry, 1893–1912

	1	*2*	*3*	*4*	*5*	*6*	*7*
1. Gasoline power		.07[a]	.07[a]	−.03[a]	.02[a]	.02[a]	.01[a]
2. Spinout status			.07[a]	−.06[a]	.08[a]	.16[a]	.19[a]
3. Founding status				.03[a]	.03[a]	.02[a]	.03[a]
4. Log of duration					−.07[a]	−.06[a]	−.05[a]
5. Density						.33[a]	.69[a]
6. Log of sales							.80
7. Cumulative contests							

NOTE: [a]p < .05

There is also a potential issue of unobserved heterogeneity when modeling the discrete hazard rates of incorporation and operational start-up. Although the control variables explicitly take into account endowments of resources, there may be unobserved factors that influence incorporation/operational start-up. Since unobserved heterogeneity is essentially an issue of unmeasured serial correlation among observations pertaining to a firm, one option is to build random-effects models that treat serial correlation of firm-specific observations as exchangeable (that is, constant). Liang and Zeger's (1986) Generalized Equations Estimator (GEE) approach to estimating a wide variety of regression models was used. PROC XTGEE in the STATA package was employed to estimate random-effects logit models with a robust estimator of variance.

RESULTS

Table 10.3 shows the results obtained in the analyses of the incorporation and operational start-ups in the American automobile industry from 1893 to 1912. Models 1 and 2 pertain to incorporation, and Models 3 and 4 concern operational start-up. Model 1 shows that entrepreneurs using gasoline technology were significantly more likely to incorporate. Spinouts and prospective founders who had commenced operations also were significantly more likely to incorporate than others. The length of the gestation period has significant negative effects. Density has positive effects rather than negative effects, indicating that density legitimated the form and induced incorporations. Cumulative contests have insignificant effects, however, and hypothesis 1a is not supported. Model 2 includes an interaction term (cumulative contests × founding-status dummy) to assess whether certification contests induce start-ups to incorporate. In these analyzes, the founding-status dummy is set to 1 if a founder has commenced operations. The effect is positive and significant, and hypothesis 2a is confirmed.[2]

---

2. In unreported analyses, including second-order density effects did not change the results. While there was a significant (.025, −.011) relationship between density and incorporation, the effect of cumulative contests remained insignificant. Adding the effect of lagged incorporations posed a problem because they were collinear with cumulative contests (.81).

Table 10.3
Random Effects Logit Models of Incorporation and Start-up

VARIABLES	Incorporation		Operational Start-up	
	MODEL 1	MODEL 2	MODEL 3	MODEL 4
Constant	-2.90^b	-2.88^b	-2.49^b	-2.51^b
	(.199)	(.201)	(.177)	(.179)
Gasoline power	$.226^b$	$.220^b$	$.257^b$	$.260^b$
	(.130)	(.131)	(.106)	(.106)
Spinout status	$.725^b$	$.719^b$	$.709^b$	$.716^b$
	(.224)	(.227)	(.207)	(.205)
Founding status	2.38^b	2.14^b	3.21^b	3.72^b
	(.154)	(.259)	(.336)	(.407)
Log of duration	$-.737^b$	$.740^b$	-1.01^b	1.02^b
	(.134)	(.134)	(.129)	(.132)
Density of organizations	$.002^a$	$.002^a$	$.009^b$	$.009^b$
	(.001)	(.001)	(.003)	(.003)
Cumulative contests	.0007	.0006	$.001^a$	$.001^a$
	(.0007)	(.0007)	(.0008)	(.0008)
Founding status × cumulative contests		$.004^b$		$-.007^b$
		(.002)		(.002)
chi-square	249.25^b	276.99^b	180.322^b	193.82^b
no. of spells	4,033	4,033	3,148	3,148
no. of events	258	258	510	510

NOTE: ^{a}p < .05, ^{b}p < .01 one-tailed tests

Models 3 and 4 concern operational start-ups. Model 3 shows that entrepreneurs using gasoline technology were significantly more likely to commence operations. Spinouts and prospective founders who had commenced operations also were significantly more likely to incorporate than others. The length of the gestation period has significant negative effects. Density has positive effects, indicating that it legitimated the form and induced operational start-ups. The effects of cumulative contests are significant and positive, and hypothesis 1b is confirmed. Model 4 includes an interaction term (cumulative contests × founding-status dummy) to test whether certification contests induce incorporated entities to commence operations. The founding-status dummy is set to 1 when a potential founder has incorporated his venture.

Contrary to prediction, the interaction term is significant and negative, imply-ing that as contests increased, incorporated producers did not commence operations. Hence, hypothesis 2b was disconfirmed.[3]

DISCUSSION

This chapter began by noting that reported research seldom analyzed how strategies of legitimation used by activists influenced foundings. It analyzed the subprocesses of incorporation and operational start-up, and hypothesized that certification contests would legitimate a new organizational form and increase incorporation and operational start-up rates.

The findings clearly show that certification contests exert different effects on the subprocesses of incorporation and operational start-up. Analyses of incorporation show that cumulative contests had insignificant main effects, but analyses of operational start-ups indicate that cumulative contests had sig-nificant positive effects. The asymmetrical effects of contests can be traced to the nature of the two founding subprocesses in question. Incorporation is an exploratory act, and the chartering of firms entails routinized legal recognition of entrepreneurial intentions by governments. By contrast, operational start-up means that resources are invested, funds are risked, and cars are produced by entrepreneurs and sold to consumers. Hence, incorporation and operational start-up differ in the amount of organizing costs incurred by founders.

Cumulative contests emphasizing speed and reliability led to perceptions of the automobile as a safe and dependable vehicle. Since races blended the prac-tice of racing with the conceptual logic of testing, they enhanced the techno-commercial viability of the automobile. Races also were opportunities for pro-ducers to enter their cars so as to gain a reputation for product quality. Thus, contests strengthened the beliefs of potential founders with prototypes about the viability of the car and the feasibility of acquiring a reputation, induced them to invest resources and risk capital, and encouraged them to commence

---

3. In unreported analyses, including the second-order effects of density did not alter results. While a significant (.031, −.006) relationship existed between density and start-ups, cumulative contests con-tinued to be significant. Inclusion of lagged prior start-ups also did not modify the findings.

production. Thus, contests encouraged high cost founding activity. By contrast, contests did not affect the enthusiasm of entrepreneurs for gaining legal recognition of their intentions. For low-cost founding activity to occur, feedback from the contests that the automobile was safe and viable was not a necessary precondition. Instead, the sheer prevalence of producers constituted enough feedback for potential founders to engage in low-cost activity.

Indeed, although population density was inserted as a control for competition and was expected to have negative effects, it had significant positive effects on incorporation and operational start-ups. This finding sheds light on the micro-foundations of ecological theory and indicates that the emphasis on legitimation is compatible with a rational-actor model of entrepreneurs. Institutional theorists, notably Zucker (1989), have argued that organizational ecologists fail to delineate the effects of legitimation on the inclinations of potential founders. The results obtained in this study suggest that the macro-level processes of density dependent legitimation affect entrepreneurial beliefs about the viability of ventures.

The findings also show that certification contests exert different effects on unincorporated producers who have commenced operations and incorporated entrepreneurs who have yet to start operations. As predicted, the cumulative number of automobile contests induced unincorporated producers who already had started operations to incorporate themselves. These results indicate that certification contests enhance legitimacy of a form, consolidate the beliefs of entrepreneurs about future growth prospects, and induce them to gain a legal identity with a view to obtaining resources from strangers. Contrary to predictions, however, the cumulative number of contests had a negative effect on the incorporated producers seeking to commence operations. Thus, contests deterred incorporated producers from becoming producers. In the automobile industry, contests not only enhanced the legitimacy of the form but also built reputations of firms. Hence, it is possible that incorporated ventures may have been deterred from starting production because they lacked a reputation, whereas other producers were already establishing reputations. Unincorporated producers who had already started operations had begun to acquire a reputation, and contests simply made it easier for them to acquire a legal identity. This interpretation suggests that there may be complex interactions between form-level legitimacy and firm-level reputation and that they exert different effects on incorporated ventures and operational start-ups.

In general, the results suggest that different mechanisms of legitimating the form can have different effects on subprocesses of founding. Social proof generated by certification contests spurred high-cost foundings in the form of operational start-ups and induced them to expand by incorporating themselves. In diametric opposition, the social proof provided by certification contests had no effect on incorporations and deterred enthusiastic founders from starting operations. In contrast, the sheer prevalence of the form generated symmetrical effects on incorporations and operational start-ups. Thus, density dependent effects of legitimation may be general and robust across founding subprocesses, whereas certification contests and other idiosyncratic methods of legitimation may have divergent effects. Indeed, while certification contests established by automobile clubs played an important role in the early automobile industry, it is possible that such enthusiasts do not play such a consequential role in other new industries. Government regulation, professional societies, or even collective action through trade associations may be more relevant building blocks of form-level legitimacy. In view of these institutional variations, density dependent approaches also have value because of their generalizability and simplicity (Hannan and Carroll 1995).

The limitations of this study point to some avenues for future research. One limitation of the study is that it did not analyze the effects of prior collaboration among founders and their prior start-up experience. Some researchers suggest that prior start-up experience, prior histories of collaboration, and the structure of the board of directors can decisively affect the pace and success of organization-building efforts (Eisenhardt and Schoonhoven 1990; Romanelli 1989; Van de Ven 1980). Additional studies are needed to assess directly the impact of founding team demography and governance structure, in particular, and resource endowments, in general, on the success of organization-building efforts. A rich area for future work is to explore interactions between the macro-level process of legitimation and micro-level resource endowments of firms and their effects on incorporation and operational start-up.

Furthermore, this study analyzed incorporation and operational start-ups in the early history of the American automobile industry. In the early history of any industry, r-strategists (first-movers in the industry) are likely to predominate but the later history of industries is characterized by the advent of K-strategists (later entrants who compete on efficiency) and the concomitant processes of concentration (Brittain and Freeman 1980). Research on incorporation and start-ups in the later history of industries is required to improve the generalizability of the results obtained in this study. Additionally, this study did not examine the effect of technological cycles on new organizations. Anderson and Tushman (1990) suggested that technological discontinuities unleash an era of ferment characterized by a struggle among rival designs that lasts until one design becomes dominant. Thereafter, an era of incremental change ensues and lasts until it is broken by the appearance of the next discontinuity. Future research needs to account explicitly for the effects of technological cycles on the selection of emerging organizations.

Moreover, this study investigated the founding subprocesses of incorporation and start-up in a population of for-profit business enterprises. Since not-for-profit nonbusiness enterprises tend to be characterized by ambiguous technologies and be susceptible to greater institutional pressures (Singh, Tucker, and House 1986), it is necessary to analyze incorporation and start-up in nonbusiness settings to ascertain the generality of the findings of this study.

Finally, researchers also need to establish whether the subprocesses of incorporation and operational start-up systematically differ from other subprocesses of founding, such as resource acquisition, social organization, and initial public offerings (Hannan and Freeman 1989). The detailed study of founding subprocesses is not only essential to expand our knowledge of organizational diversity but is also vital to shift attention from the entrepreneur to the organization building process as an object of inquiry.

11

Social Movement Theory and the Evolution of New Organizational Forms

ANAND SWAMINATHAN AND JAMES B. WADE

New organizational forms face formidable obstacles in that new roles have to be learned, external ties to supporters are often lacking, and they often must rely on social relations among strangers (Stinchcombe 1965). As a result, new organizations suffer from a liability of newness and often fail (Freeman, Carroll, and Hannan 1983). But some new organizational forms nevertheless survive and grow. In part this occurs because some new organizational populations have superior technology or simply contain organizations that fit the existing environmental contingencies. Often, however, these organizations overcome substantial obstacles through collective strategies that bear an uncanny resemblance to tactics and strategies adopted by organizations that spearhead social movements (Carroll 1997, 129–30; Hannan and Carroll 1992, 202–4). With a few notable exceptions (Aldrich and Fiol 1994; Hunt and Aldrich 1998), the entrepreneurship literature has not emphasized how strategies of collective action can promote entrepreneurial success.

Like social movements, entrepreneurs in emerging industries face the key task of gaining cognitive and sociopolitical legitimacy (Aldrich and Fiol 1994; Delacroix and Rao 1994). In attempting to achieve this legitimacy, interactions between firms often take on a social-movement–like character. Cooperation

We appreciate comments from Kim Elsbach, Elaine Romanelli, and Kaye Schoonhoven on earlier drafts of this manuscript. We also thank Violina Rindova for providing us with data on the specialty coffee industry.

rather than competition is the norm as founders attempt to mobilize resources through collective action, such as the formation of trade associations and mutual benefit societies. Also like social movements, new organizational forms need to mobilize resources to survive and grow. Our objective in this chapter is to develop a diverse set of theoretical propositions that we hope will highlight the utility of applying ideas and findings from social movement theory and research to the study of the evolution of new organizational forms. Therefore, we do not attempt to develop an overarching theoretical model of how social movement theory applies to entrepreneurship. Throughout the chapter, we use examples from the emergent phase of a variety of industries to support our propositions. In particular, we draw on descriptive data that we have gathered on craft breweries, boutique wineries, and specialty coffee shops.

RESOURCE MOBILIZATION AND ENTREPRENEURSHIP

According to resource mobilization theory, the dominant perspective on social movements, social movements grow and decline as resource levels fluctuate (Jenkins and Perrow 1977; McCarthy and Zald 1973; 1977). Four general types of resources need to be accumulated for collective action to occur. These are subsumed under the broad categories of people (both leadership and cadre), expertise or prior experience, financial and information resources, and legitimacy (Cress and Snow 1996). Builders of new organizations must acquire a similar set of resources if they are to succeed. First, the characteristics and human capital of the founders often influence the survival prospects of new organizations (Brüderl, Preisendörfer, and Ziegler 1992). Results concerning the influence of human capital on firm performance in the entrepreneurship literature are mixed. One study showed, for instance, that companies founded by individuals who had entrepreneurial parents had higher sales (Duchesneau and Gartner 1988). In contrast, Cooper, Dunkelberg, and Woo (1988a) found no relationship between family background and the survival of new ventures.

The second necessary resource is expertise or prior experience. The impact of age, education, and experience of founders on the founding and performance of new firms has also been investigated. Experience in founding prior start-ups has been shown to have both positive (Doutriax and Simyar 1987) and negative (Dunkelberg et al. 1987) effects on firm performance. Eisenhardt and Schoonhoven (1990) found no relationship between founding team experience and new firm growth. While education seems to be an important predictor of success in some instances, it appears to have a negative effect in high technology industries (Cooper and Gimeno-Gascon 1992).

The third requirement for new organizations is financial and information resources. Entrepreneurs who start businesses with greater initial capital have an increased chance of success (Cooper and Gimeno-Gascon 1992). Informal sources of capital, most often family, friends, and business associates, provide smaller amounts of funds at an earlier stage in a new venture, with formal venture capital funds playing a larger role in late-stage financing (Frear and Wetzel 1989; 1990; 1992). Entrepreneurs also network with others to gain access to sources of information, capital, and expertise (Cooper and Gimeno-Gascon 1992). The use of professionals to develop business plans and the use of accountants, for instance, is positively correlated with performance (Duchesneau and Gartner 1988). Aldrich, Rosen, and Woodward (1987) showed that initial profitability was correlated with network density and the average strength of ties, while network size was related to later profitability. Similarly, Dollinger (1985) found that the extent to which entrepreneurs devoted time to noncustomer contacts, suppliers, and trade associations was positively related to performance.

While entrepreneurship research typically focuses on resources that facilitate the founding, growth, and survival of individual organizations, we use resource mobilization theory to draw attention to the collective mobilization of resources by organizations that belong to a particular form. Resource mobilization theorists call attention to the structures and incentives that make collective action more or less costly (McCarthy and Zald 1977; Oberschall 1973). New social movements must adopt strategies that link them to supporters and other resources if they are to be successful. Often, they must also overcome determined opposition by countermovements.

Builders of new organizational forms face similar constraints. New organizations must acquire capital as well as individuals with the requisite skills and capabilities. Moreover, both social movements and new organizational forms must attain at least some degree of external legitimacy, the fourth critical resource, if they are to mobilize resources and attain their goals. Because of these similarities, the strategies and tactics used by social movements to acquire resources and sustain collective action also should be applicable to new organizational populations in the business sector. There are two important parallels between the evolution of social movements and new organizational forms. First, their emergence is facilitated by changes in the broader sociopolitical and economic environment. Second, the preexisting infrastructure or organizational field in which they are embedded influences both the strategy and performance of social movements and new organizational forms.

ENVIRONMENTAL CHANGE AND OPPORTUNITY STRUCTURE

Changes in the institutional structure and the ideology of powerful actors such as organized political parties and the state create opportunities for insurgents to organize social movements (Jenkins and Perrow 1977; McAdam 1982; Tarrow 1983; Tilly 1978). McAdam (1982), for example, attributed the diffusion of Black protest activity in the 1960s to several trends that strengthened civil rights forces, including the expansion of the Black vote and the shift of Blacks to the Democratic Party. Changes in the political power structure of a state can also open up opportunities for movements to form (Kriesi 1995). For instance, Amenta and Zylan (1991) showed that the Townsend Movement, which sought Federal pensions for the elderly in the Great Depression, was much larger in states that had passed pension laws and in states that had greater executive capacities in terms of public spending than in other states. Political opportunity for movement organizers increases when (1) the institutionalized political system becomes more open, (2) elite alignments become unstable, (3) it is possible to form alliances with elite groups, and (4) the state's capacity and propensity to repress protest decreases (McAdam 1996, 27). Changes in the political opportunity structure have been used to explain the timing of emergence and outcomes for many types of social movements. Among others, these include the Italian protest cycle (Tarrow 1989), the American women's movement (Costain 1992), and the nuclear freeze movement (Meyer 1993).

Just as favorable opportunity structures give rise to social movements, changes in the environmental opportunity structure create niches for new organizational forms. In some cases, changes on the demand side can give rise to new organizational forms. Greater affluence, changes in lifestyle, and consumer demand for greater variety led to the emergence of new organizational forms in the U.S. wine and brewing industries (Delacroix and Solt 1988; Swaminathan 1995; 1998) and in the coffee industry (Rindova and Fombrun, this volume). Technological and institutional discontinuities also open up new niches. In the semiconductor manufacturing industry, foundings seem to be driven by technological innovation (Brittain and Freeman 1980). Abernathy and Clark (1985, 18) suggested that three specific kinds of environmental changes might lead to the formation of a new niche. First, new technological options offer improved performance or new applications that cannot be met by current product designs. Tushman and Anderson (1986) accounted for product substitution through technological changes that destroy the competencies of incumbent firms. The emergence of new product classes such as cement (in 1872), airlines (in 1924), and plain-paper copying (in 1959) is attributed to basic technological innovations. Second, changes in government policy, especially in regulatory regimes, may favor revolutionary strategic developments. Deregulation allowed point-to-point air service providers and nontraditional telecommunication service providers to emerge. Third, changes in consumer preferences may impose requirements that can be met only through new designs. More recently, the rapid growth and use of the Internet opened up opportunities in electronic commerce for retail organizations, banks, and stock brokerages (Hunt and Aldrich 1998). Such a development is consistent with Romanelli's (1989b) view that any event or process that alters patterns of resource flows can create resource spaces for new organizational forms.

> **Proposition 1:** *Changes in the environmental opportunity structure create niches that allow for the emergence of new organizational forms.*

PREEXISTING INFRASTRUCTURE AND THE EVOLUTION OF NEW ORGANIZATIONAL FORMS

The preexisting infrastructure of organizational fields in which new organizational forms are embedded can affect the emergence of collective action and, in turn, influence both the strategy and performance of new organizational forms. As Olson (1965) noted, generating collective action is quite difficult. Once environmental opportunities arise, however, preexisting infrastructure reduces the cost of organizing by facilitating the acquisition of resources through collective action. Preexisting networks can aid in an industry's development by providing linkages to customers as well as sources of human capital. Because preexisting networks are a conduit of information about the industry and the individuals in it, they can also promote trust, a key factor in legitimating an industry (Aldrich and Fiol 1994). For instance, the pro-life movement's initial dependence on the infrastructure of the Catholic Church and later on that of fundamentalist Protestant churches was crucial to its growth (McCarthy 1987). Similarly, existing Black institutions, such as churches and schools, served as an infrastructure through which information and resources could be directed to the civil rights movement in the 1960s. Minkoff (1997) showed that increases in the organizational density of African American civil rights organizations promoted both protest activities by feminists and the formation of women's organizations (see also Clemens 1993). Meyer and Whittier (1994) argued that the feminist movement influenced the evolution of the peace movement. Amenta and Zylan (1991) showed that the Townsend movement to secure federal pensions for the aged was stronger in states that had other strong indigenous organizations, such as the Church of Christ, Scientist, and the Woman's Christian Temperance Union. Ingram and Simons (1998) found that the failure rate of Israeli worker cooperatives decreased with increases in the density of credit cooperatives and kibbutzim, organizations that had a similar ideology.

Preexisting networks provide a source of individuals who can potentially become decision makers in the movement (the cadre), as well as those who may become full-time members of the organization (the professional cadre) (Zald and McCarthy 1987). Preexisting networks serve similar purposes in new industries. In the early semiconductor industry, Bell Labs was a major source of both founders and expert personnel for new firms in the industry (Braun and Macdonald 1982). Besides providing a source for recruitment into the industry, the informal and formal networks at Bell Labs were a source of information that could be used to identify potential employees with the requisite skills. Similarly, pharmaceutical firms serve as a source of talent for biotech firms, and

Internet firms often recruit executives from established firms. If potential customers are also linked into networks, new industry members may have access to a conduit to generate publicity about the industry and recruit customers. Early personal computer firms could draw on numerous hobbyists who were organized into user groups. These groups not only served as potential customers but also as an organized network through which information about the industry could be channeled to the public.

A preexisting infrastructure can be used by a social movement for purposes other than that for which it was originally designed and thus represents a positive externality for the social movement. If those favoring change are linked together though preexisting relations, the prospects for mobilization are enhanced. Moreover, embeddedness in a preexisting network of relationships helps in acquiring resources and in communicating information among movement participants (Walker 1983). Thus, the fact that many entrepreneurs that later started brewpubs and microbreweries were involved in home brewing clubs and associations is likely to have created an infrastructure that facilitated the emergence of collective action in these industries. Wade, Swaminathan, and Saxon (1998) speculated that collective action will emerge more quickly in industries in which entrepreneurs have overlapping social and professional networks. The prior experiences of entrepreneurs in the craft brewing industry are likely to have promoted common understandings among industry participants. These prior relationships may be part of the reason why microbreweries have an active industry association and often cooperate by entering into joint purchasing and distribution agreements.

A preexisting infrastructure can also be an important factor in gaining institutional support. Legal mobilization of federal equal employment opportunity laws was widely used by minorities and women in their attempts to gain equality in the labor market (Burstein 1991). Similarly, organizations with new forms often have to mobilize new laws or eliminate restrictive ones to prosper. Earlier generations of organizational forms that have successfully overcome regulatory obstacles may provide a model for successful collective action for newly emerging organizational forms that face similar situations. Farm wineries have benefited from the passage of state-level farm winery laws that allowed direct sale to customers, a practice not allowed for the dominant organizational form, the mass production-based generalist winery. The operation of brewpubs, a similar organizational form that appeared much later, was also initially illegal in most states because producers of beer were generally not allowed to sell their beer on the premises. Over time, however, entrepreneurs mobilized and succeeded in changing these laws to allow for brewpub operation subject to an upper limit on the annual production level. The earlier regulatory successes of entrepreneurs in the farm winery industry may have aided them in their efforts by providing a model for successful collective action. In industries, new organizations that challenge the status quo are typically specialists that initially occupy the periphery of the resource space. Previous generations of specialist organizations provide the raw material for the entry and survival of new organizational forms.

Proposition 2: *The greater the organizational density of challenger organizational forms that entered earlier, the higher the founding rate and the lower the failure rate of organizations with a new form.*

In some cases, increasing density of organizations with the new form may lead to greater niche overlap and competition with the challenger organizations that entered the industry in an earlier period. Minkoff (1997), however, found no evidence of competition between African American civil rights organizations and women's movement organizations. To a large extent, strength of competition depends on the strategies of various challenger organizational forms. Challenger organizational forms that seek to replace the dominant incumbent organizational form may choose strategies that lead either to resource conflict and competition or to a partitioning of the resource space into nonoverlapping niches and the avoidance of competition.

Though preexisting infrastructure encourages the growth of new social movements and industries, it also constrains the range of strategies that are available to these new organizations. Existing organizations that constitute the preexisting infrastructure act as organizational templates for new organizations (DiMaggio and Powell 1983). Conell and Voss (1990) showed that the structure of the organizational field influenced both the emergence and strategy of Knights of Labor local unions among less-skilled iron and steel workers. The prior organization of both iron and steel craft workers and workers in other industries into local unions facilitated the formation of Knights of Labor unions among the less-skilled iron and steel workers. Organizing strategy, however, was constrained by strategies already adopted in the local organizational field by earlier union organizations. Less-skilled iron and steel workers were more likely to adopt a craft strategy in counties where prior craft assembly existed, whereas they were more likely to adopt a quasi-industrial strategy in counties where craft workers had previously joined less-skilled workers to form a quasi-industrial assembly.

Organizational strategy diffuses not only through time as described by Conell and Voss (1990), but also through space. There is often overlap among the memberships of various social movements. Members who cross movement boundaries carry with them models of movement organization, which then diffuse through other social movements (McAdam 1995), thus leading to protest cycles (Tarrow 1994). Thus, it may be no accident that specialty coffee shops, as described by Fombrun and Rindova (this volume), and brewpubs, which emerged at approximately the same time, bear many similarities to each other. Each of these organizational forms sharply differentiated themselves from mass producers by serving specialty (high-quality) products to an upscale clientele. In addition, each population viewed its mass producer counterparts with disdain. Possibly the similarity between these organizational forms and the overlap in their resource base (e.g., customers) led to a mutualistic relationship because the growth of each legitimated a common organizational template. Table 11.1 shows the explosive growth that each of these populations enjoyed between 1982 and 1995. The correlation between the number of brewpubs and specialty coffee shops between 1989 and 1995 was over 0.98 suggesting that these organizational forms might have had a mutualistic relationship.[1]

The emergence of new organizational forms can generate protest cycles (Tarrow 1994) or even feedback effects as the strategies and organizing models used by emerging organizational forms diffuse through the organizational community. For instance, Linda Jacobs, who teaches classes on how to set up adult on-line businesses, claims that the emergence of company web sites on the Internet has aided in legitimizing on-line pornography because these sites

---

1. Of course, this result must be viewed with extreme caution because this correlation is based on a very small number of observations.

Table 11.1

Number of Specialist Beverage Firms, 1970–1995

Year	Farm Wineries[a]	Microbreweries[b]	Brewpubs[b]	Coffee Shops[c]
1970	158	1	0	n/a
1971	163	1	0	n/a
1972	185	1	0	n/a
1973	199	1	0	n/a
1974	226	1	0	n/a
1975	251	1	0	n/a
1976	297	2	0	n/a
1977	342	2	0	n/a
1978	398	3	0	n/a
1979	484	5	0	25
1980	558	8	0	n/a
1981	631	9	0	n/a
1982	683	11	0	50
1983	739	10	1	n/a
1984	818	21	3	n/a
1985	873	26	6	n/a
1986	943	37	15	n/a
1987	1,001	46	25	n/a
1988	1,031	54	69	n/a
1989	1,051	73	110	200
1990	1,140	82	136	700
1991	1,153	109	178	1,100
1992	1,178	104	203	1,600
1993	1,213	126	265	2,100
1994	1,302	192	352	2,750
1995	1,350	291	544	4,000

[a]Farm winery densities are based on data collected by the first author.

[b]Brewpub and microbewery densities are based on data used in Carroll and Swaminathan (2000).

[c]Coffee shop densities were estimated by the Specialty Coffee Association of America. Data on the number of coffee shops were not available before 1979 and then only intermittently until 1989.

exist side by side with legitimate companies (Vinas 1998). In turn, by making money on the Internet almost immediately, the technologies developed by the on-line adult entertainment industry, such as web video and audio, have been widely imitated by both incumbents and new entrants to the Internet (Vinas 1998). Table 11.1 also shows that the growth of brewpubs was preceded by the proliferation of microbreweries and farm wineries in earlier periods.

Proposition 3: *The strategies adopted by organizations with a new form are likely to be modeled after the strategies adopted by surviving challenger organizational forms that preceded them into the same or related industries.*

Because of the importance of preexisting networks for the success of a new industry, it is both prudent and beneficial for entrepreneurs to analyze these infrastructures prior to entering an industry. In many cases, these networks can be easily identified and activated. In others, however, they may exist because of an overlap between the niche occupied by a new industry and existing niches. Resource partitioning theory suggests that concentrated industries create opportunities for specialist firms (Carroll 1985). Identifying these overlaps can make the difference between success and failure, particularly in view of research that shows that initial conditions can have profound effects on industry evolution (Arthur 1990b).

Of course, some new industries may be characterized by what is known in social movements research as an infrastructural deficit (McCarthy 1987). The pro-choice movement has experienced such an infrastructural deficit in comparison with pro-life organizations. Pro-life organizations are greater in number, have a greater number of single-issue organizations, and are more extensively linked at the local, state, and national levels (Pearce 1982). Faced with an infrastructural deficit, social movements can delay mobilizing and wait for a more favorable historical moment (Wilson and Orum 1976). While this is certainly also an option for entrepreneurs, it is probably not feasible, since the existing infrastructure will tend to change quite slowly. Another alternative is to identify another industry in which conditions are more favorable.

McCarthy (1987) also suggested that there are strategies for coping in industries that have "thin" infrastructures. For instance, the raw material for constructing a social movement exists in lists of individuals that were gathered for other purposes. These lists can serve as weak ties along which information and resources can flow. Just as a social movement organizer needs to identify these unmobilized sentiment pools, the key task for an entrepreneur faced with an infrastructural deficit is to locate resource spaces that will support the entry and survival of new organizations.

THE GENERATION OF COLLECTIVE ACTION FRAMES

For collective action to be possible, a collective action frame must emerge. According to Klandermans (1997), "collective action frames are systems of shared beliefs that justify the existence of social movements." These frames are the products of strategic efforts by groups of people to fashion shared understandings of the world and of themselves that legitimate and motivate collective action (Snow 1986; Snow and Benford 1988). Members of the pro-life movement share the common belief that abortions are wrong and must be eliminated. Similarly, members of the Women's Christian Temperance Union felt that alcohol should be banned, and this movement ultimately played a large role in the legislative success of national prohibition in 1919. In short, having a strong set of common beliefs can spur individuals to attempt social change through collective action.

Collective action frames can play a key role in the evolution of new industries. New organizational forms often try to establish a collective identity that is distinct from that of incumbent organizations. Clemens (1996, 205) argued that an organizational form "appears as a movement frame which both informs collective identity and orients groups toward other actors and institutions." More recently, Polos et al. (1998) have used the method of logical formalism to define an organizational form as a socially constructed collective identity of classes of organizations. Common sets of beliefs can lead entrepreneurs in emerging industries to undertake collective action that can aid in legitimating new organizational forms.

For a social movement, the generation of a collective identity is crucial to a movement's success (Major 1994; Kelly 1993; Melucci 1989). New social movements such as environmentalism and the women's movement have coalesced around collective identity rather than specific grievances or perceptions of injustice. According to Melluci (1989), a collective identity is generated by an interactive process in which members construct the collective "we." Collective identity is constructed through interactions with nonmembers, countermovements, and portrayals by the media. As a movement emerges boundaries are created that reinforce the "we vs. they" distinction (Taylor and Whittier 1992).

A similar process occurs when new organizational forms emerge. Romanelli (1989b), suggested that entrepreneurs in an emerging industry create opportunities for sharing information and resources by going to the same conferences and trade shows and by seeking similar resources. These interactions among entrepreneurs serve to isolate the new organizational form from competitors and other external threats (Garud and Van de Ven 1989). Cochlear implant technology gained acceptance as its proponents interacted at conferences, exchanged information, and jointly organized training programs (Garud and Van de Ven 1989). They suggested that these interactions made the organizational form less dependent on existing firms that might be threatened by the new technology. Essentially, advocates of this technology coalesced around a collective identity that differentiated cochlear implants from other hearing technologies.

Collective identity strength and distinctiveness. The success with which emerging organizational forms can respond to these threats is closely tied to the strength and distinctiveness of their collective identity. These identities can be so powerful that competing organizational populations are unable to imitate the routines of the new organizational form even when they have the resources and technology to do so. Mass production firms in the brewing industry, such as Anheuser-Busch, have the technical capabilities to produce microbrewed beer. Their attempts to do so, however, have met with very limited success because they conflict with the collective identity of microbrewers as defined by consumers. Consumers buying specialty beers seek a malt beverage brewed in a small craft-like firm according to traditional methods and using natural ingredients (Carroll and Swaminathan 2000).

The success of microbreweries in preventing imitation by the mass producers is largely due to their success in strategically deploying their identity. Bernstein (1997) identified two identity-deployment strategies. First, the "identity for critique" strategy involves confronting the identity and values of the dominant culture. For instance, some lesbian and gay groups, such as ACT UP and Queer Nation, have emphasized their differences with the mainstream culture (Bull and Gallagher 1996). Similarly, microbreweries and brewpubs emphasize their differences from beer produced by mass-production breweries. Moreover, because a dense network of relations among microbreweries and consumers maintains this identity, introductions of microbrewed beer by the mass producers are quickly detected, and the word is spread that the new product is not a "true" craft beer. Using identity-based strategies, then, microbreweries and brewpubs have successfully defined the specialty beer segment in ways that exclude the major brewers and contract brewers (Carroll and Swaminathan 2000).

The second identity-deployment strategy is referred to as identity for education (Bernstein 1997). Movements pursuing this strategy either challenge the dominant culture's perception of them or attempt to use their identity to gain legitimacy by emphasizing noncontroversial activities. Some gay activists have used this strategy in framing the passage of antidiscrimination legislation as a social justice issue. Other populations in the business sector have employed similar tactics. Although their efforts were ultimately unsuccessful, members of the brewing industry in the 1860s attempted to align their views with those advocating prohibition by professing the attitude that excessive use of hard liquor was a terrible societal problem. At the same time, they differentiated beer from spirits and asserted that beer drinkers were upstanding members of society (Baron 1962).

In contrast to microbreweries and brewpubs, contract brewers, an organizational form that emerged at about the same time, have been much less successful in establishing a robust identity. Because contract brewers brew their beer at other firms' breweries, other beer producers have labeled them as fraudulent breweries. In 1996, Anheuser Busch filed a complaint with the government alleging that the labels on the Boston Beer Company's Samuel Adams beer were misleading because the labels stated that Boston Beer Company brewed Samuel Adams. In actuality, Boston Beer Company was a contract brewer that used facilities owned by a mass-production brewery (in this case Strohs Brewing Company) to produce its beer.

Because contract brewers have had less success than brewpubs or microbreweries in differentiating their identity from that of mass-production breweries, this organizational form may have had greater difficulty in becoming established. Figures 11.1 and 11.2 offer some support for this argument. Figure 11.1 shows that from 1985 to 1995, the number of microbreweries and brewpubs grew at a much faster rate than the number of contract brewers. Figure 11.2 illustrates that contract brewers also had higher failure rates than other specialist breweries over most of the time period. Although this evidence

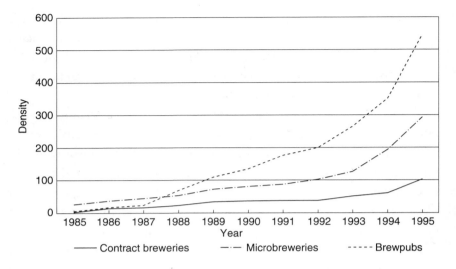

Figure 11.1 Density of contract breweries, microbreweries, and brewpubs

is purely descriptive, it suggests that new organizational forms that fail to create a collective identity that is separate and distinct from that of the dominant incumbent organizational form may suffer poorer outcomes than those that do develop a distinct identity.

> **Proposition 4:** *Organizations with new forms will be more likely to survive and grow if they can construct a collective identity that is (a) distinct from that of the dominant incumbent organizational form and (b) difficult for the dominant incumbent organizational form to assume.*

Collective action frames and preexisting infrastructure. Collective action frames can also emerge through affiliation with preexisting groups and networks, particularly if these attachments are valued. Clemen's (1993) study of women's groups over 1890–1920 showed how women's groups chose organizational forms that were recombinations of the organizational models that were available in society. The choice of a model in turn strengthens ties to some existing organizations and weakens ties to other kinds of organizations. By calling itself a "club," the New England Women's Club distanced itself from religious associations and charities and borrowed, with modification, a male

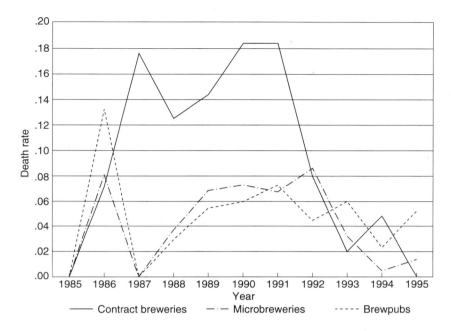

Figure 11.2 Death rates of specialist breweries

model of organization. The success of these new organizations is crucially linked to the facility with which institutional entrepreneurs can recombine existing organizational models and cultural materials to legitimate the new form (Rao 1998).

A favorable opportunity structure and preexisting infrastructure can also promote the emergence of a collective identity because they encourage early interactions among industry participants. These interactions promote interdependencies between previously isolated entrepreneurs and, thus, accelerate the legitimation process (Romanelli 1989b). Early interactions between industry participants may be particularly critical because early founders bear more of the costs in legitimating the organizational form (Delacroix and Rao 1994).

To the extent that early entrants in the industry can mobilize collectively, they can produce a bandwagon effect, as external constituencies see the form as reliable and as barriers to the capital market fall. Moreover, a community structure may evolve as other populations of organizations that support the original population emerge. Semiconductor manufacturers do not exist in a vacuum; they have interdependent relationships with producers of semiconductor equipment and associated products as well as many other populations. Similar outcomes occur in social movement industries. In achieving early success, a social movement encourages the emergence of other related movements that take advantage of the opportunity structure that the original movement has opened up (Tarrow 1991). Such a result is consistent with Arthur, Ermoliev, and Kaniovski's (1987) idea that initial conditions can have powerful effects on a system's evolution.

Proposition 5: *Organizations with new forms that model themselves after or form linkages with existing organizations with established identity characteristics will experience a greater chance of survival.*

Competition and collective action. Quite often, the emergence of a social movement arouses opposition in the form of a countermovement. The success of the women's movement in legalizing abortion led to the formation of anti-abortion groups such as Operation Rescue that opposed abortion. Similarly, movements and countermovements have emerged over a variety of issues including affirmative action, civil rights, smoking, and even marijuana use (Meyer and Staggenborg 1996).

The presence of a countermovement or antagonist plays an important role in the development of movement frames. Snow and Benford (1988) argued that three framing tasks must be accomplished for collective action to emerge, namely, diagnostic framing, prognostic framing, and motivational framing. In diagnostic framing, activists focus on a problem that demands redress and identify the agents responsible. Prognostic framing involves having a plan so that the situation can be corrected. Motivational framing provides motives or reasons why the collective action should be undertaken. A critical aspect of framing processes involves making attributions about those who support the movement (protagonists) and those who oppose it (Hunt, Benford, and Snow 1994).

In defining antagonist identities, movement actors first identify opponents to the movement and then attempt to show how their opponents' beliefs and practices conflict with their own identity (Benford and Hunt 1992; Morris

1992). A movement called Mobilization for Survival blamed multinational corporations for polluting the environment, manipulating U.S. foreign policy, and contributing to Third-World poverty (Hunt, Benford, and Snow 1994). Such actions are consistent with the idea that conflict with an out-group leads to greater cohesiveness in and commitment to a focal group (Sherif et al. 1961).

For collective action to develop, however, individuals must attribute their feelings of injustice to causes that are potentially controllable (Klandermans 1997). Thus, in the example above, Mobilization for Survival would likely have had much more difficulty in mobilizing its constituents if it attributed the social ills that it targeted to more uncontrollable causes, such as the nature of man or technological change. At first glance, these framing strategies may not seem applicable to business organizations. There is evidence, however, that such processes do occur, particularly during the early development of an industry. Brewpub and microbrewery owners view brewing as a craft and look with disdain on mass-production breweries (Carroll and Swaminathan 2000). Similarly, contract brewers, firms that brew their beer at other firm's breweries, are characterized as "pretend" breweries. Another example comes from the early telephone industry. In the early 1900s, there were numerous independent telephone companies that were competing with the Bell system. During this period, the independents lobbied to place restrictions on Bell Telephone. Bell was portrayed by the independents as an evil corporation that used anticompetitive practices (Barnett and Carroll 1993).

A similar process seems to have occurred among organizations that develop applications supporting Sun's Java language. Because Java is a software standard that can run on any chip-based system, it could reduce many software companies' dependence on Microsoft, a company that is often portrayed as a threat to the survival of other members of the computer software industry. This conflict seems to have spurred action through a variety of resource mobilization structures. For example, Sun has formed alliances with dozens of competitors in an effort to promote Java as an alternative to Windows (Lyons 1999). In addition, the president of the Java Lobby, an ad hoc association that boasts over 12,000 members, "declared war" on Microsoft after the company introduced an incompatible version of Java. Rick Ross, the association's president, stated on the lobby's web site that "the Java Lobby must abandon all hope that Microsoft will cease their antagonism to Java and to us, the community of Java developers and supporters" (Gage 1999). Collective action will emerge much more slowly in populations that fail to identify an opposing outgroup. Thus, for instance, if actors in a new population attribute their difficulties to uncontrollable causes such as poor industry conditions, a collective action frame is unlikely to develop.

Proposition 6a: *Organizations with a new form are more likely to engage in collective action when faced with competition for resources from other organizational forms.*

Interestingly, one of the implications of this process is that there is room for strategic action on the part of movement participants. Freidman and McAdam (1992) argued that social movement leaders can sometimes strategize and influence the identity formation process. Thus, it may be that it is not simply whether there is an *actual* threat to a new industry, but whether industry participants *perceive* that an out-group exists. In the case of the early telephone industry, the threat from Bell was quite real. Before it agreed to the Kingsbury Commitment, by which the industry was obliged to hook up the independents to its system at a reasonable cost, Bell was actively taking over the smaller systems and using its monopoly power to effectively crush any opposition.

Mass-production breweries, however, posed little threat to the new specialists in the brewing industry, particularly brewpubs. Because of the economies of scale associated with high concentration in the industry, mass producers had little incentive to compete with the new specialist populations, whose production accounted for only a fraction of the industry total.

At the same time, however, the mass producers were a very salient presence in the industry to the brewpubs and microbreweries. It is not surprising that brewpubs and microbreweries would view the mass producers as threatening rivals. Such a view is consistent with Porac et al.'s (1995) findings in the Scottish knitwear industry. They found that while small firms were quite likely to name larger producers as their rivals, larger producers were much less likely to perceive the smaller firms as rivals. If the process of resource partitioning leads specialists to perceive the generalists as threats, it may be a fertile ground for the emergence of collective action. Moreover, collective action may be particularly likely to succeed under these conditions because the threat is more perception than reality.

Proposition 6b: *Organizations with a new form are more likely to engage in collective action when they perceive competition with other organizational forms.*

In many cases, however, increases in the strength of the countermovement will weaken a social movement as a result of direct competition for resources. Amenta and Zylan (1991) found that growth in patronage-oriented traditional party organizations depressed the growth of the Townsend Movement. The effects of competition with a countermovement may be more complicated. Social movement organizations may benefit initially from the higher cohesion that results from competition with a countermovement, but if the countermovement continues to grow, survival chances of movement organizations should decline.

Proposition 7: *The growth of rival organizational forms will first increase and then decrease the survival chances of organizations with a new form.*

Consistent with this proposition, Ingram and Simons (1998) found that increasing concentration of economic resources among Israeli banks, a countermovement, first increased and then decreased the failure rate of Israeli worker cooperatives.

Incumbents' responses to the emergence of new organizational forms. Emerging organizational forms that achieve some success may also provoke responses from incumbent populations. Incumbent firms often respond to competence-destroying technological discontinuities by improving the price-performance characteristics of their current technology. Thus, telephone companies introduced digital subscriber lines in response to the challenge posed by cable modems.

Such a process is consistent with the idea that intense competition causes central players in an industry to adopt value-adding routines from the periphery (Leblebici et al. 1991). Incumbents may attempt to incorporate the new technology or approach that gives the new organizational form a competitive advantage. If organizations with a new form introduce a new technology, the success of incumbents in imitating the technology partially depends on whether the new technology is competence enhancing or competence destroying. Incumbent firms will have great difficulty incorporating competence-destroying technologies because they do not build on the firms' existing routines and skills (Tushman and Anderson 1986; Tushman and Murmann 1998). Incumbent organizational forms that can assume a robust identity (Padgett and Ansell 1993; Stark 1996) by adding the identity characteristics of the new organizational form to their original identity will reduce the survival chances of organizations with a new organizational form.

> **Proposition 8:** *Organizations with a new form will experience lower survival chances if incumbent organizational forms are able to assume a robust identity that includes the identity characteristics of the new organizational form.*

Proposition 8 corresponds to a process by which the goals of new organizational forms are co-opted by the existing dominant organizational form. This could occur either as a result of an independent strategic decision by the incumbent form or through the sponsorship of organizations with the new form by incumbent organizations. Sponsorship ties include acquiring partial ownership, the establishment of interfirm alliances, and the licensing of technology developed by organizations with the new form.

Bernstein (1997) suggested that emergent movements lacking a collective identity will emphasize differences and, indeed, celebrate them in order to attract adherents. Once the movement is established and has access to the polity, however, more moderate strategies will tend to emerge. Our examples from the brewing industry fit this pattern. Microbreweries and brewpubs are a relatively new and small population that is threatened by the rest of the industry. Consequently, they have emphasized differences with the dominant incumbent organizational form, the mass production brewery. In the 1860s, however, brewers had a strong association and could exercise substantial power in many state governments and, as a result, adopted more moderate identity strategies. As we discuss below, however, the very fact that a new population becomes successful and creates a strong infrastructure can ultimately lead to a decline in cooperative activity and an increase in competition.

Industry Maturation and Collective Action

As an industry ages, cooperation among firms tends to decline, and interaction among firms becomes increasingly competitive. In our view, this process occurs as threats from opposing groups subside and the population establishes a stable collective identity. That such a process occurs is not surprising, given that one important element that stimulates cooperation and the generation of a collective action frame is the identification of a threat from an opposing group (Hunt, Benford, and Snow 1994).

Events occurring in the early telephone industry provide a striking example of this process. As we noted earlier, independent telephone companies cooperated in opposing the Bell system and lobbying for restrictive legislation. To avoid the passage of such restrictive legislation, Bell agreed to abide by the Kingsbury Commitment. Among other things, the agreement stipulated that Bell must hook up the independents to its system for a reasonable cost. Interestingly, after the passage of the agreement, competition between the independents increased and mortality rates rose (Barnett and Carroll 1993). Barnett and Carroll (1993) argued that the Kingsbury Commitment triggered a competitive release. With the threat from Bell minimized, the independents entered into intense competition with each other. This result suggests an intriguing possibility, namely, that once the perception that there is an external threat disappears, collective action in an industry is substantially reduced.

A similar process seems to be occurring among supporters of the Java software standard. In November 1998, Sun prevailed in its lawsuit against Microsoft. Microsoft was barred by its license with Sun from producing incompatible versions of Java. After this victory, however, *Forbes* (Lyons 1999) reported that, "feuding factions have begun to pursue rival Java designs." Thus, success may be a double-edged sword, in that it lowers the propensity for collective action and increases intraindustry competition (Zald and McCarthy 1980).

The evolution of interorganizational relationships among organizations of a new form from cooperation to competition is consistent with density-dependent models of organizational evolution (Hannan and Carroll 1992). When an organizational form is nascent, collective action helps establish its legitimacy. Once legitimacy is attained, however, organizations compete with each other for resources within the once-new form's niche.

> **Proposition 9:** *As a new organizational form becomes legitimate and successful, the level of collective action in the industry will decrease.*

Even though collective action will decrease in a population when external threats subside, resource mobilization structures such as trade associations are still maintained. The involvement of member organizations in these associations is significantly lower than their involvement when the industry was in the process of establishing a collective identity. Today, the primary role of the Semiconductor Industry Association is the dissemination of information among industry participants, rather than encouraging cooperative activity. In many ways, the transformation of these associations resembles the changes occurring in social movements when they have achieved some degree of success.

Michels (1962) suggested that as social movements grow and acquire more resources, social movement organizations transform their goals from activism to organizational maintenance and oligarchization. Tactics become more moderate, and the leadership flows into the hands of a few members. This conservative transformation is partly driven by movement growth. As growth continues, there is increasing structural differentiation and professionalization of roles. Rose (1967) suggested that as organizations age and grow in size, the number of staff increases while the rights of members decrease. In a sample of trade associations, Leblebici and Salancik (1989) generally found that there were significant negative correlations between the age and size of an association and members' rights.[2]

The evolution of resource mobilization structures such as industry associations parallels those of movements that Zald and Ash (1966) have referred to

---

2. In one analysis, Leblebici and Salancik (1989) split their sample into associations that had specific purpose statements and those that had general statements. The correlation between size and members' rights was not significant for those associations that had specific purpose statements, although it was in the expected negative direction.

as "becalmed." Becalmed movements have not achieved complete success but have influenced the course of events leading up to the present. Moreover, their goals are still relevant. Similarly, industry associations and other mobilization structures have played an important role in the evolution of the industry, and their goals are still important to industry members. Thus, population members are willing to contribute resources to maintain these structures but are no longer intimately involved. The maintenance of these structures is potentially useful because they serve as an infrastructure that the industry can draw upon if a significant threat to its viability emerges. At the same time, however, it might be difficult for firms to mobilize these structures effectively in the face of a new threat if they have only been indirectly involved for a long period of time. Thus, as a new form becomes legitimated, the goals of the resource mobilizing structures representing the form will tend to focus on the survival and the maintenance of the resource mobilizing structures themselves. In turn, this transformation will act as a segregating process that increasingly differentiates the resource mobilization structures from the organizational form itself.

Proposition 10: *As a new organizational form gains legitimacy, the resource mobilization structures representing the form will become increasingly segregated and differentiated from the organizational form.*

Proposition 11: *As a new organizational form gains legitimacy, the goals of the resource mobilization structures representing the form will be transformed from activism to organizational maintenance.*

Table 11.2 shows how the population of specialist breweries has grown over time. Membership in the industry association, however, seems to be losing its appeal to more recent entrants into the specialty brewing segment. The proportion of specialty breweries that are members of the industry's trade association, the Institute for Brewing Studies, has fallen from a peak of almost 52% in 1995 to roughly 42.5% by September 1998. Casual observation also suggests that involvement in running the trade association and organizing key activities, such as an annual trade convention, has become the province of a few key players in the industry, supplemented by a professional staff. As the

Table 11.2

Membership of Specialist Breweries in the Institute of
Brewing Studies (IBS), 1991–1998[a]

Year	Number of Specialist Breweries	Number of IBS Members	Percentage of Specialist Breweries Holding IBS Membership
1991	267	70	26.22%
1992	307	99	32.25%
1993	391	150	38.36%
1994	544	239	43.93%
1995	835	434	51.98%
1996	1,067	485	45.45%
1997	1,306	581	44.49%
1998	1,370	582	42.48%

[a]Data for 1991 to 1995 include specialist breweries alive at any point during a
particular year. Data for 1996, 1997, and 1998 reflect specialist breweries alive on
December 23, 1996, December 30, 1997, and September 11, 1998, respectively.
These data have been compiled from North American brewery lists published by
the Institute of Brewing Studies.

number of members in an association increases over time, free-riding may
become a significant problem, as many members gain the informational
benefits afforded by membership without being significantly involved in the
association's activities. In turn, this process may accelerate the rate at which
the association's primary goals are transformed from those of activism for the
organizational form to the maintenance of the association and its professional
staff.

Collective Action and the Choice of Organizational Form

Thus far, we have primarily discussed how collective action can influence the
emergence and success of new organizational forms. Of course, new organizational forms can emerge and thrive in the absence of collective action (see
Romanelli 1991 for a review). Even in the presence of infrastructural deficits,
changes in technology, government policies, and consumer preferences can create resource spaces for new organizational forms. And, as we discussed above,
collective action often fades over time in an industry. This raises the question
of what kinds of organizations benefit when collective action is absent and

when it is present. The answer to this question boils down to the choice of an appropriate organizational form. Organizational forms can be defined along two dimensions: r versus K strategists and specialists versus generalists (Brittain and Freeman 1980). R-strategists are first-movers, who move rapidly into new niches when organizational density is far below the population's carrying capacity. K-strategists enter the population at a later stage, when density approaches the carrying capacity, and compete on the basis of efficiency. Specialist organizations depend on a narrow range of resources for survival, whereas generalist organizations depend on a broad range of resources for survival. Gamson (1990, 44–46) found that single-issue social movement organizations were more likely than multiple-issue social movement organizations to be accepted by antagonist groups and gain new advantages for their constituents. Because of their narrow focus, single-issue social movements are able to develop a more distinct social identity that allows them to attract resources and execute strategy more effectively. Similarly, specialist organizations tend to develop a sharper identity that allows them to target distinct, relatively uncontested niches that can sustain them in the early phase of an industry. Internal coordination costs are also lower for specialist organizations that have a restricted set of activities (Barnett and Freeman 1997), a crucial advantage in emerging industries in which organization-building resources are often scarce. Finally, because of their narrow focus, specialists are less likely to provoke a response from incumbent organizations that would threaten their survival (Péli and Nooteboom 1999).

Proposition 12: *In an emerging industry, specialist organizations will have a survival advantage over other organizational forms.*

Older and larger social movement organizations are able to mobilize more resources and survive (Cress and Snow 1996; Edwards and Marullo 1995; McCarthy and Wolfson 1996). Large, single-issue social movement organizations can be classified as K-specialists since they complement their focus on a narrow movement niche with the efficiency of a formal organization. In emerging industries, as we have previously discussed, organizations can take collective action to enhance the cognitive legitimacy of the organizational form. Collective action often occurs in the development of technical standards and regulatory regimes (Hunt and Aldrich 1998; Van de Ven and Garud 1994). Other collective strategies include the establishment of trade associations, research consortia, and interfirm alliances (Aldrich and Fiol 1994). The presence of collective action reduces technological and, more generally, environmental uncertainty in an industry and allows K-specialists to be more successful (Hunt and Aldrich 1998).

Proposition 12a: *When collective action is present within an emerging industry, K-specialist firms will have a survival advantage over other organizational forms.*

In the absence of collective action, emerging industries are characterized by competition between rival technological designs. Both the future technological trajectory and market potential are uncertain. In this era of ferment, r-specialist firms with their emphasis on speed and flexibility are more likely to be successful (Brittain and Freeman 1980; Hunt and Aldrich 1998, 281).

Proposition 12b: *When collective action is absent within an emerging industry, r-specialist firms will have a survival advantage over other organizational forms.*

CONCLUSION

With few exceptions (e.g., Davis and Thompson 1994), social movement theory has not been used to explain outcomes for business organizations. Many strands of organization theory, including institutional theory (Clemens 1993; Conell and Voss 1990), organizational ecology (Edwards and Marullo 1995; Minkoff 1997), and social network theory (Gould 1993; Snow, Zurcher, and Ekland-Olson 1980), have influenced social movement theorists. In this chapter, we derived implications for the evolution of new organizational forms from a variety of perspectives in social movement theory, particularly those that focus on the mobilization of resources and the generation of collective action frames. Social movement theory is especially useful in explaining the emergence and survival of new organizational forms because collective action is often required to establish the form's legitimacy. New organizational forms also typically seek to replace the dominant incumbent organizational form, much as social movement organizations challenge elite organizations. The formation of a distinct and inimitable collective identity by organizations with a new form is crucial to the success of this endeavor.

An interesting avenue for future research would be to examine similarities in demographics and experience among entrepreneurs in new industries and determine whether they are positively related to the emergence of collective action. Such demographic similarity may occur because founders in new industries tend to enter from populations that are similar to the new population. Consequently, entrepreneurs in emerging industries may have an overlap in their prior industry experience that will provide them with a basis for collective action. Entrepreneurs can likely be seen as lone pioneers, but the survival of the new organizational forms they promote seems to depend on their linking with similar others to create a collective identity they can all share and that will contribute to the growth of the population as a whole.

12

Entrepreneurship in Context

Strategic Interaction and the Emergence of Regional Economies

ARI GINSBERG, ERIK R. LARSEN, AND
ALESSANDRO LOMI

Long regarded as an intriguing legacy of pre-capitalist modes of economic organization, industrial districts and other similar patterns of interorganizational division of labor based on geographical proximity are reemerging as distinct forms of the post-fordist organization of production (Piore and Sabel 1984; Pyke and Sengenberger 1992). The flexible specialization allowed by a high level of division of labor organized on a spatial basis has sparked a wideranging discussion on the various forms of geographical concentration, such as industrial districts, as possible historical alternatives to mass production and industrialization (Beccattini 1991; Best 1990; Degli Ottati 1994; Locke 1995; Sabel and Zeitlin 1985; 1997).

Building on this debate, researchers have found geographical concentrations of economic and organizational activities to be a prominent feature of the industrial landscape in advanced capitalist economies as diverse as those of Italy (Lazerson and Lorenzoni 1999), Japan (Friedman 1988), Germany (Herrigel 1996), and the United States (Saxenian 1994). In the U.S., for example, *Business Week*

Support for this research was provided by the Berkley Center for Entrepreneurial Studies, New York University, and is gratefully acknowledged. An earlier version of this paper was presented at the 3rd Conference on Cellular Automata For Research and Industry, Trieste, Italy, October 7–9, 1998.

(1992) estimated that in 1992 600,000 Americans were employed in 15 clusters of high-tech firms, with many still emerging. In 1994, *Fortune* reported that in the previous year alone about 540,000 people had moved to the Southeast and the mountain states to work in entrepreneurial clusters of knowledge-driven industry, which were poised to become key players in America's economic future. In Italy—admittedly a more conventional context for studying industrial districts—the share of manufacturing employment accounted for by industrial districts grew from 32 to 42 percent between 1971 and 1991 (Brusco 1999).

The increasingly important role of "hot spots" (as these geographical clusters of start-up and high-growth firms are called by the popular business press) as sources of job creation and technological innovation makes it particularly important to understand the effects of regional development on the success of firms in those entrepreneurial settings. At the same time, the geographical concentration of organizational activity that is observable in many industries (Krugman 1991) poses a number of problems for current theories of entrepreneurship and organization creation.

In particular, questions about the evolution of geographical clusters of start-up firms have never been satisfactorily addressed (Scott 1989). Although researchers in economic geography (Melecki 1985) and organizational ecology (e.g., Lomi 1995) have confirmed the tendency of firms within industries to form regional clusters, the evolution of such clusters has generally been understudied in the organizational sciences literature (DeNoble and Galbraith 1992). To narrow the gap in theory development, in this chapter, we seek to shed light on the relationship between localized decision making and the evolution of regional clusters.

To establish the theoretical background of our study, we begin with the conceptual issues induced by the spatial dimensions of entrepreneurial action. More specifically we emphasize the local nature of many elements typically associated with processes of organizational founding, such as information search, competitive interaction, resource dependencies, imitation, and learning (Aldrich 1999; Hannan and Carroll 1992; Leifer and White 1987; Levinthal and March 1981; March 1993; Odorici and Lomi 2000). We develop a connection between entrepreneurship and the game-theoretic interpretation of strategic interaction that, in our view, underlies the emergence of organizational activities in geographic space.

SPATIAL DIMENSIONS OF ENTREPRENEURIAL ACTION

An awareness of the conceptual problems induced by the spatial dimensions of organizational environments is particularly important to an understanding of the process of entrepreneurship. This is because the creation of a new business involves a conscious effort to mobilize resources in pursuit of economic opportunities (Aldrich, Rosen, and Woodward 1987) and access to key resources (Aldrich and Zimmer 1985). But how can the local action of individual entrepreneurs—which, by definition, is heavily dependent on information embedded in local networks—give rise to regular patterns of industry structure whereby companies come to cluster around a few selected locations? What models of entrepreneurship can we use to explain the evolution of such clusters? In this chapter, we try to articulate a credible answer to these questions by focusing on what experienced observers of industrial districts are beginning to consider as the most fundamental process underlying the evolution of regional economies, namely, the interaction process by which individual strategies propagate within specific geographical boundaries to give rise to specific collective forms of action defined by a mix of competition and cooperation (Brusco 1999; Degli Ottati 1994).

Bridging Macro and Micro Models of Entrepreneurship

As a prominent theory of the birth, survival, and death of organizations, organizational ecology has provided an enduring model for entrepreneurship (Bygrave 1993), and studies by organization ecologists have supported the notion of the spatial heterogeneity of organizational birth and death rates (Carroll and Wade 1991; Lomi 1995; Swaminathan and Wiedenmayer 1991). But organizational ecologists' macro perspective on organizations is silent about the role, if any, of individual action (Hannan and Carroll 1992). According to this macro perspective, the process of organizational evolution is driven by competitive and institutional forces outside the control of any one individual actor. As a consequence, some scholars consider organizational ecology to be still too far from an ideal model of entrepreneurship, which has at its core the actions of individual entrepreneurs (Bygrave 1993).

Building on the notion of bounded rationality introduced by Simon (1957) and March and Simon (1958), theories based on the psychology and economics of choice (Kahneman, Slovic, and Tversky 1982) have taken the opposite route to understanding entrepreneurial phenomena. They have started from the micro foundations of purposive action to try to reduce organizational structures and routines to cognitive limits in the information processing capacities of individual agents (e.g., Busenitz and Barney 1994; Manimala 1992). Critics of this way of thinking about organizations question the value of this research approach and wonder "whether there is a tight coupling between motives of participants and the collective action of organizations [given] the frequency with which unanticipated consequences of organizational action dominated the intended consequences" (Hannan 1986, 179).

Cluster Development

For the reasons discussed above, neither a micro nor a macro perspective appears to provide an adequate theoretical framework for explaining the emergence of regional clusters in entrepreneurial settings. Such clusters have been described as "network-based industrial systems that promote collective learning and flexible adjustment" and that "encourage experimentation and entrepreneurship" (Saxenian 1994, 2). SRI International, the research firm that pioneered the field of industry cluster analysis a decade ago, defines a cluster by the industrial employment bulges in a particular geographic area. So, for example, when the employment for an industry is 5% nationally and it is 15% in a local area, that area has a cluster (Saunders 1998). California's Silicon Valley, Boston's Route 128, Manhattan's Silicon Alley, and France's Scientific City in Toulouse are examples of regional clusters in emergent industries in which competitors have formed complex networks of interdependent relationships.

One of the essential characteristics of industrial regions is their status as "collectivities of producers, i.e., as clusters of interdependent activities whose mutual proximity to one another engenders complex, dynamic, flows of agglomeration economies" (Scott 1995, 60). Scott (1995) argued that such economies (e.g., cost reductions resulting from proximity to specialized firms) are not only activated by and consumed through the operation of simple market mechanisms but are also engendered by institutional infrastructures that lie outside of the sphere of market relations (e.g., regional development policy). Agents of collective order such as municipal governments, can play an important and positive role in regional industrial development. But centralized policy making is fraught with heavy risks (Scott 1995).

Clusters may develop with or without state or regional planning. Whereas North Carolina's Research Triangle was the result of an economic development program, Silicon Valley happened on its own (Saunders 1998). Without a central authority to coordinate collective decision making, how does cluster development occur? If individual entrepreneurs compete locally, but regional clusters are affected by global evolutionary forces, what level of analysis is the most appropriate, and, more important, how might different levels of action be linked? We will try to address these and related questions by developing a computational model of how individual behavior evolves into aggregates with complex collective properties that determine the structural context of future action. In other words, we will illustrate how, from a micro-foundation with only local rational entrepreneurs and no central coordination, clusters of cooperation can emerge. We do not dispute, as stated above, that macro forces can also play a significant role in the formation or later development of clusters, but we emphasize that clusters could emerge by themselves without central planning. In our approach, the formation of clusters is the unintended consequence of these deliberate micro activities, that is, the decision making by the individual entrepreneur. To illustrate how such a modeling approach can make a useful theoretical contribution, we demonstrate below how it can be applied to answering a set of research questions about the emergence of regional development in entrepreneurial settings.

The Rules of the Game in Industrial Districts[1]

The dynamics of competition and cooperation provide a valuable starting point for exploring possible links between macro theories based on the sociology of organizations and micro theories based on the economics and psychology of individual choice. Competition over scarce resources is one of the

---

1. We deliberately titled this section after Brusco's (1999) essay to emphasize the continuity between the research concerns expressed by specialists on industrial districts and regional economies and our own modeling efforts.

central mechanisms responsible for the evolution of organizational populations and the diversity of organizational forms observed in society (Hannan and Freeman 1989). At the same time, individuals in organizations, and organizations in markets, interact to secure control over scarce resources and allocate these resources efficiently. During processes of strategic interaction, actors form expectations about the behavior of rivals and act in reaction to, or anticipation of, this expected behavior.

The existence of competition in the form of conflicting claims over scarce resources makes possible the game theory representation of a wide range of individual-level decisions and strategic choices that are of interest to economists and social scientists (Shubik 1982). In general terms, expectation formation can be seen as a basic computational process according to which individual actors perform a series of logical operations on inputs coming from the environment through a set of connections. The result of this computation is a set of courses of action, or strategies, that are dependent on the agents' current knowledge and on the position that they occupy in a structure of interaction emerging from the accumulation of individual micro-level behaviors (Huberman and Glance 1993; Krackhardt and Porter 1985). It is the game-theoretic nature of strategic decision that provides the mechanism for the evolution of cooperation (Axelrod 1984).

Game theory provides a number of concepts that can be used to model the interaction among individuals in a population and to formalize abstract evolutionary systems (Maynard-Smith 1982). More specifically, we can model such systems as a population of agents playing a spatial variation of the Repeated Prisoner's Dilemma (RPD) game. The Prisoner's Dilemma (PD) is a two-person non-zero-sum game, frequently used in experimental and theoretical investigations of strategic interaction in populations of self-interested individuals (Axelrod 1984). The computational model employs the infinitely repeated version of the PD (RPD), in which in every round of the game, each firm can choose between two possible actions, D for "defect" and C for "cooperate." Figure 12.1 shows the payoff matrix (M) of the RPD. The environmental assumptions are that the game will be played for an indefinite number of times and that the discounted value of the payoff for the next exchange is sufficiently high. An additional specification is that $2R > T$, which prevents players from taking turns exploiting each other and earning higher profits.

	Cooperate	Defect
Cooperate	R, R	S, T
Defect	T, S	P, P

Figure 12.1 The payoff matrix for the repeated prisoner's dilemma game

The rules of the PD game can be employed to develop a model of coevolution of strategies in a population of individuals playing a spatial variation of the repeated Prisoner's Dilemma game. In the computational model, the game is played by agents (in our case, entrepreneurs or start-up firms, represented as cells) arranged on a two-dimensional spatial array, or lattice, of size $n \times n$ (May and Nowak 1992). At any given time, every cell on the array can occupy only one of the two states (C or D). The strategy of a cell can be seen as emerging from the results of a series of games played with cells living in a neighborhood of radius K.

Such a computational model can be simulated under a variety of local conditions to clarify how regional development in entrepreneurial settings occurs through the interaction of ecological macro-dynamics with firm-level processes. Given the analytical complexities involved in specifying and estimating such a model empirically, a computer simulation can be used to learn whether and how the ecological processes that are frequently observed in the study of empirical organizational populations are sensitive to different forms of localized interaction among individual organizations. Such a computer simulation can be used to answer key questions about the influence of localized interactions, on the evolution of regional clusters in entrepreneurial settings.

RESEARCH QUESTIONS

Processes of competition and cooperation in industries organized along a relevant spatial dimension pose a fundamental challenge to new-venture founders. Spatial proximity tends to make information on prices, costs, and even production processes more transparent to customers and suppliers. Not only must new-venture founders convince skeptics of their organization's ability to survive, they must also fend off competitors offering slightly different versions of their products or services. When founders with imitable products or services realize that their innovations are leaking to competitors and potential new entrants, they gain a strong incentive to cooperate on stabilizing conditions in the industry (Aldrich and Fiol 1994). Implicit cooperation in establishing a dominant design, common standards, and the interfirm movement of personnel, which are made possible by conditions of imitability, in turn serve to increase the level of shared competencies.

Collaboration and Proximity

Regional clusters are particularly important to the development of shared competencies among firms in an emergent industry. They afford their members proximity-based learning and cost- and time-saving advantages that are difficult for firms outside the cluster to imitate. Competitors within such clusters have access to a highly skilled technical labor force and may share ties to a research base, such as research universities or government laboratories. Such access is particularly important during the early stages of industry evolution, when firms are engaged in basic research (Melecki 1985; Porter 1990). Within the cluster, time to market and barriers to entry are lowered because of the experience and capabilities of researchers, suppliers, labor, and venture capitalists in the region (Saxenian 1994). Agglomeration economies occur as new firms generate more new ventures, which are attracted by the technical and resource base or are created from spin-offs in the region (Melecki 1985).

In addition to deriving cost advantages, competitors within the cluster help create industry infrastructure and credibility rapidly through their affiliation and nearness (Scott 1989). On one hand, proximity among rivals creates institutional legitimacy and helps stimulate a local infrastructure and expanded supply of skilled labor and resources (Porter 1990). Proximity also enhances cooperation in interorganizational relationships by facilitating the information flows that create trust and mitigates perceived differences (Porter 1990). On the other hand, proximity makes it harder to strike the right balance between uniqueness and comparability, which is the key to success for many entrepreneurial ventures (Aldrich 1999).

Magnitude of initial collaboration. Initial collaborations begin informally in networks of interfirm relations, but some later develop into more formalized strategic alliances, consortia, and trade associations (Powell 1990). Studies of high-technology industries, such as the cochlear implant industry, have found that brand-new innovations tend to be pursued by a handful of parallel, independent actors. These actors come to know one another rapidly through personal interaction and through traveling in similar social and technical circles, such as attending the same industry conferences and technical committee meetings (Garud and Rappa 1994). If founders can resist the temptation to cheat or defect, they can rise above the level of their initial ventures and run together "in packs" (Van de Ven 1993).

The magnitude of initial collaboration plays an important role in the dynamics of regional development. Analysis of multiple-player prisoner dilemma situations suggests that a minimum level of cooperative activity, that is, critical mass, is needed to make the activity self-sustaining (Schelling 1978). Moreover, analysis of industry developmental trajectories suggests that the evolution of regional clusters of industrial activity can only be understood in terms of a path-dependent process of evolution and adjustment structured by the phenomenon of localized increasing returns (Arthur 1990a; Romer 1986; Scott 1995). Therefore, we seek to answer the following question:

Question 1: *How does the magnitude of initial collaboration influence regional development in entrepreneurial settings?*

Individual Competitive Strategy

A shared resource base, network of alliances, agglomeration of economies, lower entry barriers, faster time to market, and entrepreneurial climate all serve to generate an environment that is not only conducive to high levels of innovation but is also characterized by a tension between cooperation and intense competition (Scott 1989). Although regional networks may be marked by cooperation among competitors in their formative stage, research suggests that such relationships may quickly deteriorate and lead to increased competition and industry-level innovation (Van de Ven and Garud 1989). Because firms within the network are in more direct competition for human, financial, and technological resources, rivalry may become more intense within a regional cluster than within the industry.

Although the initial benefits of conformity and collaboration (legitimacy, stability, access to resources, and the ability to attract skilled personnel) provide the sources of growth and profitability in the initial stages of regional development, over time these same institutional processes can generate deleterious effects. To break the pattern of inertia, homogeneity, and deteriorating innovative capacity that conformity and collaboration may bring, firms in the regional cluster are likely to have to undergo a period of crisis or shock. Following a protracted period of convergence and cooperation, firms within regional clusters are susceptible to a significant environmental jolt, such as a technological shift, changes in who buys the product and how they use it, or governmental policy changes.

Research suggests that those that are among the first to respond to technological shifts obtain competitive benefits of volume and experience that may not accrue to followers (Lieberman and Montgomery 1988), and that decision heuristics, or strategies, used by entrepreneurs influence the innovativeness of new ventures (Manimala 1992). From a game-theoretic perspective, we would expect initial defections to bring very high payoffs to the defecting firm, but the premise that individual competitive strategies make a difference in terms of the overall development of a regional cluster has not been directly examined. Thus, we seek to answer the following question:

Question 2: *Do individual competitive actions systematically influence regional development in entrepreneurial settings?*

Computational Capabilities

The close proximity that exists among members of a regional cluster makes it likely that they will know more about each other than about competitors outside the cluster. The same logic obtains for competitors within a neighborhood of the region, for example, a district such as Silicon Alley in New York, which is concentrated in the Soho neighborhood. Managers tend to give more weight to opinions expressed by individuals they consider to be more socially proximate (e.g., because they are insensitive to similar sets of issues or face similar constraints) or to imitate individuals they consider to be more prominent—and therefore visible—in their social networks (Kahneman, Slovic, and Tversky 1982). Managers develop mental models that serve to orient them toward proximate and similar competitors and thereby increase their cognitive efficiency (Porac and Thomas 1990). But research suggests that such simplification and narrowing of focus may come at the expense of competitive blind spots, such as incorrect generalization (Nisbett and Ross 1980) and insensitivity to challenges from unexpected directions (Ginsberg 1995).

Cognitive theories explain how proximity to competitors influences the computational capabilities of managers and their strategic choices. When managers are able to compare or benchmark their performance with that of a larger number of direct competitors, they are likely to form better judgments and to receive higher payoffs from their decisions. From a game-theoretic perspective, we would therefore expect the average gains received from strategic interactions to vary positively with the number of direct competitors that a firm considers in its strategic interactions. Because we have little understanding of how the overall evolution of the system is influenced when members of a regional cluster compare their performance with that of a larger, or smaller, set of competitors, however, we seek to answer the following question:

Question 3: *How do the computational capabilities of managers influence regional development in entrepreneurial settings?*

Indirect Connectivity

Although industry systems are usually represented as generic resource spaces without spatial extension, individual organizations are embedded in multiple networks of exchange relations characterized by recognizable geographical boundaries. The fact that not every individual company interacts with every other in a given competitive domain implies the existence of an imperfect connectivity at the industry level. Individual organizations are likely to be directly connected only to a limited number of other organizations (e.g., suppliers or competitors) and indirectly connected to many others through the first-level contacts (e.g., suppliers of suppliers, suppliers of competitors, competitors of suppliers). As a consequence of this complex chain of relations, the effects of competitive strategies adopted by individual companies will affect the immediate contacts in their "neighborhood" directly and will diffuse to more distant organizations through a chain of indirect and partially overlapping connections (Lomi and Larsen 1996).

From a theoretical point of view, this characterization of organizational environments in terms of imperfect sets of partially overlapping connections among companies is challenging for current theories of regional development, because it implies that individual companies may be subject to (and react to) competitive pressures that are scattered and do not originate from the action of recognizable rivals. This implication opens up important questions about the influence of attribution and interpretation on strategic interaction.

Even if managers have a relatively high level of computational ability, their strategic interactions may be severely limited by mental models that lack important information about the broader competitive context. As mentioned above, the proximity-based advantages afforded to members of a regional cluster may also serve to engender blind spots and judgmental biases. This is consistent with the behavior of managers of firms in the Route 128 cluster who viewed mini-computers as the focal point of industry innovation, despite the fact that the national and international population of firms in the industry had begun to focus on personal computers (Saxenian 1994). In addition, studies have found that entrepreneurs appear to be strongly prone to biases of overconfidence and representativeness, defined as a relation between a hypothetical process and some event associated with the process (e.g., Busenitz and Barney 1994; Cooper, Dunkelberg, and Woo 1988).

From a game-theoretic perspective, our focus on the network structure of organizational environments implies that patterns of indirect connectivity determine, at least in part, if and how innovative behaviors will spread out in a system and how and when competitors will react to individual strategic moves. Specifically, we know relatively little about how the overall evolution of the system is influenced when individual entrepreneurs are more or less sensitive to the consequences of competition outside of their neighborhood. Therefore, we seek to answer the following question:

Question 4: *How does sensitivity to indirect connectivity affect regional development in entrepreneurial settings?*

METHODOLOGY

There are three main motivations for relying on simulation methods to study the relationship between micro-behavior and macro-dynamics in the evolution of regional networks of start-up firms. First, rules and routines that regulate the behavior and performance of individual organizations are essentially unobservable at the population level. Second, ecological theories of organizations are silent on the role of individual action, while behavioral theories of organizations are silent on the role of population evolution. Hence, no guidance is available to discipline the search for empirical specification, and it is difficult to discriminate empirically between alternative micro-evolutionary processes and to test their macro-implications for the dynamics of organizational populations (Levinthal 1990). Finally, simulation methods are increasingly being used to further our understanding of key issues in organizational ecology, such as the relationship between learning and evolution (Mezias and Lant 1994) and adaptation and selection (Levinthal 1990). This literature indicates that computer simulation can be as important as systematic empirical analysis for extending the frontiers of organizational ecology research (Masuch 1995).

To simulate the computational model in which the Prisoner's Dilemma game is played by agents (represented as cells) arranged on a two-dimensional spatial array, or lattice, we used a program designed to give agents three key computational and behavioral features.[2] First, they have the capability to process only local information; second, their states get updated synchronously

---

2. The program used for the simulation was written in Turbo Pascal Version 7.0. A version of the program can be obtained from the authors.

at discrete points in time; and third, their states are defined in terms of the two actions available, cooperation and defection (Lindgren and Nordahl 1994).

In any one round, the payoff for each individual cell is computed as the sum of the payoffs across the games played with the neighboring cells. For example, when K = 1, the game will only be played with the eight cells that touch a given cell c_{ij}. When K = 2, the number of games each cell plays per round is 24, and, for K = 3, the number of games per round is increased to 48. In every round, the state of every cell in the lattice is updated in two steps: (1) computation of the maximum payoff received by any cell in the neighborhood and (2) occupation of each site by either the original "owner" or by one of its neighbors, depending on who obtains the highest score in that round. In that sense, the propagation of strategy across the system is strictly related to its adaptive value or "fitness." Appendix A formalizes the assumptions underlying these rules, and Appendix B provides an overview of the process for a single cell in a time period. These qualitative features of our framework make the model similar to a two-dimensional cellular automata model (Packard and Wolfram 1985).

Cellular Automata Models

To apply concepts from computation theory to the sociology of regional development, we must first find a relationship between the observable qualitative behavior of a social system (in our case, a high-technology firm, or a cluster of firms in an emergent industry) and the operation of a computing machine.

Cellular automata (CA) are mathematical models of dynamic systems that provide a convenient framework with which to address this modeling problem. Their connection with collective social entities made up of elementary decision units, performing logical operations on their inputs, and the operations of a parallel computer, is particularly transparent (Gutowitz 1991; Hogeweg 1988). In both cases, the solution of a global problem and the efficiency of this solution do not depend on the power and speed of a central control mechanism but on the coordination of a large number of decentralized processors (Lomi and Larsen 1999). Thus, cellular automata lend themselves particularly well to portraying the macrobehavior produced by diffused positional externalities among micro-elements processing local information, a situation that may represent the single most important problem in developing a theory of regional development in entrepreneurial settings.[3]

A two-dimensional CA model of pair-wise interactions can be seen as an *n* × *n* chess board on which each square has some computational power to perform a local action depending on the state of the neighborhood.[4] A formal representation of such a CA is:

$$x_{i,j}^{t} = \phi\left(\sum_{h=i-k}^{h=i+k} \sum_{g=j-k}^{g=j+k} x_{h,g}^{t-1} \right)$$

where x_{ij}^{t} is the value of cell i,j at time t and ϕ is a Boolean function that specifies the rule of the automata. The parameter k determines the range of the rule, that is, how many neighboring sites are taken into account (and affected by) the evolution of the automata. In other words, the parameter k defines how local is local, or the propagation feature of the automation. The value of a given site depends at most on $2k+1$ sites, and the region affected by a given site grows at most k sites in each direction every time step t.

Methodological Issues

Before simulating the model, we needed to deal with two important methodological issues, the first concerning the boundary conditions of the system under investigation, a problem that is commonly encountered in the application of dynamic lattice models (Wolfram 1983). There are two acceptable methods for dealing with this problem. One is to impose periodic boundary conditions whereby the lattice is "folded" and the cells arranged on a torus, (i.e., the shape of a doughnut), and the other is to assign a null value to the cells nearest to the boundary. In this study, we followed the second method, that is, we assume that the m cells nearest to the boundary will always cooperate. We use $m = 5$ and accordingly reduce the number of effective cells on the lattice to $(n-2m)^{2}$. The model used in this paper has $n = 70$, so the total

---

3. Cellular automata (CA) models have been increasingly used in a variety of research areas, including physics, chemistry, artificial life, and computer science. The application of cellular automata has found its way less frequently into economics and other social sciences (e.g., Albin 1987; 1998; Keenan and O'Brian 1993; Lomi and Larsen 1996).

4. See Packard and Wolfram (1985) for a more detailed description of two dimensional CAs.

number of active cells in the simulation is 3,600. The number of active cells stays constant in all the results presented in this paper.

A second methodological issue concerns the initialization of the system, that is, the starting assignment of strategies to lattice sites. One possible analytical approach is to start from a single "seed," typically placed in the center of the lattice. In the present context, this would involve placing a single defector in a sea of cooperators to study how strategic interactions unfold over time. A second approach is to start from a cluster of seeds, also placed in the center of the lattice, in which the number of sites may be generated according to some random mechanism. In this study, we used both of these approaches. We began by using the second approach to examine how the magnitude of initial cooperation in the cluster-formation stage influences cluster growth over time. We used the first option to examine the influence of individual competitive strategies on cluster evolution when one member of a cluster of cooperators defects in response to an environmental shock.

RESULTS

The evolutionary dynamics generated by the spatial distribution of D-strategists and C-strategists in an entrepreneurial setting can be seen in Figures 12.2, 12.3, and 12.5. These figures show geographical coverage on the horizontal axis and the payoffs received on the vertical axis. The valleys in these figures represent clusters of D-strategists, while the peaks represent clusters of cooperators. All players located in the "valley of defectors" get the payoff (= 0) corresponding to the DD combination in M (the payoff matrix). The height of the clusters is defined in terms of the payoff achieved by C-strategists, each of which gets 8, corresponding to the CC combination in M multiplied by the number of players in the neighborhood.

Initial Size of the Cooperative

Our first question was, how does the size of the cooperative cluster affect the overall evolution of the cluster, or how many cooperators are needed to create (and expand) cooperation in an environment dominated by defectors? As

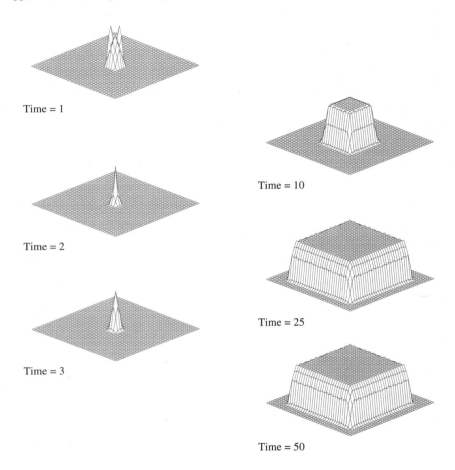

Figure 12.2 Spatial evolution of the model initialized
by a cluster of 16 cooperators

expected, initial size is critical in determining the viability of the cluster. We
experimented with different initial magnitudes to establish first the minimum
size for the cluster of cooperators to achieve critical mass. To do this, we
placed a cluster of cooperators in the middle of the automata, that is, in a sea
of defectors, since that the total number of active cells is 3,600. We found that
a size of 3*3 (9) cooperators will always die out. A minimum cluster size of 16
cooperators was necessary for the cluster of cooperators to become self-
sustaining. Figure 12.2 shows an example in which we start from 4*4 (16)

Random

K = 1

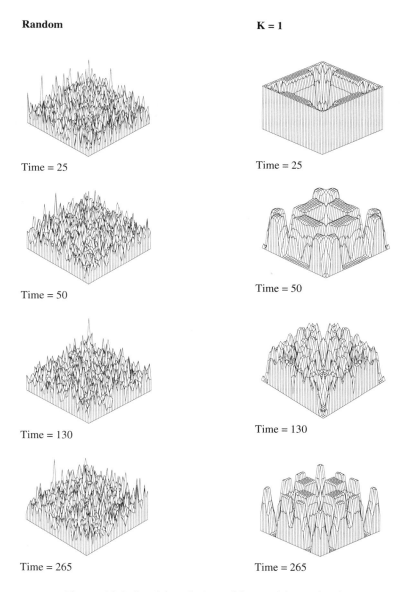

Time = 25

Time = 25

Time = 50

Time = 50

Time = 130

Time = 130

Time = 265

Time = 265

Figure 12.3 Spatial evolution of the model initialized
by a single defector

cooperators in the middle of the automata. The automata reaches a stable configuration at time = 25.

As shown in Figure 12.2, the progression of growth is nonlinear early on. Since there has been no previous defection in the strategic interactions of these firms at time = 1, the payoff that is decided by the value of T at time 1 is equal to 4. This means that as soon as one time-step has elapsed, there will be many defectors as a result. In turn, the value of T will drop dramatically at time 2, because the value of T at time 2 is given by the number of defectors at time 1, where all except 16 were defectors (e.g., adhered to different technological standards). From time 2 onward, T starts to increase until time 25, when there is a balance between the temptation to defect and the reward for cooperating.

The Impact of Defection

To understand the effects of defection in an environment completely dominated by cooperation, we asked two key questions. First, what do the evolutionary dynamics of a system look like when individual firms use a game-theoretic logic to decide whether or not to defect? And, second, how does this compare with the dynamics when local interaction is random? In other words, how will the introduction of a strategy of defecting influence a community of cooperators? Figure 12.3 reports four space-time frames illustrating the evolution of strategic interaction starting from a single defector located in the center of the lattice. The first column shows individual action generated randomly, and the second column shows individual action generated by game-theoretic rules. As expected, in a system in which individual agents choose and update their local strategies according to the game-theoretic rules described earlier (i.e., when they play the spatial version of the RPD specified in Appendixes A and B with their nearest neighbors), and (K = 1 and α = −0.001), the evolutionary dynamics of regional development display a tendency toward self-organization over time. This pattern of spatial evolution stands in stark contrast to one in which firms act on the basis of a "coin toss."

When individual firms choose a strategy based on a game-theoretic logic, the dynamics of regional development reflect a series of continuously changing symmetric spatial patterns, with cooperators (C-strategists) and defectors (D-strategists) persisting indefinitely but in fluctuating proportions. At time

= 25, there is a large area in the center where firms are defecting, which is the reason they are winning nothing. At this point in time, the advantage of winning by defecting has almost disappeared, and shortly thereafter, new patterns of strategic interaction begin to emerge. At time = 50, there are now 12 areas where cooperation dominates, four that are fairly large and eight that are relatively small. At time = 130, some of the cohesion seen earlier disappears. There are now many more smaller clusters of cooperatives, but no dominating ones, in contrast to the spatial distribution seen at the time = 50. At time = 265, after which point the system reaches equilibrium, we once again see increased cohesion and size of cooperative clusters.

Figure 12.4 shows time-series plots of the diffusion of defectors and industry revenues. The number of defectors grows very rapidly during the first 30 generations. The effect of diffuse competition then sets in, and the number of D-strategists fluctuates as a function of T. Similarly, total industry revenue drops drastically during the first 30 generations and then fluctuates as a function of T. After 265 generations, the system reaches a stable equilibrium, at which point no further change occurs. In other words, no single firm changes its strategy, and total industry revenues remain stable after this point.

The interesting conclusion suggested by Figures 12.3 and 12.4 is that strategic interaction at the individual level results in regional clusters of industrial activity partitioned into well-defined clusters of D- and C-strategists with no tendency toward change. The conclusion of this preliminary analysis is not only that individual strategies have relevant system-level implications for regional development but, more important, that the long-run equilibrium implies the coexistence of dominant and dominated firm strategies.

Computational Capability

To further understand the connection between local strategic interactions and the collective development of the system, we asked a third question, How do the computational capabilities of local decision makers influence the evolutionary dynamics of our simplified geographical region? The range of local interaction, as measured by K, reflects the computational power of the firms that operate in the region. For example, where K = 1, in every round every cell plays against the eight others in its neighborhood, where K = 2, in every

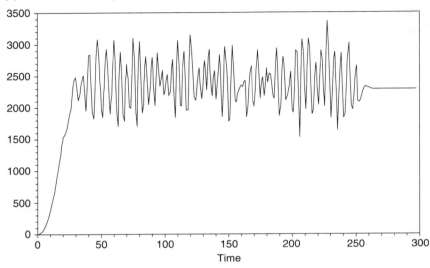

(a) Number of D-strategies

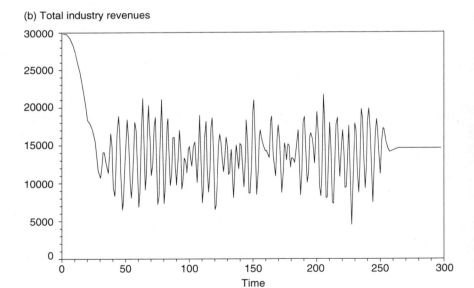

(b) Total industry revenues

Figure 12.4 Temporal evolution of the model initialized by a single defector

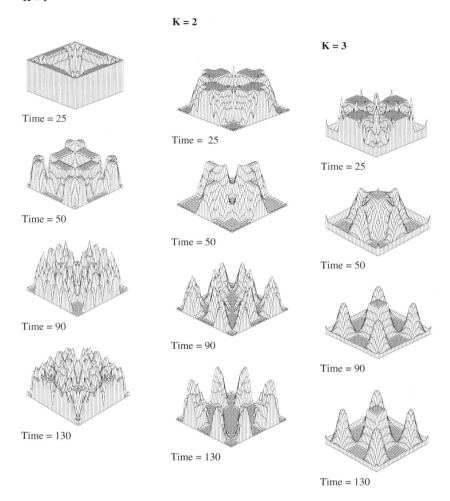

K = 1

Time = 25

Time = 50

Time = 90

Time = 130

K = 2

Time = 25

Time = 50

Time = 90

Time = 130

K = 3

Time = 25

Time = 50

Time = 90

Time = 130

Figure 12.5 The influence of interaction range (K) on the spatial evolution of the model

round every cell plays against the 24 others in its neighborhood, and where K = 3, in every round every cell plays against the 48 others in its neighborhood. Thus, increasing K means that local decision makers are now able to compare their performance with that of a larger number of direct competitors.

Figure 12.5 shows how variations in evolutionary dynamics across space-time frames reflect differences in the range of local interaction (K) for a given $\alpha = -0.001$. The vertical dimension in Figure 12.5 captures time variations within models for a given range of local interaction. Each column contains four space-time frames of the model to illustrate the different configurations reached by the system after 25, 50, 90, and 130 generations, respectively, as a function of K. Only K is changed experimentally, while everything else, including the initial conditions, is kept constant across models.

As shown in Figure 12.5, the extent to which computational capability is increased significantly changes the spatial and temporal distribution of C- and D-strategists and the payoffs they receive. Specifically, as K increases, clusters of adjacent firms adopting the same strategy increase in size, and they do so earlier on. This results in fewer and fewer independent clusters and a more concentrated spatial distribution of strategies. This implies that as K increases, that is, as the region becomes socially constructed as better organized and more cooperative, the permanence of suboptimal local strategies decreases. This also results in the realization of equilibrium at an earlier point in time. When K = 3, the system reaches a periodic solution at time = 90, at which point it reaches the same solution every five periods (e.g., at time = 130).

Figure 12.6 shows time-series plots of the diffusion of maximum winnings over time. For all three ranges, maximum winnings plunge drastically after the initial defection, but the plunge is much more severe and comes much earlier when computational ability, as measured by K, is higher. Following an initial plunge, maximum winnings fluctuate as a function of T. Whereas K = 1 produces a model with a stable solution, K = 3 produces a model with a periodic solution. After some initial oscillations, the stable solution model reaches equilibrium at time t = 226, as shown in Figure 12.6. In contrast, the periodic solution model, after an initial transient, repeats a certain pattern or sequence over and over again as the model evolves. Each sequence has fixed periodicity with an arbitrary length: when K = 3, the model enters a periodic motion with a period of 5.

Awareness of Indirect Connectivity

In our final question, we sought to understand how the overall evolution of regional clusters is influenced when individual entrepreneurs are more or less sensitive to the consequences of indirect connectivity, as reflected in competition

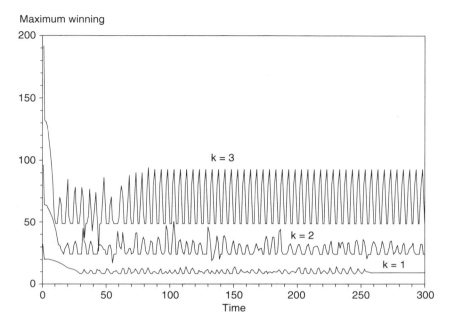

Figure 12.6 The influence of interaction range (K) on the temporal distribution of maximum payoffs

outside of their neighborhood. The intensity of the relation between the aggregate number of defectors and the expected payoff of defecting—α—reflects the sensitivity to indirect connectivity of the firms that operate in the region. By experimentally varying α, we analyze what happens to the evolutionary dynamics of the regional system as the individual short-term advantage of defecting decreases as a function of the aggregate number of existing D-strategists.

Figure 12.7 illustrates the impact of sensitivity to indirect connectivity on regional development by plotting both the average number of defectors and total industry profits from time t = 450 to t = 600 against α. Results are based on 100 simulations for a system in which cellular agents play the RPD with their eight nearest neighbors (K = 1). As the decision heuristic becomes negative, that is, as sensitivity to indirect connectivity becomes stronger, the average number of D-strategists becomes fewer. While the advantage of defecting decreases linearly as the number of D-strategists increases, the average number of D-strategists α = −0.0008 to α = −0.002 reduces the population of D-strategists from around

(a) Average number of D-strategists

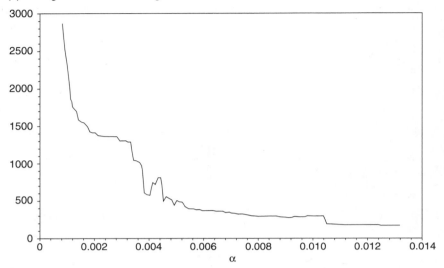

(b) Total average industry profit

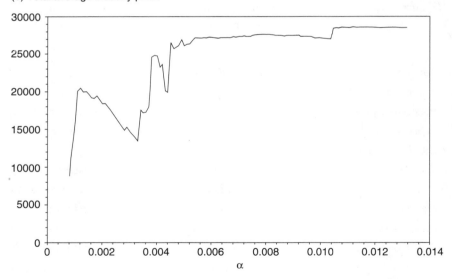

Figure 12.7 The influence of interorganizational connectivity (α) on evolutionary dynamics

3,700 to around 1,100, corresponding to a reduction of around 70 percent. Changing the strength of diffuse competition from $\alpha = -0.01$ reduces the population of D-strategists from around 1,100 to 200, or approximately 80 percent.

As shown in the lower half of Figure 12.7 (b), there is a relatively good fit between the number of D-strategists and the total average industry profit. In other words, from an industry point of view, cooperation between and among regional clusters pays off. Profitability is not only a function of the number of cooperators or defectors in the population, however, but also of their spatial organization. Larger cluster sizes represent higher levels of connectivity through which the negative impact of defecting can spread. When there is a higher level of fragmentation, that is, when clusters are smaller, the opposite is true. This explains why in the area of $\alpha = -0.0015$ to $\alpha = -0.0035$, average industry profits decline, even as a becomes more negative and the number of defectors does not go up. At these points, there are still so many defectors in the population that profitability is still strongly influenced by the spatial distribution of cooperators and defectors. Specifically, when defectors are organized in small regional clusters, average industry profitability is higher than when they are organized in one big one, for example.

As indirect competition reduces the adaptive value of adopting a rational competitive strategy in any one individual game, D-strategists are confined to a progressively narrower region of the system, and only rarely can they propagate through space to form stable clusters. These effects are consistent with conjectures about the ecological consequences of niche desegregation and institutional change, which, by breaking the boundaries around technical or institutional sectors, make individual organizations more sensitive to competitive pressures coming from more remote sites (Hannan and Freeman 1986). Similar processes of diffuse competition are triggered when markets, or populations, expand to transcend national or regional boundaries (Hannan and Carroll 1992).

DISCUSSION AND CONCLUSIONS

We began by drawing attention to the weakness of the theoretical linkage between existing micro and macro perspectives on entrepreneurship, in spite of, or perhaps because of, the important results independently achieved by research conducted at different levels of analysis. We argued that the weakness of the micro-to-macro linkage is particularly apparent when one tries to analyze regional development in entrepreneurial settings. In such settings, the unit of observation is frequently the entrepreneur (or a set of entrepreneurs), but the unit of analysis is a complex composite actor with spatial extension, such as an industrial district or a regional economy. We proposed a theoretical framework to address this problem, based on the image of social actors as units performing a complex collective computation by processing strictly local, and therefore incomplete, information. These can be individual entrepreneurs or organized groups, depending on the context.

We used computational techniques inspired by the theory of cellular automata to link this image to a formal evolutionary model in which individual agents operate in a spatially extended environment and play the infinitely repeated version of the Prisoner's Dilemma with their neighbors. Finally, we simulated the model under a variety of evolutionary conditions to illustrate how local entrepreneurs with limited computational and cognitive capacities interact to impose and sustain order in their environment.

At a general level, the findings show clearly that while the connection between individual behavior and its aggregate system-level consequences is not easily predictable, social order cannot arise spontaneously from random interaction and is heavily path dependent. Small differences in initial size may be amplified over time by positive feedback mechanisms and result in huge differences in terms of regional development. Aggregate regional structures with clear boundaries emerge from, but at the same time shape, the patterns of interaction at the micro level. Not only can such regional systems evolve and persist without any intentional design or central coordination, but they can also partition the population into sharply distinct clusters characterized by persistent performance differences.

In more specific terms, we found that cooperative clusters below a certain initial size will not survive in an industry characterized by a lack of convergence on a dominant design and fierce competition. Once above the critical mass of initial size, however, such clusters evolve on the basis of a growing stock of cooperative economics. These results are consistent with studies that show a tendency for regional development in emerging industries to follow a recursive development trajectory, referred to by David (1985) as a "lock-in." They are also consistent with the tendency for certain geographical regions (e.g., Hollywood, Detroit, Silicon Valley) to become virtually synonymous with a particular type of product (Scott 1995).

The very existent of path dependence and lock in also means that regions will eventually find it very difficult to adapt to certain kinds of external jolts as they grow to increased cooperation and convergence (Scott 1995). This is consistent with anecdotal evidence on shifts in the relocation of the dominant spatial nexus of industries in entrepreneurial settings (Saxenian 1994; Scott 1998). For example, in the 1980s, Route 128 minicomputer companies were not prepared for the technological shift toward personal computers, and in the early 1990s, Silicon Valley firms were not well prepared for the technological and consumer shift toward the Internet.

Our results suggest, however, that individual response to such jolts may plunge the region into considerable fragmentation and turmoil before stabilization and equilibrium conditions are reached. We found that strategies with different fitness values not only persist over time but also coexist in varying proportions and are localized in clearly bounded clusters. The key insight here is that these dynamics are self-organizing because the agents (in our case, the individual entrepreneurs) are not programmed to form stable clusters.

The second set of results suggested by the analysis is that cognitive capabilities and sensitivities can significantly alter the spatial and temporal distribution of cooperation and competition, and strongly affect the dynamics of regional development. When social norms and managerial practices facilitate a greater range of interaction, they also increase computational power. Here, there is both good and bad news. As individual agents are given the computational power to compare their performance with that of a larger number of direct competitors, the distribution of strategic types or product standards becomes less spatially fragmented but more temporally unstable. Specifically, when the range of local interaction increases, the system no longer reaches a unique equilibrium configuration, and, when $K = 3$, it enters a periodic collective motion in which the same state will be visited every five periods, or generations, infinitely many times.

Our results suggest that as individual entrepreneurs become more sensitive to the collective consequences of their actions, that is, as they become more sensitive to the effects of indirect connectivity, D-strategies are confined to a limited region around the initial defector and do not spread beyond the local level. This result is the consequence of the simple frequency-dependent selection mechanism that we set up, according to which the payoff from defection is a monotonically decreasing function of the aggregate number of defectors. What is interesting, however, is that relatively small changes in the intensity of the relationship between the density of D-strategists and individual rewards associated with defection produce relatively large differences in regional development.

These results support arguments made by Scott (1995), among others, that there is an important and positive role for agents of collective order to play in local industrial development. Regional industrial consortia and forums that regularly bring together major local constituencies (e.g., employment agencies, banks, workers' organizations, and municipal governments) can provide an important mechanism for developing social norms and managerial practices that facilitate greater awareness of the consequences of indirect connectivity.

Limitations

Although we believe that these results are important for understanding the dynamics of regional development in entrepreneurial settings, we need to recognize the limitations of our study. These can be divided into limitations that are inherent in the modeling framework and those that are inherent to assumptions that are restrictive in the present context but that do not necessarily imply a loss of generality.

The first basic limitation of the modeling framework is its synchronous updating mechanism. The state of every site on the lattice is updated in the same discrete time steps. While this computational structure is generally considered a reasonable assumption in models of physical and chemical systems (Wolfram 1986), its realism for modeling the mechanics of social and ecological processes can be questioned (Hogeweg 1988). For example, Huberman and Glance (1993) convincingly argued that the behavior of the system is extremely sensitive to the assumption of synchronous updating.

The second limitation of our modeling framework concerns the fact that the same rule of local interaction is used to update the state of every cell in the lattice. In principle, it is possible to think of different rules competing for sites or to design individual cells that draw rules of interaction from a distribution of possible rules. We are not aware of any work that has implemented such a model, however, possibly because the computational burden would quickly become prohibitive if the number of possible combinations were left unconstrained.

Future Directions

To simulate the behavior of our models, we relied on a number of auxiliary assumptions that correspond to a set of constraints that can be relaxed in future studies. For example, we assumed that all players have equal information (or understanding) of the global consequences of individual action. Future studies can relax this assumption by adding a random, time-varying and/or location-specific disturbance term in the relation, defining the advantage of defecting as a function of the density of D-strategists. We also assumed that each player can consistently and readily emulate the strategy that satisfies a local fitness criterion. Future studies can modify this assumption by allowing players to make mistakes, for example, by designing an updating mechanism according to which there is a small probability that players will choose a local strategy that is the opposite of what they intend (Lindgren and Nordahl 1994).

A third assumption on which we relied is that memory of past events does not influence players' expectation about future encounters. Future studies can abandon this assumption by following the pioneering work of Axelrod (1984) and including history as a determinant of future strategy, with memory structure operating as a sort of genetic code (Lindgren and Nordahl 1994). Alternatively, future studies can incorporate into the model the less Pavlovian processes of expectation formation suggested by Huberman and Glance (1993). The final constraint to be addressed by future studies is a product of the structure of the game, which allows the entrepreneurs to choose only between two strategies that define the state space on each individual cell on the lattice. Although models with more than two states are not conceptually difficult to design, they are computationally more expensive to simulate. The cost of such simulations should decrease significantly in the future, however, as computational technology becomes more efficient.

In conclusion, we believe that the current research illustrates the great potential of computational models to further our understanding of a wide range of emergent phenomena underlying the dynamics of regional development by revealing the connections between organized collectivities and complex computational systems. Strategic interactions in geographic space reflect the micro-macro dichotomy pervading organizational research particularly well because, while individual firms act in reaction to and anticipation of each other's reaction, the final result of their local activities is invariably mediated by collective outcomes, that is, by the forces of indirect competition.

In attempting to establish an explicit connection between strategies of local interaction and their global population consequences, we sought to shed light on the emergence and evolution of regional clusters in entrepreneurial settings. The approach we proposed reflects an autogenetic perspective of strategic behavior, which emphasizes the role of the self-organizing capacities of individual interaction in a social field (Drazin and Sandelands 1992; Ginsberg, Larsen, and Lomi 1997). We hope that our study opens new frontiers for theories of regional development in entrepreneurship.

Appendix A

Mathematical Formulation of the Spatial Model

To incorporate the effects of diffuse competition, the advantage of defecting (T) in any one round is not fixed as in the usual RPD but is a function of the global number of defectors. Let f_i be a function that relates the aggregate number of agents choosing D to the payoff of defection expected by each individual player. Thus T^t—the expected payoff associated with defection at time t—is:

$$T^t = f_i (D^{t-1}) \tag{2}$$

Let $a_{i,j}^{t-1}$ be the state of cell c_{ij} at time t−1 (i.e., D or C), $a_{h,g}^{t-1}$ the state of any other cell $c_{h,g}$ in the neighborhood s_K directly playing with c_{ij}, T^t, R, P, S the payoffs associated with the different strategies in M, and let K be the range of the local interaction. Then the total payoff for cell ij at time t, which is repeated for all $n \times n$ cells in the lattice, can be computed as:

$$\Pi_{i,j}^t = \sum_{h=i-K}^{h=i+K} \sum_{g=i-K}^{g=i+K} (a_{i,j}^{t-1}, a_{h,g}^{t-1}, T^t, R, P, S) \tag{3}$$

Every round, the state of every cell in the lattice is updated in two steps. The first step involves the computation of $\pi_{i,j}^t$. This quantity can be computed as:

$$\pi_{i,j}^t = \text{Max}(\Pi_{h,g}^t \ for \ (((i-K)< h < (i+K)) \wedge ((i-K)< g < (i+K))) \tag{4}$$

where $\pi_{i,j}^t$ is the maximum payoff received by any cell c_{ij} in a K-neighborhood.

In the second step, every site is either occupied by the original "owner" or by one of the neighbors, depending on who obtains the highest score in that round. Another way of saying this is that agent c_{ij} will abandon the strategy chosen in the previous round if a neighbor with a different strategy out competed all the others in the neighborhood, that is, managed to obtain the highest payoff. So in every round c_{ij} updates its strategy according to the rule:

$$a_{i,j}^t = \begin{cases} D \ if \ \exists \ a_{h,g}^{t-1} \in \sigma_K = D \mid \Pi_{h,g}^t \rightarrow \pi_{i,j}^t \\ C \ if \ \exists \ a_{h,g}^{t-1} \in \sigma_K = C \mid \Pi_{h,g}^t \rightarrow \pi_{i,j}^t \end{cases} \tag{5}$$

This equation reflects the idea that agents evaluate their strategy relative to (or "given") their knowledge of what the other players in the K-neighborhood received at t−1.

At every generation (or round) all the cells in the system revise their strategy according to this two-step updating process and adopt the locally "best" course of action.

Appendix B

Mathematical Formulation of the Payoff Function

We define f_1 in equation (1) as a linear function of the global number of defectors where α is the slope of the line, N the total number of defectors, and 4 is the payoff for defecting if no cell defects (i.e., if N = 0). The relationship is given as:

$$T^t = \alpha \, N^t + 4 \tag{6}$$

where

$$N^t = \sum_{i=1+m}^{i=n-m} \sum_{j=1+m}^{j=n-m} \begin{cases} 1 \; if \, a_{i,j}^{t-1} = D \\ 0 \; if \, a_{i,j}^{t-1} = C \end{cases} \tag{7}$$

The slope of the line is an expression for how sensitive individual agents are to the aggregate consequence of their actions or—if $\alpha < 0$—it could be seen as a global level penalty for defecting. When $\alpha = 0$, there is no diffuse effect and the model becomes similar to May and Nowak's model (1992). A positive α is associated with increasing returns on defection, and a negative α—as we use in the baseline case where $\alpha = -0.001$—puts a penalty on individual defection which increases with the aggregate number of other agents choosing the same uncooperative course of action.

Appendix C

Decision Routine for an Individual Cell

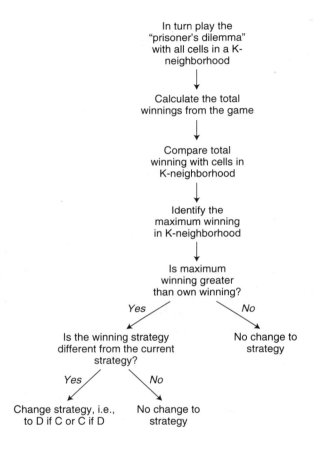

13

The Legal Environment of Entrepreneurship

Observations on the Legitimation of
Venture Finance in Silicon Valley

MARK C. SUCHMAN, DANIEL J. STEWARD,

AND CLIFFORD A. WESTFALL

New firms vary widely in structure, strategy, and situation. This is hardly surprising, given that popular images of entrepreneurship often emphasize novelty, innovation, and product differentiation. Most start-ups, however, generally resist the temptation to reinvent the wheel. Entrepreneurs rarely, if ever, create companies from whole cloth; rather, they build on organizational models present in the larger social environment. In this chapter, we explore the "institutional ecology" of Silicon Valley to illustrate how such organizational models emerge and diffuse within a new organizational community. Our exploration highlights the impact of the legal environment on both the founding of new firms and the institutionalization of new organizational forms.

This chapter bridges two previously distinct lines of scholarship. The first, more theoretical line has examined the interplay between law, understood broadly, and general organizational activity (Edelman and Suchman 1997), while the second, more empirical line has examined the role of law firms in

Research for this chapter was supported in part by NSF grants #SBR-9201121 and SBR-9702605. The authors would like to thank the editors of this volume, the participants in the Entrepreneurship Dynamic Conference, and the members of the University of Wisconsin Seminar on Law, Innovation and Entrepreneurship for their helpful comments on earlier drafts. Thanks also go to Lauren Edelman for her collaboration in developing the typology on which our discussion of law and entrepreneurship rests.

Silicon Valley (Friedman et al. 1989; Suchman 1994b; Suchman and Cahill 1996). Here, to explore the impact of law on entrepreneurial activity, we consider the connection between the legal environment and the emergence of persistently entrepreneurial organizational communities, as exemplified by Silicon Valley. Although law firms play a large part in our story, we examine other elements of the legal environment as well, to construct a more rounded account of the multifaceted relationship between law and entrepreneurship.

ENTREPRENEURSHIP, INNOVATION, AND ORGANIZATIONAL ENVIRONMENTS

Entrepreneurship and innovation, while closely related, are not synonymous. Entrepreneurship—the process of constructing and promoting new endeavors—emphasizes initiative and advocacy.[1] In contrast, innovation—the process of conceiving and elaborating novel approaches—emphasizes imagination and originality. A reclusive laboratory scientist can be innovative without being entrepreneurial; an enterprising franchisee can be entrepreneurial without being innovative. In many contexts, of course, innovation and entrepreneurship go hand in hand; however, beyond a certain point, the urge to innovate may have the perverse effect of diverting precious resources from the crucial task of implementing stable routines to the less productive activity of exploring infinite alternatives. For the typical entrepreneur, novelty, like a trace mineral, can be deadly both in absence and in surfeit.

Stated more prosaically, the entrepreneur faces two distinct, but interrelated problems: an economic problem and a cognitive problem. To launch an economically viable enterprise, the entrepreneur must assemble an initial stock of resources (raw materials, labor, capital, etc.), configure those resources into a stable organizational structure, and position that structure within a munificent environmental niche. By separating the new firm from potential competitors,

---

1. We limit ourselves here to the entrepreneurial construction of new formal organizations. In reality, of course, entrepreneurial activity can also yield both broader social movements, as in the case of "moral entrepreneurship" (Becker 1963), and narrower reforms within preexisting organizations, as in corporate intrapreneurship (Geisler 1993). This chapter, however, does not address either of these two kindred phenomena.

innovation can help in these tasks. Significantly, however, start-up firms depend not only on material resources but also on cultural understandings, and this gives rise to the second half of the entrepreneurial challenge: To launch a cognitively viable enterprise, the entrepreneur must construct a mental map of underexploited opportunities, generate a coherent model for organizing around those opportunities, and communicate a legitimating account of the endeavor to potential stakeholders. Together, maps, models, and accounts make up a cognitive framework—a cultural understanding of how to perceive, act upon, and describe the world.[2] In the absence of adequate maps, models, and accounts, even sizable "real" niches may go unnoticed and untapped; conversely, in the presence of particularly compelling maps, models and accounts, even purely "imaginary" niches may become self-fulfilling prophecies (cf. Weick 1979, 273–75). Thus, entrepreneurial success often depends as much on the articulation of cognitive frameworks as on the mobilization of economic resources, and excessive novelty can render a new firm too unfamiliar to survive.

The economic and cognitive problems of entrepreneurship do not arise in a vacuum. Rather, both sets of challenges derive from conditions in the interorganizational environment. Both economic resources and cognitive frameworks originate, in large part, outside the new firm itself. Unfortunately, at the environmental level, responses to the economic and cognitive challenges of entrepreneurship can often work at cross purposes. If an effective organizing model becomes common knowledge, thereby easing the cognitive problem, new enterprises will proliferate until they exhaust available resources, thereby exacerbating the economic problem.[3] Conversely, if an ample resource supply becomes indiscriminately available, thereby easing the economic problem, deviant organizing models will tend to proliferate until they obscure any established conventions, thereby exacerbating the cognitive

---

2. This chapter focuses primarily on cognitive models, since these are the key cultural blueprints that allow entrepreneurs to create stable organizational structures. Obviously, however, a blueprint is useless without a map of the terrain and an account of the project, so our statements about cognitive models apply generally to maps and accounts as well.

3. This insight underlies the familiar density dependence argument in organizational ecology, discussed below. New populations generally lack widely accepted organizing models, and hence they multiply only slowly. As cognitive legitimacy rises, however, founding rates increase and failure rates decline, until the environmental carrying capacity becomes taxed, and competitive forces brake the entrepreneurial bandwagon.

problem.[4] Overall, then, widespread entrepreneurship would seem to depend on a relatively rare conjunction of environmental conditions: resources must be plentiful, but at the same time, models for identifying and capturing those resources must be clear. Such conditions are generally transitory, as environments pass from certainty to scarcity or from plenty to confusion.

Nonetheless, the occasional emergence of persistently entrepreneurial environments such as Silicon Valley suggests that certain conditions can suspend these transitions in mid-course, perhaps indefinitely. While few researchers have yet addressed the origins of such persistently entrepreneurial environments (but see Saxenian 1994), one key precondition would seem to be the emergence of interorganizational structures that (a) stabilize resource flows without either binding or dissipating them and (b) systematize cognitive models without either rigidifying or deconstructing them.[5] In most real-world settings, such structures will involve complex mixtures of ecological and institutional elements.

AN INSTITUTIONAL ECOLOGY OF ENTREPRENEURSHIP

To understand persistent entrepreneurialism, one must draw from several distinct theoretical perspectives. Most prominent among these are organizational ecology and neo-institutional theory. Although neither approach offers a self-contained theory of entrepreneurship, both provide valuable insights into the workings of organizational environments, with numerous implications for the study of persistent entrepreneurialism. Moreover, read in conjunction, these two literatures suggest the outlines of an emerging institutional ecology,

---

4. This second dynamic is not as widely acknowledged as the first, but hints appear in the literatures on slack search (March 1988, 4), superstitious learning (Levitt and March 1988), and competence-destroying innovation (Anderson and Tushman 1990; Tushman and Anderson 1986).

5. In addition to sustaining entrepreneurship by stabilizing resource flows and systematizing cognitive models, some environments also (or alternatively) sustain entrepreneurship by fostering competence-destroying innovations (Tushman and Anderson 1986) that create a near-perpetual state of economic disequilibrium. Although Silicon Valley arguably displays elements of both persistent entrepreneurship and persistent innovation, this chapter focuses primarily on the former, emphasizing the ways in which environmental structures support the relatively routine creation of new business enterprises.

an integrative perspective with even clearer relevance to entrepreneurship than either of its component parts.

Organizational Ecology

Organizational ecologists (e.g., Astley 1985; Baum 1996; Hannan and Freeman 1977; 1989; Singh and Lumsden 1990) apply a biological metaphor to the study of organizational life. In general terms, the ecological approach examines organizations as though they were biotic organisms emphasizing the competition for material resources among populations of similar firms, and highlighting the correspondence between organizational forms and environmental niches. Further, the classic ecological formulation posits that most organizations are rigidly inertial and that population-level change therefore occurs less through firm-level adaptation than through the disproportional founding and/or failure of some types of organizations relative to others (e.g., Hannan and Freeman 1984; 1989; cf. Aldrich 1979; Baum and Singh 1994b). What changes, in this view, is not the individual organization, but rather the competence pool, the organizational equivalent of a gene pool, comprising all of the structural and procedural blueprints embodied in an entire population.[6] Competitive selection creates differential net mortality within and between populations, raising the prevalence of adaptive competences and lowering the prevalence of maladaptive competences in the surviving pool.

Entrepreneurship, from an ecological perspective, primarily reflects the impact of resource pressures on organizational founding rates. Entrepreneurial activities arise when environmental change opens a previously nonexistent or unoccupied niche. The availability of unbound resources creates a temporary period of disequilibrium, and during this window of opportunity, founding rates are likely to rise, as new firms proliferate to exploit the open environmental space. As the previously vacant niche approaches its carrying capacity, however, foundings and failures begin to equalize. Heightened com-

---

6. In the lexicon of organizational ecology, a competence or "comp" is the organizational equivalent of a gene, the basic unit of constitutive information, encoding fundamental rules about how to produce an organizational structure, operational procedure, or behavioral pattern (Suchman, forthcoming; cf. Hannan and Freeman 1989, 48–50; McKelvey 1982).

petition raises the failure rate and suppresses the founding rate until a new equilibrium emerges, with the niche housing exactly as many organizations as it can support—no more, no less.

Admittedly, the reemergence of equilibrium does not necessarily imply a low rate of entrepreneurship. Even a full niche can support persistently high founding rates, provided that the corresponding failure rates remain equally high. Under stable environmental conditions, however, elevated rates of founding and failure will generally involve some waste of resources, leaving persistently entrepreneurial populations vulnerable to eventual displacement by less volatile forms. This insight lies at the heart of ecological models of community "succession" (Astley 1985, 235).[7] Thus, traditional ecological analysis suggests that entrepreneurship ultimately stems from economic disequilibrium, of either the short-run or the long-run variety. Sooner or later a changing niche structure will elevate organizational founding rates, and sooner or later a stable niche structure will depress them.

Neo-Institutional Theory

Neo-institutional theorists (e.g., DiMaggio and Powell 1983; Meyer and Rowan 1977; Meyer and Scott 1983; Powell and DiMaggio 1991) draw their inspiration from theories of culture and discourse rather than from biology. This perspective portrays organizations as highly ritualized enactments of taken-for-granted cultural models, emphasizing the diffusion of such models within fields of interacting firms. As they become institutionalized in formal laws, informal norms, and tacit assumptions, these cultural models acquire a quasi-rulelike status, and conformity brings organizations both legitimacy and social support. Seeing organizational behavior as a response to such environmental constraints, institutional theorists generally assume that organiza-

---

7. In such models, ecologists differentiate between r-specialist and K-specialist strategies, with r-specialist populations emphasizing high reproduction rates, while K-specialists emphasize maximal exploitation of available resources. A full niche can exhibit a high level of entrepreneurial activity, as long as r-specialists predominate; as communities mature and niches become increasingly stable, however, K-specialists will tend to out-compete r-specialists, and entrepreneurship will consequently tend to decline. Thus, the filling of a niche by r-specialists represents only a temporary culmination of one stage in a succession, not a permanent equilibrium point (see Hannan and Freeman 1989, 118–20).

tion-level change reflects broader cultural shifts at the level of interorganizational fields, industrial sectors, societal polities, or even the world system.

Although institutional theory currently lacks a comprehensive account of entrepreneurship, the literature implicitly links entrepreneurial activity with at least three distinct cultural processes: diffusion, recombination, and sensemaking. Diffusion introduces preexisting models into new fields, as expanded accounts of relevance erase the cognitive boundaries between previously separate domains. In this process, entrepreneurship may simply involve imitating the organizational forms of one field when launching new endeavors in another. Recombination goes one step further, constructing novel organizational forms, but from preexisting standardized components. Here, the entrepreneur creatively rearranges chunks of already-institutionalized activity into new permutations. As Meyer and Rowan (1977, 45) put it, "the building blocks for organizations [are] littered around the societal landscape; it takes only a little entrepreneurial energy to assemble them into a structure." Finally, sensemaking, the most radical form of institutional entrepreneurship, involves the construction of genuinely novel cultural accounts to address unexpected and anomalous events. Unlike diffusion and recombination, sensemaking engages entrepreneurs in all phases of the social construction process from the interpretation of problematic interactions, to the formulation of shared typifications, to the assembly of appropriate institutions (cf. Berger and Luckmann 1967; Weick 1995).

Nonetheless, sensemaking remains simply a variation on the central institutionalist theme: entrepreneurship emerges when cultural understandings are in flux. In this, neo-institutional theory echoes organizational ecology's claim that entrepreneurship stems primarily from disequilibrium. The only difference is that, here, the disequilibrium is cultural, not material, a product of underinstitutionalized cognitive models, not of under-exploited economic niches. As understandings become increasingly taken for granted, both the need and the opportunity for entrepreneurial diffusion, recombination, and sensemaking tend to decline. Thus, ecological accounts of community succession, in which high-turnover entrepreneurial populations give way to low-turnover bureaucratic populations, find their counterpart in institutional accounts of "field structuration" (DiMaggio and Powell 1983, 65), in which haphazard local interactions give way to coherent collective institutions. In their conventional guises, it seems, neither ecology nor institutionalism allow much room for the possibility of more persistent entrepreneurship.

Institutional Ecology

While ecological theories of entrepreneurship focus on resource flows and vacant niches, and institutional theories focus on cultural understandings and available models, actual entrepreneurship emerges from a complex interplay of both niches and models, in conjunction. Thus, to capture the workings of persistently entrepreneurial environments, a more integrated theoretical account may be needed. Fortunately, in the past few years, debates between scholars in ecology and institutionalism have inspired a nascent literature on what might be termed institutional ecology (e.g., Baum and Oliver 1996; Fombrun 1988; Hannan and Carroll 1992; Haveman and Rao 1997; Singh, Tucker, and Meinhard 1991; Suchman, forthcoming). Although the initial formulations in this literature were of only limited relevance to the study of entrepreneurship, recent trends hold more promise.

For the most part, early works of institutional ecology treated institutional processes as little more than exogenous resource constraints within the traditional ecological framework. Hypothesizing that institutionally legitimated organizations receive a disproportionate amount of material support from the social environment, researchers explored the impact of laws, regulations, and other societywide institutions on organizational failure rates. Although not entirely irrelevant to the study of entrepreneurship, such investigations tended to focus on inappropriately macroscopic levels of analysis and on inappropriately advanced stages of the organizational life cycle. Arguably, an adequate account of entrepreneurship demands equal or greater attention to the impact of community-level institutions on organizational founding rates. By structuring access to economic resources and cognitive models, local institutions may play a particularly important role in the construction of new firms, even if global conditions play a larger part in the survival of going enterprises.

Expanding institutional ecology to address the impact of local institutions on organizational foundings has several advantages for the study of entrepreneurship. First, this approach emphasizes that the creation of start-ups is a complex social process. Foundings do not simply materialize as random events, and institutions do not merely allocate resources among existing organizations; rather, institutions determine, at least in part, which types of new organizations emerge in the first place. Second, this approach suggests that cognitive models may matter as much as economic resources. Institutions do not merely provide material sustenance, they also promulgate cultural understandings, and frequently, the primary institutional constraints on entrepreneurship involve access to legitimate models for organizing, rather than access to land, labor, and capital. Third, this approach highlights the importance of local, community-level institutions. Not all institutional forces operate on a societal scale; some of the most important ones operate more narrowly, within particular geographically or functionally bounded organizational communities. Fourth, this approach illuminates the endogeneity of many entrepreneurship dynamics. As the level of analysis moves downward, from whole societies to specific communities, the scales of institutional and entrepreneurial activity become more nearly equivalent, and one begins to see that while local institutions may be affecting entrepreneurship, entrepreneurship is also affecting local institutions.

Two examples from the emerging literature may help to illustrate this expanded approach. The first is the familiar density dependent selection model from organizational ecology, which invokes institutional conceptions of cognitive legitimacy to address ecological questions about population dynamics (e.g., Hannan and Carroll 1992).[8] In suggesting that founding rates rise as organizational forms acquire taken-for-grantedness, density dependence theory moves organizational ecology beyond a purely resource-oriented view of institutions to consider the impact of institutions on the availability of cognitive models. While resource acquisition remains a central concern of this literature, these analyses acknowledge that new organizations are difficult to assemble and sustain without adequate models and that access to such models is an important constraint in the institutional environment.

For the study of entrepreneurship, however, the density dependence literature suffers from two drawbacks. First, most empirical investigations have

---

8. Neo-institutional theorists (e.g., Baum and Powell 1995; Zucker 1989) have often criticized this work for emphasizing cognitive taken-for-grantedness at the expense of more moral and pragmatic forms of legitimation (Suchman 1995a). Arguably, however, it is precisely the decision to define legitimacy in cognitivist terms that allows density dependence theory to avoid reducing legitimation to a question of resource acquisition.

simply inferred the legitimacy of organizational forms from the size of observed populations, rather than examining the actual structure of cultural discourses or the actual transmission of institutionalized models (but cf. Hannan et al. 1995). This yields a rather impoverished account of how specific models acquire legitimacy and how specific entrepreneurs acquire models. Second, the density dependence literature has made little effort to link reproduction, the process of founding new firms, to speciation, the process of generating new populations. For the most part, this literature has only paid lip service to the analysis of what Hannan and Freeman (1989, 54) termed "blending [and] segregating processes," the consolidation and differentiation of emerging organizational forms.

Both of these critiques have particular relevance for studies of entrepreneurship. In the construction of new firms, the availability of relevant models becomes a crucial issue. Because density dependence theory fails to examine how cognitive models actually diffuse, it is at a disadvantage in predicting where and how new firms will arise. At the same time, because density dependence theory fails to link reproduction and speciation, it is poorly suited to address either the relationship between innovation and entrepreneurship or the effects of entrepreneurship on larger organizational environments. Although the model can provide useful insights into the effects of cognitive legitimacy on population-level founding rates, it cannot explain the genealogies of particular firms, nor account for patterns of mutation, speciation, and structuration.

Such questions about the interrelation of organization-level reproduction, population-level speciation, and community-level structuration lie at the heart of an alternative approach to institutional ecology, developed by Suchman (1994b) to explain the role of law firms in Silicon Valley. This approach likens the relationship between organizational ecology and institutional theory to the relationship between biological ecology and genetics: just as genes provide the blueprints for new organisms, cognitive models provide the blueprints for new organizations. And just as mating patterns shape organic populations by structuring the flow of constitutive genetic blueprints, institutional patterns—definitions, typologies, accounts of relevance, theories of causation, and so on—shape organizational populations by structuring the flow of constitutive cognitive models. Cognitive models carry the scripts for organizational competences (see note 7, above), and in structuring the transmission of such models, cognitive institutions function as organizational reproduction mechanisms.

Elaborating on this analysis, Suchman (1994b; forthcoming) distinguished two modes of organizational reproduction—filiation and compilation—differentiated by how the constitutive models (competences) are transmitted from progenitors to progeny. In filiation, new organizations draw competences directly from specific existing organizations that embody those competences themselves. A classic example of such filiation is the traditional spin-off process, in which personnel leave one organization to found another, constituting the new firm around models that they acquired at the old. Figure 13.1, a depiction of the semiconductor industry's Shockley/Fairchild/Intel "family tree," illustrates this process, with each line of descent indicating a direct flow of managerial and/or technical personnel: Bell Labs (1) begat Shockley Semiconductor (2), which begat Fairchild Semiconductor (3) and its numerous "fairchildren"—including such prominent firms as National Semiconductor (4), Intel (5), and Advanced Micro Devices (6).[9]

Contrastingly, in compilation, new organizations draw competences not from specific progenitors but, rather, from summary accounts of the overall competence pool, generated by observing multiple alternative approaches. Although entrepreneurs could theoretically conduct such observations on their own, in practice, compilation generally operates through third-party intermediaries. These intermediaries act as interorganizational pollinators, synthesizing competences from a wide range of sources and then providing new organizations with preprocessed infusions of relevant know-how. Figure 13.2 illustrates this pollination process. An intermediary observes some subset of the organizational population, constructs a summary account of the determinants of success and failure, and formulates corresponding blueprints for action (competences). The intermediary then imparts this constitutive information to new firms, allowing them to build their structures around the compiled model, rather than around direct observations of specific exemplars.

Significantly, this genetic approach to institutional ecology suggests that entrepreneurship can simultaneously both reflect and affect community-level

9. This set of companies comprises roughly half the population of Silicon Valley semiconductor manufacturers (see Rogers and Larsen 1984, 43–45).

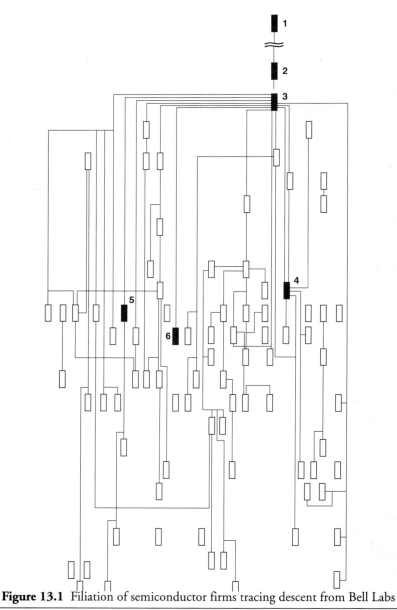

Figure 13.1 Filiation of semiconductor firms tracing descent from Bell Labs

KEY: (1) Bell Labs; (2) Shockley Semiconductor; (3) Fairchild Semiconductor; (4) National Semiconductor; (5) Intel; and (6) Advanced Micro Devices.

SOURCE: Rogers and Larsen (1984, 44), citing Semiconductor Equipment and Materials Institute, Mountain View, California.

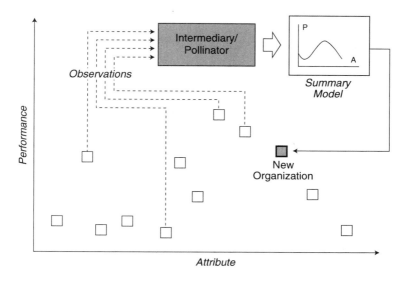

Figure 13.2 Compilation of competences by an intermediary organization

institutions. Whether a particular population reproduces primarily through filiation or compilation depends on a number of institutional factors—whether
competences are guarded as trade secrets, whether spin-offs are discouraged by
traditions of lifetime employment, whether suitable pollinators are present, and
so on. At the same time, the mix of filiational and compilational reproduction
may have a reciprocal affect on the pace, level, and character of institutionalization within the community. By promoting firm-level mixing and recombination of competences, filiation produces loose organizational kinship networks, with firms scattered along a continuous range of variation. In contrast,
by fostering community-level standards and typologies, compilation produces
distinct but internally homogeneous subpopulations, with firms clustered into
discontinuous uniform categories. Thus, community-level patterns of filiation
and compilation—the institutional foundations of organizational genetics—
are among the most fundamental of blending and segregating processes.

In summary, entrepreneurship is embedded within institutional frameworks.
Some of these frameworks are global; others are local. Some structure material
resource flows; others structure cultural information flows. While entrepreneurship often reflects transitory material and cultural disequilibria, under

appropriate conditions, more persistent forms of entrepreneurial activity can emerge as well. Taken as a whole, the institutional ecology perspective suggests that persistent entrepreneurship depends, at least in part, on the support of institutional structures that regulate the flow of resources and models to new firms, so as to produce a steady but controlled release of entrepreneurial energy. Among the various institutional structures that might regulate the flow of resources and models to new firms, law occupies a particularly important place.

LAW AND ENTREPRENEURSHIP

Because law offers a public statement of prevailing social norms, couched in a rhetoric of "explicit, authoritative and coercive" state power (Edelman and Suchman 1997, 480), legal institutions enjoy high salience in the minds of modern managers. Even if the law in action is often ambiguous, contested, and largely symbolic, the legalization of managerial consciousness (cf. Sitkin and Bies 1993) virtually ensures that the legal environment will command organizational attention. Indeed, because people generally believe that legal rules carry significant consequences, whether this is true or not, ambiguity and uneven enforcement may actually heighten law's cognitive salience, as organizations struggle to construct coherent interpretations and shared symbols of compliance (see Edelman 1992). Thus, the salience of law becomes a self-fulfilling prophecy (Merton 1957).

Law can exert a substantial influence on the entrepreneurial character of organizational communities, but this influence is multifaceted, not unitary. The legal environment of entrepreneurship has at least four dimensions, each with distinct implications for the prevalence, persistence, and viability of entrepreneurial activity. Extending a typology originally proposed by Edelman and Suchman (1997; Suchman 1993), we label these dimensions facilitative, regulative, constitutive, and professional law, respectively.

Facilitative Law

At their most passive, legal institutions provide facilities for various interorganizational interactions that might otherwise occur elsewhere. Litigation is the most familiar feature of the facilitative legal environment. Before they even enter a courtroom, however, organizations may "bargain in the shadow of the law," framing promises and demands in light of legal rights (Mnookin and Kornhauser 1979, 950; cf. Macaulay 1963). Beyond the courthouse, administrative law in the form of the Freedom of Information Act facilitates corporate espionage (Casey, Marthinsen, and Moss 1983; Farrell 1984), and regulatory law in the form of rate-setting commissions facilitates oligopolistic collusion (Breyer 1982). By providing the places and procedures for such activities, the facilitative legal environment lends institutional support, and occasionally institutional restraint, to interactions that, in law's absence, might have been pursued by other means.

Start-up companies may be particularly vulnerable to certain aspects of facilitative law, most notably litigation. New firms often find themselves at a competitive disadvantage in their legal encounters. Unlike more established companies, start-ups generally lack the internal legalistic structures that might buffer them from the external legal environment (cf. Dobbin et al. 1993; Edelman and Suchman 1998; Sitkin and Bies 1993). The youngest start-ups may suffer a further handicap because they are not yet repeat players in the legal system, and, as a result, they cannot reap the benefits of routinized long-term litigation strategies (see Galanter 1974). Further, whether they win or lose in court, start-ups are likely to suffer disproportionately from the burden of litigation, since they generally have only limited slack resources from which to fund legal expenses or to cover adverse judgments. To make matters worse, young companies also tend to be thinly staffed, and the distractions of litigation may divert scarce executive attention away from other important tasks.

Recent complaints about the proliferation of shareholder derivative suits in Silicon Valley highlight the importance of the facilitative legal environment for real-world entrepreneurs. In theory, these suits allow shareholders to seek compensation from corporate officers, and to demand reform of corporate practices, when mismanagement undercuts stock prices. Industry leaders argue, however, that unscrupulous plaintiffs' attorneys have abused this opportunity, bringing a flood of groundless "strike suits" on the basis of ordinary stock volatility, with the sole purpose of extorting large fee payments and private settlements (Buffone 1995). Hard data on this phenomenon are largely absent, and previous alarms about supposed litigation crises have proven notoriously unreliable

(Galanter 1983; Hayden 1991); nonetheless, few would deny the cognitive salience of such threats from the facilitative legal environment. Of course, it also bears noting that facilitative law is not entirely inhospitable to entrepreneurial activity. Antitrust lawsuits, for example, have occasionally opened previously monopolized niches to entrepreneurial competition, as when MCI (following the lead of the Justice Department) sued to break AT&T's hold on the long-distance telephone market (Chen 1997).

Regulative Law

Law's second dimension reflects the role of legal institutions as vehicles for societal control over organizational activity. The formal regulation of industry by state agencies provides the archetype of regulative law, but this sphere also includes numerous privately enforced public-policy initiatives, such as rights to sue against workplace discrimination and market fraud. In both guises, the regulative legal environment operates not merely as a neutral arena but also as a structure of incentives, precepts, and enforcement mechanisms designed to channel organizational behavior in particular directions. Admittedly, regulative law may not always accomplish (or even sincerely pursue) its official goals, but the distinguishing features of this dimension of the legal environment nonetheless remain its pervasive rhetoric of intentional sovereign authority and its pervasive concern with organizational compliance and evasion. Organizations ignore regulative law at their peril.

In one way or another, regulative law structures virtually every major flow of resources and information into the emerging firm.[10] Thus, for example, intellectual property law regulates the flow of innovations (Tushman and Murmann, this volume); securities law regulates the flow of capital; and labor, antidiscrimination, and immigration law all regulate the flow of personnel. In the aggregate, these regulations affect not only the fates of individual firms but also the structure of entire communities.

---

10. Admittedly, start-ups often confront a somewhat less pervasive regulative environment than do their larger corporate counterparts, because many laws explicitly exempt businesses below a certain size. This formal exemption is counterbalanced, however, by the fact that start-ups are less likely than established firms to enjoy the informal protection of ongoing ties with enforcement agencies.

The comparison between California's Silicon Valley and Massachusetts' Route 128 Technology Corridor offers an interesting illustration of the potential impact of regulative law on entrepreneurship. Saxenian (1994) argued that Silicon Valley's success has stemmed from the region's flexible small-firm network structure and from the interorganizational flows of personnel and ideas that this structure engenders (see also Perrow 1992). She contrasted this with Route 128, where, she claimed, tightly bounded corporate monoliths have stifled economic growth and undercut indigenous entrepreneurship. While Saxenian seldom referred to law in this analysis, subsequent commentators have suggested that these differences in organizational structure may themselves have reflected differences in the regulative regions' legal environments (e.g., Hyde 1998; see also Al-Hibri 1997; Kahn 1999). Well before the advent of high technology in either locale, the two jurisdictions had adopted quite divergent approaches toward the regulation of noncompetition clauses in employment contracts. Such clauses discourage departing employees from entering related lines of business and, thereby, afford employers a greater degree of control over organizational boundaries. Massachusetts has long enforced such clauses, provided that they are not unreasonable (Hyde 1998); California has deemed them unenforceable as a matter of statute since 1941 (California Business and Professions Code §16600). Thus, the regulative environment of Route 128 favors relatively hermetic firms and long-term employment relations, while the regulative environment of Silicon Valley favors more porous firms and a freer flow of personnel and ideas.

Constitutive Law

Although accounts of regulative law emphasize the imposition of sanctions and the proclamation of norms, the primary significance of the legal environment often lies not in the law's overt ability to deter or inveigh but, rather, in its more subtle ability to define fundamental social categories and to delineate taken-for-granted cognitive models and, thereby, to provide the basic building blocks of human consciousness and activity (e.g., Boyle 1985; Gabel 1980; Gordon 1984; Kennedy 1980). This perspective reveals a third, constitutive dimension of the legal environment, grounded in the role of legal institutions as frameworks for understanding and reproducing socially constructed reality. The archetype of constitutive law is the doctrine of corporate personhood, which defines a particular type of social group as a coherent collective actor with legal identity, interests, and capacities equivalent to natural individuals (Rao, this volume; see also Coleman 1974; 1990; Creighton 1990; Roy 1990; cf. Masten 1991). The constitutive legal environment does more than simply construct the corporation, however; it also underpins understandings of contracts and securities (Suchman 1994b), of intellectual property (Campbell and Lindberg 1990), and even of corporate insolvency (Delaney 1989; Carruthers and Halliday 1994).

More generally, the constitutive legal environment offers a toolkit (Swidler 1986) of basic institutional scripts and labels, which organizations combine and recombine (but rarely question) to construct various practical legal devices (Powell 1993). These devices, and the constitutive legal rights that they comprise, are among the most important of the organizational building blocks that "litter the societal landscape" (Meyer and Rowan 1977, 345). And as Meyer and Rowan (1977) suggested, the existence of such building blocks substantially eases the cognitive challenges of entrepreneurship. Legal devices—proprietary information agreements, technology licenses, equipment leases, employment contracts, stock options, and the like—encode a wide range of crucial entrepreneurial competences, making legal documents, in many ways, the equivalent of organizational DNA.[11]

The impact of such legal blueprints on the constitution of entrepreneurial start-ups becomes particularly evident in the Silicon Valley venture capital financing process, which we discuss in greater detail below. Venture capital financing contracts are relatively high-order legal devices, each composed of narrower documents—such as stock purchase agreements, investors' rights agreements, and articles of incorporation—which are in turn constructed of still more basic legal elements, such as affirmative and negative covenants, liquidation preferences, and stock registration rights (see Daunt 1989; Testa 1991). For Silicon Valley start-ups, these legal devices carry both material and cultural import. The signing of a venture capital financing contract obviously

---

11. Competences are, of course, encoded in other sites and on other media as well. Unlike biological organisms, organizations do not store their entire constitutive blueprint in a single nucleus (Suchman, forthcoming; see also McKelvey 1982).

results in a substantial infusion of financial resources; at the same time, however, it also represents a central legitimating rite of passage, a sort of baptism into the Silicon Valley faith. Somewhere between these purely pecuniary and purely ceremonial poles, the venture capital contract scripts the competences that maintain organizational purpose and coherence in the face of a dramatically complexified organizational coalition. In short, these legal devices (and their underlying bodies of corporate, contract, and securities law) provide the constitutive underpinning for one of the key gestational events in the genesis of a new Silicon Valley start-up.

Professional Law

The fourth way in which law affects entrepreneurship is through the routine organizational activities of the various entities that make up the legal system. Behind the abstract principles and procedures of the law, the legal environments of organizations are composed of concrete social actors who are often organizations themselves. As the label "professional legal environment" implies, the corporate law firm provides the archetype here. Law firms act both as representatives of, and representatives to, the larger legal system, but at the same time, they also act as ordinary organizations, embedded within the wider organizational community.[12] Their role in the legal system provides these firms with a unique raison d'être, but even as they pursue this professional charter, much of their ecological and institutional relevance stems from the more generic needs and activities that they have in common with the lay organizations around them (see Edelman and Suchman 1997, 498–502).

To understand how the professional legal environment affects the institutional ecology of entrepreneurship, one must recognize that within many organizational communities, and particularly within young communities such as Silicon Valley, law firms occupy a privileged structural position. Their network ties and their institutional identities leave them well situated to mediate

---

12. It is worth noting that, although the following pages focus exclusively on lawyers and law firms, the professional legal environment includes other professions and other organizations as well. In their capacity as formal organizations, legislatures, regulatory agencies, police departments, compliance offices, etc., all contribute to the professional dimension of law.

flows of both material resources and cognitive models among the nonlegal organizations with whom they interact. Suchman (1994a, 17–26) referred to these activities as the lawyer's "dealmaking" and "counseling" roles, respectively.

As dealmakers, law firms use their ties within the local business community to engage in sorting and steering, for example, matching start-ups with investors. To quote one Silicon Valley attorney,[13]

> Clients choose us because we know a lot of people in the venture capital community. [Our top partners] can get [leading venture capitalists] on the phone and say, "Hey, I've got this great business plan, take a look at it." Clients are looking for that "in," and venture capitalists need some way to sort out the wheat from the chaff.

Such interventions channel the flow of resources within the organizational community, with potentially significant ecological consequences. Law firm dealmaking opens community resource pools to entrepreneurial newcomers and yet, by being selective, protects those pools from unwarranted depletion. Investors will be most willing to accept the uncertainties of funding entrepreneurship when investment opportunities arrive prescreened, with a community insider's legitimating imprimatur.

As counselors, law firms use their observations of client companies to engage in compilation and pollination, advising start-ups on the promises and pitfalls of particular organizing models. As a prominent local attorney put it,

> Good lawyers are a wonderful resource for business advice, because the problems that growing companies encounter are similar, and even if a problem is new

---

13. The following pages draw on quotations from a series of roughly 25 semistructured interviews conducted during the summer of 1991 with various participants in the Silicon Valley organizational community. Interviews were divided approximately equally among lawyers, venture capitalists, and entrepreneurs, as well as including several individuals who had played multiple roles over the course of their careers. The analysis was further enriched by informal conversations with journalists, academics, and other informed community-watchers. The sampling frame for these interviews was a systematic, multiple-snowball sample of individuals who were active in Silicon Valley during the formative period from 1970 to 1990. To capture as full a range of accounts as possible, the sample was informally stratified along such dimensions as industry, seniority, tenure in the community, geographic location, and the like. In two months of interviewing, the response rate (ratio of interviews to initial contacts) was over 85%.

to an entrepreneur who's never been president of a company before, the outside counsel has seen various ways people have dealt with it.

In dispensing such business advice, lawyers channel the flow of constitutive information within the organizational community, observing a wide range of organizational forms, constructing summary accounts of efficacy and appropriateness, and then disseminating coherent compiled models. By delineating which lessons and which competences are relevant for whom, law firm counseling institutionalizes organizational reproduction and eases the cognitive challenges of entrepreneurship. At the same time, by allowing creative recombination and sensemaking, counseling also facilitates adaptation to changing circumstances.

Significantly, neither dealmaking nor counseling necessarily has much to do with formal law. As dealmakers, law firms primarily trade on their social networks, to support nonlegal reputational brokerage (cf. Gilson 1984; see also Bernstein 1992); as counselors, law firms primarily trade on their vicarious experiences, to support nonlegal business consulting. Because they are not acting in a purely legal capacity, law firms are not alone in their ability to perform these activities, and their professional monopoly does not guarantee them a niche free from competitors. In Silicon Valley, for instance, lawyers share the dealmaking and counseling roles with substantial populations of venture capitalists and "corporate angels," as well as with various consultants, incubators, networking clubs, and the like (cf. Nohria 1992).

Nonetheless, as suggested above, law firms (or at least Silicon Valley law firms) do occupy a privileged structural position within the surrounding organizational community, affording them several advantages in the dealmaking and counseling process. Specifically, law firms benefit from the threefold advantages of exposure, access, and trust. First, law firms benefit from broad exposure to a wide range of organizational activity. They routinely encounter large numbers clients facing similar challenges and seeking similar opportunities, and this helps to ensure that, as dealmakers, they will be a reliable source of referrals, and, as counselors, they will be a reliable source of advice. Second, law firms enjoy the benefits of access and timing (cf. Burt 1992). They typically encounter new entrepreneurs quite early in the start-up process, often, during the pre-founding period when the entrepreneur is still extricating him-

or herself from a previous employer. This early involvement enables law firms, as dealmakers, to be first in line to sign the freshest talent, and it enables law firms, as counselors, to impart advice while companies are still relatively malleable and receptive, before structures have solidified and inertia has set in (cf. Freeman 1982; Hannan and Freeman 1984).

Finally, law firms benefit from a substantial degree of trust, on the part of both community insiders and start-up clients. As dealmakers, law firms are reputationally bonded (cf. Gilson 1984; Gilson and Kraakman 1984) by their ongoing participation in the organizational community. While a one-shot entrepreneur may have little track record and little to lose by deception, a repeat-player law firm must operate under the shadows of both the past and the future (Axelrod 1984), and if such a firm chooses to extend its good name to a client, others in the community are likely to take that endorsement seriously (cf. Uzzi 1996). As one Silicon Valley attorney put it,

> Our firm is encouraging attorneys to take into account whether the reputation of the client will create problems with other clients and whether the proposal of the client is so outlandish as to be unreasonable. We want to make sure that we are not making an introduction that will ultimately backfire on us.

At the same time, as counselors, law firms also benefit from a different sort of trust, grounded not in firm-level reputation but in larger institutional accounts of the lawyer as personal champion. This imagery tends to reduce the perception of opportunism between lawyer and client and to increase clients' receptivity to lawyers' advice. To put it epigrammatically, your lawyer is yours in a way that your venture capitalist, your Environmental Protection Agency inspector, and your auditor will never be yours.

To the extent that other organizational populations can develop similar levels of exposure, access, and trust, they will prove to be worthy contenders for the law firm's dealmaking and counseling niches. In practice, however, this combination is rare, especially in very young organizational communities. In the early stages of the structuration process, law firms draw extraordinary strength from their position within an institutional order that creates (a) the basis for free-standing legal representatives with diverse clienteles, (b) the need for early and frequent legal advice in the entrepreneurial process, and (c) the foundation for lawyer-client trust under an ethic of zealous advocacy. Thus, the law firm's capacities as a dealmaker and a counselor ultimately rest on its charter within the larger legal system. It is precisely this propensity of legal institutions to empower organizational emissaries—and to shape the capacities of those emissaries even in nonlegal encounters—that represents the defining characteristic of the professional legal environment.

By empowering law firms to fill the otherwise problematic roles of deal-maker and counselor, the professional legal environment affects not only individual start-ups but also the surrounding organizational community. At the most general level, such law-firm activities tend to speed the structuration process, reducing the perceived level of uncertainty, both about viable strategies ("What should you do?") and about plausible outcomes ("What will happen next?"). This uncertainty reduction, and the attendant stabilization of interorganizational relations, helps to fix free resources within the community and to prevent encroachment by outside claimants. In addition, of course, the belief systems and exchange networks that law firms foster during the early stages of structuration often carry long-term consequences for the character of the emerging field (Suchman and Cahill 1996).

As structuration proceeds, law firms' activities may also serve to sustain persistent entrepreneurship while, at the same time, taming the start-up process by embedding it within community norms. This has clearly been the case in Silicon Valley. As dealmakers, Silicon Valley lawyers mediate a steady but selective flow of resources within the community, helping to secure adequate funding for new ventures but also encouraging behavior that comports with the prevailing order. At the same time, as counselors, Silicon Valley lawyers also mediate a flexible but selective flow of models within the community, helping to provide cognitive structure to new ventures but also facilitating recombination and sensemaking in the face of novel situations. In conjunction, these efforts allow for a steady release of entrepreneurial energy, maintaining the community's vitality and adaptability, while not overwhelming its supporting institutional structures.[14]

---

14. As suggested above, these roles are largely comparable with the roles played by venture capitalists, although these two professional populations draw their legitimacy from distinct institutional realms.

Finally, in addition to acting as dealmakers and counselors, law firms also occasionally act as proselytizers, exporting community models to the larger institutional environment and defending the community against alternative models that might be imposed upon it from outside (Suchman and Cahill 1996). Thus, for example, in speaking of his firm's efforts to open a branch office in Southern California, one prominent Silicon Valley attorney observed,

> In Southern California I've encountered many entrepreneurs who could hardly believe that venture capitalists weren't really "vulture capitalists." I felt like our office in Newport Beach had a sort of missionary mode to at least encourage the entrepreneurs to consider that venture capital could be an alternative, because some of the other options are really awful. Some of the things that they think they want to do are really bad news stuff.

As this comment illustrates, law firms often go well beyond agnostically offering clients a range of morally neutral alternatives and engage, instead, in a sort of imperialistic paradigm-pushing. When particular organizing models become emblematic and constitutive of particular organizational communities, the propagation of those models takes on overtones of patriotic duty and manifest destiny. As Swaminathan and Wade (in this volume) note, entrepreneurship often displays many of the characteristics of a social movement. By creating opportunities and justifications for proselytizing on behalf of community customs, the professional legal environment empowers law firms to act as social-movement leaders.

In short, the professional legal environment places law firms, as organizational actors, in a particularly favorable position from which to mediate flows of resources and information within new organizational communities. By giving law firms the tripartite advantages of exposure, access, and trust, the legal system empowers these organizations to act as both dealmakers and counselors, filling a linchpin niche in the community's emerging institutional ecology (Van de Ven and Garud 1989). To the extent that this niche might otherwise go unoccupied, the professional legal environment can exert a potentially significant influence on community development—speeding structuration, facilitating persistent entrepreneurship, and mobilizing the defense of core indige-nous practices against incompatible external alternatives.

SILICON VALLEY VENTURE CAPITAL FINANCING CONTRACTS

Although distinct in theory, the facilitative, regulatory, constitutive, and professional dimensions of the legal environment nonetheless intersect and interact with one another in practice. The emergence of standardized ven-ture capital financing in Silicon Valley nicely demonstrates one such inter-action, in this case, between constitutive and professional law. As suggested above, venture capital financing contracts represent central, constitutive legal devices in the Silicon Valley community. At the same time, the circu-lation of venture capital dollars is perhaps the most crucial resource flow that Silicon Valley law firms mediate in their professional capacity as dealmakers, and the diffusion of models for managing venture capital relationships is per-haps the most crucial competençe flow that Silicon Valley law firms medi-ate in their professional capacity as counselors. Thus, this intersection between constitutive and professional law allows these firms to play an important role in establishing the character of entrepreneurship within the community as a whole. In the words of a senior Silicon Valley attorney and part-time venture capitalist, "venture capital [law] is a specialty which is practiced very well in Silicon Valley, yet it is not even understood in a lot of other places in the country, let alone the rest of the world." The emergence of these distinctive, community-defining activities reveals the structuration process at work.

The standardization of venture capital transactions was not necessarily the only or even the most important way in which legal institutions shaped the environment of entrepreneurship in Silicon Valley. The impact of law has been rich and multidimensional, and the facilitative, regulative, constitutive, and professional aspects of law have all played significant roles. Nonetheless, the standardization of start-up financing clearly contributed considerably to the community's development. A closer examination of this standardization process can usefully illustrate the real-world connections between legal forces and persistent entrepreneurship, and can demonstrate the amenability of such connections to empirical study.

Contractual Standardization

To capture the structuration of Silicon Valley's investment practices, we conducted a quantitative content-analysis of the underlying venture capital financing contracts themselves. For this purpose, we used an original data set (Suchman 1994b), covering 100% of the first-round, high-technology venture capital financing contracts entered into by two of Silicon Valley's leading venture capital funds between 1975 and 1990. This data set contains a total of 108 contracts, spanning much of the community's formative period. Each of these agreements was coded on over 400 elements of contractual structure. Measured items included (a) formal issues, such as the length of the agreement and the number of separate contractual instruments involved; (b) substantive issues, such as stock redemption provisions, antidilution protections, and dividend structures; and (c) exogenous information, such as the age, industry, and valuation of the company, the structure of the investor syndicate, and the identity of the lead investor and of the drafting law firm.[15]

From this data set, one can compute a summary measure of contractual standardization/idiosyncrasy, indicating the degree to which a given contract contains "nonstandard," "counter-normative," or "deviant" terms—unusual provisions absent both from prescriptive models and from other observed financing agreements (Suchman 1995b, 52). In the current data set, these idiosyncrasy scores are roughly normally distributed, over a range from −3.621 to 3.703, with a mean of 0.02 and a standard deviation of 1.534. In theory, if venture capital financings are becoming more routinized and institutionalized over time, one would expect to see idiosyncrasy scores declining over the course of the observation period. As Figure 13.3 illustrates, this is indeed the case. The average level of contractual idiosyncrasy drops sharply

---

15. The empirical evidence presented below draws heavily on the principal author's prior research. Readers who are interested in methodological and/or computational details beyond those reported here should refer to Suchman (1994b).

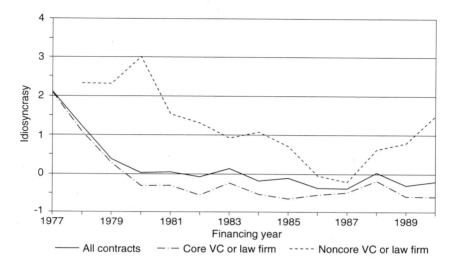

Figure 13.3 Overall idiosyncrasy of venture capital financing contracts

from 1977 to 1980, and it continues to decline slightly from 1980 until about 1987.

Significantly, in addition to showing this secular trend of standardization, the data also suggest that the eventually dominant financing norms may have originated in Silicon Valley, and then gradually diffused outward to other regions (Suchman 1995b). The upper and lower lines in Figure 13.3 indicate average idiosyncrasy levels for two subsets of the contract sample: (a) those agreements involving either a lead investor or a drafting law firm from Silicon Valley, and (b) those involving neither a lead investor nor a drafting law firm from Silicon Valley. The results closely follow the classic pattern associated with sociotechnical diffusion processes (Rogers 1995). At all points, the Silicon Valley contracts are more standardized than the non–Silicon Valley agreements, and over time, the Silicon Valley agreements become standardized relatively rapidly, while the non–Silicon Valley agreements retain substantial levels of idiosyncrasy even into the late 1980s.

In summary, this first set of analyses suggests that venture capital financings became increasingly routinized from 1975 to 1990 and that this routinization originated within Silicon Valley and then gradually diffused outward. Not only do these findings provide concrete empirical evidence of contractual standardization, they also demonstrate the importance of a vanguard local community in this developmental process.

Law Firm Effects

In addition to revealing strong time trends and a clear differentiation between Silicon Valley and other regions, the venture capital financing contract data also shed light on the role of local law firms in creating this Silicon Valley effect. Suchman (1995b) reported that, even after controlling for historical time, multivariate regression models indicate a significant correlation between the standardization of venture capital financing contracts and the drafting law firm's proximity to the core of Silicon Valley. To further explore this association, one can compute a simple path model, based on the assumption that most new companies first choose a geographic location, then select a law firm, then locate a venture capital backer, and, finally, enter into a financing agreement. Figure 13.4 presents such a model.

This path model supports the general thrust of the institutional ecology perspective, while at the same time portraying the law firm's role as somewhat more modest than the qualitative data might imply. In Figure 13.4, the strongest direct determinant of contractual standardization (net of time) is the proximity of the lead venture capital fund to the core of Silicon Valley. Thus, one might argue, investors and not lawyers are the key interorganizational pollinators in the financing domain. Despite this, however, the path model concurs with the qualitative evidence in suggesting that the structuration of venture capital financing is a multistage, fundamentally systemic process. Figure 13.4 illustrates that, rather than simply reflecting isolated economic choices, Silicon Valley financings are in fact deeply embedded in community-level networks of entrepreneurs, lawyers, and venture capitalists, with each population contributing significantly to the final outcome. Local law firms influence contractual idiosyncrasy only indirectly, by steering clients toward more conventional local investors; nonetheless, the legal community provides a crucial link in the causal chain. The bulk of the Silicon Valley entrepreneur's propensity to enter into standardized financings appears to stem from his or her greater likelihood of selecting a local law firm, not from personal encultura-

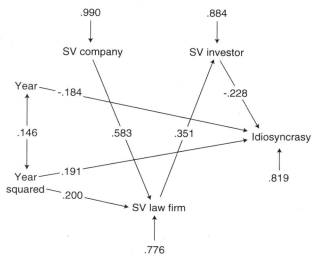

NOTE: Path coefficients are standardized betas. For further
computational details, see Suchman 1994b, 144–74.

Figure 13.4 Effects of Silicon Valley setting on contractual idiosyncrasy

tion or from personal access to local investors. Thus, law firms act as gatekeepers and matchmakers, channeling their clients into the community's inner
circles and, in the process, helping to institutionalize the community's distinctive financing practices.

Contractual Typification

Taken alone, the observation that contracts have become increasingly standardized says little about the nature of the developing regime. A decline in
idiosyncrasy is equally compatible with the ascendance of a single dominant
design or the emergence of a fixed menu of multiple acceptable alternatives.
A full discussion of Silicon Valley's emergent contractual archetypes lies beyond
the scope of this chapter (see Suchman 1994b), but even a more limited
examination of the venture capital financing contract data set offers clear evidence of such typification-without-homogenization. One example is the contractual provision known as a "mandatory stock conversion trigger." In a typ-

ical venture capital financing, the investor syndicate purchases a block of pre-ferred stock, which carries various protective rights and privileges over and against the founders' common stock. While these preferences provide crucial reassurance to early stage investors, they also imperil the company's future access to public capital markets, since arm's-length investors will tend to shy away from an offering of common stock if shares with preferential rights remain outstanding. Consequently, many financing contacts contain "manda-tory conversion" provisions that automatically convert investors' preferred shares into common shares when the start-up concludes an initial public offer-ing (IPO) of a specified magnitude. Financing contracts frequently indicate this conversion trigger in terms of the total proceeds of the anticipated pub-lic offering, and the dollar value thus specified both indicates the parties' expectations for corporate growth and serves as a transition point in interor-ganizational power relations. In this sense, the conversion trigger clearly encodes a particular organizational competence. Nonetheless, at the time of a first-round financing, the future market value of the start-up will necessarily be somewhat speculative, and the choice of a specific IPO target, largely sym-bolic (cf. Daunt 1989, 10).

Figure 13.5 depicts the distribution of mandatory conversion triggers in the financing contract data set, plotted against the financing date. In the early years, a substantial minority of venture capital financing contracts omitted mandatory conversion provisions entirely, and those that do include these clauses adopt a wide range of trigger values, between $2 million and $10 mil-lion. By the mid-1980s, however, the number of contracts lacking mandatory conversion language has dropped effectively to zero, and trigger values have coalesced around three standard sizes. Indeed, after 1985, only two agreements in the entire data set specify any trigger values other than $5 million, $7.5 mil-lion, or $10 million. Clearly, this particular contractual provision shows strong evidence of typification: as venture capital financing becomes more institu-tionalized, ever larger numbers of agreements include IPO thresholds, yet variation narrows to a ritualized choice of small ($5 million), medium ($7.5 million), or large ($10 million).

The exact role of law firms in the construction of such typologies cannot easily be determined from an examination of this single clause alone. Nonethe-less, the broader body of quantitative and qualitative evidence suggests that law

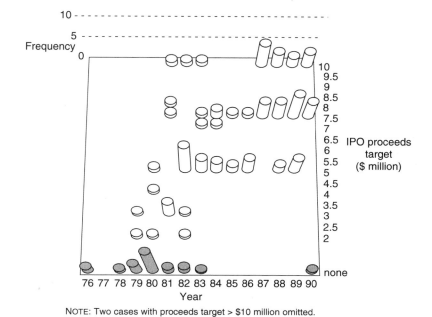

Figure 13.5 Mandatory conversion triggers by financing date

firms have, indeed, accelerated the typification of Silicon Valley financings, both by promoting law-firm-specific archetypes and by organizing advice around categorical classification schemes. Thus, for example, Suchman (1994b, 261–72) identified five distinct contractual archetypes in the venture financing data set, and he reported consistent bivariate and multivariate associations between particular law firms and particular archetypes.[16] A prominent Silicon Valley attorney offered a somewhat more evocative, emic account of the legal community's role in the typification process:

> I think there are law firms out there that have three cookie cutters, and they just ask: "Is it A, B, or C?" They're going to force these things into one of those cookie cutters and just ignore the fact that you may not fit the profiles. They'll just pretend you do, and they'll just cram you into the structure.

---

16. Venture capital funds, too, display fund-specific preferences for some archetypes over others.

While this account makes law firm interventions sound rather procrustean and even a bit sinister, the institutionalization of the venture capital financing process may carry some distinct advantages as well. The emergence of taken-for-granted start-up practices eases both the economic and the cognitive burdens of entrepreneurship, allowing new enterprises not only to obtain resources from well-defined sources but also to deploy those resources under well-defined models. The comments of a local venture capitalist capture this more positive side of routinization:

> In Silicon Valley, you sort of learn by example. If it's not broken, you don't have to fix it, and you don't have to invent. There's a way to do this—so just do it. It's not like this is the first time a new company has been created. So just execute. Go like hell.

CONCLUSION

We have argued here that persistent entrepreneurship depends as much on convention as on innovation. Standards and routines are not merely cookie-cutter constraints, they also act as an armature or brace that allows new companies to stand without squandering valuable muscle energy. Facing both economic and cognitive challenges, entrepreneurs require either exaggerated opportunities, grounded in disequilibrium, or minimized obstacles, grounded in routinization. Almost by definition, however, disequilibrium tends to be a transitory phenomenon. As a result, persistently entrepreneurial environments generally rest not merely on a steady stream of economic opportunities but also on a coherent social infrastructure that actively facilitates sustained organizational reproduction.

In this sense, entrepreneurship is both an ecological and an institutional phenomenon. Transitory entrepreneurial activity can stem either from a temporary fluctuation in niche structure or a temporary fluctuation in discourse structure. If entrepreneurship is to continue indefinitely, however, organizational reproduction itself must become institutionalized. Presumably, such institutionalized reproduction patterns can involve both filiational and compilational elements. Either way, though, community-level context is crucial. In the long run, persistent entrepreneurial activity will be more common where the local institutional ecology promotes open but structured resource flows and standardized but flexible organizing models. In the absence of these conditions, the community structure is likely either to degenerate into chaos or to ossify into rigidity.

In the fragile institutional ecology of entrepreneurship, law plays several significant roles. In its facilitative capacity, the legal environment establishes forums and procedures for organizational interactions, enabling such activities as patent searches, antitrust claims, and shareholder-derivative suits. In its regulative capacity, the legal environment establishes societal control over organizational activity, imposing such strictures as securities regulations, labor laws, and environmental protection provisions. In its constitutive capacity, the legal environment establishes the basic building blocks of organizational structure, reifying such legal devices as articles of incorporation, stock purchase agreements, and investors rights agreements.

Importantly, however, legal institutions comprise more than merely a set of disembodied, doctrinal principles; rather, law is interpreted, carried, and implemented by concrete organizational actors. In this sense, alongside its facilitative, regulatory, and constitutive facets, law also serves as a professional environment, empowering particular populations of agents whose legal charter colors (but hardly precludes) their more generic organizational activities. Many of these agents, of course, operate within local organizational communities, where they are themselves enmeshed in community-level ecological and institutional dynamics. Although the degree of embeddedness may vary from site to site, these local processes inevitably shape both the fates of legal organizations and the effects of global laws. Thus, rather than representing a unilateral external force, the legal environment of entrepreneurship is, in many regards, fundamentally endogenous to the process of community structuration.

In Silicon Valley, this endogeneity manifests itself in the distinctive niche that local law firms occupy as dealmakers, counselors, and proselytizers. Over time, the region's lawyers have successfully parlayed their initial assets of exposure, access, and trust into an important and lucrative linking-pin role in the institutional ecology of organizational reproduction and community structuration. At the same time, the law that these firms practice has subtly come to reflect Silicon Valley's unique configuration of industrial, financial, and legal forces. The future of this particular organizational environment remains to be seen, of course. In their activities to date, however, Silicon Valley law firms provide clear evidence that legal institutions, legal agents, and legal devices can indeed play an integral role in constructing and institutionalizing a local climate of persistent entrepreneurship.

14

Emergent Themes and the Next Wave of Entrepreneurship Research

CLAUDIA BIRD SCHOONHOVEN

AND ELAINE ROMANELLI

We noted in Chapter 1 that the Balboa Bay Conference was a convocation, a gathering of scholars and active researchers to discuss the vital dynamic entrepreneurship plays in the creation and evolution of industries. Our goals for this conference bordered on the immodest, perhaps. Our intention was, and it remains, to influence the next wave of entrepreneurship research. This book is based on the premise that now is the time to focus theoretical and empirical attention on both the local and the global origins and impact of *The Entrepreneurship Dynamic*. In the past, entrepreneurship research has focused on the attributes of individual entrepreneurs and their propensity to found new companies. In contrast, we argue that the important questions of today concern the mass effects of entrepreneurial activity on the creation of new firms and industries, the pioneering of emerging markets, the evolution of existing industries, the development of regional economies, and even their impact on the competitiveness of nations. To understand these mass effects, a much broader understanding of contexts that produce the entrepreneurship dynamic is essential.

In the next few pages, we hope to put to rest two pervasive but, in our view, inappropriate beliefs about entrepreneurship. Then, we will review the contributions this book makes by highlighting the emergent themes from the Balboa Bay Conference. Last, we will consider questions to be asked in the next wave of entrepreneurship research. Because the theoretical and empirical papers in any book cannot be expected to weave a taut tapestry of "answers" to questions posed therein, we will identify unanswered questions, highlight needed theory development, and suggest a stream of research for the entrepreneurship dynamic into the next decade. As such, we offer this book as an invocation to future research.

PUTTING MYTHS TO REST

As we discussed in Chapter 3, theory about the origins of entrepreneurial activity in society has centered on a debate about whether the supply of individuals or the demand for entrepreneurial activity fundamentally accounts for rates of organizational founding (Hunt and Aldrich 1998; Peterson 1980; Thornton 1999). As the chapters in this book make clear, neither view is wholly correct or incorrect. While individuals play important roles in the creation of new organizations and new market spaces (see Burton; Abrahamson and Fairchild; and Rindova and Fombrun, all in this volume), the simple supply of entrepreneurial personalities in a society does not account for changes in the rates of organizational founding. At the same time, while opportunity for entrepreneurial activity, whether born of developments in economic, technological, or regulatory conditions, may be important to the rise or decline of organizational founding rates (see Murmann and Tushman, this volume), opportunity alone does not drive the phenomenon. Entrepreneurial activity arises, rather, from the collective activity of entrepreneurs and others, such as venture capitalists, lawyers, and industry professionals, who together actively create and sustain legitimate market space for new products, services, and technologies.

This idea of entrepreneurship as the purposive and collective market space–creating activities of entrepreneurs and others is the central contribution of our book, and, if nothing more, it should lay to rest the persistent and, in our view, nonproductive debate between supply and demand theories. While both perspectives make certain contributions to our understanding of some aspects of entrepreneurial activity, in formulating their arguments as an either-or proposition, they inappropriately and too narrowly concentrate attention on the characteristics of individuals or the conditions of environments. Thus, they miss the central and critical dynamic of entrepreneurship as a transforming agent in industry and society, one that is born of existing conditions and one that, at the same time, redeploys resources toward new organizational and industry arrangements.

At the heart of supply-side theories of entrepreneurial activity is what we call the Myth of the Lonely Only Entrepreneur. Although the origins of this argument are obscure, decades of anecdote, especially in American biography, celebrate the larger-than-life and seemingly unique individuals who single-handedly, it often appears, create the organizations that transform both industries and the ways of day-to-day life in a society. The theoretical idea of the entrepreneur as a distinct and uncommon character in society emerges more or less full-blown in Schumpeter's (1934) discussion of the need for "deviant" individuals, the relatively rare people who can withstand social pressures for conformity and so take advantage of economic and technological opportunities. The idea of the entrepreneurial personality was grounded more formally as a psychological trait by McClelland (1961), who argued in *The Achieving Society* that entrepreneurial activity in society depends on the number of individuals who possess what he called a high "need for achievement." Although he was mainly seeking to explain the microfoundations of the "Protestant work ethic" (Weber 1958 [1904–5]), and though he located the phenomenon in culture, as depicted in the stories that mothers tell their children, McClelland's work set the stage for countless investigations of psychological traits that might identify and distinguish the entrepreneurial personality (see Brockhaus 1982, for a review). The idea persists today, both in popular culture—check any bookstore for a long shelf of entrepreneurs' biographies—and in theory. It is implicit in Venkataraman's argument that "people are different and these differences matter" and that "by emphasizing and illuminating individual differences entrepreneurship can emerge as a legitimate field with its own distinctive domain within the broader field of business research and education" (1997, 123).

Despite the persistence and prevalence of this belief in the rare and special entrepreneur, a growing body of research emphasizes the role of teams of individuals who work collectively, whether formally or informally, to found new organizations and to create legitimate new market spaces. At the organization level, several theorists (e.g., Boeker 1989; Eisenhardt and Schoonhoven 1990;

Reynolds 1994) have explored the shared industry experiences of the typically several individuals who work collectively to start a new venture. For example, in their extensive study of foundings in the semiconductor industry, Schoonhoven, Eisenhardt, and Lyman (1990) showed that most founders of new organizations have previously worked for several firms in their industry before founding a new organization. Founding teams tend to be formed from among existing networks of colleagues, and key employees are typically recruited from prior places of employment. New organizations take shape not from the singular knowledge or personal proclivities of an individual entrepreneur but, rather, from the collective knowledge and experience of a founding team and its advisors and investors. The importance of teams is further underscored by recent studies of venture financing (e.g., Schoonhoven and Eisenhardt 1992), which emphasize the important role of venture capitalists, not only as sources of funds for the new organizations but also as critical players in the strategies and governance structures of the new organizations. In other words, it takes a collective.

At the organizational level, entrepreneurial teams, including the founders and their investors and advisors, overcome liabilities of newness (Stinchcombe 1965) both as they draw upon a broader body of knowledge and experience than any single individual can bestow and as they extend the network of other individuals and organizations that can support the development of the new organization. Although more research is needed to understand the role of entrepreneurial networks in the success or survival of new organizations (Aldrich and Zimmer 1986), it should be taken for granted in today's theory that the singular resources of isolated individuals, no matter how impressive, are rarely sufficient to meet the challenges of organization creation. It takes a collective.

Teams of entrepreneurs are even more critical to the successful formation of new industries or organizational populations. While most new organizations are created to replicate the forms and strategies of existing organizations in established populations (Aldrich 1999; see also Burton, and Romanelli and Schoonhoven, both in this volume), when organizations are founded to introduce fundamentally new products or services, including new technologies, liabilities of newness are substantially greater. New organizational forms confront direct competitive challenges from established organizations and industries that depend on old forms and technologies for their ongoing income and survival (Tushman and Anderson 1986). Moreover, they face the amorphous challenge of communicating to the general marketplace even the possibility of new and better ways of doing things.

As all of the chapters in Part Two of this volume elucidate, only collective action by entrepreneurs and investors from many organizations can produce the cognitive and sociopolitical legitimacy (Aldrich and Fiol 1994) that is needed for creation of a viable new market space. Whether through informal agreements to represent their new products in the language of old products and services (see Aldrich and Baker, this volume), through certification contests that publicize the general benefits of a new product or service (see Rao) or through the more formal creation of standards-bodies and professional associations (see Saxenian; Rindova and Fombrun; and Swaminathan and Wade), new market spaces develop principally from the concerted, and typically conscious, cooperation and interaction of large numbers of entrepreneurs working together to legitimate the new organizational form. These ideas, while they echo the legitimation processes that Hannan and Freeman (1989) ascribed to increases in population density, go further in that they emphasize the need for space-creating collective activity. Increases in density do not merely generate legitimacy; legitimacy is a product of collective activity.

As we look at this book as a whole, then, perhaps the clearest argument that runs through almost every chapter is that entrepreneurship is a collective activity. Whether we are speaking about the formation of a single organization or the formation and development of a new population, collective action is required. As a consequence, at least one previous answer to the question, "Where do new firms come from?" can be eliminated. Neither new organizations nor the new populations they spawn are the creation of single individuals. The Myth of the Lonely Only Entrepreneur can be and should be laid to rest.

The second belief that should be put to rest develops from demand-side theories of entrepreneurial activity, which focus on opportunities for the creation of new goods and services. Though no author has formally explicated any specific arguments of a demand-side theory of entrepreneurship, which contrasts McClelland's quite specific proposal of entrepreneurial supply, sociologists (e.g., Hunt and Aldrich 1998; Peterson 1980; Thornton 1999) have argued generally that entrepreneurial activity arises whenever an opportunity for such activity exists, quite independent of any supply of entrepreneurs. Many studies from economics, sociology, and organization theory have examined rates of organizational founding as a function of economic, technological, cultural, and political conditions. Although this literature is itself in need of systematic review to discover when and how these various contextual influences may combine or dominate one another, its central implicit thesis is that entrepreneurial activity will arise whenever conditions are "right." Thus, Venkataraman (1997, 120) pointed to the question of "why, when and how opportunities for the creation of goods and services in the future arise in an economy" as one of the central concerns for the field of entrepreneurship. While the studies in this volume do not suggest that context or the existence of opportunity is unimportant, they indicate that favorable conditions alone are insufficient to foster the formation of new organizations and especially new organizational populations.

At the level of the individual organization, recent studies of innovation in established organizations have shown that opportunity recognition is neither mysterious nor problematic for the majority of potential entrepreneurs, which, according to demand-side theory, includes virtually everyone, depending on the nature of the opportunity. Within existing organizations and organizational communities, there is no dearth of ideas for innovative new products or technologies, even ideas that launch new industries. Idea creation and opportunity recognition are ongoing and continuous processes, as the following examples from three information technology firms indicate (Jelinek and Schoonhoven 1993, 165, 253, and 311):

> All of the time, we have more ideas than we can use. We select innovative ideas . . . through an on-going discussion.
> —*Peter Rosenbladt, Hewlett-Packard*

> We have too many ideas. It is hard to decide which ones to develop.
> —*Gordon Moore, Intel*

> We get product ideas all of the time. If you look at the ratio of product ideas to the stuff that gets built around here, it's a very big number.
> —*Jim Williams, National Semiconductor*

These comments suggest that the generation and recognition of economic "opportunities" is neither difficult nor rare, at least in many organizations. Rather, the challenge is for the innovators to obtain buy-in from area experts and from those who influence resource allocation for new product development. "Buy-in" obtains from a social influence process through which individuals combine sufficient technical and economic information to convince others to support an idea. Here, again, the ideas of knowledge networks and the active creation of an entrepreneurial team arise. Moreover, the problem of persuading others of the market viability of an innovation is evident. At firms like Intel, individuals who recognize and seek to pursue an innovative opportunity must pass a tough review before the Technical Review Group. Only after an idea has passed the stiff technical review does Intel investigate potential returns on investment or costs associated with development. In keeping with our arguments above, we should point out that this is precisely the kind of training that many entrepreneurs receive from their former places of employment, experience that is readily transferred into a new venture. Entrepreneurial teaming, it seems, is increasingly an integral part of existing organizations' cultures.

Recognizing and demonstrating the technical viability of an opportunity is only the first step. Potential entrepreneurs must still influence investors to support an idea for a new venture, whether the resources derive from family, friends, wealthy individuals, or institutional venture capitalists. And they must persuade the larger and ultimate community of decision makers, that is, the market, that the new product or service is worth the costs of replacing the old product or service that performed the same or similar function. Hence, the realization of entrepreneurial "opportunities" in society depends both on the social networks that teams of entrepreneurs can mobilize and on their activities to publicize and legitimate a new product form. Entrepreneurship, whether at the firm or population level, is a process of mobilizing resources and of actively creating a new market space. The presence of opportunity alone is insufficient.

Overall, then, the belief that the origins of entrepreneurial activity lie at the "nexus of opportunity and individual differences" (Venkataraman 1997, 123) needs to be cast aside in favor of a broader conception of collective activity as the principal agent in the process of organization and population creation. Neither new firms nor new populations arise solely as a function of entrepreneurially distinctive individuals, whatever their numbers; nor do they simply emerge whenever opportunity demands. Nor, we believe, is it the simple coexistence of entrepreneurial opportunity and entrepreneurial individuals that produces this essential phenomenon. As Gartner (1988) pointed out, the key question is not "Who is an entrepreneur?" nor, we would add, "When will entrepreneurship occur?" but, rather, "What is entrepreneurship?" As the chapters of this book make clear, it is the market-creating activities of entrepreneurial teams and collectivities that merit the attention of researchers.

EMERGENT THEMES FROM THE BALBOA BAY CONFERENCE

As we review the empirical and theoretical contributions of this book, several themes emerge on the entrepreneurship dynamic in the creation and evolution of industries. We have already noted that entrepreneurship depends on *collective action*. Closely related to the collective action notion is the idea of *community*. Collective entrepreneurial action does not arise in a vacuum, nor does it simply fill a vacant space in the existing fabric of organizational populations. Community, we believe, is the context that both produces and is transformed by entrepreneurial activity.

The concept of *organizational community* has recently emerged, primarily in ecological theory, to help explain the rise of new organizational populations. As discussed by Carroll (1984) and Astley (1985), while ecological studies of population development have provided rich and consistent evidence for the effects of population density on founding rates within populations (e.g., Hannan and Freeman 1987, 1989), they have not accounted for the appearance of new populations. To understand how new populations arise, it is necessary to posit and examine conditions outside of the demographics and dynamics of existing populations or industries themselves. Organizational community, which is most simply defined as a set of interdependent organizational populations, is the logical, extended context for examining the origins of new populations and industries.

At least three papers in this volume have explored communities of knowledge as contexts for the generation of entrepreneurial ideas: Miner and colleagues, in Chapter 5; Abrahamson and Fairchild, in Chapter 6; and Murmann and Tushman, in Chapter 7. Each of these papers shifts our attention to a broader notion of an originating context, a context that may contain several communities—as in knowledge and technical communities. For example, Abrahamson and Fairchild outline the structure and dynamics of knowledge industries, whose existence depends on the rapid production of new and improved technical knowledge. They describe how specific knowledge industries, for example, consulting and mass media, which are quite interdependent, nonetheless form a community of knowledge purveyors, both populated by idea entrepreneurs. Taking management as a salient and demanding market for such ideas, and quality circles as the empirical "idea" for solving certain practical problems in management, the authors explore whether new ideas emerge primarily from suppliers or their buyers. While some evidence suggests that new ideas emerge from the buyers, it is the suppliers who popularize and elaborate ideas for use and diffusion over a broad population. In an ever-constant need for new ideas, suppliers, much more than buyers, promote the supplanting of old ideas with new ideas. Suppliers are the initial beneficiaries and thus are the entrepreneurs of the knowledge industries.

MENTAL MODELS

Closely related to the ideas of *collective action* and *community* is the concept of the *mental model*. As discussed by Burton in Chapter 2, a mental model is a coherent idea, held in this case by organizational founders, about right and appropriate ways of organizing their firms. Such ideas, which vary over entrepreneurs even in the same organizational population, develop from prior educational and organizational work experiences, whether in replication or explicit deviance from those experiences. Mental models also emerge among members of an organizational population. Such models are evident in Rindova and Fombrun's chapter and Swaminathan and Wade's chapter, which discuss actively promulgated and shared understandings about right and appropriate organizational forms in the coffee and microbrew industries, respectively. Finally, some mental models extend well beyond the ken of individual entrepreneurs, whether with respect to their organizations or their populations. As Miner and her colleagues make clear in Chapter 5, the dramatic increases in wealth in the United States over the past 20 years, especially as represented in the now-iconic Silicon Valley, have led to a general understanding among business and policy leaders throughout the world of right and appropriate contexts for entrepreneurial activity. The mental model is the cognitive instantiation of institutionalized understandings.

Suchman and his colleagues, in Chapter 13, provide a detailed description of the emergence and diffusion of a mental model among law firms in Silicon Valley about right and appropriate ways of incorporating a new firm, structuring stock purchase agreements, and constructing financial contracts with investors. The mental models Silicon Valley law firms present to their entrepreneur clients constitute a package of routinized methods for efficiently dealing with questions common to those starting companies. More generally, a population of firms within a community may contribute to institutionalizing ways of dealing with common problems faced by entrepreneurs. In the case Suchman and his colleagues discuss, law firms and venture capitalists are prominent populations within a community of organizations that are especially influential during the early founding period of a firm, during its incorporation and the formalization of equity agreements with investors.

On a more global scale, Miner and her colleagues also found evidence of a strong mental model among university technology-transfer officers in multiple countries about the role of technology transfer from universities to industrial start-ups in a region. The mental model collectively espoused was an idealized account or belief about how successful entrepreneurship in the Silicon Valley has been created. In reality, however, universities worldwide are embedded in relatively idiosyncratic cultures, political systems, and, in some cases, centuries-old customs to which the Silicon Valley idealized mental model must be adapted—if it is used at all. Because cultural contexts vary worldwide, a wholesale adoption of best practices from Silicon Valley may not be possible given variation in local conditions. Therefore, the process of implementing the Silicon Valley model is likely to produce variation, more consistent with the variable mental models Burton (this volume) actually found among Silicon Valley entrepreneurs with respect to the employment relationship in their new firms.

In many ways, the U.S. model of institutional venture capital has become a sort of mental model, although it has a unique and strong reliance on pension funds and its features have not diffused throughout the world as *the* model for financing new ventures. Nevertheless, a number of developed countries are attempting to create a venture capital industry in the presence of taken-for-granted, institutionalized constraints on entrepreneurs' conceptualizations about sources of capital in their own countries. For example, historically, new ventures in Europe have been backed by wealthy individuals rather than by institutionalized venture capitalists, whose funds come from others. Spanish King Ferdinand and Queen Isabella's bankrolling of Christopher Columbus in 1492 is a prime example of privileged wealthy individuals supporting entrepreneurial ventures, a practice that has continued up to the present. Venture capital is still a nascent industry in Europe. A question to be investigated is whether financial contracts in countries other than the U.S. are driven by the variable preferences of wealthy individuals or whether the mental models about appropriate forms of contracting more closely mirror national histories, regulations, and policies. Indeed, are there contracts at all? Investigation of entrepreneurs' mental models about sources of capital and its availability may shed light on entrepreneurs' behavior and thus more light on the impact of mental models in the entrepreneurial dynamic.

THE LOCAL ORIGINS AND PROCESSES
OF ORGANIZATION CREATION

The final insight to emerge from the Balboa Bay Conference is also related to ideas about collective action, community, and mental models. There is both theory and evidence throughout this volume that *entrepreneurship is a local process.* That is, new firms are derived from the local communities and populations of organizations residing within a given region. Recall that Rindova and Fombrun observed in Chapter 9 that, in the specialty coffee industry, a regional base characterized the initial organization of this new industry. Founders were living and working in either Seattle or Boston when the first Starbucks and the first Coffee Connections were founded in those cities. Once the new firms were founded, their entrepreneurs actively altered the structure of the existing coffee industry and its surrounding community by setting new standards for coffee bean quality and by creating a new consumer-direct delivery system for beans and brewed coffee beverages, the coffee bar. From local, regional origins to a national presence, the specialty coffee industry was formed, and in time it has altered the product offerings of the existing old-line coffee producers.

In Saxenian's research in Chapter 4, educated Chinese and Indian immigrants employed in Silicon Valley technology companies perceived limits on their abilities to advance professionally in existing companies, invariably run by non-Asian executives. Through local, collective action, both ethnic groups founded professional and technical associations to share information with one another and with younger generations of Indian and Chinese entrepreneurs. Between 1989 and 1996 fourteen of these associations were formed in the region, creating yet another subpopulation of organizations in this particular region. By 1998, 58 publicly traded technology companies were either founded or run by ethnic Chinese or Indians, growth heavily attributable to localized collective behavior among potential entrepreneurs.

Evidence for the local origins and processes of organizational creation can also be found in other research. At the individual level of the founder, Cooper and Dunkelberg (1987) noted a highly localized start-up pattern among new firms in two regions of the U.S.: Austin, Texas, and Palo Alto, California. In these localities, approximately 90% of new firms had a founder already working in the local region. Similarly, in a study of over 350 entrepreneurs who founded new firms in 18 regions of the U.S., Schoonhoven and Eisenhardt (1990) found that, on average, 63% of founding team members had previously worked together at the same company. The majority of prior workplaces were organizations in the same region in which the new firms were founded.

Emphasis on the local origins of entrepreneurial activity points to a kind of organizational community, the regional community, consisting of all entrepreneurs, investors, supply and professional support organizations, and others who reside and work within relatively small geographic areas. Especially for entrepreneurs, who cannot alone, or even in teams, acquire sufficient resources for founding, a local, geographic circumscription of community seems important. As many of the papers in this volume point out, however, entrepreneurs are not members only of their local, geographic communities. As Wade pointed out (1995), organizations and their founders also participate nationally, and even internationally, in technological communities. More research into the boundaries of organizational communities, which are probably multiple and overlapping for entrepreneurs in most industries, is needed to enrich our understanding of both the origins of entrepreneurial activity and the community "stages" on which they play.

FROM EMERGENT THEMES TO REMAINING QUESTIONS

The themes that emerged from the Balboa Bay Conference are in sharp contrast to prevailing notions about entrepreneurship. We have argued from the research and theory reported in this volume that the field of entrepreneurship is substantially broader, richer, and more complex theoretically and has more levels of analysis than prevailing conceptualizations of its "distinctive domain." Beyond individual differences and opportunity recognition, the research presented here suggests that entrepreneurial activity has an overlay with contextual conditions that can be characterized as communities of knowledge, technology, organizations, and populations—often operating at a local level. We also identified an underpinning that corresponds with entrepreneurial activities, the cognitive processes of entrepreneurs—the mental models they form and that inform their entrepreneurial actions.

In a sense, the papers in this volume address the context of entrepreneurship at both the local and global levels of analysis. Entrepreneurial action is constrained by the cognitions of entrepreneurs and by the organizational, knowledge, and technology communities in which they are embedded. The social context for an individual or nascent entrepreneur also has roots in the existing organization within which he or she is working. As places of employment, prior organizations provide technical knowledge, business and industry knowledge, and knowledge of talented individuals. Earlier work organizations also influence mental models regarding what the new start-up should look like and how it should be structured. Prior organizations essentially provide the gene pool for new organizations. Moving along a continuum of local sources of entrepreneurial activity are increasing layers of context emanating from the individual in an existing organization, itself a member of a local organizational population, which in turn is embedded in a local community of organizational populations, typically within a region. This provides the local context for entrepreneurship. Moving further along a continuum of global sources of entrepreneurial activity, one encounters the global population of the existing organization, the technological community within which knowledge is created and shared, and perhaps a community of organizational populations that may well have different attributes than the local community populations. Viewed from both a local and a global perspective, the study of entrepreneurship ultimately means the study of entrepreneurship within and across regions, nations, and in non-U.S. settings.

One of the problems with asking "Where do new firms and industries come from?" is that we are trying to examine something before it comes into existence. How, for example, do researchers measure the existence of an open environmental space before new or existing firms act to occupy it? Given the large body of research that exists on entrepreneurship, broadly construed, it is not surprising, then, how little attention has been paid to the question, "Where do new firms come from?"

There is evidence that this lack of attention to origins is a continuing problem. In the 1999 edition of *Frontiers of Entrepreneurship Research* there are 130 papers on entrepreneurship theory and research. Of these, only 1.5 % address where new firms come from. Among 35 (!) different topic areas, only two even suggest an inquiry into the origins of new firms. One paper (Surlemont, Leleux, and Denis 1999, 213), in a promising section labeled "contextual effects on new firms," compares differences in personal bankruptcy laws across nations and their impact on firm formation, bankruptcy, and growth rates. Finding that lack of personal bankruptcy laws decreases the formation rate of new firms, the authors attribute declines to states' failures to create a safety net to minimize the personal financial costs of entrepreneurial failure. A second paper, on the role of social networks in new business creation, documents how a social network facilitated creation of independent bookseller enterprises in Southern California (Weinstein 1999). Neither of these two papers is characteristic of contemporary research on entrepreneurship, and they remain among the few that investigate or theorize about the originating contexts of new organizations. For the most part, the papers in the *Frontiers* volume assume that entrepreneurial activity and new firms simply exist and that their origins either need not be questioned or are of little interest.

FUTURE THEORY AND RESEARCH
ON THE ENTREPRENEURSHIP DYNAMIC

We believe that entrepreneurship is a fundamental dynamic of change in industries, economies, and societies. The explicit focus on sources and consequences of entrepreneurial activity in this book is intended to open and expand the fairly narrow domain of entrepreneurship theory and research as it stands today. In our view, a richer more sophisticated set of research questions has been raised and implied within this volume. Of the many questions and avenues for theory development and research that reside in our expanded view of the entrepreneurship dynamic, we will focus on merely a few in the next paragraphs.

THEORETICAL DIMENSIONS OF CONTEXT AND COMMUNITY

The themes that emerged from the Balboa Bay Conference suggest fertile areas for theory development. As we have argued throughout this volume, context constrains rates and kinds of new organizations that are founded and simultaneously motivates the creation of new organizations. What is it about context, theoretically, that either constrains or motivates the entrepreneurship dynamic? At least three basic theoretical problems face investigators interested in questions related to the development and change of new industries and populations. The first is to define the *dimensions of context* that matter. We have a starting point with the concept of the organizational community, itself a major component of the entrepreneurial context. Second, what are the *boundaries of an organizational community?* DiMaggio (1994) called this the most fundamental challenge of community research, and he noted that boundaries can be defined differently, and appropriately differently, depending on the research question of interest. Third and last, what are the characteristic *dimensions of an organizational community?* Theoretical dimensions must be established to support cumulative investigation of the development and change of communities and especially their influences on the appearance and disappearance of organizational populations or industries.

Role of the state. We have urged that the entrepreneurship dynamic be viewed in context. Powerful actors in most contexts are political institutions, whether they are states, provinces, or federal or regional governments. Actions taken by governments are likely to have a strong impact on the creation of new firms and new industries because they may significantly alter the context for entrepreneurial activity. For example, deregulation of the American telecommunications industry in the early 1980s loosened regulatory constraints and revealed fertile fields for new firms and technologies to explore. In contrast to the monopolistic hold of AT&T and its affiliates that characterized the industry before deregulation, the multifaceted telecommunications industry in the U.S. today is replete with new firms, competition, and promising technologies. Similarly, an agency of the U.S. government, the National Science Foundation, enabled commercialization of the Internet when it added the "dot com" domain to signify a commercial organization rather than a government (.gov), nonprofit (.org), or university (.edu) organization. It has been documented that between 1990 and 1999, several thousand new Internet-based commercial firms, that is, the "dot.coms," were founded in the U.S. alone. Federal as well as regional governments have strong interests in promoting economic development. By varying countries and regions that are studied, we introduce variation in policies used to promote (or not) new business start-ups. Entrepreneurship is a field rife with policy-relevant implications and yet we have little knowledge of the role of states in the entrepreneurship dynamic.

Elite entrepreneurship and privileged contexts. It could be argued that several of the studies reported here focus on elite entrepreneurs and privileged entrepreneurial contexts. Three of the ten empirical papers in this volume are based on data collected in the Silicon Valley region of Northern California, certainly a rich and privileged context for entrepreneurship (Schoonhoven and Eisenhardt 1992). Are we in danger of generalizing from research on the mobilization of entrepreneurs in especially privileged regional contexts?

Many of the inquiries in this book concern the origins of new firms that, once established, are identified empirically as "emerging growth" companies, new firms with the potential for the creative destruction of existing technologies, industries, and organizational competencies. Highly trained specialist engineers, scientists, and production and service personnel are typically required in these start-ups. In the service sector, the new ventures of interest utilize contemporary information technology in new ways for service delivery, even though they may reside in more conventional industries like financial services, publications, and booksellers. The combination of dependence on leading-edge science and technology, the requirement for specialist employees, and a focus on emerging and growth markets suggests that these firms are likely to require substantial capital at founding and for growth. Although not intentionally, the research reported here does not focus on slow and low-growth-potential industries and small businesses that are likely to remain small in size. Neither is there a focus on family-owned businesses although the establishment of private firms is certainly included here.

Despite our intention not to impose narrow scope conditions on the ideas presented or to limit the range of applications of the ideas developed here, the research reported here does perhaps reflect a strong interest in elite entrepreneurs and elite entrepreneurial activity, which can be defined as the founding of new firms targeted for emerging or high-growth markets and which typically depend on leading-edge, science-based technologies. Certainly this focus reflects research opportunities that abound at the close of the twentieth and in the early twenty-first centuries. When one studies science-based industries, the likelihood is high that one will see new technologies, products, and markets developing rapidly. This in turn increases the likelihood that we may observe high variation in new organizations, populations, and communities within a short period of time.

Rather than labeling this elite entrepreneurship, however, perhaps it is more appropriate to think of relatively *privileged contexts* for entrepreneurial activity, how they are created, and how variation in contexts influences new firm formation, new population and industry emergence, and modified community and industrial structures. Relatively privileged contexts for entrepreneurship may be based on the greater concentration of resources vital to new firm start-up, whether these are based on variation in resources across nation-states or regional differences within a given country. For example, in the United States, there are substantial differences across regions in the concentration of venture capital firms and the total dollars invested in new organizations within a given time period (Florida and Smith 1990; Schoonhoven and Eisenhardt 1993). Some argue that venture capital investment follows entrepreneurial activity and especially the rise of large numbers of new organizations in a region, rather than causing higher rates of start-up activity. The formation rate of new firms in Silicon Valley is at an all-time high, and venture capital-ists have invested $13.4 billion in the Santa Clara Valley region of Northern California in 1999 alone, up from $3.5 billion in 1997. This can be compared with the $134.9 million captured by new ventures in the South Central region of California and $133.5 million invested in start-ups in the Sacramento region in 1999, the latter receiving the smallest infusion of venture capital in the U.S, among the eighteen regions that have received venture-capital funds (Walden 1999). Following from an organizational community perspective, other organizational populations may also provide needed resources, like the regional concentration of universities with engineering programs or the con-centration of manufacturing employees or software engineers within a region.

An unanswered question concerns the critical mass of existing organizations and populations necessary, and of what types, for an increase in the new-firm formation rate. This, of course, is the question that interests entrepreneurs, investors, and regional development officials alike. It should interest scholars of entrepreneurship as well. Do differences in the concentration of resources (communities of knowledge and technology, populations of organizations residing in a community) across regions give rise to significant differences in the formation rate of new firms? One can imagine creating a resource con-centration index to measure the extent to which a given region or context varies in the opportunities provided for entrepreneurial activity, essentially a measure of the extent to which privileged contexts for entrepreneurship exist.

In other parts of the world, wealthy individuals, families, and corporations are often the sources of risk capital. In the U.S., wealthy individuals (often, cashed-out entrepreneurs), called "angels," are much less visible than the high-profile and well-organized venture capital industry, though angel networks and groups are taking an increasingly prominent and formal role in entrepreneur-ial investment processes. Comparative cross-national research on the degree of formal and informal arrangements of investment in regions and countries, concentration of financial resources, resource visibility, and modes of resource acquisition may yield greater insight into the sources, rates, and consequences of entrepreneurial activity. For example, one can imagine that socioeconomic status, social networks, and family connections may play a larger role in nar-rowing access to entrepreneurial resources in other countries than they appear to do in the U.S., but this remains an empirical question.

International contexts for entrepreneurship. It should be clear that the ideas discussed above about collective activity, community, and mental models are not limited to U.S.-based organizations. In this volume, Miner and her colleagues, in Chapter 5, and Murmann and Tushman, in Chapter 7, address entrepreneurship in a more global context and in non-U.S. settings. Miner and her colleagues' work demonstrates the power of population-level learning achieved across national boundaries. Highly publicized Northern California's Silicon Valley "successes" have shaped how those in distant countries conceive of sources of entrepreneurship as well as their perceptions of the role of universities in commercializing new technology. Miner and her colleagues' research suggests that some global homogenization is likely to be found through attempts to mimic Silicon Valley best practices. Yet sources of new firm variation are also likely to be present in the varying contexts resulting from country- and region-specific differences. The impact of these country and regional differences as contexts for entrepreneurship needs to be explored. The emerging economies of Eastern Europe, countries of the former Soviet Union, and the vast People's Republic of China all present fascinating contexts for the study of entrepreneurship, its sources, and its consequences. We hope readers of this book will embrace the challenge that research in these settings presents.

Population and sample biases. In the United States, entrepreneurial actions that result in the founding of a new venture may capture substantial resources from the U.S. venture capital industry. The small number of firms that are successful in attracting venture capital funding, and eventually in going public, typically receive a disproportionate share of attention from the business press and from commercial companies that gather firm-level data. To focus too narrowly on entrepreneurial activity that is widely publicized or only on those new firms with venture capital funding will surely limit the range of variation we observe empirically. Much like studying only *Fortune* 500 companies, studying only the rapid-growth firms of the *Inc.* 500 or only new ventures financed by venture capital firms rules out thousands of new organizations founded annually. Those who study the relatively small number of venture capital–backed firms in the U.S. or only the *Inc.* 500, or only new ventures that have made an initial public offering (IPO) are essentially sampling on the dependent variable of new-firm success.

The *Inc.* 500 organizations are successfully founded ventures that have flourished and grown in size. The venture capital industry is concentrated in a few regions in the U.S. and is dominated by elite-university–trained MBAs whose business and social circles are narrow. The social structuring of the venture capital industry along with its limited regional clustering in turn eliminates thousands of entrepreneurs and new ventures that have limited or no access to the institutionalized venture capital industry. These sources of sample and population bias in turn bias coefficients and the interpretation of our findings. Clearly we need to think carefully about research designs, samples, and population selection for studying the entrepreneurship dynamic.

Local contexts. It may be useful to compare different founding contexts and conditions, especially those in which sources of capital are neither institutionalized nor well organized with those in which the acquisition of capital is well understood and institutionalized. Access to capital is highly variable. Among new ventures that obtain large sums of money at founding, what created the initial inflow of substantial cash? Is it a social network process by individual entrepreneurs? Is it experience working in a prior firm that is dominant in a region, which in turn may provide higher visibility and legitimacy for its former employees?

Beyond originating work organizations, what are the other organizations, institutions, and populations that play a role in the creation of new ventures? Consider the role of universities in the entrepreneurship dynamic. It is an empirical question whether elite-university graduates are advantaged in obtaining capital and other social network–derived resources for start-ups in the region in which their universities are located. Or is this a myth derived from limited anecdotal observations about Stanford and MIT graduates, for example, whose regions are legendary sources for the entrepreneurship dynamic? Or do the children of successful former entrepreneurs or venture capitalists have differential access to scarce resources within a region, perhaps akin to the children of Hollywood-based movie stars who eventually become successful in their own right within the Hollywood milieu? Anecdotal observations may provide the basis for a more systematic investigation of the role of local institutions, populations, and social networks in the entrepreneurship dynamic.

We have argued that entrepreneurship is a local phenomenon that relies on and builds from business skills of individuals with experience in a related industry and within existing organizations in a region. The local nature of entrepreneurship arguments needs to be tested across regions and with cross-national samples of new ventures. As with the similar argument that the U.S.-dominated field of organizational behavior is a parochial dinosaur (Boyacigiller and Adler 1991), it is essential to test our theories and to develop our notions about the entrepreneurship dynamic in organizations, populations, and communities throughout the rest of the world. In larger-scale international studies we may find some global homogenization of best practices based on attempts to mimic Silicon Valley successes. Yet it is local contexts that will constrain the choices available and in turn create requisite variation from the observed U.S. practices. Comparative regional and international studies will better inform our conclusions about the entrepreneurship dynamic in the creation and evolution of industries.

A more specific focus is to tackle directly the question of why some contexts, that is, regions, produce large numbers of new organizations. This is a simple question that may involve daunting work. Local organizational communities, that is, the cities and regions that promote or impede the founding of new organizations, must be fully described and characterized. We need to know the number and diversity of organizational populations that make up the local organizational communities over time. And we need to observe the rates and locations of organizational foundings over time to observe whether they are inside or outside the boundaries of existing populations.

The role of time. What is missing in research on the entrepreneurship dynamic—and also absent in much contemporary research on organizations— is a conceptualization of the role of time and historical timing on the entrepreneurial dynamic. Because we have focused for so long on easily identified new firms and their entrepreneurs, scholars have paid scant attention to *pre-start-up* phenomena and contexts. Most entrepreneurship research has focused on new-venture performance (Venkataraman 1997), and performance is typically measured at one point in time. Similarly, we have failed to ask about the implications of the entrepreneurship dynamic for industry creation and evolution. We need to work on conceptualizing the role of time and time-based phenomena in the entrepreneurship dynamic. With some solid theoretical and empirical work ahead of us, we can seek new-venture populations and communities that can be followed over time or, alternatively, about which ample historical context data are available.

Entrepreneurship, new firms, and the transformation of contexts. Last, understanding the impact of new firms on existing firms and industries involves a host of relatively uninvestigated phenomena. Stated broadly, how do we move conceptually from the contexts that create new organizations and populations to the modification of entire communities or industry structures? The question is, "What is the impact of new firms on the evolution of existing industries?" The importance of answering this question can be seen in the impact of one new firm, Netscape Communications Corporation, a computer software firm credited with launching the browser industry. Netscape was founded in 1993 by Jim Clark and Marc Andreeson to commercialize Mosaic, a web browser co-developed by Andreeson as a student at the University of Illinois. Netscape's browser software provided a missing link in web-use technology. Released in December 1994, Navigator 1.0 offered an easy to use graphical user interface for browsing the world wide web, enabling efficient movement among the thousands of sites already on the web. Long dominated by Microsoft, the software industry now had a new product category, the web browser, developed by a newly founded firm, which in turn allowed scores of other new companies to launch products and services on the Internet, efficiently enabled by browser software. By September 2000, the longer-range impact of Netscape on a wider range of industries could be observed. Browsers enabled computer users to efficiently locate firms like Yahoo!, an Internet "portal" founded in 1995 as the first on-line navigational guide to the world wide web and itself founded on innovative software technology. With the improvements Yahoo! made in its search-engine software, users could easily look up information on nearly every imaginable topic. Internet portals like Yahoo! and its competitors, Lycos, Alta Vista, and Excite@Home, now provide a range of global Internet communications, commerce, and media services offered by a comprehensive brand-named network of service providers. By entering portals, computer users have efficient access to a wide range of industries, including media, travel, entertainment, and sports, to name a few. At portals, users can directly engage in electronic commerce, buying such things as airline and concert tickets, clothing, cosmetics, and jewelry from a wide range of providers whose services and prices can be easily compared. While Netscape cannot be credited with creating what is today described as a multi-billion-dollar market for Internet-enabled software, products, and services, nonetheless, it was an early and significant start-up company that has had a demonstrable impact on a wide range of existing industries as well as on new industries established since 1995.

This question, "What is the impact of new firms on the evolution of existing industries?" has not been addressed by either organizational ecologists or strategy theorists. We begin with contexts, communities, and populations as the settings from which the entrepreneurship dynamic emerges. For scholars of entrepreneurship, to stop short of addressing the impact of new firms on the evolution of industries is to miss what we argue is one of the most important questions to be resolved among the mass effects of the entrepreneurship dynamic.

CONCLUSION

The purpose of this book has been to provide a richer rendering of the context of entrepreneurship. In our attempts to broaden the field of inquiry, we have focused attention on two questions we believe are essential for a more sophisticated view of this important dynamic in the creation and evolution of industries. First, "Where do new firms come from, and what are the conditions that promote the rise of entrepreneurial activity in general?" Second, "How do new organizations affect the development and evolution of industries and the creation of new organizational populations?" Twelve original papers have diversely addressed either or both of these questions.

Collectively, the research reported in this book broadens in at least four ways what some regard as the distinctive domain of entrepreneurship theory and research. First, we ask what precedes entrepreneurial activity, rather than assuming that entrepreneurship begins with individual rational behavior and the identification of a market opportunity. Specifically, we ask what are *the antecedents of entrepreneurship* and the contexts from which entrepreneurship derives (organizations, populations, industries, and communities of organizations)? This broadens the distinctive domain of entrepreneurship substantially by recognizing that the context of new organization creation is substantially more complex than a focus on individual rational action suggests.

The existence of *mental models*, documented by research reported here (see

Burton; Miner et al.), suggests that social cognition plays an important role in the unfolding of entrepreneurial activities. The distinctive domain of entrepreneurship also includes individuals' perceptual processes, which are influenced by founders' prior workplaces and organizational contexts. Population-level learning may also precede entrepreneurial activity. Socially constructed perceptions of the Silicon Valley template of entrepreneurship play a role internationally. With the global diffusion of the "Magic Beanstalk" conception of the role of universities in technology transfer and the formation of new firms, we find good evidence of learning across a global population of universities.

Then we ask where new firms come from, more generally. Among the answers is that entrepreneurship is a local process. New firms are formed in particular and local regions, predominantly by individuals who live, who are educated, and who work in local organizations in the regions. The business and technical knowledge necessary to found a new organization, as well as potential new employees, derives from individuals learning the business and technical knowledge in their prior organizational contexts.

Next, we ask what are the consequences of entrepreneurial activity, beyond the founding of a new firm, which is sometimes accompanied by genuine innovation and typically by the creation of new jobs? An important and relatively unaddressed consequence of entrepreneurship is its impact on the *creation of new industries*. New firms may create innovative new products and services that in turn spawn new industries to exploit previously untouched markets. For example, Steve Wozniak and Steve Jobs created the first commercially successful personal computer and pioneered the PC industry by founding Apple Computer in 1983. As thousands of new PC users emerged, scores of new PC firms were founded, and the PC industry itself was firmly launched. By 1995, from an initial base of zero, the PC industry has created more than $250 billion in net shareholder value (Meeker et al. 1995). Now nearly 20 years old, the industry has continued to evolve, liberating users from their desktops with ever lighter, portable, and wireless computing devices. More generally, the domain of entrepreneurship includes investigation of the conditions under which such entrepreneurial activity contributes to the creation of new industries. In the year 2000, products are being offered that capitalize on the increasing miniaturization and functionality of semiconductor chips, growth of the Internet as a communication medium, and the increasing sophistication of wireless devices like mobile telephones and computers to gain Internet access. These small products and their emerging industry offer many of the same advantages of personal computers without their size, weight, and limited mobility. The battle for dominance in this rapidly forming industry continues to be waged. *How* this new industry will develop is yet to be seen, but we know that multiple knowledge and organizational communities will play important roles as the new industry emerges.

An additional consequence of entrepreneurial activity is its influence on the *evolution of existing industries*. Once a new firm has been created, dynamics are set in motion that may have multiple consequences for the existing industrial structure. The organizational context is now changed, sometimes in fundamental ways, such that new industries are launched and existing industries have altered competitive landscapes. The entrepreneurship dynamic also helps blur the boundaries between existing industries, as Netscape's founding suggests. As the battle for sophisticated hand-held devices with Internet access continues to be waged, we are witnessing a blurring of the boundaries of the computer, telecommunications, and wireless industries, industries previously thought to be discrete.

Last, in the process of exploring where new firms come from and their impact on the creation and evolution of industries, multiple theoretical perspectives have been applied to address these questions. We have seen the development of a community ecology theory of organizational foundings. Future research on the sources of entrepreneurship, new firms, and their impact on the creation and evolution of industries should consider this developing community perspective. Other theoretical lenses have been used to illuminate the phenomena of interest from different angles. In this volume, scholars have relied on neo-institutional theory, social movement theory, organizational ecology arguments, social cognition arguments, population-level learning processes, organization evolution arguments, and community ecology theory to frame their inquiries and to interpret their research findings. This suggests that the rational assumptions that have strongly influenced the study of entrepreneurship for decades should be relaxed and the phenomenon re-illuminated by varying theories and their assumptions.

We all have much work to do. Building more theory and applying a variety of assumptions and theoretical perspectives in our research will enhance our ability to learn more, more quickly. The emergent themes derived from the research we report here help set the stage for a new era of research on the entrepreneurship dynamic. We invite others to join us in this fascinating realm of inquiry.

REFERENCES

Abernathy, W. 1978. *The Productivity Dilemma*. Baltimore: Johns Hopkins University Press.

Abernathy, W., and K. B. Clark. 1985. "Innovation: Mapping the Winds of Creative Destruction." *Research Policy* 14: 3–22.

Abernathy, W., and J. Utterback. 1978. "Patterns of Industrial Innovation." *Technology Review* 80: 40–47.

Abrahamson, E. 1990. "Fads and Fashions in Administrative Technologies." Ph. D. dissertation, Graduate School of Business, New York University.

———. 1991. "Managerial Fads and Fashions: The Diffusion and Rejection of Innovations." *Academy of Management Review* 16: 586–612.

———. 1996a. "Management Fashion." *Academy of Management Review* 21: 254–85.

———. 1996b. "Technical and Aesthetic Fashion." In B. Czarniawska and G. Sevon, eds., *Translating Organizational Change*, 117–37. Berlin and New York: DeGruyter.

———. 1997. "The Emergence and Prevalence of Employee-Management Rhetorics: The Effect of Long Waves, Labor Unions, and Turnover, 1875 to 1992." *Academy of Management Journal* 40: 491–533.

Abrahamson, E., and G. Fairchild. 1999. "Management Fashion: Lifecycles, Triggers, and Collective Learning Processes." *Administrative Science Quarterly* 44: 708–40.

Abrahamson, E., and C. Fombrun. 1992. "Forging the Iron Cage: Interorganizational Networks and the Production of Macro-culture." *Journal of Management Studies* 29: 175–94.

———. 1994. "Macro-cultures: Determinants and Consequences." *Academy of Management Review* 19: 728–55.

Acs, Z. J. 1996. "Does Research Create Jobs?" *Challenge* 39: 32–38.

Acs, Z. J., D. B. Audretsch, and M. P. Feldman. 1994. "R&D Spillovers and Recipient Firm Size." *Review of Economics and Statistics* 76: 336–40.

Al-Hibri, A. Y. 1997. "The American Corporation in the Twenty-First Century: Future Forms of Structure and Governance." *University of Richmond Law Review* 31: 1399–1406.

Alarcon, R. 1999. "Recruitment Processes Among Foreign-Born Engineers and Scientists in Silicon Valley." *American Behavioral Scientist* 42: 1381–97.

Albert, S., and D. Whetten. 1985. "Organizational Identity." In L. L. Cummings and B. M. Staw, eds., *Research in Organizational Behavior* 7: 263–95. Greenwich, Conn.: JAI Press.

Albin, P. 1987. "Microeconomic Foundation of Cyclic Irregularities or 'Chaos.'" *Mathematical Social Research* 13: 185–214.

————. 1998. *Barriers and Bounds to Rationality*. Princeton, N.J.: Princeton University Press.

Aldag, R. 1997. "Moving Sofas and Exhuming Woodchucks: On Relevance, Impact, and the Following of Fads." *Journal of Management Inquiry* 6: 8–16.

Aldrich, H. E. 1979. *Organizations and Environments*. Englewood Cliffs, N.J.: Prentice-Hall.

————. 1999. *Organizations Evolving*. London: Sage.

Aldrich, H. E., and C. M. Fiol. 1994. "Fools Rush In? The Institutional Context of Industry Creation." *Academy of Management Review* 19: 645–70.

Aldrich, H. E., and A. Fortune. 2000. "Can't Buy Me Love (But I Know Where You Can Rent It): The Emerging Organizational Community Around Application Service Providers." Paper presented at the annual meeting of the Academy of Management, Toronto.

Aldrich, H. E., H. Rosen, and W. Woodward. 1987. "The Impact of Social Networks on Business Foundings and Profit: A Longitudinal Study." In N. Churchill, J. Hornaday, B. Kirchhoff, O. Krasner, and K. Vesper, eds., *Frontiers in Entrepreneurship Research*, 154–68. Wellesley, Mass.: Center for Entrepreneurial Studies, Babson College.

Aldrich, H. E., and U. H. Staber. 1988. "Organizing Business Interests: Patterns of Trade Association Foundings, Transformations, and Deaths." In G. R. Carroll, ed., *Ecological Models of Organization*, 111–26. Cambridge, Mass.: Ballinger.

Aldrich, H. E., and R. Waldinger. 1990. "Ethnicity and Entrepreneurship." *Annual Review of Sociology* 16: 111–35.

Aldrich, H. E., and G. Wiedenmayer. 1993. "From Traits to Rates: An Ecological Perspective on Organizational Foundings." *Advances in Entrepreneurship, Firm Emergence, and Growth*, 1: 145–95. Greenwich, Conn.: JAI Press.

Aldrich, H., and C. Zimmer. 1986. "Entrepreneurship Through Social Networks." In D. L. Sexton and R. W. Smilor, eds., *The Art and Science of Entrepreneurship*, 3–23. Cambridge, Mass.: Ballinger.

Amenta, E., and Y. Zylan. 1991. "It Happened Here: Political Opportunity, the New Institutionalism, and the Townsend Movement." *American Sociological Review* 56: 250–65.

American Association for Engineering Societies. 1995. "Report of the Engineering Manpower Commission." New York.

Anders, G., P. McGeehan, and K. Kranhold. 1998. "Milestones Hit by Schwab and E*Trade." *Wall Street Journal*, December 2, p. C1.

Anderson, C. 1996. "Specialty Coffee Market, Coffee Drinkers Maturing." *Gourmet News*, April, pp. 25–26.

Anderson, P., and M. Tushman. 1990. "Technological Discontinuities and Dominant Designs: A Cyclical Model of Technological Change." *Administrative Science Quarterly* 35: 604–33.

Andrews, M. 1992. "Avenues for Growth." Report for the Specialty Coffee Association of America. Long Beach, Calif.

Applebaum, E., and R. Batt. 1994. *The New American Workplace: Transforming Work Systems in the United States*. Ithaca, N.Y.: Cornell University Press.

Appold, S. 1995. "Agglomeration, Interorganizational Networks, and Competitive Performance in the U.S. Metalworking Sector." *Economic Geography* 71: 27–54.

Argyres, N. S., and J. P. Liebeskind. 1998. "Privatizing the Intellectual Commons: Universities and the Commercialization of Biotechnology." *Journal of Economic Behavior and Organization* 35: 427–54.

Arrow, K. 1962. "Economic Welfare and the Allocation of Resources for Invention." In R. R. Nelson, ed., *The Rate and Direction of Inventive Activity*, 609–26. Princeton, N.J.: Princeton University Press.

Arthur, W. B. 1990a. "Silicon Valley Locational Clusters: When Do Increasing Returns Imply Monopoly?" *Mathematical Social Sciences* 19: 235–51.

———. 1990b. "Positive Feedbacks in the Economy." *Scientific American* no. 262, pp. 92–99.

Arthur, W. B., Y. M. Ermoliev, and Y. M. Kaniovski. 1987. "Path Dependence Processes and the Emergence of Macro-structure." *European Journal of Operational Research* 30: 294–303.

Asian Americans for Community Involvement (AACI). 1993. *Qualified, But . . . A Report on Glass Ceiling Issues Facing Asian Americans in Silicon Valley.* San Jose, Calif.: AACI.

Association of University Technology Managers (AUTM). 1995. "Licensing Survey FY 1991–FY 1995 Executive Summary." *1995 Survey Summary.* Norwalk, Conn.: AUTM.

———. 1998. "Survey Shows Small Companies Are Biggest Users of Academic Research Innovations." *1996 Survey Summary.* Norwalk, Conn.: AUTM.

Astley, W. G. 1985. "The Two Ecologies: Population and Community Perspectives on Organizational Evolution." *Administrative Science Quarterly* 30: 224–41.

Astley, W. G., and C. J. Fombrun. 1983. "Technological Innovation and Industrial Structure." *Advances in Strategic Management,* 1: 205–29. Greenwich, Conn.: JAI Press.

Atkinson, S. H. 1994. "University-Affiliated Venture Capital Funds." *Health Affairs* 13: 159–72.

Audretsch, D. B., and P. E. Stephan. 1996. "Company-Scientist Locational Links: The Case of Biotechnology." *American Economic Review* 86: 641–52.

Auster, E., and H. E. Aldrich. 1984. "Small Business Vulnerability, Ethnic Enclaves and Ethnic Enterprise." In R. Ward and R. Jenkins, eds., *Ethnic Communities in Business,* 39–54. Cambridge: Cambridge University Press.

Axelrod, R. 1984. *The Evolution of Cooperation.* New York: Basic Books.

Bania, N., R. Eberts, and M. Fogarty. 1993. "Universities and the Start-up of New Companies: Can We Generalize from Route 128 and Silicon Valley?" *Review of Economics and Statistics* 75: 761–64.

Bardham, A. D., and D. K. Howe. 1998. "Transnational Social Networks and Globalization: The Geography of California's Exports." Working paper no. 98–262, Fisher Center for Real Estate and Urban Economics, University of California at Berkeley.

Barley, S. 1990. "The Alignment of Technology and Structure Through Roles and Networks." *Administrative Science Quarterly* 35: 61–103.

Barley, S. R., and G. Kunda. 1992. "Design and Devotion: Surges of Rational and Normative Ideologies of Control in Managerial Discourse." *Administrative Science Quarterly* 37: 363–400.

Barley, S., G. Meyer, and D. Gash. 1988. "Cultures of Culture: Academics, Practitioners, and the Pragmatics of Normative Control." *Administrative Science Quarterly* 33: 24–60.

Barnett, W. P., and G. R. Carroll. 1987. "Competition and Mutualism Among Early Telephone Companies." *Administrative Science Quarterly* 32: 400–421.

———. 1993. "How Institutional Constraints Affected the Organization of Early U.S. Telephony." *Journal of Law, Economics, and Organization* 9: 98–126.

Barnett, W. P., and J. Freeman. 1997. "Too Much of a Good Thing? Product Proliferation and Organizational Failure." Working paper, Graduate School of Business, Stanford University.

Baron, J. N., M. D. Burton, and M. T. Hannan. 1996. "The Road Taken: The Origins and Evolution of Employment Systems in Emerging High-Technology Companies." *Industrial and Corporate Change* 5: 239–76.

———. 1999. "Engineering Bureaucracy: The Genesis of Formal Policies, Positions, and Structures in High Technology Firms." *Journal of Law, Economics, and Organization* 5: 1–41.

Baron, J. N., M. T. Hannan, and M. D. Burton. 1999. "Building the Iron Cage: Determinants of Managerial Intensity in the Early Years of Organizations." *American Sociological Review* 64: 527–47.

Baron, R. A., and G. D. Markman. 1998. "Social Skills and Entrepreneurial Success: A Framework and Initial Data." Working paper, Lally School of Management and Technology, Rensselaer Polytechnic Institute, Troy, N.Y.

Baron, S. 1962. *Brewed in America.* Boston: Little, Brown.

Basalla, G. 1988. *The Evolution of Technology.* New York: Cambridge University Press.

Bateson, P. 1988. "The Biological Evolution of Cooperation and Trust." In D. Gambetta, ed., *Trust: Making and Breaking Cooperative Relations,* 14–30. New York: Basil Blackwell.

Baum, J. A. C. 1996. "Organizational Ecology." In S. Clegg, C. Hardy, and W. R. Nord, eds., *Handbook of Organization Studies,* 77–114. New York: Oxford University Press.

Baum, J. A. C., H. J. Korn, and S. Kotha. 1995. "Dominant Designs and Population Dynamics in Telecommunications Services: Founding and Failure of Facsimile Transmission Service Organizations, 1965–1992." *Social Science Research* 24: 97–135.

Baum, J. A. C., and S. Mezias. 1992. "Localized Competition and Organizational Failure in the Manhattan Hotel Industry." *Administrative Science Quarterly* 37: 580–604.

Baum, J. A. C., and C. Oliver. 1992. "Institutional Embeddedness and the Dynamics of Organizational Populations." *American Sociological Review* 57: 540–59.

———. 1996. "Toward an Institutional Ecology of Organizational Founding." *Academy of Management Journal* 39: 1378–1427.

Baum, J. A. C., and W. A. Powell. 1995. "Cultivating an Institutional Ecology of Organizations: Comment on Hannan, Carroll, Dundon, and Torres." *American Sociological Review* 60: 529–38.

Baum, J. A. C., and J. V. Singh. 1994a. "Organizational Hierarchies and Evolutionary Processes: Some Reflections on a Theory of Organizational Evolution." In J. A. C. Baum and J. V. Singh, eds., *Evolutionary Dynamics of Organizations,* 3–22. New York: Oxford University Press.

———. 1994b. "Organizational Niche Overlap and the Dynamics of Organizational Founding." *Organizational Science* 5: 483–502.

Baumol, W. J. 1993. *Entrepreneurship, Management, and the Structure of Payoffs.* Cambridge, Mass.: MIT Press.

Beardsley, J., and D. Dewar. 1977. *Quality Circles.* San Jose, Calif.: Beardsley and Associates.

Beccattini, G. 1991. "The Industrial District as a Creative Milieu." In G. Benko and M. Dunford, eds., *Industrial Change and Regional Development,* 102–16. London: Belhaven Press.

Becker, H. S. 1963. *Outsiders: Studies in the Sociology of Deviance.* New York: Free Press.

Beeson, P., and E. Montgomery. 1993. "The Effects of Colleges and Universities on Local Labor Markets." *Review of Economics and Statistics* 75: 753–61.

BenDanile, D. K. Szafara, and A. Broder. 1997. "What Aspects of the Culture of Technical Professors and the Structure of Research Universities Help or Hinder the Transfer of Technology to Start-up Ventures?" Technical report, Center for Entrepreneurial Leadership, the Ewing Marion Kauffman Foundation, and the Johnson Graduate School of Management, Cornell University.

Benford, R. D., and S. A. Hunt. 1992. "Dramaturgy and Social Movements: The Social Construction and Communication of Power." *Sociological Inquiry* 62: 36–55.

Benoit, W. 1995. *Accounts, Excuses, and Apologies: A Theory of Image Restoration Strategies.* Albany, N.Y.: SUNY Press.

Berger, P., and T. Luckmann. 1967. *The Social Construction of Reality.* New York: Doubleday.

Bernstein, L. 1992. "Opting Out of the Legal System: Extralegal Contractual Relations in the Diamond Industry." *Journal of Legal Studies* 21: 115–57.

Bernstein, M. 1997. "Celebration and Suppression: The Strategic Uses of Identity by the Lesbian and Gay Movement." *American Journal of Sociology* 103: 531–65.

Best, M. 1990. *The New Competition: Institutions of Industrial Restructuring.* Cambridge, Mass.: Harvard University Press.

Bijker, W., T. Hughes, and T. Pinch. 1987. *The Social Construction of Technological Systems.* Cambridge, Mass.: MIT Press.

Birch, D. L. 1979. *The Job Generation Process.* Cambridge Mass.: MIT Program on Neighborhood and Regional Change.

———. 1987. *Job Creation in America: How Our Smallest Companies Put the Most People to Work.* New York: Free Press.

———. 1989. "Change, Innovation, and Job Generation." *Journal of Labor Research* 10: 33–38.

Birley, S. 1986. "The Role of New Firms: Births, Deaths, and Job Generation." *Strategic Management Journal* 7: 361–76.

Boeker, W. P. 1988. "Organizational Origins: Entrepreneurial and Environmental Imprinting at the Time of Founding." In G. R. Carroll, ed., *Ecological Models of Organizations,* 33–51. Cambridge, Mass.: Ballinger.

———. 1997. "Executive Migration and Strategic Change: The Effect of Top Manager Movement on Product-Market Entry." *Administrative Science Quarterly* 42: 213–36.

Bonacich, E., and J. Modell. 1980. *The Economic Basis of Ethnic Solidarity: Small Business in the Japanese American Community.* Berkeley: University of California Press.

Borjas, G. J. 1994. "The Economics of Immigration." *Journal of Economic Literature* 32: 1667–1717.

————. 1995. "The Economic Benefits from Immigration." *Journal of Economic Perspectives* 9: 3–22.

Boyacigiller, N., and N. Adler. 1991. "The Parochial Dinosaur: The Organizational Sciences in a Global Context." *Academy of Management Review* 16: 262–91.

Boyle, J. 1985. "The Politics of Reason: Critical Legal Theory and Local Social Thought." *University of Pennsylvania Law Review* 133: 685–780.

Braun, E., and S. Macdonald. 1982. *Revolution in Miniature: The History and Impact of Semiconductor Electronics*. Cambridge: Cambridge University Press.

Bresnahan, T. F., and F. Malerba. 1999. "Industrial Dynamics and the Evolution of Firms' and Nations' Competitive Capabilities in the World Computer Industry." In D. C. Mowery and R. R. Nelson, eds., *Sources of Industrial Leadership: Studies of Seven Industries*, 79–133. New York, Cambridge University Press.

Brett, A. M., D. V. Gibson, and R. Smilor, eds. 1991. *University Spin-off Companies: Economic Development, Faculty Entrepreneurs, and Technology Transfer*. Savage, Md.: Rowman and Littlefield.

Breyer, S. 1982. *Regulation and Its Reform*. Cambridge, Mass.: Harvard University Press.

Brint, S., and J. Karabell. 1991. "Institutional Origins and Transformations: The Case of American Community Colleges." In W. W. Powell and P. DiMaggio, eds., *The New Institutionalism in Organizational Analysis*, 337–60. Chicago: University of Chicago Press.

Brittain, J., and J. Freeman. 1980. "Density Dependent Selection and the Proliferation of Organizations." In R. H. Miles and J. R. Kimberly, eds., *The Organizational Life Cycle*, 291–338. San Francisco: Jossey-Bass.

————. 1986. "Entrepreneurship in the Semiconductor Industry." Paper presented at the annual meeting of the Academy of Management, Chicago.

Brockhaus, R. H. 1982. "The Psychology of the Entrepreneur." In C. A. Kent, D. L. Sexton, and K. H. Vesper, eds., *Encyclopedia of Entrepreneurship*, 39–71. Englewood Cliffs, N.J.: Prentice-Hall.

Brüderl, J., P. Preisendörfer, and R. Ziegler. 1992. "Survival Chances of Newly Founded Business Organizations." *American Sociological Review* 57: 227–42.

Brusco, S. 1999. "The Rules of the Game in Industrial Districts." In A. Grandori, ed., *Interfirm Networks: Organization and Industrial Competitiveness*, 17–40. London: Routledge.

Buffone, D. C. 1995. "Note: Predatory Attorneys and Professional Plaintiffs: Reforms Are Needed to Limit Vexatious Securities Litigation." *Hofstra Law Review* 23: 655–92.

Bull, C., and J. Gallagher. 1996. *Perfect Enemies: The Religious Right, the Gay Movement, and the Politics of the 1990s*. New York: Crown.

Burstein, P. 1991. "Legal Mobilization as a Social Movement Tactic: The Struggle for Equal Employment Opportunity." *American Journal of Sociology* 91: 1201–25.

Burt, R. S. 1992. *Structural Holes: The Social Structure of Competition*. Cambridge, Mass.: Harvard University Press.

Burton, M. D. 1995. *The Evolution of Employment Systems in High Technology Firms*. Ph.D. dissertation, Stanford University.

Busenitz, L.W., and J. B. Barney. 1994. "Biases and Heuristics in Strategic Decision Making:

Differences Between Entrepreneurs and Managers in Large Organizations." *Academy of Management Best Paper Proceedings*, 85–89.

Business Week. 1992. "Hot Spots: America's New Growth Regions Are Blossoming Despite the Slump." October 19, pp. 80–88.

Bygrave, W. D. 1993. "Theory Building in the Entrepreneurship Paradigm." *Journal of Business Venturing* 8: 255–80.

California Business and Professions Code §16600. 1999. Deerings California Codes Annotated.

Campbell, J. L., and L. N. Lindberg. 1990. "Property Rights and the Organization of Economic Activity by the State." *American Sociological Review* 55: 634–47.

Cantillon, R. 1931. *Essai sur la nature du commerce en general.* Ed. and trans. H. Higgs. London: Macmillan.

Cantlon, J. E., and H. E. Koenig. 1991. "Global Economic Competitiveness and the Land-Grant University." In A. M. Brett, D. V. Gibson, and R. Smilor, eds., *University Spin-off Companies: Economic Development, Faculty Entrepreneurs, and Technology Transfer*, 3–30. Savage, Md.: Rowman and Littlefield.

Carland, J., F. Hoy, W. Boulton, and J. A. Carland. 1984. "Differentiating Entrepreneurs from Small Business Owners: A Conceptualization." *Academy of Management Review* 9: 354–59.

Carlsson, B., and P. Braunerhjelm. 1998. "Industry Clusters: Biotechnology/Biomedicine and Polymers in Ohio and Sweden." Working paper, Weatherhead School of Management, Case Western Reserve University.

Carlton, D. W. 1983. "The Location and Employment Choices of New Firms: An Econometric Model with Discrete and Continuous Endogenous Variables." *Review of Economics and Statistics* 65: 440–49.

Carroll, G. R. 1984. "Organizational Ecology." *Annual Review of Sociology* 10: 71–93.

———. 1985. "Concentration and Specialization: Dynamics of Niche Width in Populations of Organizations." *American Journal of Sociology* 90: 1262–83.

———. 1988. *Ecological Models of Organizations.* Cambridge, Mass.: Ballinger.

———. 1997. "Long-Term Evolutionary Change in Organizational Populations: Theory, Models, and Empirical Findings in Industrial Demography." *Industrial and Corporate Change* 6: 119–43.

Carroll, G. R., J. Delacroix, and J. Goodstein. 1988. "The Political Environment of Organizations: An Ecological View." *Research in Organizational Behavior* 10: 359–92.

Carroll, G. R., H. A. Haveman, and A. Swaminathan. 1992. "Careers in Organization: An Ecological Perspective." *Life-Span Development and Behavior* 11: 112–14.

Carroll, G. R., and A. Swaminathan. 1991. "Density Dependent Organizational Evolution in the American Brewing Industry from 1633 to 1988." *Acta Sociologica* 34: 155–75.

———. 2000. "Why the Microbrewery Movement? Organizational Dynamics of Resource Partitioning in the American Brewing Industry After Prohibition." *American Journal of Sociology* 106: 715–62.

Carroll, G. R., and J. Wade. 1991. "Density Dependence in the Organizational Development of the American Brewing Industry Across Different Levels of Analysis." *Social Science Research* 20: 217–302.

Carruthers, B. G., and T. C. Halliday. 1984. *Rescuing Business: The Making of Corporate Bankruptcy Law in England and the United States.* New York: Oxford University Press.

Casey W. L., J. E. Marthinsen, and L. S. Moss. 1983. *Entrepreneurship, Productivity, and the Freedom of Information Act: Protecting Circumstantially Relevant Business Information.* Lexington, Mass.: Lexington Books.

Cerna, M. 1993. "New Performance Measures Will Yield Comparative Data on HMOs." *Hospitals and Health Networks* no. 67, p. 48.

Chang, S. L. 1992. "Causes of Brain Drain and Solutions: The Taiwan Experience." *Studies in Comparative International Development* 27: 27–43.

Chen, J. 1997. "The Legal Process and Political Economy of Telecommunications Reform." *Columbia Law Review* 97: 835–73.

Chesbrough, H. 1998. "The Role of Institutional Environment on Innovation." Working paper, Harvard Business School.

Chicago Tribune. 1990. "Plantation Coffee for New Cup of Joe." November 15, p. 2.

Chrisman, J. J., T. Hynes, and S. Fraser. 1995. "Faculty Entrepreneurship and Economic Development: The Case of the University of Calgary." *Journal of Business Venturing* 19: 267–81.

Christensen, C., F. Suarez, and J. Utterback. 1998. "Strategies for Survival in Fast-Changing Industries." *Management Science* 44: S207–20.

Citizens' Internet Empowerment Coalition (CIEC). 1998. *http://www.ciec.org* (December).

Clark, T., and G. Salaman. 1996. "The Management Guru as Organizational Witchdoctor." *Organization* 3: 85–107.

Clemens, E. S. 1993. "Women's Groups and the Transformation of U.S. Politics, 1892–1920." *American Journal of Sociology* 98: 755–98.

———. 1996. "Organizational Form as Frame: Collective Identity and Political Strategy in the American Labor Movement, 1880–1920." In D. McAdam, J. D. McCarthy, and M. N. Zald, eds., *Comparative Perspectives on Social Movements: Politcal Opportunities, Mobilizing Structures, and Cultural Framings,* 205–26. Cambridge: Cambridge University Press.

Cockburn, I., and R. Henderson. 1996 "Public-Private Interaction in Pharmaceutical Research." *Proceedings of the National Academy of Science of the United States of America* 93: 12725–30.

Cole, R. 1979. *Work, Mobility and Participation: A Comparative Study of American and Japanese Industry.* Berkeley: University of California Press.

———. 1985. *The Macropolitics of Organizational Change: A Comparative Study of American and Japanese Industry.* Berkeley: University of California Press.

———. 1989. *Strategies for Learning: Small Group Activities in American, Japanese, and Swedish Industry.* Berkeley: University of California Press.

Coleman, J. 1974. *Power and Structure of Society.* New York: Norton Books.

———. 1990. *Foundations of Social Theory.* Cambridge, Mass.: Belknap Press of Harvard University Press.

Conell, C., and K. Voss. 1990. "Formal Organization and the Fate of Social Movements: Craft Association and Class Alliance in the Knights of Labor." *American Sociological Review* 55: 255–69.

Cooper, A. C. 1973. "Technical Entrepreneurship: What Do We Know?" *R&D Management* 3: 50–65.

———. 1985. "The Role of Incubator Organizations in the Founding of Growth-Oriented Firms." *Journal of Business Venturing* 1: 75–86.

Cooper, A. C., and W. C. Dunkelberg. 1987. "Entrepreneurial Research: Old Questions, New Answers, and Methodological Issues." *American Journal of Small Business* 11: 11–24.

Cooper, A. C., W. C. Dunkelberg, and C. Y. Woo. 1988a. "Survival and Failure: A Longitudinal Study." In B. Kirchhoff, W. Long, W. E. McMullan, K. Vesper, and W. E. Wetzel, Jr., eds., *Frontiers in Entrepreneurship Research*, 225–37. Wellesley, Mass.: Center for Entrepreneurial Studies, Babson College.

———. 1988b. "Entrepreneurs' Perceived Chances for Success." *Journal of Business Venturing* 2: 97–108.

Cooper, A. C., and F. J. Gimeno-Gascon. 1992. "Entrepreneurs, Processes of Founding, and New-Firm Performance." In D. L. Sexton and J. D. Kasarda, eds., *The State of the Art of Entrepreneurship*, 301–40. Boston: PWS-Kent.

Cooper, A. C., F. J. Gimeno-Gascon, and C. Y. Woo. 1994. "Initial Human Capital as Predictors of New Venture Performance." *Journal of Business Venturing* 9: 371–95.

Cooper, A., and C. Smith. 1992. "How Established Firms Respond to Threatening Technologies." *Academy of Management Executive* 6: 55–70.

Costain, A. W. 1992. *Inviting Women's Rebellion: A Political Process Interpretation of the Women's Movement.* Baltimore: Johns Hopkins University Press.

Creighton, A. L. 1990. "The Emergence of Incorporation as a Legal Form for Organizations." Ph.D. dissertation, Department of Sociology, Stanford University.

Cress, D. M., and D. A. Snow. 1996. "Mobilization at the Margins: Resources, Benefactors, and the Viability of Homeless Social Movement Organizations." *American Sociological Review* 61: 1089–1109.

Cringely, R. X. 1996. *Accidental Empires: How the Boys of Silicon Valley Make Their Millions, Battle Foreign Competition, and Still Can't Get a Date.* New York: HarperCollins.

Cusumano, M., Y. Mylonadis, and R. Rosenbloom. 1992. "Strategic Maneuvering and Mass Market Dynamics: The Triumph of VHS over Beta." *Business History Review* 66: 51–94.

Dasgupta, P., and P. A. David. 1994. "Toward a New Economics of Science." *Research Policy* 23: 487–521.

Daunt, J. A. 1989. *Venture Capital Strategies for High Technology Companies.* Palo Alto, Calif.: Fenwick, Davis and West.

David, P. A. 1985. "Clio and the Economics of QWERTY." *American Economic Review* 75: 332–37.

Davis, G. F., and T. A. Thompson. 1994. "A Social Movement Perspective on Corporate Control." *Administrative Science Quarterly* 39: 141–73.

Davis, S. J., and J. C. Haltiwanger. 1994. "Small Business and Job Creation: Dissecting the Myth and Reassessing Facts." *Business Economics* 29: 13–21.

Davis, S. J., J. C. Haltiwanger, and S. Schuh. 1996. *Job Creation and Destruction.* Cambridge, Mass.: MIT Press.

Dedrick, J., and K. L. Kraemer. 1998. *Asia's Computer Challenge: Threat or Opportunity for the United States and the World.* New York: Oxford University Press.

Degli Ottati, G. 1994. "Competition and Cooperation in the Industrial District as an Organizational Model." *European Planning Studies* 2: 463–83.

Delacroix, J., and H. Rao. 1994. "Externalities and Ecological Theory: Unbundling Density Dependence." In J. A. C. Baum and J. V. Singh, eds., *Evolutionary Dynamics of Organizations*, 255–68. New York: Oxford University Press.

Delacroix, J., and M. E. Solt. 1988. "Niche Formation and Foundings in the California Wine Industry, 1941–84." In G. R. Carroll, ed., *Ecological Models of Organizations*, 53–70. Cambridge, Mass.: Ballinger.

Delacroix, J., A. Swaminathan, and M. Solt. 1989. "Density Dependence Versus Population Dynamics: An Ecological Study of Failings in the California Wine Industry." *American Sociological Review* 54: 245–62.

Delaney, K. J. 1989. "Power, Intercorporate Networks, and Strategic Bankruptcy." *Law and Society Review* 23: 643–66.

DeNoble, A., and C. Galbraith. 1992. "Competitive Strategy and High Technology Regional/Site Location Decisions: A Cross-Country Study of Mexican and U.S. Electronic Component Firms." *Journal of High Technology Management Research* 3: 19–37.

Denzin, N. K., and Y. S. Lincoln, eds. 1999. *Collecting and Interpreting Qualitative Materials.* Thousand Oaks, Calif.: Sage Publications.

DiMaggio, P. J. 1988. "Interest and Agency in Institutional Theory." In L. G. Zucker, ed., *Institutional Patterns and Organizations: Culture and Environment*, 3–21. Cambridge, Mass.: Ballinger.

———. 1991. "Constructing an Organizational Field as a Professional Project: U.S. Art Museums, 1920–1940." In W. W. Powell and P. J. DiMaggio, eds., *The New Institutionalism in Organizational Analysis*, 267–92. Chicago: University of Chicago Press.

———. 1997. "Culture and Cognition." *Annual Review of Sociology* 23: 263–87.

DiMaggio, P. J., and W. W. Powell. 1983. "The Iron Cage Revisited: Institutional Isomorphism and Collective Rationality in Organizational Fields." *American Sociological Review* 48: 147–60.

———. 1991. "Introduction." In W. W. Powell and P. J. DiMaggio, eds., *The New Institutionalism in Organizational Analysis*, 1–40. Chicago: University of Chicago Press.

Dobbin, F. R., J. R. Sutton, J. W. Meyer, and W. R. Scott. 1993. "Equal Opportunity Law and the Construction of Internal Labor Markets." *American Journal of Sociology* 99: 396–427.

Dollinger, M. J. 1985. "Environmental Contacts and Financial Performance of the Small Firm." *Journal of Small Business Management* 23: 24–30.

Dosi, G. 1980. "Technological Paradigms and Technological Trajectories." *Research Policy* 11: 147–62.

———. 1988. "Sources, Procedures, and Microeconomic Effects of Innovation." *Journal of Economic Literature* 26: 1120–71.

Douglas, M. 1986. *How Institutions Think.* Syracuse, N.Y.: Syracuse University Press.

Doutriaux, J., and F. Simyar. 1987. "Duration of the Comparative Advantage Accruing from Some Start-up Factors in High-Tech Entrepreneurial Firms." In N. Churchill, J. Hornaday, B. Kirchhoff, O. Krasner, and K. Vesper, eds., *Frontiers in Entrepreneurship Research*, 436–51. Wellesley, Mass.: Center for Entrepreneurial Studies, Babson College.

Drazin, R., and L. Sandelands. 1992. "Autogenesis: A Perspective on the Process of Organizing." *Organization Science* 3: 230–49.

Drucker, P. 1993. *Innovation and Entrepreneurship: Practice and Principles.* New York: Harper-Business.

Duchesneau, D. A., and W. B. Gartner. 1988. "A Profile of New Venture Success and Failure in an Emerging Industry." In B. Kirchhoff, W. Long, W. E. McMullan, K. Vesper, and W. E. Wetzel, Jr., eds., *Frontiers in Entrepreneurship Research*, 372–86. Wellesley, Mass.: Center for Entrepreneurial Studies, Babson College.

Dunkelberg, W. C., A. C. Cooper, C. Y. Woo, and W. Dennis. 1987. "New Firm Growth and Performance." In N. Churchill, J. Hornaday, B. Kirchhoff, O. Krasner, and K. Vesper, eds., *Frontiers in Entrepreneurship Research*, 307–21. Wellesley, Mass.: Center for Entrepreneurial Studies, Babson College.

Edelman, L. B. 1992. "Legal Ambiguity and Symbolic Structures: Organizational Mediation of Law." *American Journal of Sociology* 97: 1531–76.

Edelman, L. B., and M. C. Suchman. 1997. "The Legal Environments of Organizations." *Annual Review of Sociology* 23: 479–515.

———. 1998. "When the 'Haves' Hold Court: The Internalization of Law in Organizational Fields." Paper presented at the University of Wisconsin Institute for Legal Studies Conference on the Twenty-Fifth Anniversary of Marc Galanter's "Why the 'Haves' Come Out Ahead: Speculations on the Limits of Legal Change." Madison, Wisc.

Edwards, B., and S. Marullo. 1995. "Organizational Mortality in a Declining Social Movement: The Demise of Peace Movement Organizations in the End of the Cold War Era." *American Sociological Review* 60: 908–27.

Edwards, R. C. 1979. *Contested Terrain: The Transformation of the Workplace in the Twentieth Century.* New York: Basic Books.

Eisenhardt, K. M. 1989. "Building Theories from Case Study Research." *Academy of Management Review* 14: 532–50.

Eisenhardt, K. M., and C. B. Schoonhoven. 1990. "Organizational Growth: Linking Founding Team, Strategy, Environment, and Growth Among U.S. Semiconductor Ventures, 1978–1988." *Administrative Science Quarterly* 35: 504–29.

Epstein, R. C. 1928. *The Automobile Industry: Its Economic and Commercial Development.* Chicago: A.W. Shaw and Co.

Farley, M. 1992. "Matching Investors with Inventions at MIT." *Boston Globe*, August 16, p. 65.

Farrell, K. 1984. "Competition: Using Freedom of Information." *Venture* 6: 39–40.

Fernandez, M. 1998. "Asian Indian Americans in the Bay Area and the Glass Ceiling." *Sociological Perspectives* 42: 119–49.

Fetterman, D. M. 1989. *Ethnography Step by Step.* Newbury Park, Calif.: Sage.

Finkelstein, S., and D. C. Hambrick. 1996. *Strategic Leadership: Top Executives and Their Effect on Organizations.* St. Paul, Minn.: West.

Fligstein, N. 1987. "The Intraorganizational Power Struggle: The Rise of Finance Presidents in Large Corporations." *American Sociological Review* 52: 44–58.

————. 1990. *The Transformation of Corporate Control.* Cambridge, Mass.: Harvard University Press.

————. 1996. "Markets as Politics: A Political Cultural Approach to Market Institutions." *American Sociological Review* 61: 656–73.

Flink, J. J. 1970. *America Adopts the Automobile, 1895–1910.* Cambridge, Mass.: MIT Press.

————. 1988. *The Automobile Age.* Cambridge, Mass.: MIT Press.

Florida, R., and D. F. Smith. 1990. "Venture Capital, Innovation, and Economic Development." *Economic Development Quarterly* 4: 345–60.

Fombrun, C. J. 1986. "Structural Dynamics Within and Between Organizations." *Administrative Science Quarterly* 31: 403–21.

————. 1988. "Crafting an Institutionally Informed Ecology of Organizations." In G. R. Carroll, ed., *Ecological Models of Organizations*, 223–39. Cambridge, Mass.: Ballinger.

Fortune. 1994. "The Geography of an Emerging America." June 27, pp. 88–94.

Foster, R. 1986. *Innovation: The Attacker's Advantage.* New York: Summit Books.

Frear, J., and W. E. Wetzel, Jr. 1989. "Equity Capital for Investors." In R. H. Brockhaus, Sr., N. C. Churchill, J. A. Katz, B. A. Kirchhoff, K. H. Vesper, and W. E. Wetzel, Jr., eds., *Frontiers in Entrepreneurship Research*, 230–44. Wellesley, Mass.: Center for Entrepreneurial Studies, Babson College.

————. 1990. "Who Bankrolls High-Tech Entrepreneurs?" *Journal of Business Venturing* 5: 77–89.

————. 1992. "The Informal Venture Capital Market in the 1990s." In D. L. Sexton and J. D. Kasarda, eds., *The State of the Art of Entrepreneurship*, 463–86. Boston: PWS-Kent.

Freeman, J. 1982. "Organizational Life Cycles and Natural Selection Processes." In B. Staw and L. L. Cummings, eds., *Research in Organizational Behavior*, 4: 1–34. Greenwich, Conn.: JAI Press.

————. 1986. "Entrepreneurs as Organizational Products: Semiconductor Firms and Venture Capital Firms." In G. Libecap, ed., *Advances in the Study of Entrepreneurship, Innovation, and Economic Growth.* Greenwich, Conn.: JAI Press.

Freeman, J., G. R. Carroll, and M. T. Hannan. 1983. "The Liability of Newness: Age Dependence in Organizational Death Rates." *American Sociological Review* 48: 692–710.

Frenzen, J., P. Hirsch, and P. Zerillo. 1994. "Consumption, Preferences, and Changing Lifestyle." In N. Smelser and R. Swedberg, eds., *Handbook of Economic Sociology*, 403–25. New York: Russell Sage Foundation.

Friedman, D. 1988. *The Misunderstood Miracle.* Ithaca, N.Y.: Cornell University Press.

Friedman, D., and D. McAdam. 1992. "Collective Identity and Activism: Networks, Choices, and the Life of a Social Movement." In A. D. Morris and C. M. Mueller, eds., *Frontiers in Social Movement Theory*, 156–73. New Haven, Conn.: Yale University Press.

Friedman, L. M., R. W. Gordon, S. Pirie, and E. Whatley. 1989. "Law, Lawyers, and Legal Practice in Silicon Valley: A Preliminary Report." *Indiana Law Journal* 64: 555–67.

Gabel, P. 1980. "Reification in Legal Reasoning." *Research in Law and Sociology* 3: 25–51.

Gage, D. 1999. "Java Lobby Declares War on Microsoft." *http://www.zdnet.com/eweek/news/0309/11ajava.html.*

Galanter M. 1974. "Why the 'Haves' Come Out Ahead: Speculations on the Limits of Legal Change." *Law and Society Review* 9: 95–160.

————. 1983. "Reading the Landscape of Disputes: What We Know and Don't Know (and Think We Know) About Our Allegedly Contentious and Litigious Society." *UCLA Law Review* 31: 4–84.

Galbraith, C., and A. F. De Noble. 1988. "Location Decisions by High Tech Firms." *Entrepreneurship, Theory and Practice* 13: 31–47.

Galbraith, J. 1980. "Applying Theory to the Management of Organizations." In W. Evans, ed., *Frontiers in Organizations and Management*, 151–67. New York: Praeger.

Gamson, W. A. 1990. *The Strategy of Social Protest.* Belmont, Calif.: Wadsworth Publishing Co.

Gartner, W. B. 1985. "A Conceptual Framework for Describing the Phenomenon of New Venture Creation." *Academy of Management Review* 10: 696–706.

————. 1988. " 'Who Is an Entrepreneur?' Is the Wrong Question." *American Journal of Small Business* 12: 11–32.

Garud, R., and M. Rappa. 1994. "A Sociocognitive Model of Technological Evolution." *Organization Science* 5: 344–62.

Garud, R., and A. H. Van de Ven. 1989. "Innovation and the Emergence of Industries." In A. H. Van de Ven, H. Angle, and M. S. Poole, eds., *Research on the Management of Innovations*, 489–532. Cambridge, Mass.: Ballinger.

Geertz, C. 1963. *Peddlers and Princes.* Chicago: University of Chicago Press.

Geisler, E. 1993. "Middle Managers as Internal Corporate Entrepreneurs: An Unfolding Agenda." *Interfaces* 23: 52–63.

Gendron, G. 1995. "Small Is Beautiful! Big Is Best!" *Inc.* 17: 39–45.

Geranios, N. K. 1992. "Growth in Specialty Coffee, Not Just Beans." *Chicago Tribune*, December 20, p. 10C.

Ghosh, S. 1998. "Making Business Sense of the Internet." *Harvard Business Review* 76: 126–35.

Gill, J., and S. Whittle. 1993. "Management by Panacea: Accounting for Transience." *Journal of Management Studies* 30: 281–95.

Gilson, R. J. 1984. "Value Creation by Business Lawyers: Legal Skills and Asset Pricing." *Yale Law Journal* 94: 239–313.

Gilson, R. J., and R. H. Kraakman. 1984. "The Mechanisms of Market Efficiency." *Virginia Law Review* 70: 549–643.

Ginsberg, A. 1995. "Minding the Competition: From Mapping to Mastery." *Strategic Management Journal* 15: 153–74.

Ginsberg, A., E. R. Larsen, and A. Lomi. 1997. "Generating Strategy from Individual Behavior: A Model of Structural Embeddedness." In J. A. C. Baum and J. Dutton, eds., *Advances in Strategic Management: The Embeddedness of Strategy*, 13: 121–47. Greenwich, Conn.: JAI Press.

Glaeser, E. L., H. D. Kallal, J. A. Schenkman, and A. Shleifer. 1992. "Growth in Cities." *Journal of Political Economy* 100: 1126–52.

Glaser, J., and A. Strauss. 1967. *The Discovery of Grounded Theory.* Chicago: Aldine Publishing Co.

Glassmeier, A. 1991. "Technological Discontinuities and Flexible Production Networks: The Case of Switzerland and the World Watch Industry." *Research Policy* 20: 469–85.

Gong, Margie. 1996. "A Forward Look Towards the Origin of AAMA—Part 1." Asian American Manufacturing Association, *AAMA News*, October 1996.

Gordon, R. W. 1984. "Critical Legal Histories." *Stanford Law Review* 36: 57–125.

Gould, R. 1993. "Collective Action and Network Structure." *American Sociological Review* 58: 182–96.

Granovetter, M. 1995. "The Economic Sociology of Firms and Entrepreneurs." In A. Portes, ed., *The Economic Sociology of Immigration: Essays on Networks, Ethnicity, and Entrepreneurship*, 128–65. New York: Russell Sage Foundation.

Guillen, M. F. 1994. *Models of Management: Work, Authority, and Organization in a Comparative Perspective*. Chicago: University of Chicago Press.

Gutowitz, H. 1991. *Cellular Automata: Theory and Experiment*. Cambridge, Mass.: MIT Press.

Halliday, T., M. J. Powell, and M. W. Granfors. 1987. "Minimalist Organizations: Vital Events in State Bar Associations, 1870–1930." *American Sociological Review* 52: 456–71.

Han, S. 1994. "Mimetic Isomorphism and Its Effect on the Audit Services Market." *Social Forces* 73: 637–63.

Hannan, M. T. 1986. "Ecological Theory: General Discussion." In S. Lindenberg, J. S. Coleman, and S. Nowak, eds., *Approaches to Social Theory*. New York, N.Y.: Russell Sage Foundation.

———. 1988. "Social Change, Organizational Diversity, and Individual Careers." In M. Riley, ed., *Social Change and the Life Course*, 161–74. Newbury Park, Calif.: Sage.

Hannan, M. T., M. D. Burton, and J. N. Baron. 1996. "Inertia and Change in the Early Years: Employment Relations in Young, High-Technology Firms." *Industrial and Corporate Change* 5: 503–36.

Hannan, M. T., and G. R. Carroll. 1992. *Dynamics of Organizational Populations: Density, Legitimation, and Competition*. New York: Oxford University Press.

———. 1995. "Theory Building and Cheap Talk About Legitimation: Reply to Baum and Powell." *American Sociological Review* 60: 539–44.

Hannan, M. T., G. R. Carroll, E. A. Dundon, and J. C. Torres. 1995. "Organizational Evolution in a Multinational Context: Entries of Automobile Manufacturers in Belgium, Britain, France, Germany, and Italy." *American Sociological Review* 60: 509–29.

Hannan, M. T., and J. Freeman. 1977. "The Population Ecology of Organizations." *American Journal of Sociology* 82: 929–64.

———. 1984. "Structural Inertia and Organizational Change." *American Sociological Review* 49: 149–64.

———. 1986. "Where Do New Organizational Forms Come From?" *Sociological Forum* 1: 50–72.

———. 1987. "The Ecology of Organizational Founding: American Labor Unions, 1836–1985." *American Journal of Sociology* 92: 910–43.

———. 1989. *Organizational Ecology*. Cambridge, Mass.: Harvard University Press.

Harrison, B. 1994. "The Myth of Small Firms as the Predominant Job Generators." *Economic Development Quarterly* 8: 3–18.

Harrison, L. 1993. "Starbucks' Caffeine Rush—Firm's Aim: Underpromise, Overdeliver." *Seattle Times*, p. D1.

Haunschild, P. 1994. "How Much Is that Company Worth? Interorganizational Relationships, Uncertainty, and Acquisition Premiums." *Administrative Science Quarterly* 39: 391–411.

Haunschild, P., and A. S. Miner. 1997. "Modes of Interorganizational Imitation: The Effects of Outcome Salience and Uncertainty." *Administrative Science Quarterly* 42: 472–99.

Haveman, H. A. 1993. "Organizational Size and Change: Diversification in the Savings and Loan Industry after Deregulation." *Administrative Science Quarterly* 38: 20–50.

Haveman, H. A., and H. Rao. 1997. "Structuring a Theory of Moral Sentiments: Institutional and Organizational Coevolution in the Early Thrift Industry." *American Journal of Sociology* 102: 1606–51.

Hawley, A. H. 1986. *Human Ecology: A Theoretical Essay.* Chicago: University of Chicago Press.

Hayden, R. M. 1991. "The Cultural Logic of a Political Crisis: Common Sense, Hegemony, and the Great American Liability Insurance Famine of 1986." *Studies in Law, Politics, and Society* 11: 95–117.

Hebert, R. F., and A. N. Link. 1988. *The Entrepreneur: Mainstream Views and Radical Critiques.* New York: Praeger.

Heeks, R. 1996. *India's Software Industry: State Policy, Liberalisation and Industrial Development.* New Delhi: Sage.

Henderson, R. 1995. "Of Life Cycles Real and Imaginary: The Unexpectedly Long Old Age of Optical Lithography." *Research Policy* 24: 631–43.

Henderson, R., and K. Clark. 1990. "Architectural Innovation: The Reconfiguration of Existing Product Technologies and the Failure of Existing Firms." *Administrative Science Quarterly* 35: 9–30.

Henderson, R., and I. Cockburn. 1994. "Measuring Competence? Exploring Firm Effects in Pharmaceutical Research." *Strategic Management Journal* 15: 63–84.

Herrigel, G. 1996. *Industrial Constructions.* New York: Cambridge University Press.

Hewitt, J. P. 1994. *Self and Society.* Boston: Allyn and Bacon.

Hidefjall, P. 1997. *The Pace of Innovation: Patterns of Innovation in the Cardiac Pacemaker Industry.* Linkoping University.

Hing, B. O., and R. Lee, eds. 1996. *The State of Asian Pacific America: Reframing the Immigration Debate.* Los Angeles: Leadership Education for Asian Pacifics and UCLA Asian American Studies Center.

Hogeweg, H. 1988. "Cellular Automata as a Paradigm for Ecological Modeling." *Applied Mathematics and Computation* 27: 81–100.

Hsu, J. 1997. *A Late Industrial District? Learning Networks in the Hsinchu Science-Based Industrial Park.* Ph.D. dissertation, University of California at Berkeley.

Huberman, B., and N. Glance. 1993. "Evolutionary Games and Computer Simulations." *Proceedings of the National Academy of Science* 90: 7716–18.

Huczynski, A. 1993. *Management Gurus.* New York: Routledge.

Hunt, C. S., and H. E. Aldrich. 1998. "The Second Ecology: Creation and Evolution of Organizational Communities." In B. M. Staw and L. L. Cummings, eds., *Research in Organizational Behavior,* 20: 267–301. Greenwich, Conn.: JAI Press.

Hunt, S., R. D. Benford, and D. A. Snow. 1994. "Identity Fields: Framing Processes and the

Social Construction of Movement Identities." In E. Larana, H. Johnston, and J. R. Gusfield, eds., *New Social Movements: From Ideology to Identity*, 185–208. Philadelphia: Temple University Press.

Hybels, R. C., A. Ryan, and S. Barley. 1994. "Alliances, Legitimation and Founding Rates in the U.S. Biotechnology Field, 1971–1989." Paper presented at the Academy of Management Conference, Dallas.

Hyde, A. September 1998. "The Wealth of Shared Information: Silicon Valley's High-Velocity Labor Market, Endogenous Economic Growth, and the Law of Trade Secrets." *http://andromeda.rutgers.edu/hyde/WEALTH.htm* (May 25, 1999).

Iansiti, M., and T. Khanna. 1995. "Technological Evolution, System Architecture, and the Obsolescence of Firm Capabilities." *Industrial and Corporate Change* 4: 333–61.

Ingram, P., and T. Simons. 1998. "State Formation, Ideological Competition, and the Ecology of Israeli Workers' Cooperatives, 1920–1992." *Administrative Science Quarterly* 45: 25–53.

Institute for Information Industry, Market Intelligence Center (III-MIC). Tapei, 1997.

Ishikawa, K. 1968. *QC Circles Activities*. Tokyo: Union of Japanese Scientists and Engineers.

Jackson, B. 1996. "Reengineering the Sense of Self: The Manager and the Management Gurus." *Journal of Management Studies* 33: 571–90.

Jacobs, J. 1969. *The Economy of Cities*. New York: Random House.

Jaffe, A. B. 1989. "Real Effects of Academic Research." *American Economic Review* 79: 957–70.

Jaffe, A. B., M. Trajtenberg, and R. Henderson. 1993. "Geographic Localization of Knowledge Spillovers as Evidenced by Patent Citations." *Quarterly Journal of Economics* 108: 577–98.

Jelinek, M., and C. B. Schoonhoven. 1993. *The Innovation Marathon: Lessons from High-Technology Firms*. Oxford: Basil Blackwell.

Jenkins, J. C., and C. Perrow. 1977. "Insurgency of the Powerless: Farm Workers' Movements, 1946–1972." *American Sociological Review* 42: 249–68.

Johnson, J. M. 1998. *Statistical Profiles of Foreign Doctoral Recipients in Science and Engineering: Plans to Stay in the United States*. Arlington, Va.: National Science Foundation, Division of Science Resources Studies, NSF 99–304.

Johnson, J. M., and M. C. Regets. 1998. "International Mobility of Scientists and Engineeers to the United States—Brain Drain or Brain Circulation?" *National Science Foundation Issue Brief*, NSF 98–316.

Jones-Evans, D., F. Steward, K. Balazs, and K. Todorov. 1998. "Public Sector Entrepreneurship in Central and Eastern Europe: A Study of Academic Spin-offs in Bulgaria and Hungary." *Journal of Applied Management Studies* 7: 59–76.

Juran, J. 1967. "The QC Circle Phenomenon." *Industrial Quality Control* 23: 329–36.

Kahn, M. A. 1999. "I. Intellectual Property: D. Trade Secret: 1. Non-Compete Agreements: (a) California Law: Application Group Inc v. Hunter Group Inc." *Berkeley Technical Law Journal* 14: 283–90.

Kahneman, D., P. Slovic, and A. Tversky. 1982. *Judgment Under Uncertainty: Heuristic and Biases*. Cambridge: Cambridge University Press.

Kalakota, R., and A. B. Whinston. 1996. *Frontiers of Electronic Commerce*. Reading, Mass.: Addison-Wesley.

Kaplan, D. A. 1999. *The Silicon Boys and Their Valley of Dreams*. New York: William Morrow.

Karpik, L. 1978. "Organizations, Institutions, and History." In L. Karpik, ed., *Organizations and Environment: Theory, Issues, and Reality*, 15–68. Beverly Hills, Calif.: Sage.

Keenan, D., and M. O'Brien. 1993. "Competition, Collusion and Chaos." *Journal of Economic Dynamics and Control* 17: 327–53.

Kelly, C. 1993. "Group Identification, Intergroup Perceptions and Collective Action." In W. Stroebe and M. Hewstone, eds., *European Review of Social Psychology* 4: 59–83. Chichester, Eng.: Wiley.

Kennedy, D. 1980. "Toward an Historical Understanding of Legal Consciousness: The Case of Classical Legal Thought in America, 1850–1940." *Research in Law and Sociology* 3: 3–24.

Kidder, T. 1981. *The Soul of a New Machine*. Boston: Little, Brown.

Kimberly, J. R., and H. Bouchikhi. 1995. "The Dynamics of Organizational Development and Change: How the Past Shapes the Present and Constrains the Future." *Organization Science* 6: 9–18.

Kimes, B. R. 1985. *Standard Catalogue of Cars, 1805–1942*. Iola, Wisc.: Krause Publications.

Kimes, B. R., and H. A. Clark. 1989. *Standard Catalogue of Cars, 1805–1942*. Iola, Wisc.: Krause Publications.

Kirzner, I. 1973. *Competition and Entrepreneurship*. Chicago: University of Chicago Press.

Klandermans, B. 1997. *The Social Psychology of Protest*. Cambridge, Mass.: Basil Blackwell.

Klofsten, M., and D. Jones-Evans. 1996. "Stimulation of Technology-Based Small Firms—A Case Study of University-Industry Cooperation." *Technovation* 16: 187–93.

Knight, F. H. 1921. *Risk, Uncertainty, and Profit*. Chicago: University of Chicago Press.

Kochan, T. A., H. C. Katz, and R. B. McKersie. 1992. *The Transformation of American Industrial Relations*. Ithaca, N.Y.: Industry and Labor Relations Press.

Krackhardt, D., and L. Porter. 1985. "When Friends Leave: A Structural Analysis of the Relationship Between Turnover and Stayers' Attitudes." *Administrative Science Quarterly* 30: 242–61.

Kriesi, H. 1995. "The Political Opportunity Structure of New Social Movements: Its Impact on Their Mobilization." In J. C. Jenkins and B. Klandermans, eds., *The Politics of Social Protest: Comparative Perspectives on States and Social Movements*, 167–98. Minneapolis: University of Minnesota Press.

Krugman, P. 1991. *Geography and Trade*. Cambridge, Mass.: MIT Press.

———. 1995. *Development, Geography, and Economic Theory*. Cambridge, Mass.: MIT Press.

Kunda, G. 1992. *Engineering Culture: Control and Commitment in a High-Tech Corporation*. Philadelphia: Temple University Press.

Landes, D. 1983. *Revolution in Time*. Cambridge, Mass.: Harvard University Press.

Lant, T., and J. A. C. Baum. 1995. "Cognitive Sources of Socially Constructed Competitive Groups: Examples from the Manhattan Hotel Industry." In W. R. Scott and

S. Christensen, eds., *The Institutional Construction of Organizations*, 15–39. Thousand Oaks, Calif.: Sage Publications.

Lant, T., and C. Phelps. 1999. "A Situated Learning Prospective of Strategic Groups." In A. S. Miner and P. Anderson, eds., *Industry and Population Level Learning.* Greenwich, Conn.: JAI Press.

Latour, B., and S. Woolgar. 1986. *Laboratory Life: The Construction of Scientific Facts.* Princeton, N.J.: Princeton University Press.

Lawler, E., and S. Mohrman. 1985. "Quality Circles After the Fad." *Harvard Business Review* 63: 65–71.

Lawrence, P., and J. G. Lorsch. 1967. *Organizations and Environment.* Cambridge, Mass.: Harvard University Press.

Lazerson, M., and G. Lorenzoni. 1999. "The Firms That Feed Industrial Districts: A Return to the Italian Source." *Industrial and Corporate Change* 8: 235–66.

Leblebici, H., and G. R. Salancik. 1989. "The Rules of Organizing and the Managerial Role." *Organization Studies* 10: 301–25.

Leblebici, H., G. R. Salancik, A. Copay, and T. King. 1991. "Institutional Change and the Transformation of Interorganizational Fields: An Organizational History of the U.S. Radio Broadcasting Industry." *Administrative Science Quarterly* 36: 333–63.

Leifer, E., and H. C. White. 1987. "A Structural Approach to Markets." In M. Mizruchi and M. Schwartz, eds., *Intercorporate Relations: The Structural Analysis of Business*, 85–108. New York: Cambridge University Press.

Levinthal, D. 1990. "Organizational Adaptation: Environmental Selection and Random Walks." In J. Singh, ed., *Organizational Evolution*, 201–33. Newbury Park, Calif.: Sage.

Levinthal, D. A., and J. G. March. 1981. "A Model of Adaptive Organizational Search." *Journal of Economic Behavior and Organization* 2: 307–33.

Levitt, B., and J. G. March. 1988. "Organization Learning." *Annual Review of Sociology* 14: 319–40.

Liang, K. Y., and S. L. Zeeger. 1986. "Longitudinal Data Analysis for Discrete and Continuous Outcomes." *Biometrika* 42: 121–30.

Lieberman, M., and D. Montgomery. 1988. "First-Mover Advantage." *Strategic Management Journal* 11: 35–59.

Light, I. 1972. *Ethnic Enterprise in America.* Berkeley: University of California Press.

Light, I., and E. Bonacich. 1988. *Immigrant Entrepreneurs.* Berkeley: University of California Press.

Lin, O. 1998. "Science and Technology Policy and Its Influence on Economic Development in Taiwan." In H. S. Rowen, ed., *Beyond East Asian Growth: The Political and Social Foundations of Prosperity.* London: Routledge.

Lindgren, C., and M. Nordahl. 1994. "Evolutionary Dynamics of Spatial Games." *Physica D* 75: 292–309.

Link, A. N., and L. L. Bauer. 1989. *Cooperative Research in U.S. Manufacturing: Assessing Policy Initiatives and Corporate Strategies.* Lexington, Mass.: Lexington Books.

Locke, R. 1995. *Remaking the Italian Economy: Policy Failures and Local Successes.* Ithaca, N.Y.: Cornell University Press.

Lomi, A. 1995. "The Population Ecology of Organizational Founding: Location

Dependence and Unobserved Heterogeneity." *Administrative Science Quarterly* 40: 121–44.

Lomi, A., and E. R. Larsen. 1996. "Interacting Locally and Evolving Globally: A Computational Approach to the Dynamics of Organizational Populations." *Academy of Management Journal* 39: 1287–1321.

———. 1999. "Evolutionary Models of Local Interaction: A Computational Perspective." In J. A. C. Baum and B. McKelvey, eds., *Variations in Organizational Science*, 255–78. Newbury Park, Calif.: Sage.

Louis, K. S., D. Blumenthal, M. Gluck, and M. Stoto. 1989. "Entrepreneurs in Academe: An Exploration of Behaviors Among Life Scientists." *Administrative Science Quarterly* 34: 110–31.

Lumsden, C. J., and J. V. Singh. 1990. "The Dynamics of Organizational Speciation." In J. V. Singh, ed., *Organizational Evolution: New Directions*, 145–63. Newbury Park, Calif.: Sage.

Lynn, L. H., and T. J. McKeown. 1988. *Organizing Business: Trade Associations in America and Japan.* Washington, D.C.: American Enterprise Institute for Public Policy Research.

Lyons, D. 1999. "Java in Jeopardy." *Forbes*, January 11. *http://www.forbes.come/99/0111/6301110a.html.*

Macaulay, S. 1963. "Non-contractual Relations in Business: A Preliminary Study." *American Sociological Review* 28: 55–67.

Macmillan, I. C., R. Siegel, and P. N. Subba Narasimha. 1985. "Criteria Used by Venture Capitalists to Evaluate New Venture Proposals." *Journal of Business Venturing* 1: 119–28.

Major, B. 1994. "From Social Inequality to Personal Entitlement: The Role of Social Comparisons, Legitimacy Appraisals, and Group Membership." *Advances in Experimental Social Psychology* 26: 293–355.

Malecki, E. J. 1991. *Technology and Economic Development: The Dynamics of Local, Regional, and National Change.* New York: Wiley.

Manimala, M. J. 1992. "Entrepreneurial Heuristics: A Comparison Between High PI (High Pioneering) and Low PI Ventures." *Journal of Business Venturing* 6: 477–504.

March, J. G. 1988. *Decisions and Organizations.* Oxford: Basil Blackwell.

———. 1993. "The Myopia of Learning." *Strategic Management Journal* 14: 95–112.

March, J. G., and J. P. Olsen. 1976. *Ambiguity and Choice in Organizations.* Bergen, Norway: Universitetsforlaget.

March, J. G., and H. Simon. 1958. *Organizations.* New York: Wiley.

Marshall, A. 1919. *Industry and Trade.* London: Macmillan.

Martin, R., and P. Sunley. 1995. "Paul Krugman's Geographical Economics and Its Implications for Regional Development Theory: A Critical Assessment." *Economic Geography* 70: 259–92.

Masten, S. E. 1991. "A Legal Basis for the Firm." In O. E. Williamson and S. G. Winter, eds., *The Nature of the Firm: Origins, Evolution, and Development*, 196–212. New York: Oxford University Press.

Masuch, M. 1995. "Computer Simulation." In N. Nicholson, ed., *The Dictionary of Organizational Behavior.* London: Basil Blackwell.

Mathews, J. 1997. "A Silicon Valley of the East: Creating Taiwan's Semiconductor Industry." *California Management Review* 39: 26–54.

May, R. M., and M. A. Nowak. 1992. "Evolutionary Games and Spatial Chaos." *Nature*, no. 359, pp. 826–29.

Maynard-Smith, J. 1982. *Evolution and the Theory of Games.* Cambridge: Cambridge University Press.

McAdam, D. 1982. *Political Process and the Development of Black Insurgency, 1930–1970.* Chicago: University of Chicago Press.

———. 1995. "Initiator and Spin-off Movements: Diffusion Processes in Protest Cycles." In M. Traugott, ed., *Repertoires and Cycles of Collective Action,* 217–39. Durham, N.C.: Duke University Press.

———. 1996. "Political Opportunities: Conceptual Origins, Current Problems, Future Directions." In D. McAdam, J. D. McCarthy, and M. N. Zald, eds., *Comparative Perspectives on Social Movements: Political Opportunities, Mobilizing Structures, and Cultural Framings,* 23–40. Cambridge: Cambridge University Press.

McCarthy, J. D. 1987. "Pro-Life and Pro-Choice Mobilization: Infrastructure Deficits and New Technologies." In M. N. Zald and J. D. McCarthy, eds., *Social Movements in an Organizational Society,* 49–66. New Brunswick, N.J.: Transaction Publishers.

McCarthy, J. D., P. Smith, and M. Zald. 1996. "Accessing Public, Media, Electoral and Governmental Agendas: Political Opportunities, Mobilizing Structures, and Cultural Framings." In D. McAdam, J. D. McCarthy, and M. N. Zald, eds., *Comparative Perspectives on Social Movements,* 291–312. New York: Cambridge University Press.

McCarthy, J. D., and M. Wolfson. 1996. "Resource Mobilization by Local Social Movement Organizations: Agency, Strategy, and Organization in the Movement Against Drinking and Driving." *American Sociological Review* 61: 1070–88.

McCarthy, J. D., and M. N. Zald. 1973. *The Trend of Social Movements in America: Professionalization and Resource Mobilization.* Morristown, N.J.: Global Learning Press.

———. 1977. "Resource Mobilization and Social Movements: A Partial Theory." *American Journal of Sociology* 82: 1212–41.

McCarthy, K. F., and G. Vernez. 1997. *Immigration in a Changing Economy: California's Experience.* Santa Monica, Calif.: RAND.

McClelland, D. C. 1961. *The Achieving Society.* Princeton, N.J.: Van Nostrand.

McGuire, M. 1993. "Grounds for Change." *Chicago Tribune,* May 3, p.1.

McKelvey, W. 1982. *Organizational Systematics: Taxonomy, Evolution, Classification.* Berkeley: University of California Press.

McQueen, D. H., and J. T. Wallmark. 1982. "Spin-off Companies from Chalmers University of Technology." *Technovation* 1: 305–15.

———. 1985. "Support for New Ventures at Chalmers University of Technology." In J. A. Hornaday, ed., *Frontiers of Entrepreneurship Research,* 609–20. Wellesley, Mass.: Center for Entrepreneurial Studies, Babson College.

Meeker, M., C. DePuy, and S. McCuen. 1995. *The Internet Report.* New York: Morgan Stanley U.S. Investment Research.

Melecki, E. J. 1985. "Industrial Location and Corporate Organization in High-Tech Industries." *Economic Geography* 61: 345–69.

Melucci, A. 1989. *Nomads of the Present: Social Movements and Individual Needs in Contemporary Society.* Philadelphia: Temple University Press.

Merton, R. K. 1957 [1940]. *Social Theory and Social Structure.* Glencoe, Ill.: Free Press.

Methé, D., A. Swaminathan, and W. Mitchell. 1996. "The Underemphasized Role of Established Firms as Sources of Major Innovations." *Industrial and Corporate Change* 5: 1181–1204.

Meyer, D. S. 1993. "Peace Protest and Policy: Explaining the Rise and Decline of Antinuclear Movements in Postwar America." *Policy Studies Journal* 21: 29–51.

Meyer, D. S., and S. Staggenborg. 1996. "Movements, Countermovements, and the Structure of Political Opportunity." *American Journal of Sociology* 101: 1628–60.

Meyer, D. S., and N. Whittier. 1994. "Social Movement Spillover: The Effects of the Women's Movement on the Peace Movement." *Social Problems* 41: 277–98.

Meyer, J. W., and B. Rowan. 1977. "Institutionalized Organizations: Formal Structure as Myth and Ceremony." *American Journal of Sociology* 83: 340–63.

Meyer, J. W., and W. R. Scott. 1983. *Organizational Environments: Ritual and Rationality.* Beverly Hills, Calif.: Sage.

Meyer, M. 1994. "Measuring Performance in Economic Organizations." In N. Smelser and R. Swedberg, eds., *Handbook of Economic Sociology,* 556–78. Princeton, N.J.: Princeton University Press.

Mezias, S., and T. Lant. 1994. "Mimetic Learning and the Evolution of Organizational Populations." In J. A. C. Baum and J. V. Singh, eds., *Evolutionary Dynamics of Organizations,* 179–98. New York: Oxford University Press.

Mian, S. A. 1996. "Assessing Value-Added Contributions of University Technology Business Incubators to Tenant Firms." *Research Policy* 25: 325–35.

Michels, R. 1962. *Political Parties.* New York: Free Press.

Micklethwait, J., and A. Wooldridge. 1996. *The Witch Doctors: Making Sense of the Management Gurus.* New York: Times Books.

Miles, M., and A. M. Huberman. 1984. *Qualitative Data Analysis: A Sourcebook of New Methods.* Beverly Hills, Calif.: Sage.

Miles, S. 1998. "Do You Know Tony Podesta?" *Wired Magazine,* December, pp. 80–89.

Miller, M. 1997. "Venture Forth." *Far Eastern Economic Review* 161: 62–63.

Miller, R., M. Hobday, T. Leroux-Demers, and X. Olleros. 1995. "Innovation in Complex System Industries: The Case of Flight Simulation." *Industrial and Corporate Change* 4: 363–400.

Miner, A. S. 1993. "Review of Dynamics of Organizational Populations: Density, Competition, and Legitimation." *Academy of Management Review* 18: 355–67.

Miner, A. S., and P. Anderson. 1999. "Interorganizational and Population-Level Learning: Implications for Strategic Management." In J. A. C. Baum, A. S. Miner, and P. Anderson, eds., *Advances in Strategic Management: Population-Level Learning and Industry Change.* Greenwich, Conn.: JAI Press.

Miner, A. S., and P. Haunschild. 1995. "Population Level Learning." In B. Staw and L. L. Cummings, eds., *Research in Organizational Behavior,* 17: 115–66. Greenwich, Conn.: JAI Press.

Miner, A. S., and I. Holzinger. 1998. "The Fountain of Eternal Growth: Interorganizational

Observation as a Source of Variation." WAGE presentation, University of Wisconsin, Madison.

Miner, A. S., J. Y. Kim, I. Holzinger, and P. R. Haunschild. 1999. "Fruits of Failure: Organizational Failure and Population-Level Learning." In J. A. C. Baum, A. S. Miner, and P. Anderson, eds., *Advances in Strategic Management: Population-Level Learning and Industry Change*. Greenwich, Conn.: JAI Press.

Miner, A. S., and S. Raghavan. 1999. "Interorganizational Imitation: A Hidden Engine of Selection." In J. A. C. Baum and B. McKelvey, eds., *Variations in Organization Science: In Honor of Donald T. Campbell*, 35–62. Newbury Park, Calif.: Sage.

Minkoff, D. C. 1997. "The Sequencing of Social Movements." *American Sociological Review* 62: 779–99.

Mintzberg, H. 1978. "Patterns in Strategy Formation." *Management Science* 24: 934–48.

Mitchell, W. 1989. "Using Academic Teaching: Transfer Methods and Licensing Incidence in the Commercialization of American Diagnostic Imaging Equipment Research, 1954–1988." *Research Policy* 20: 203–16.

Mnookin, R. H., and L. Kornhauser. 1979. "Bargaining in the Shadow of the Law: The Case of Divorce." *Yale Law Review* 88: 950–97.

Morris, A. D. 1992. "Political Consciousness and Collective Action." In A. D. Morris and C. M. Mueller, eds., *Frontiers in Social Movement Theory*, 351–73. New Haven, Conn.: Yale University Press.

Mowery, D. C. 1990. "The Development of Industrial Research in U.S. Manufacturing." *American Economic Review* 80: 345–49.

———. 1999. "The Computer Software Industry." In D. C. Mowery and R. R. Nelson, eds., *Sources of Industrial Leadership: Studies of Seven Industries*, 133–68. New York: Cambridge University Press.

Murmann, J. P. 1998. "Knowledge and Competitive Advantage in the Synthetic Dye Industry, 1850–1914: The Coevolution of Firms, Technology, and National Institutions in Great Britain, Germany, and the United States." Ph.D. dissertation, Graduate School of Arts and Sciences, Columbia University, New York.

Murmann, J. P., and R. Landau. 1998. "On the Making of Competitive Advantage: The Development of the Chemical Industries in Britain and Germany Since 1850." In A. Arora, R. Landau, and N. Rosenberg, eds., *Chemicals and Long-Term Economic Growth: Insights from the Chemical Industry*, 27–70. New York: John Wiley and Sons.

Nadler, D., and M. Tushman. 1997. *Competing by Design*. Oxford: Oxford University Press.

Naughton, B., ed. 1997. *The China Circle: Economics and Technology in the PRC, Taiwan, and Hong Kong*. Washington, D.C.: Brookings Institution Press.

Nelson, R. R., ed. 1993. *National Innovation Systems*. New York: Oxford University Press.

———. 1994. "Evolutionary Theorizing About Economic Change." In N. Smelser and R. Swedberg, eds., *Handbook of Economic Sociology*, 108–36. Princeton: Princeton University Press.

Nisbett, R., and L. Ross. 1980. *Human Inference: Strategies and Shortcomings of Social Judgment*. Englewood Cliffs, N.J.: Prentice-Hall.

Nohria, N. 1992. "Information and Search in the Creation of New Business Ventures: The Case of the 128 Venture Group." In N. Nohria and R. J. Eccles, eds., *Networks and Orga-*

nizations: Structure, Form, and Action, 240–61. Cambridge, Mass.: Harvard University Press.

Oberschall, A. 1973. *Social Conflict and Social Movements.* Englewood Cliffs, N.J.: Prentice-Hall.

Odorici, V., and A. Lomi. 2000. "Classifying Competition: An Empirical Study on the Cognitive Social Structure of Strategic Groups." In Z. Shapira and T. Lant, eds., *Managerial and Organizational Cognition*, 273–304. Mahwah, N.J.: Lawrence Erlbaum.

Olson, M., Jr. 1965. *The Logic of Collective Action.* Cambridge, Mass.: Harvard University Press.

Packard, N., and S. Wolfram. 1985. "Two-dimensional Cellular Automata." *Journal of Statistical Physics* 38: 901–46.

Padgett, J. F., and C. K. Ansell. 1993. "Robust Action and the Rise of the Medici, 1400–1434." *American Journal of Sociology* 98: 1259–1319.

Parthasarathy, B. 1999. "The Indian Software Industry in Bangalore." Ph.D. dissertation, University of California at Berkeley.

Pearce, K. 1982. "Pro-Choice Organizational Structure, 1973–1980." Manuscript. Department of Sociology, Catholic University, Washington, D.C.

Péli, G., and B. Nooteboom. 1999. "Market Partitioning and the Geometry of Resource Space." *American Journal of Sociology* 104: 1132–53.

Pennings, J. M. 1982. "Organizational Birth Frequencies: An Empirical Investigation." *Administrative Science Quarterly* 27: 120–44.

Perrow, C. 1992. "Small-Firm Networks." In N. Nohria and R. J. Eccles, eds., *Networks and Organizations: Structure, Form, and Action*, 445–70. Boston: Harvard Business School Press.

Peterson, R. A. 1980. "Entrepreneurship and Organization." In P. C. Nystrom and W. H. Starbuck, eds., *Handbook of Organization Design*, 65–83. New York: Oxford University Press.

Pettigrew, A. 1979. "On Studying Organizational Culture." *Administrative Science Quarterly* 24: 570–81.

Pfeffer, J. 1994. *Competitive Advantage Through People: Unleashing the Power of the Work Force.* Boston: Harvard Business School Press.

Pfeffer, J., and G. Salancik. 1978. *The External Control of Organizations: A Resource Dependence Perspective.* New York: Harper and Row.

Phillips, A. 1960. "A Theory of Interfirm Organization." *Quarterly Journal of Economics* 74: 602–13.

Piore, M., and C. Sabel. 1984. *The Second Industrial Divide.* New York: Basic Books.

Podolny, J. M. 1994. "Market Uncertainty and the Social Character of Economic Exchange." *Administrative Science Quarterly* 39: 458–83.

Polos, L., M. T. Hannan, G. R. Carroll, and G. Peli. 1998. "Forms and Identities (On the Structure of Organizational Forms)." Manuscript. University of Amsterdam.

Porac, J., and H. Thomas. 1990. "Taxonomic Mental Models in Competitor Definition." *Academy of Management Review* 15: 224–40.

Porac, J., H. Thomas, and C. Baden-Fuller. 1989. "Competitive Groups as Cognitive Communities: The Case of the Scottish Knitwear Industry." *Journal of Management Studies* 26: 397–416.

Porac, J., H. Thomas, F. Wilson, D. Paton, and A. Kanfer. 1995. "Rivalry and the Industry Model of Scottish Knitwear Producers." *Administrative Science Quarterly* 40: 203–27.

Porter, M. E. 1990. *The Competitive Advantage of Nations.* New York: Free Press.

———. 1998. "Clusters and the New Economics of Competition." *Harvard Business Review* 76: 77–90.

Portes, A., ed. 1995. *The Economic Sociology of Immigration: Essays on Networks, Ethnicity and Entrepreneurship.* New York: Russell Sage Foundation.

Powell, M. J. 1993. "Professional Innovation: Corporate Lawyers and Private Lawmaking." *Law and Social Inquiry* 18: 423–52.

Powell, W. W. 1990. "Neither Market nor Hierarchy: Network Forms of Organizations." In L. L. Cummings and B. M. Staw, eds., *Research in Organizational Behavior* 12: 295–336. Greenwich, Conn.: JAI Press.

Powell, W. W., and P. Brantley. 1991. "Competitive Cooperation in Biotechnology: Learning Through Networks." In N. Nohria and R. Eccles, eds., *Networks and Organizations*, 336–94. Boston: Harvard Business School Press.

Powell, W. W., and P. J. DiMaggio, eds. 1991. *The New Institutionalism in Organizational Analysis.* Chicago: University of Chicago Press.

Powell, W. W., K. W. Koput, and L. Smith-Doerr. 1996. "Interorganizational Collaboration and the Locus of Innovation: Networks of Learning in Biotechnology." *Administrative Science Quarterly* 41: 116–45.

Press, E., and J. Washburn. 2000. "The Kept University." *Atlantic Monthly*, March, pp. 39–54.

Pyke, F., and W. Sengenberger. 1992. *Industrial Districts and Local Economic Regeneration.* Geneva: International Institute for Labor Studies.

Quick, R. 1998. "Gawkers or Shoppers? Selling Bras on the Web." *Wall Street Journal*, December 29, p. B1.

Rae, J. B. 1959. *American Auto Manufacturers: The First Forty Years.* Philadelphia: Chilton.

Ragin, C. C. 1987. *The Comparative Method: Moving Beyond Qualitative and Quantitative Strategies.* Berkeley: University of California Press.

Rao, H. 1994. "The Social Construction of Reputation: Certification Contests, Legitimation, and the Survival of Organizations in the American Automobile Industry, 1895–1912." *Strategic Management Journal* 15: 29–44.

———. 1998. "Caveat Emptor: The Construction of Non-Profit Consumer Watchdog Organizations." *American Journal of Sociology* 103: 912–61.

Rao, H., and J. V. Singh. 1999. "Sources of Variation in Organizational Populations: The Speciation of New Organizational Forms." In J. A. C. Baum and B. McKelvey, eds., *Variations in Organization Science.* Newbury Park, Calif.: Sage.

Rauch, J. E. 1993. "Productivity Gains from Geographic Concentration of Human Capital: Evidence from the Cities." *Journal of Urban Economics* 34: 380–400.

Reese, J. 1996. "Starbucks: Inside the Coffee Cult." *Fortune*, December 9, p. 190.

Reitan, B. 1997. "Fostering Technical Entrepreneurship in Research Communities: Granting Scholarships to Would-Be Entrepreneurs." *Technovation* 17: 287–96.

Reynolds, P. D. 1991. "Sociology and Entrepreneurship: Concepts and Contributions." *Entrepreneurship Theory and Practice* 16: 47–69.

———. 1994. "Reducing Barriers to Understanding New Firm Gestation: Prevalence and Success of Nascent Entrepreneurs." Paper presented at the annual meeting of the Academy of Management, Dallas.

Reynolds, P. D., B. Miller, and W. R. Maki. 1995. "Explaining Regional Variation in Business Births and Deaths: U.S., 1976–88." *Small Business Economics* 7: 389–407.

Reynolds, P. D., and S. B. White. 1997. *The Entrepreneurial Process: Economic Growth, Men, Women, and Minorities.* Westport, Conn.: Quorum Books.

Rindova, V. 1998. "Competing for the Mind: Corporate Communications and Observers' Interpretations of Specialty Coffee Chains." Ph.D. dissertation, Stern School of Business, New York University.

Rindova, V., and C. J. Fombrun. 1999. "Constructing Competitive Advantage: The Role of Firm-Constituent Interactions." *Strategic Management Journal* 20: 691–710.

Roberts, E. B. 1991. "The Technological Base of the New Enterprise." *Research Policy* 20: 283–98.

Roberts, E. B., and D. H. Peters. 1981. "Commercial Innovation from University Faculty." *Research Policy* 10: 108–26.

Rogers, E. M. 1986. "The Role of the Research University in the Spin-off of High-Technology Companies." *Technovation* 4: 169–81.

———. 1995. *Diffusion of Innovations.* New York.

Rogers, E. M., and J. K. Larsen. 1984. *Silicon Valley Fever: Growth of High Technology Culture.* New York: Basic Books.

Romanelli, E. 1985. Performance and Persistence of New Firm Strategies in Organizational Evolution: The Case of Minicomputers. Ph.D. dissertation, Columbia University.

———. 1989a. "Environments and Strategies of Organization Start-up: Effects on Early Survival." *Administrative Science Quarterly* 34: 369–87.

———. 1989b. "Organization Birth and Population Variety: A Community Perspective on Origins." In B. M. Staw and L. L. Cummings, eds., *Research in Organizational Behavior* 11: 211–46. Greenwich, Conn.: JAI Press.

———. 1991. "The Evolution of New Organizational Forms." *Annual Review of Sociology* 17: 79–103.

Romanelli, E., and M. L. Tushman. 1994. "Organizational Transformation as Punctuated Equilibrium: An Empirical Test." *Academy of Management Journal* 37: 1141–67.

Romer, Paul. 1986. "Increasing Returns and Long-Run Growth." *Journal of Political Economy* 94: 1002–87.

Rose, A. 1967. "Voluntary Associations." In A. Rose, ed., *The Power Structure*, 213–52. New York: Oxford University Press.

Rosenkopf, L., and M. Tushman. 1994. "The Coevolution of Technology and Organization." In J. A. C. Baum and J. Singh, eds., *Evolutionary Dynamics of Organizations.* New York: Oxford University Press.

———. 1998. "The Coevolution of Community Networks and Technology: Lessons from the Flight Simulator Industry." *Industrial and Corporate Change* 7: 311–46.

Roy, W. 1990. "Functional and Historical Logics in Explaining the Rise of the American Industrial Corporation." *Comparative Social Research* 12: 19–44.

Ryan, A., J. Freeman, and R. C. Hybels. 1995. "Biotechnology Firms." In Glenn R. Carroll and Michael T. Hannan, eds., *Organizations in Industry: Strategy, Structure, and Selection,* 332–57. New York: Oxford University Press.

Sabel, C., and J. Zeitlin. 1985. "Historical Alternatives to Mass Production: Politics Markets and Technology in Nineteenth-Century Industrialization." *Past and Present* 108: 134–76.

———. 1997. *Worlds of Possibility: Flexibility and Mass Production in Western Industrialization.* Paris: Maison des Sciences de l'Homme.

Sager, I. 1997. "Cloning the Best of the Valley." *Business Week,* August 25, p. 146.

Sanderson, S., and M. Uzumeri. 1995. "Product Platforms and Dominant Designs: The Case of Sony's Walkman." *Research Policy* 24: 583–607.

Saunders, S. 1998. "Competitive Advantages When You Move into an Area That Does What You Do." *Plant Sites and Parks,* February/March.

Saxenian, A. 1994. *Regional Advantage: Culture and Competition in Silicon Valley and Route 128.* Cambridge, Mass.: Harvard University Press.

———. 1999. *Silicon Valley's New Immigrant Entrepreneurs.* San Francisco: Public Policy Institute of California.

Schein, E. 1983. "The Role of the Founder in Creating Organizational Culture." *Organizational Dynamics* 12: 13–29.

Schelling, T. C. 1978. *Micromotives and Macrobehavior.* New York: W. W. Norton.

Schlenker, B. R. 1980. *Impression Management.* Monterey, Calif.: Brooks/Cole.

Schoonhoven, C. B., and K. M. Eisenhardt. 1990. "Speeding Products to Market: Waiting Time to First Product Introduction in New Firms." *Administrative Science Quarterly* 35: 177–207.

———. 1992. "Regions as Industrial Incubators of New Technology-Based Firms: Implications for Economic Development." In E. S. Mills and J. F. McDonald, eds., *Sources of Metropolitan Growth,* 9–21. New Brunswick, N.J.: Rutgers University Press.

———. 1993. Entrepreneurial Environments: Incubator Region Effects on the Birth of New Technology-Based Firms. In M. Lawless and L. Gomez-Mejia, eds., *Advances in Global High-Technology Management,* 3: 149–75. Greenwich, Conn.: JAI Press.

Schuler, R. 1992. "Strategic Human Resource Management: Linking the People with the Strategic Needs of the Business." *Organizational Dynamics,* Summer, pp. 18–32.

Schumpeter, J. A. 1934. *The Theory of Economic Development: An Inquiry into Profits, Capital, Credit, Interest, and the Business Cycle.* Cambridge, Mass.: Harvard University Press.

———. 1950. *Capitalism, Socialism, and Democracy.* New York: Harper and Row.

Scott, A. J. 1989. *New Industrial Spaces: Flexible Production, Organization and Regional Development in North America and Western Europe.* London: Pion.

———. 1995. "The Geographic Foundations of Industrial Performance." *Competition and Change* 1: 51–66.

Scott, W. R. 1987. "The Adolescence of Institutional Theory." *Administrative Science Quarterly* 32: 493–511.

———. 1995. *Institutions and Organizations.* Thousand Oaks, Calif.: Sage Publications.

————. 1998. *Organizations: Rational, Natural, and Open Systems.* Upper Saddle River, N.J.: Prentice-Hall.

Segal, N. S. 1986. "Universities and Technological Entrepreneurship in Britain: Some Implications of the Cambridge Phenomenon." *Technovation* 4: 189–205.

Shane, S. 1999. "Prior Knowledge and the Discovery of Entrepreneurial Opportunities. Working paper, Sloan School of Management, Massachusetts Institute of Technology.

————. 2000. "Prior Knowledge and the Discovery of Entrepreneurial Opportunities." *Organization Science,* 11: 448–69.

Shane, S., and R. Khurana. 1999. "Career Experiences and Firm Foundings." Working paper, Sloan School of Management, Massachusetts Institute of Technology.

Shenhav, Y. 1995. "From Chaos to Systems: The Engineering Foundations of Organization Theory." *Administrative Science Quarterly* 40: 557–85.

Sherif, M., O. J. Harvey, B. J. White, W. R. Hood, and C. Sherif. 1961. *Intergroup Conflict and Cooperation: The Robbers Cave Experiment.* Norman, Okla.: Institute of Intergroup Relations.

Shubik, M. 1982. *Game Theory in the Social Sciences: Concepts and Solutions.* Cambridge, Mass.: MIT Press.

Siegel, R., E. Siegel, and I. C. MacMillan. 1993. "Characteristics Distinguishing High-Growth Ventures." *Journal of Business Venturing* 8: 169–79.

Simon, H. 1957. *Administrative Behavior.* New York: Free Press.

Singh, J. V., and C. Lumsden. 1990. "Theory and Research in Organizational Ecology." *Annual Review of Sociology* 16: 161–95.

Singh, J. V., D. Tucker, and R. House. 1986. "Organizational Legitimacy and the Liability of Newness." *Administrative Science Quarterly* 31: 171–93.

Singh, J. V., D. J. Tucker, and A. G. Meinhard. 1991. "Institutional Change and Ecological Dynamics." In W. W. Powell and P. J. DiMaggio, eds., *The New Institutionalism and Organizational Analysis,* 390–422. Chicago: University of Chicago Press.

Sitkin, S. B., and R. J. Bies, eds. 1993. *The Legalistic Organization.* Newbury Park, Calif.: Sage.

Smith, A. 1994 [1776]. *The Wealth of Nations.* New York: The Modern Library.

Smith, J. P., and B. Edmonston, eds. 1997. *The New Americans: Economic, Demographic, and Fiscal Effects of Immigration.* Washington, D.C.: National Academy Press.

Smith, R. 1973. *The Social History of the Bicycle.* New York: American Heritage Press.

Snow, D. A. 1986. "Organization, Ideology, and Mobilization: The Case of Nicheren Shoshu of America." In D. G. Bromley and P. E. Hammond, eds., *The Future of New Religious Movements.* Macon, Ga.: Mercer University Press.

Snow, D. A., and R. D. Benford. 1988. "Ideology, Frame Resonance, and Participant Mobilization." In B. Klandermans, H. Kriesi, and S. Tarrow, eds., *From Structure to Action: Comparing Movement Participation Across Cultures, International Social Movement Research,* 197–218. Greenwich, Conn.: JAI Press.

————. 1992. "Master Frames and Cycles of Protest." In A. Morris and C. Mueller, eds., *Frontiers in Social Movement Theory,* 133–55. New Haven: Yale University Press.

Snow, D. A., L. A. Zurcher, Jr., and S. Ekland-Olson. 1980. "Social Networks and Social

Movements: A Microstructural Approach to Differential Recruitment." *American Sociological Review* 51: 464–81.

Sobocinski, P. 1999. *Creating Hi-Tech Business Growth in Wisconsin: University of Wisconsin–Madison Technology Transfer and Entrepreneurship*. Madison, Wisc.: University of Wisconsin System Board of Regents.

Sonnenfeld, J. A., and M. A. Peiperl. 1988. "Staffing Policy as a Strategic Response: A Typology of Career Systems." *Academy of Management Review* 13: 588–600.

Spender, J. C. 1989. *Industry Recipes: The Nature and Sources of Managerial Judgment*. Oxford: Basil Blackwell.

Stark, D. 1996. "Recombinant Property in East European Capitalism." *American Journal of Sociology* 101: 993–1027.

Starr, J. A., and I. C. Macmillan. 1990. "Resource Cooptation via Social Contracting: Resource Acquisition Strategies for New Ventures." *Strategic Management Journal* 11: 79–92.

Stevenson, H., M. Roberts, and H. Grousbeck. 1989. *New Business Ventures and the Entrepreneur*. Homewood, Ill.: Irwin.

Stinchcombe, A. L. 1965. "Social Structure and Organizations." In J. G. March, ed., *Handbook of Organizations*, 142–93. Chicago: Rand McNally.

Strang, D., and M. W. Macy. 1999. "'In Search of Excellence': Fads, Success Stories, and Communication Bias." Paper presented at Academy of Management, Chicago.

Strauss, A., and J. Corbin. 1998. *Basics of Qualitative Research*. Thousand Oaks, Calif.: Sage Publications.

Stuart, T. 1998. "Network Positions and Propensities to Collaborate." *Administrative Science Quarterly* 43: 668–98.

Stuart, T., H. Hoang, and R. Hybels. Forthcoming. "Interorganizational Endorsements and the Performance of Entrepreneurial Ventures." *Administrative Science Quarterly*.

Suarez, F. F., and J. M. Utterback. 1995. "Dominant Designs and the Survival of Firms." *Strategic Management Journal* 16: 415–30.

Suchman, M. C. 1993. "Conceptualizing the Legal Environments of Organizational Activity." Paper presented to the Stanford Conference on Organizations, Asilomar, Calif.

————. 1994a. "On the Role of Law Firms in the Structuration of Silicon Valley." Institute for Legal Studies Disputes Processing Research Program, Working paper DPRP 11-7.

————. 1994b. "On Advice of Counsel: Law Firms and Venture Capital Funds as Information Intermediaries in the Structuration of Silicon Valley." Ph.D. dissertation, Department of Sociology, Stanford University.

————. 1995a. "Managing Legitimacy: Strategic and Institutional Approaches." *Academy of Management Review* 20: 571–610.

————. 1995b. "Localism and Globalism in Institutional Analysis: The Emergence of Contractual Norms in Venture Finance." In W. R. Scott and S. Christensen, eds., *The Institutional Construction of Organizations*, 39–63. Thousand Oaks, Calif.: Sage Publications.

————. Forthcoming. "Constructed Ecologies: Reproduction and Structuration in Emerging Organizational Communities." In W. W. Powell, ed., *Remaking the Iron Cage: Institutional Dynamics and Processes*. Chicago: University of Chicago Press.

Suchman, M. C., and M. L. Cahill. 1996. "The Hired Gun as Facilitator: Lawyers and the Suppression of Disputes in Silicon Valley." *Law and Social Inquiry* 21: 679–712.

Sull, D., R. Tedlow, and R. Rosenbloom. 1997. "Managerial Commitments and Technological Change in the U.S. Tire Industry." *Industrial and Corporate Change* 6: 461–501.

Swaminathan, A. 1995. "The Proliferation of Specialist Organizations in the American Wine Industry, 1941–1990." *Administrative Science Quarterly* 40: 653–80.

———. 1998. "Entry into New Market Segments in Mature Industries: Endogenous and Exogenous Segmentation in the U.S. Brewing Industry." *Strategic Management Journal* 19: 389–404.

Swaminathan, A., and G. Wiedenmayer. 1991. "Does the Pattern of Density Dependent in Organizational Mortality Rates Vary Across Levels of Analysis? Evidence from the German Brewing Industry?" *Social Science Research* 20: 45–73.

Swidler, A. 1986. "Culture in Action: Symbols and Strategies." *American Sociological Review* 51: 273–86.

Tang, J. 1993. "The Career Attainment of Caucasian and Asian Engineers." *Sociological Quarterly* 34: 467–96.

Tarrow, S. 1983. "Struggling to Reform: Social Movements and Policy Change During Cycles of Protest." Western Societies Program, Occasional paper no. 15. Center for International Studies, Cornell University.

———. 1989. *Democracy and Disorder: Protest and Politics in Italy, 1965–1975.* Oxford: Oxford University Press.

———. 1991. "Struggle, Politics and Reform: Collective Action, Social Movements and Cycles of Protest." Western Societies Program, Occasional paper no. 21, 2d ed. Center for International Studies, Cornell University.

———. 1994. *Power in Movement: Social Movements, Collective Action and Politics.* New York: Cambridge University Press.

Taylor, V., and N. E. Whittier. 1992. "Collective Identity in Social Movement Communities: Lesbian Feminist Mobilization." In A. Morris and C. M. Mueller, eds., *Frontiers of Social Movement Theory*, 104–30. New Haven, Conn.: Yale University Press.

Teece, D. 1987. "Profiting from Technological Innovation: Implications for Integration, Collaboration, Licensing, and Public Policy." In D. Teece, ed., *The Competitive Challenge*, 185–219. Cambridge, Mass.: Ballinger.

Tenenbaum, J. M., T. S. Chowdhry, and K. Hughes. 1997. *The eCo System: CommerceNet's Architectural Framework for Internet Commerce.* White paper and prospectus, Draft 1, January 15. CommerceNet Inc.

Testa, R. J. 1991. "The Legal Process of Venture Capital Investment." In S. M. Pratt and J. Morris, eds., *Pratt's Guide to Venture Capital Sources*, 15th ed., 57–70. Needham, Mass.: Venture Economics, Inc.

Thomas, R. P. 1977. *An Analysis of the Patterns of Growth of the Automobile Industry, 1895–1929.* New York: Arno Press.

Thompson, J. D. 1967. *Organizations in Action.* New York: McGraw-Hill.

Thornton, P. H. 1999. "The Sociology of Entrepreneurship." *Annual Review of Sociology* 25.

Tilly, C. 1978. *From Mobilization to Revolution.* Reading, Mass.: Addison-Wesley.

———. 1997. *Roads from the Past to the Future.* New York: Rowman and Littlefield.

————. 1998. *Durable Inequality.* Berkeley: University of California Press.

Tornatzky, L., A. Waugaman, and L. Casson. 1995. "Benchmarking Best Practices for University-Industry Transfer: Working with Start-Up Companies." Report of the Southern Technology Council, Southern Growth Policies Board.

Tripsas, M. 1997a. "Surviving Radical Technological Change Through Dynamic Capability." *Industrial and Corporate Change* 6: 341–77.

————. 1997b. "Unraveling the Process of Creative Destruction: Complementary Assets and Incumbent Survival in the Typesetter Industry." *Strategic Management Journal* 18: 119–42.

Tuma, N. B., and M. T. Hannan. 1984. *Social Dynamics: Models and Methods.* San Francisco: Academic Press.

Turner, J. 1995. "Universities and Their Intellectual Property Commercialization Companies from the Viewpoint of the Company." Working paper presented at the WIPO Asian Regional Seminar on University Relations with Industry, Beijing.

Tushman, M. L., and P. C. Anderson. 1986. "Technological Discontinuities and Organizational Environments." *Administrative Science Quarterly* 31: 439–65.

Tushman, M. L., and J. P. Murmann. 1998. "Dominant Designs, Technology Cycles, and Organizational Outcomes." In B. M. Staw and L. L. Cummings, eds., *Research in Organizational Behavior* 20: 231–66. Greenwich, Conn.: JAI Press.

Tushman, M. L., and L. Rosenkopf. 1992. "On the Organizational Determinants of Technological Change: Towards a Sociology of Technological Evolution." In B. Staw and L. L. Cummings, eds., *Research in Organization Behavior*, 14. Greenwich, Conn.: JAI Press.

Uzzi, B. 1996. "The Sources and Consequences of Embeddedness for the Economic Performance of Organizations: The Network Effect." *American Sociological Review* 61: 674–98.

Van de Ven, A. H. 1980. "Early Planning, Implementation, and Performance of New organizations." In J. R. Kimberly and R. H. Miles, eds., *The Organizational Life Cycle*, 83–134. San Francisco: Jossey-Bass.

————. 1993. "A Community Perspective on the Emergence of Innovations." *Journal of Engineering and Technology Management* 10: 23–51.

Van de Ven, A. H., and R. Garud. 1989. "A Framework for Understanding the Emergence of New Industries." R. S. Rosenbloom and R. Burgelman, eds., *Research on Technological Innovation, Management and Policy*, 4: 195–225.

————. 1991. "Innovation and Industry Development: The Case of Cochlear Implants." Manuscript. Strategic Management Research Center, University of Minnesota.

————. 1994. "The Coevolution of Technical and Institutional Events in the Development of an Innovation." In J. A. C. Baum and J. V. Singh, eds., *Evolutionary Dynamics of Organizations*, 425–43. New York: Oxford University Press.

Vedovello, C. 1997. "Science Parks and University—Industry Interaction: Geographical Proximity Between the Agents as a Driving Force." *Technovation* 17: 491–502.

Venkataraman, S. 1997. "The Distinctive Domain of Entrepreneurship Research." In *Advances in Entrepreneurship, Firm Emergence, and Growth*, 3: 119–38. Greenwich, Conn.: JAI Press.

Ventresca, M., and M. Washington. 1998. "Organizational Fields: Bringing Conflict Back In." Working paper, Kellogg Graduate School of Management, Northwestern University.

Vinas, T. 1998. "X-Rated and on the A-List." *Industry Week*, September 21, pp. 11–12.

Von Braun, C. F. 1997. *The Innovation War*. Upper Saddle River, N.J.: Prentice-Hall.

Von Hippel, E. 1988. *Sources of Innovation*. New York: Oxford University Press.

Wade, J. 1995. "Dynamics of Organizational Communities and Technological Bandwagons: An Empirical Investigation of Community Evolution in the Microprocessor Market." *Strategic Management Journal* 16: 111–33.

———. 1996. "A Community-Level Analysis of Sources and Rates of Technological Variation in the Microprocessor Market." *Academy of Management Journal* 39: 1218–44.

Wade, J., A. Swaminathan, and M. S. Saxon. 1998. "Normative and Resource Flow Consequences of Local Regulations in the American Brewing Industry, 1845–1918." *Administrative Science Quarterly* 43: 905–35.

Wald, M. L. 1998. "Senate Spares Internet from Taxes." *New York Times,* October 9, 1998.

Walden, K. 1999. Moneytree U.S. Report. PriceWaterhouse Coopers.

Waldinger, R., H. Aldrich, R. Ward, and Associates. 1990. *Ethnic Entrepreneurs: Immigrant Business in Industrial Societies*. Newbury Park, Calif.: Sage.

Walker, J. 1983. "The Origins and Maintenance of Interest Groups in America." *American Political Science Review* 77: 390–406.

Weber, Max. 1958 [1904–5]. *The Protestant Ethic and the Spirit of Capitalism*. New York: Charles Scribner's Sons.

Weick, K. E. 1979. *The Social Psychology of Organizing*. Reading, Mass.: Addison-Wesley.

———. 1995. *Sensemaking in Organizations*. Thousand Oaks, Calif.: Sage Publications.

Weiss, L. 1987. "Explaining the Underground Economy: State and Social Structure." *The British Journal of Sociology* 38: 216–34.

———. 1988. *Creating Capitalism: The State and Small Business Since 1945*. Oxford: Basil Blackwell.

Welles, E. O. 1999. "Not Your Father's Industry." *Inc.*, January, pp. 25–28.

Werth, B. 1994. *The Billion-Dollar Molecule: One Company's Quest for the Perfect Drug*. New York: Simon and Schuster.

Westhead, P. 1995. "Survival and Employment Growth Contrasts Between Types of Owner-Managed High-Technology Firms." *Entrepreneurship Theory and Practice* 20: 5–27.

White, H. 1980. "A Heteroskedeastcity-Consistent Covariance Matrix Estimator and a Direct Test for Heteroskedastcity." *Econometrica* 48: 817–30.

———. 1992. *Identity and Control*. Princeton: Princeton University Press.

Wicksteed, S. Q. 1985. *The Cambridge Phenomenon*. Thetford, Eng.: Thetford Press.

Wiley, J. D. 1999. Testimony of John D. Wiley, Provost, University of Wisconsin, Madison, Before the Special Committee on State Strategies for Economic Development. January 11, Madison, Wisc.

Wilson, K. L., and A. M. Orum. 1976. "Mobilizing People for Collective Action." *Journal of Political and Military Sociology* 4: 187–202.

Wolffe, R. 1998. "Software Baron." *The New Republic*, November 16, pp. 22–25.

Wolfram, S. 1983. "Statistical Mechanics of Cellular Automata." *Review of Modern Physics* 55: 471–526.

———. 1986. "Cellular Automata Fluids: Basic Theory." *Journal of Statistical Physics* 45: 601–44.

Womack, J. P., D. T. Jones, and D. Roos. 1990. *The Machine That Changed the World.* New York: Rawson Associates.

Wong, B. 1998. *Ethnicity and Entrepreneurship: The New Chinese Immigrants in the San Francisco Bay Area.* Needham Heights, Mass.: Allyn and Bacon.

Woodward, J. 1965. *Industrial Organization: Theory and Practice.* New York: Oxford University Press.

Zald, M. N., and R. Ash. 1966. "Social Movement Organizations: Growth, Decay, and Change." *Social Forces* 44: 327–41.

Zald, M. N., and M. A. Berger. 1990. "Social Movements in Organizations: Coup d'Etat, Bureaucratic Insurgency, and Mass Movement." In M. N. Zald and J. D. McCarthy, eds., *Social Movements in an Organizational Society,* 185–222. New Brunswick, N.J.: Transaction Publishers.

Zald, M. N., and J. D. McCarthy. 1980. "Social Movement Industries: Competition and Cooperation Among Movement Organizations." In L. Kriesberg, ed., *Research in Social Movements, Conflict and Change,* 3: 1–20. Greenwich, Conn.: JAI Press.

———. 1987. *Social Movements in an Organizational Society.* New Brunswick, N.J.: Transaction Publishers.

Zucker, L. G. 1986. "Production of Trust: Institutional Sources of Economic Structure, 1840–1920." In B. M. Staw and L. L. Cummings, eds., *Research in Organizational Behavior,* 8: 53–112. Greenwich, Conn.: JAI Press.

———. 1989. "Combining Institutional Theory and Population Ecology: No Legitimacy, No History." *American Sociological Review* 54: 542–45.

Zucker, L. G., M. R. Darby, and J. Armstrong. 1998. "Geographically Localized Knowledge: Spillovers or Markets?" *Economic Inquiry* 36: 65–86.

Zucker, L. G., M. R. Darby, and M. B. Brewer. 1998. "Intellectual Human Capital and the Birth of U.S. Biotechnology Enterprises." *American Economic Review* 88: 290–306.

INDEX

AAMA, *see* Asian American Manufacturers Association (AAMA)
Abernathy, W., 178, 189, 290
Abrahamson, E., 5, 6, 135–36, 147–77, 391
Academic publishing, *see* Scholarly knowledge industry
Access advantages, 369–70
Acs, Z. J., 131
ALAM, *see* Association of Licensed Automobile Manufacturers (ALAM)
Aldrich, H. E., 2, 7, 61, 65, 207–35, 288
Amazon.com, 63
Amenta, E., 289, 291, 305
American Association of Junior Colleges, 266
American Express, 47–48
American Society for Quality Control (ASQC), 160, 171
Anderson, P. C., 53, 285, 290
Andreeson, Marc, 404
Angel investors, 89–90, 97, 369, 400
Argyes, N. S., 123–24
Armstrong, J., 133
Arthur, W. B., 302
Ash, R., 308–9
Asia, 83–84. *See also* Chinese entrepreneurs; Japan
Asian American Manufacturers Association (AAMA), 79, 84–86
ASQC, *see* American Society for Quality Control (ASQC)
Association of Licensed Automobile Manufacturers (ALAM), 272
Association of University Technology Managers (AUTM), 121–22
Associations, *see* Professional associations; Trade associations
Astley, W. G., 390

Attachment, 17
Audretsch, D. B., 47, 131, 133
AUTM, *see* Association of University Technology Managers (AUTM)
Autocracy model, 18–19
Automobile Association of America, New York club, 273
Automobile industry, 56, 61, 270–74; certification contests in, 270–74; founding subprocesses in, 274–75; methods in study of, 274–80. *See also* Certification contests

Baker, T., 7, 61, 207–35
Bakshi, Naren, 89
Balboa Bay Conference, 4, 7, 9–10, 383, 390–95
Bangalore, India, 98–101
Bania, N., 125, 133
Bankruptcy law, 396
Barley, S., 263
Barnett, W. P., 307
Basu, Radha, 98, 99
Baum, J. A. C., 263
Baumol, W. J., 197
Beardsley, Jeff, 163–64, 171
"Becalmed" movements, 308–9
Beeson, P., 130–31
Bell Labs, 291, 307, 360
Benford, R. D., 302
Bernstein, L., 298, 306
Between-population strategies: cognitive, 221–23; sociopolitical, 231–32
Bezos, Jeff, 63
Biotechnology industry, 197, 231–32
Birch, D. L., 126–27
Birley, S., 2
"Blending and segregating processes," 358

"Body-shopping," 100

Books, and dissemination of ideas, 161–62, 164, 165

Bosack, Leonard, 47, 57

"Bots," 234

Bouchikhi, H., 20

Boundaries: community, 63–65, 397; organizational, 222–23

Bounded rationality, 316–17

"Brain circulation," 68

Braunerhjelm, P., 129, 132

Brewer, M. B., 125–26, 132–33

Brewpubs, *see* Microbreweries and brewpubs

Brint, S., 266

Brittain, J., 50–51

Brusco, S., 318n

Bureaucracy model, 18, 19

Burt, R. S., 59

Burton, M. D., 3–4, 13–39, 391, 392

Business-education knowledge management industry, 152, 153, 155. *See also* Management-knowledge community; Scholarly knowledge industry

Business Week, 314–15

"Buy-in," 389

Café Espresso Roma, 238

Cambridge University, 122–23

CA models, *see* Cellular automata (CA) models

Carlsson, B., 129, 132

Carroll, G. R., 270, 278, 307, 390

Cellular automata (CA) models, 327–28

Certification contests: defined, 277; divergent effects of, 280–84; in early U.S. auto industry, 270–74; form-level effects of, 268–69; future research and, 284; hypothesized effects based on number of, 269–70, 280–82; incorporation and, 276, 278, 280, 281; operational start-up and, 276, 278, 280, 281; as source of legitimacy, 264, 267–70

Certifying institutions, 225–26

Chalmers University, Gothenburg, Sweden, 122–23

Chandra, Prakash, 87

Chang, Herbert, 102–3

Charisma, 228

Chesbrough, H., 180

Chinese entrepreneurs: Chinese professional associations and, 78–86; as proportion of workforce, 72–73; relationship with Taiwan, 83–84, 94–98; sectoral concentrations and, 77–78. *See also* Immigrant entrepreneurs

Chinese Institute of Engineers (CIE), 82–84

Chrisman, J. J., 122

CIE, *see* Chinese Institute of Engineers (CIE)

CIEC, *see* Citizens Internet Empowerment Coalition (CIEC)

Cisco Systems, 47, 57

Citizens Internet Empowerment Coalition (CIEC), 229

Claimmaking strategies: legitimacy and, 263, 266–67; resource claims and, 250–58, 259. *See also* Certification contests

Clark, H. A., 276, 277

Clark, Jim, 404

Clark, K. B., 280

Clemens, E. S., 297, 300

Coffee bar, 245–47. *See also* Specialty coffee industry

Coffee industry, *see* Specialty coffee industry

Cognitive legitimacy, 211, 232

Cognitive models, 357, 358–59

Cognitive strategies, 211, 213–26, 324; between-population, 221–23; community-level, 223–26; organization-level, 213–15; within-population, 215–21

Cole, R., 160, 164, 166, 171

Collaboration, *see* Collective action

Collective action: choice of organizational form and, 310–11; collective identity and, 297–300; competition and, 302–5, 322–23, 332–33, 340–41; early collaborations and, 321–22; emerging populations and, 212–13, 219–21, 228–31, 387; frame generation and, 297–312; industry maturation and, 307–8; legitimacy and, 263, 264–74, 308; myths about entrepreneurship and, 384, 385–86; preexisting networks and, 291–93, 300–2; resource mobilization and, 287–89. *See also* Community

Columbus, Christopher, 393

Commitment model, 18, 19, 31

Communications Decency Act, 229, 232

Community: of knowledge, 391–92; organizational, 390–91; regional, 45–46, 58–59, 63–64, 65, 394–95; theory and, 6–7, 396–405. *See also* Organizational community

Community ecology, 64

Community-level strategies: cognitive, 223–26; sociopolitical, 231–32

Competitive strategy: change in, 50–51; choice of employment model and, 24–27, 37, 38; collective action and, 302–5, 321–22; industry categories and, 25–27; regional clusters and, 322–23, 332–33, 340–41

Compilation, 359–61

Computational capabilities, 323–24, 333–36, 341

Computer industry, 180, 197, 210

Conell, C., 293–94

Conferences, 266

Consequential legitimacy, 227

Constitutive law, 365–67

Consulting industry, 152, 153, 155, 160, 171, 172. *See also* Management-knowledge community

Consumer activists, 265

Consumers: preferences of, and opportunity, 290; response to novel technology, 271

Context: changes in, and opportunity structure, 289–90; dominant design and, 180–81, 196–200; international, 401; local, 402–3; privileged, 398–400; in process of organization creation, 2; role of the state and, 397–98; role of time and, 403; sample biases and, 401–2; transformation of, 2–3, 404–5. *See also* Knowledge communities; Legal environment; Local processes; Organizational community; Organizational environment; Regional clusters

Control, *see* Coordination and control

Cooper, A. C., 287, 394

Coordination and control, 17

Cosmopolitan, 272

Creative destruction, 236

Credit reporting agencies, 52–53

Cross-generational mentoring, 88–91

Cross-national research, 400

Darby, M. R., 125–26, 132–33

David, P. A., 341

Davis, S. J., 127–28

Delacroix, J., 213

Demand theories, *see* Supply vs. demand theories of entrepreneurship

De Noble, A. F., 132

Density: auto industry and, 277–78; organiza-

tional community and, 56–58; organizational forms and, 262–63, 291, 293

Density dependence theory, 357–58

Devaughan, M., 5, 109–46

Dewar, Donald, 163–64, 171

Diazo reaction, 187, 188

Diffusion: idea entrepreneurs and, 155–56; institutional theory and, 355; learning in emerging populations and, 210–11; organization strategy and, 294–96; technology cycles and, 202–3

DiMaggio, P. J., 397

Disk-drive technology, 180

Dissertations, and dissemination of ideas, 161–62, 165

Dollinger, M. J., 288

Dominant design, 179, 186–87, 190–92, 195; convergence on, 216–19; emergence of, 192, 193–95; emerging populations and, 210–11, 216–19; national differences and, 179, 196–200; nested-hierarchy concept and, 179, 186–87, 190–92, 195; research on, 189–92, 196–200; technology cycles and, 190–92, 196–200

"Dot.coms," 398

Dunkelberg, W. C., 287, 394

Duryea brothers, 270–71

Eberts, R., 125, 133

E-commerce (electronic commerce): cognitive strategies in, 208, 215–26; defined, 208; sociopolitical strategies in, 227–32

Economic growth: immigrant entrepreneurs and, 70–78, 106–8; university links with, 111, 114, 117–20, 127–30

Edelman, L. B., 230, 362

EDI, *see* Electronic data interchange (EDI)

Educational institutions, *see* Universities

Edwards, R. C., 18

Eesley, D. T., 5, 109–46

Eisenhardt, K. M., 288, 386, 394

Electric cars, 272

Electronic data interchange (EDI), 223

Electronics industry, 31

Emerging populations: collective action and, 212–13, 219–21, 228–31, 387; individual strategies and, 212–13; learning and, 208, 210–11; legitimacy and, 208; sociopolitical strategies and, 209–13, 226–32; strategies

Emerging populations *(continued)*
for population creation and, 209–13; threats
to, 207–8
Employee selection, 17
Employment model diversity, 13–39; and, 16–
18, 19; dimensions of models and, 17–18,
19–20, 21; experience of founders and, 27–
28, 33–34, 36–37; external partners and,
29–30, 34–35; factors in, 27, 28, 29, 30–
35; founders' approaches and, 38; industry
categories and, 20, 22–24, 27; Silicon Valley
start-ups and, 15–30, 31; strategic focus and,
24–27, 37, 38
Engineering model, 18, 19
England, 129, 181–89
Enhancer strategy, 25–26
Entrepreneurial personality, 42–43
Entrepreneurial teams, 33, 36, 386. *See also*
Founders
Entrepreneurship, 383; as dynamic, 2–3; vs.
innovation, 350; institutional ecology of,
352–62; macro-cognitive approach to, 237;
macro vs. micro models of, 316–17; myths
about, 384–90; as restructuring of social
space, 258; spatial dimensions of, 316–20;
themes from Balboa Bay Conference and, 9–
10, 390–95
Entrepreneurship research: organizational ori-
gins and, 1–2, 3–7; outcomes and, 2, 3; past
emphases of, 13–14, 383, 396; questions for,
1–3, 284, 343–44
Environment, *see* Context; Legal environment;
Local processes; Organizational community;
Organizational environment; Regional
clusters
Eras of ferment, 190, 194–95, 199–200
Eras of incremental change, 190, 195
Ermoliev, Y. M., 302
Ethnic networks: benefits of, 91–92; globalization of, 92–103; origins of, 78–92
Existing organizations: change in strategy in,
50–51; as entrepreneurial context, 4, 43–45,
65, 395; growth of, 51–52; opportunity
recognition in, 47–50, 53, 388–89; work-
form diversity in, 52–55. *See also* Experience
of founders; Local processes; Organizational
community
Experience of founders: choice of employment
model and, 27–28, 33–34, 36–37; identification of opportunities and, 47–50

Expertise claims, 254–58, 287–88
Exposure advantages, 369
External partners, 29–30, 34–35. *See also* Ven-
ture capital

Facilitative law, 362–64
Fairchild, G., 5, 6, 147–77, 391
Farley, M., 122
Feldman, M. P., 131
Filiation, 359–61
Financial resources, 288. *See also* Venture capital
Fiol, C. M., 208
Fogarty, M., 125, 133
Fombrun, C. J., 7, 8, 61, 220, 236–61, 294,
391
Fortune, 315
Founders: deviance from dominant industry
models and, 27–35; employment model and,
17–28, 33–34, 36–37, 38; experience of,
27–28, 33–34, 36–37, 47–50, 287–88;
strategy of, 24–27, 37, 38. *See also* Entrepre-
neurial teams; Immigrant entrepreneurs
France, 181–89, 317
Fraser, S., 122
Freeman, J., 45, 50–51, 60, 358, 387
Freidman, D., 304
Frenzen, J., 270
Frontiers of Entrepreneurship Research (1999 edi-
tion), 396

Galbraith, C., 132, 155
Game theory, 318–20, 325–26
Gamson, W. A., 311
Gartner, W. B., 390
Garud, R., 298
Geographic clusters, *see* Regional clusters
Germany: biotechnology industry in, 231–32;
dominant designs and, 181–89, 197;
synthetic dye industry and, 181–89
Gill, J., 156–57
Ginsberg, A., 9, 314–48
Glance, N., 343
Glass ceiling hypothesis, and immigrant entre-
preneurs, 74–75, 87–88
Glickman, David, 47–48
Glidden tour, 273, 274
Global System for Mobile Communication
(GSM) standard, 180, 197–98
Gloria Jean's Coffee Bean, 238, 256
Goel, Prabhu, 88

Government policies, 397–98; dominant designs and, 184, 189, 192, 218; legitimacy and, 211–12, 226, 227–28, 229, 230–31, 271; opportunity and, 290; organizational forms and, 292–93; regional clusters and, 318. *See also* Legal environment

GSM standard, *see* Global System for Mobile Communication (GSM) standard

Gupta, Satish, 88, 90

Haltiwanger, J. C., 127–28

Han, K. W., 95–96

Hannan, M. T., 56, 60, 270, 358, 387

Harrison, B., 128

Haunschild, P., 145–46

Hawley, A. H., 57–58

Henderson, R., 133

Hewlett-Packard (HP), 98, 99

Hirsch, P., 270

Historical timing, 403

HP, *see* Hewlett-Packard (HP)

Hsinchu companies, *see* Taiwan

Huberman, B., 343

Huczynski, A., 157

Human resource strategy, *see* Employment model diversity

Hunt, C. S., 219

Hybels, R. C., 263

Hynes, T., 122

IAQC, *see* International Association of Quality Circles (IAQC)

Idea entrepreneurs, 147–49; competition and, 175; diffusion stage and, 155–56; disciples and, 156–58; dynamics of knowledge entrepreneurship and, 154–56; gurus and, 156–58, 162–63, 168–71; hypercompetition and, 174–77; introduction stage and, 154–55; knowledge communities and, 149–58; management-knowledge entrepreneurs and, 152–54; management-knowledge market and, 152; methods in study of, 158–63; results of study of, 163–72; tactics and, 175–76

Identity claims, 254–58

IISs, *see* Indian Institutes of Science (IISs)

IITs, *see* Indian Institutes of Technology (IITs)

Immigrant entrepreneurs, 68–108; cross-generational mentoring and, 88–91; economic impact of, 70–78, 106–8; educational attainments of, 73–74; ethnic representation and, 72–73; glass ceiling hypothesis and, 74–75; globalization of ethnic networks and, 92–103; immigration system and, 71–72; local processes and, 394; origins of ethnic networks and, 78–92; as presence in technology industry, 75–78; Silicon Valley economy and, 70–78, 104, 106–8; ties with home countries, 83–84, 93–103

Immigration Act of 1965 (Hart-Celler Act), 71

Impression management theory, 250, 266

Inc. 500, 47–49, 401–2

Incentives: technology cycle and, 194–95; university-linked new ventures and, 115–16

India, 98–101

Indian entrepreneurs: Indian professional associations and, 78–82, 87–91; as proportion of workforce, 72; relationship with India, 98–101; sectoral concentrations and, 77–78. *See also* Immigrant entrepreneurs

Indian Institutes of Science (IISs), 87

Indian Institutes of Technology (IITs), 87, 101

Indirect connectivity, 324–26, 336–39, 341–42

Individual entrepreneurs: competitive strategies and, 321–23; existing organizations and, 43–45, 46; immigrant entrepreneurs and, 78; local processes and, 42–45, 316, 394; Myth of the Lonely Only Entrepreneur and, 385–87; new population strategies and, 212–13

The Indus Entrepreneur (TiE), 82, 88–91

Industrial districts, *see* Organizational community; Regional clusters

Industry associations, *see* Professional associations; Trade associations

Industry category: employment model and, 20, 22–24; university-linked new ventures and, 122–24, 125

Industry clusters, 45–46, 221. *See also* Regional clusters

Industry creation, 404–5, 406

Industry evolution, 407

Industry formation: collective action and, 386; university-linked ventures and, 142–45

Information resources, 288

Infrastructural deficit, 296

Infrastructure changes, 239, 249, 250–52, 290–96

Ingram, P., 291, 305

Initial public offering (IPO), 133

Innovation vs. entrepreneurship, 350

Innovator strategy, 24–26

Institutional activists: collective action by, 264–74; legitimating strategies and, 263–64

Institutional ecology, 349, 356–62, 381. *See also* Law firms in Silicon Valley

Integrated Silicon Solutions, Inc. (ISSI), 95–96

Intel, 51

International Association of Quality Circles (IAQC), 160, 166–67, 184

International contexts, 401

Internet, 63. *See also* E-commerce

Internet Tax Freedom Act, 212, 232

InveStar Capital, 102

ISSI, *see* Integrated Silicon Solutions, Inc. (ISSI)

Jacobs, J., 52

Jacobs, Linda, 294

Jaffe, A. B., 133

Japan: quartz technology and, 179–80, 198–99; video technology and, 180

Java software standard, 303, 307

Job creation, and university-linked new ventures, 117–20, 127–30

Jones-Evans, D., 131, 132

Journalists, *see* Popular press

Juran, Joseph, 163, 164, 166

JUSE, *see* Union of Japanese Scientists and Engineers (JUSE)

Kaniovski, Y. M., 302

Karabel, J., 266

Kekulé, Friedrich August, 185

Khosla, Vinod, 90

Kidder, T., 23, 53n

Kimberley, J. R., 20

Kimes, B. R., 276, 277

Klandermans, B., 297

Klofsten, M., 131

Knights of Labor, 293–94

Knowledge communities, 147, 148, 391–92; dynamics of, 173–74; idea entrepreneurship and, 149–58; management-knowledge community and, 152

Knowledge industries, *see* Idea entrepreneurs

Knowledge market, *see* Knowledge communities

Koput, K. W., 144–45

K-strategists, 311–12

Kunda, G., 23

Lam, David, 75, 82, 86

Larsen, E. R., 9, 314–48

Law firms in Silicon Valley, 349, 358, 367–80, 381–82, 392; advantages of, 369–70, 372–73; contractual standardization and, 373–75; contractual typification and, 377–80; deal-making and counseling roles of, 367–73; professional roles of, 367–73; as proselytizers, 372; role in Silicon Valley effect and, 376–77; structuration process and, 371

Lawler, Edward, 171

Leadership claims, 252–54

Leaders vs. laggards, 153, 154, 156–58, 168, 172. *See also* Management gurus; Publications

Learning, and emerging populations, 208, 210–11, 218–19. *See also* Cognitive strategies

Leblebici, H., 308

Lee, David, 75, 82

Lee, Jimmy, 95–96

Lee, Lester, 75, 82, 84

Legal environment, 362–73; constitutive law and, 365–67; facilitative law and, 362–64; professional law and, 367–73; regulative law and, 364–65. *See also* Law firms in Silicon Valley

Legitimacy, 208; certifying institutions and, 225–26; claimmaking strategies and, 263; cognitive, 211, 213–26; collective action and, 263, 264–74, 308; cooperation between firms and, 286–87; definition of, 211; evolutionary model and, 208–9; industry associations and, 220; institutional activists and, 263–64; restructuring framework and, 250–52; sociopolitical, 211–12, 226–32, 387. *See also* Cognitive strategies

Lerner, Sandra, 47, 57

Liang, K. Y., 280

Liebeskind, J. P., 123–24

Liu, Gerry, 83

Local processes, 40–67, 393–95; bridging macro and micro models and, 316–17; cluster development and, 317–18; collaboration and, 321–22, 329–32, 340–41; community boundaries and, 63–65; community origins and, 58–69; competitive strategy and, 322–23, 332–33, 340–41; computational capabilities and, 323–24, 333–36, 341; game theoretic approach and, 318–20, 325–26; indirect connectivity and, 324–26, 336–39, 341–42; intellectual capital and, 46–47; macro and micro models and, 316–17; organizational populations and, 55–62; resources

and, 45–46; spatial dimensions of action and, 315, 316–20; university-linked ventures and, 140, 143–44. *See also* Existing organizations; Organizational community
Local social issues, 119–20, 130–33
Lockheed Aerospace Corporation, 163, 166
"Lock-in," 341
Lomi, A., 9, 314–48
Low-cost strategy, 25–26
Lyman, K., 386

Magic Beanstalk Vision: evidence on beliefs in, 120–35; shared beliefs in, 113–20; sources of shared beliefs in, 135–38
Management fads, 135–36
Management gurus, 156–58, 162–63, 168–71; backgrounds of, 157–58, 162–63, 170–71; defined, 157; leading-edge publications and, 168–71
Management-knowledge community, 151, 152; interdependent industries in, 152, 153, 155; introduction of techniques in, 155; management-knowledge entrepreneurs and, 152–54. *See also* Idea entrepreneurs; Quality circles
"Mandatory stock conversion trigger," 377–79
March, J. G., 317
Marketer strategy, 25–26
Market processes, and dominant designs, 193
Market space creation, 384, 385–86, 387
Massachusetts, 117, 122, 129, 317, 341
Maxim, Hiram, 271
McAdam, D., 289, 304
McCarthy, J. D., 296
McClelland, D. C., 43n, 385, 387
Medical industry, 31
Mental models, 145–46, 391–93, 405–6. *See also* Magic Beanstalk Vision
Methé, D., 194
Meyer, D. S., 291
Meyer, J. W., 355, 366
Mian, S. A., 127
Michels, R., 308
Micklethwait, J., 157
Microbreweries and brewpubs, 292, 294, 298–300, 304, 306
Microsoft, 230, 303, 307
Miner, A. S., 5–6, 109–46, 391, 392, 401
Minkoff, D. C., 291, 293
MIT, 122, 124–26
Mitchell, W., 194

Mobile telephony, 180
Mobilization for Survival, 303
Mohrman, Susan, 171
Monte Jade Science and Technology Association, 79
Montgomery, E., 130–31
Moral legitimacy, 211
Murmann, J. P., 5, 6, 178–203, 391, 401
Myths about entrepreneurship: the Lonely Only Entrepreneur and, 385–87; opportunity and, 387–90

Naipaul, V. S., 91
Naranjo, John, 242–43
National Association of Automobile Manufacturers, 272
National Coffee Association, 240, 242
National Committee on Quality Assurance, 266–67
National differences, 181–89, 196–200
National Science Foundation, 398
National Taiwan University Alumni Association, 83
Negotiation, and dominant designs, 193, 201
Neo-institutional theory, 354–56
Netscape, 230, 404–5
News media, 63
Non-resident Indians (NRIs), 99
North Carolina, 117
NRIs, *see* Non-resident Indians (NRIs)

Ohio, 129
Oliver, C., 263
Olson, M., Jr., 291
Online pornography industry, 227, 229, 294–95
Operating system technology, 180, 197
Opportunity: environmental change and, 289–90; identification of, 47–50, 236; myths about entrepreneurship and, 387–90; technology cycles and, 179, 193–94
OrderTrust (company), 221–22
Organizational community, 4, 390–91; boundaries of, 63–65, 397; dimensions of, 397; diversity of populations in, 59; new population formation and, 60–62; number of populations in, 59; origins of, 58–59; population density in, 56–58; regional differences and, 65. *See also* Local processes; Mental models; Regional clusters

Organizational ecology, 262–63, 316, 353–54.
See also Institutional ecology
Organizational environment: change in, and
opportunity structure, 289–90;
entrepreneurial challenges and, 350–52. *See
also* Legal environment
Organizational forms, 4; collective action and,
386–87; empirical research on, 262–63;
incumbents' responses and, 305–7; infrastructure changes and, 290–96; institutional
entrepreneurs and, 263–64; opportunity
structure and, 287–90; origins of diversity in,
13–39. *See also* Employment model diversity
Organizational knowledge, diffusion of, 210–11
Organizational populations: constraints on
emergence of, 207–35; density and, 56–58;
formation of, 60–62; number of, 59; population-level learning and, 145–46. *See also*
Emerging populations
Organizational theory: geography and, 66;
industry-dominant models and, 14, 36; local
processes and, 45–46
Organization-level strategies: cognitive, 213–
15; sociopolitical, 227–28

Patil, Suhas, 88
Peet, Alfred, 243–45, 253, 255
Peet's Coffee and Tea Company, 243–45, 253
Personal legitimacy, 228
Personnel search organizations, 53, 54
Peterson, R. A., 42
Pettigrew, A., 214
Polos, L., 297
Popular press, 152, 153, 155, 160–61, 164,
167, 171, 172, 273. *See also* Management-
knowledge community
Populations, *see* Organizational populations
Porac, J., 304
"Portal wars," 234
Porter, M. E., 59
Powell, W. W., 144–45
Pragmatic legitimacy, 211
Pre-start-up phenomena, 403
Prisoner's Dilemma (PD), 319–20, 326–27,
348
Procedural legitimacy, 227–28
Professional associations, 63, 78–92, 265
Professional law, 367–73
Progressive norms, 149–51
Publications: leading- vs. lagging-edge, 153,

154, 157–58, 162–63, 168–71; waves of
content publishing and, 165–68

Quality circles, 158; gurus and, 168–71; introduction of, 163–65; publishing history and,
165–68

Ramp Networks, 101–3
Rao, H., 7, 8, 61, 213, 262–85
Rational norms, 149–51
Recombination, 355
Regional clusters, 314–48; conclusions of study
of, 339–42; limitations to study of, 342–43;
mathematical formulation of model, 345–46;
mathematical formulation of payoff function,
347; research methodology and, 326–29;
research questions regarding, 320–26, 343–
44; results of simulation study of, 329–39;
spatial dimensions of action and, 316–20.
See also Local processes; Organizational com-
munity; Route 128 in Massachusetts; Silicon
Valley
Regional community, 45–46, 58–59, 63–64,
65, 394–95. *See also* Organizational community
Regulative law, 364–65. *See also* Government
policies
Rekhi, Kanwal, 88
Repeated Prisoner's Dilemma (RPD), 319–20
"Report cards," 266–67
Resource claims, 250–58, 259; expertise claims
and, 254–58, 287–88; identity claims and,
254–58; leadership claims and, 252–54;
value claims and, 250–52
Resource concentration, 400
Resource mobilization theory, 287–89
Resource partitioning theory, 296
Restructuring of social collectives framework,
248–58
Riekar, Wayne, 163–64, 171
Rindova, V. P., 7, 8, 61, 220, 236–61, 294, 391
Roberts, E. B., 125
Rogers, E. M., 127
Romanelli, E., 1–10, 40–67, 298, 383–408
Rose, A., 308
Rosen, H., 288
Rosenbloom, R., 194
Ross, Rick, 303–4
Route 128 in Massachusetts, 117, 129, 317,
341, 365

Rowan, B., 355, 366
R-strategists, 311–12
Rura-Polley, T., 5, 109–46
Ryan, A., 263

SAE, *see* Society of Automotive Engineers (SAE)
Salancik, G. R., 308
San Francisco, CA, 84
Saxenian, A., 3–5, 66, 68–108, 129, 394
Saxon, M. S., 291
SCAA, *see* Specialty Coffee Association of America (SCAA)
Scholarly knowledge industry, 160–61, 167, 171, 172
Schoonhoven, C. B., 1–10, 40–67, 288, 383–408
Schuh, S., 127–28
Schultz, Howard, 246, 260
Schumpeter, J. A., 2, 50, 53n, 198
Scientific field patterns in venture creation, 122–24
Scott, W. R., 317–18, 342
Segal, N. S., 130
Self-regulation, 229
Semiconductor industry, 291, 359, 360
Sensemaking, 355
Shane, S., 126
Shekar, Chandra, 89–90
Shockley, William, 47
Siliconindia (journal), 101
Silicon Valley: Asian presence in, 69–70, 101–3; as distinct region, 317, 376–77; elite entrepreneurship and, 398–99; employment models in, 15–30, 31; ethnic professional associations in, 78–92; globalization of ethnic networks and, 92–103; government regulation and, 231; immigrant-run companies in, 106–8; legal environment and, 349, 358, 365, 367–80, 381–82, 392; organizational community and, 63, 66; relationship with India, 98–101; relationship with Taiwan, 94–98; universities and, 117, 118, 128–29. *See also* Immigrant entrepreneurs; Law firms in Silicon Valley
Silicon Valley Indian Professionals Association (SIPA), 87–88
Simon, H., 316–17
Simons, T., 291, 305
Simulation methods, 326. *See also* Regional clusters

SIPA, *see* Silicon Valley Indian Professionals Association (SIPA)
Smith, Adam, 57
Smith-Doerr, L., 144–45
Snow, D. A., 302
Sobocinski, P., 123
Social movements: emergence of organizational forms and, 286–313; frame generation and, 297–312; institutional entrepreneurship and, 263, 266; Magic Beanstalk Vision and, 136–37; opportunity structure and, 289–90; pre-existing infrastructure and, 290–96; resource mobilization theory and, 287–89. *See also* Collective action
Social networks, 396
Social structure changes, 238–39
Society of Automotive Engineers (SAE), 272
Sociopolitical legitimacy, 211–12, 226–32; collective action and, 228–31, 387; consequential, 227; personal, 228; procedural, 227–28; structural, 228
Sociopolitical strategies: between-population, 231–32; community-level, 231–32; organization-level, 227–28; within-population, 228–31
Sociostructure changes, 239, 249, 252–54
Software Technology Parks (STPs), 99
Spatial dimensions of entrepreneurship, *see* Local processes
Specialization, 57–58
Specialty Coffee Association of America (SCAA), 247
Specialty coffee industry: activities as resource claims in, 248–58, 259; change in U.S. coffee industry and, 236–39, 242–48; competition in, 247–48, 255, 256; creation of, 243–45; growth of, 243, 247–48; key industry changes and, 248, 249; local processes and, 61, 394; opportunity creation in, 245–47; organizational form and, 294; research approach to, 239–42; sources of evidence on, 241
SPEC study, *see* Stanford Project on Emerging Companies
SRI International, 317
Standards, *see* Dominant design
Stanford Project on Emerging Companies (SPEC), 15–16. *See also* Silicon Valley
Stanford University, 136, 224–25
Starbucks Coffee Company, 246, 247–48, 253–54, 256, 257–58

Star model, 18, 19
Start-ups studied, *see Inc.* 500 founders
State, role of the, *see* Government policies
Stephan, P. E., 47, 133
Steward, D. J., 9, 349–82
Stinchcombe, A. L., 50, 174
STPs, *see* Software Technology Parks (STPs)
Strategy, *see* Competitive strategy; Emerging populations; employment model diversity
Structural legitimacy, 228
Suchman, M. C., 9, 211, 227, 230, 349–82, 392
Sull, D., 194
Sun Microsystems, 303, 307
Superstructure changes, 239, 249, 254–58
Supply vs. demand theories of entrepreneurship, 42–43, 155, 164–65, 172, 175
Swaminathan, A., 7, 8, 194, 278, 286–313, 372, 391
Sweden, 129, 131
Switzerland: synthetic dye industry and, 181–89; watch industry in, 179–80, 198–99
Symbols, 61
Synthetic dye industry, 181–89, 196, 199–200

Tai, Ken, 102–3
Taiwan, 83–84, 94–98
Technical community, 152, 153, 155, 160, 171, 172. *See also* Knowledge communities; Management-knowledge community
Technological innovation, and opportunity, 289–90
Technology cycles: dominant design concept and, 190–92, 196–200; entrepreneurial opportunity and, 192–95; eras of ferment and, 190, 194–95, 199–200; eras of incremental change and, 190, 195
Technology industry, 75–78. *See also* Immigrant entrepreneurs
Technology transfer, *see* Universities
Tedlow, R., 194
Terman, Frederick, 224–25
Theory development, 397–400
TiE, *see* The Indus Entrepreneur (TiE)
Times-Herald auto race, 272
Tire industry, 194
Total quality management (TQM), 162
Townsend Movement, 289, 305
TQM, *see* Total quality management (TQM)
Trade associations, 219–21, 265, 271, 309–10

Trajtenberg, M., 133
Trika, Mohan, 92–93
Trust advantages, 369–70
Tushman, M. L., 5, 6, 53, 178–203, 285, 290, 391, 401

Union of Japanese Scientists and Engineers (JUSE), 163, 171
United States, and dominant designs, 180, 197
Universities: beliefs about new venture creation and, 113–20; commercialization of inventions from, 110–13; commonality of beliefs across, 114, 135–38; dominant designs and, 185–86, 197; immigrant entrepreneurs and, 73, 83; impact of commercialization and, 120–35; implications of commercialization and, 138–46; links between new ventures and, 111–12; links with economic growth, 111, 114, 117–19, 139–40; mental models and, 145–46, 392; national differences and, 185–86; role of, 110, 402; spin-off capabilities of, 115–17, 121–27; values and, 140–41. *See also* Magic Beanstalk Vision
University-linked ventures, 111–12; compared with other new ventures, 126–27; implications for policy, 138–41; Magic Beanstalk Vision of, 113–20; research on creation process, 124–26; scientific field patterns and, 122–24; theories of entrepreneurial process and, 141–42; unexpected outcomes and, 138–39, 140–41
University of Wisconsin-Madison, 122, 123
Utterback, J., 178, 189

Value claims, 250–52
Van de Ven, A. H., 298
Vedovello, C., 132
Veerina, Mahesh, 101–3
Venkataraman, S., 41, 201, 385, 388
Venture capital: Asian entrepreneurs and, 92, 95, 97, 102–3; collective action and, 386; contractual standardization and, 373–75; legal environment and, 366–67, 367–68; mental model and, 393; privileged contexts and, 399–400; sample biases and, 401–2; Silicon Valley law firms and, 373–80. *See also* Angel investors; External partners; Law firms in Silicon Valley
Vicarious learning, and Magic Beanstalk Vision, 137–38

Video technology, 180
Virtual organizations, 174
Vision Software, 89
Voss, K., 293–94

Wade, J. B., 7, 8, 286–313, 372, 391, 394–95
Welles, E. O., 220
Western Europe, 129
Westfall, C. A., 9, 349–82
Westhead, P., 129, 131
White, H., 267
Whittier, N., 291
Whittle, S., 156–57

Within-population strategies: cognitive, 215–21; sociopolitical, 228–31
Woo, C. Y., 287
Woodward, W., 288
Wooldridge, A., 157
world wide web, *see* E-commerce; Internet

Zald, M. N., 308–9
Zeger, S. L., 280
Zerrillo, P., 270
Zucker, L. G., 125–26, 132–33, 283
Zylan, Y., 289, 291, 305